automotive air conditioning

automotive
air conditioning

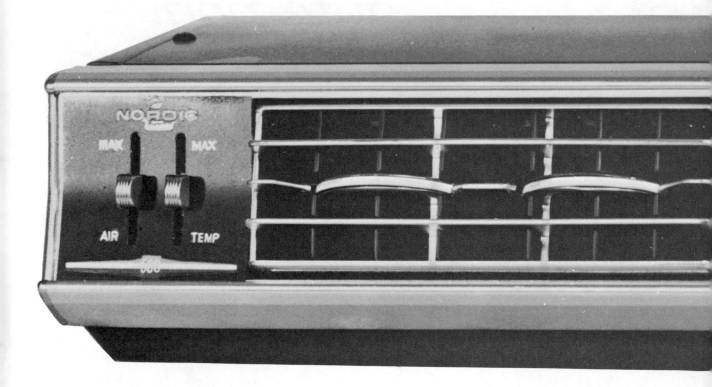

DELMAR PUBLISHERS
COPYRIGHT © 1973
BY LITTON EDUCATIONAL PUBLISHING, INC.

LIBRARY OF CONGRESS CATALOG CARD NUMBER: 73 – 2167

PRINTED IN THE UNITED STATES OF AMERICA

Boyce H. Dwiggins,
Assistant Supervisor
Vocational Technical Education
Broward County Board of Public Instruction
Fort Lauderdale, Florida

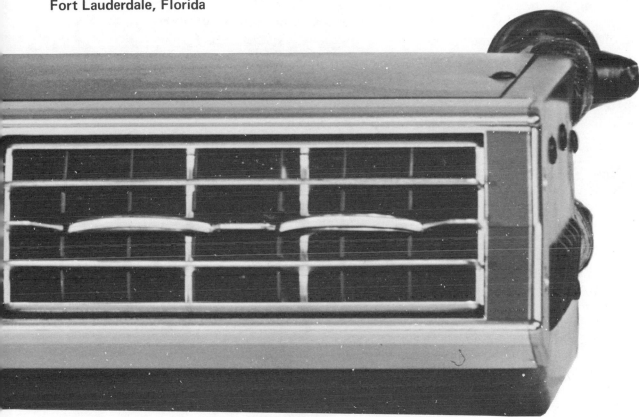

DELMAR PUBLISHERS • ALBANY, NEW YORK 12205

A DIVISION OF LITTON EDUCATIONAL PUBLISHING, INC.

Preface

Automotive air conditioning in the past few years has grown in popularity to unexpected proportions. In the next few years it is estimated that up to three-quarters of all cars built will be equipped with air conditioning. Many other automobiles will be air conditioned after delivery to owners.

Perhaps you heard about the fellow who rolled up the windows of his car a few blocks from his home so the neighbors would not know that he couldn't afford air conditioning. Not so much of a joke anymore — the price of units now are within the reach of most budgets.

The information contained in this book is designed to give the student basic knowledge of automotive air conditioning theory and service diagnosis procedures. In addition, it is intended to help the student develop correct working habits and good judgment in the performance of his duties as an air conditioning mechanic.

This text would not have been possible without the generous cooperation of the many manufacturers of automobile air conditioners and components, whose material is used to supplement this text.

Particular thanks is expressed to Mr. Richard G. Herd, former Associate, Vocational-Industrial Education State of New York, for his invaluable assistance and encouragement.

This book is dedicated to Eddie and Judy.

Boyce H. Dwiggins

AUTOMOTIVE AIR CONDITIONING

Automotive air conditioning serves three main purposes:

● It provides a background of principles of science, refrigeration and air conditioning, which must be understood by the craftsmen and technicians. This information is fundamental to all types of mobile air conditioning and servicing.

● The instructional units are "terminal" for those who apply immediately the basic skills developed in the class and shop with this background information.

● The instructional units are "preparatory" for those who plan to move into advanced phases of refrigeration and air conditioning work, including refrigeration systems not related to automobiles.

This book contains three basic sections. Section I is arranged in the natural order of dependence of one principle, law or set of conditions upon another Section II is System diagnosis. The material within a unit proceeds in an orderly, organized pattern which is planned to help the student see relationships. Section III is planned to give the student step-by-step instruction in the performance of a particular service procedure. It is suggested that each topic in this section be considered as an assignment that is to be carried out by the student.

Many line drawings, cutaway sections, photographs, and charts are used in the text to supplement appropriate descriptions. These illustrations have been selected to improve the instructional effectiveness of the text material through emphasis, by simplifying a description, or by helping to identify parts in relation to the complete functioning of a system.

REFERENCE SECTION

The Reference Section is designed to give basic and fundamental facts relating to certain areas not covered specifically in the text. Basic wiring and vacuum diagrams as well as refrigeration circuits and various other helpful information may be found in this section.

GLOSSARY OF TERMS

A Glossary of Terms is included as an aid in identifying component parts and phrases in the text of this and other textbooks on the subject of air conditioning. It includes, whenever possible, slang, or shop terms, for various components of the system.

SUGGESTED APPLICATIONS

There are variations within each training program on the need for instructional material to meet exacting local requirements. With the pattern of organization employed in this text, the material should be adaptable to many different types of training programs and for a number of levels on which instruction may be given. Here are a few suggestions on how the material in this book may be used effectively.

- As a textbook in schools where the student must develop a broad understanding of refrigeration and air conditioning terms, principles, devices, components and systems, and must learn how to apply the skills and related technical information to practical problems.

- As a basic textbook in vocational-industrial-technical education for organized class, group, or individual instruction.

- As a basic practical refrigeration and air conditioning textbook and resource manual for apprentice training, in-shop training courses for mechanics, salesmen, service personnel and other persons.

- As a basic textbook for industrial cooperative work experience students and classes.

- As a textbook or source book for adult programs, occupational extension or supplemental courses where a sound, practical working knowledge of refrigeration and air conditioning gives meaning to work in related occupations and technologies.

- As a resource book in teacher-training classes for preparing courses of study and for studying the organizational pattern and the teaching content.

- As an on-the-job shop manual and reference book for air conditioning mechanics.

INSTRUCTOR'S GUIDE

An Instructor's Guide contains solutions to all of the objective questions and problems. Suggested answers are given wherever there may be variations in which an answer may be stated by individual students. The guide is intended to conserve valuable teaching time and to provide a uniform basis to the solutions for the problem material.

A complete air conditioning training package is available from Scott Engineering Sciences, Pompano Beach, Florida, developed by the author for use with this book.

Contents

SECTION III   SERVICE PROCEDURES

SECTION IV   REFERENCES

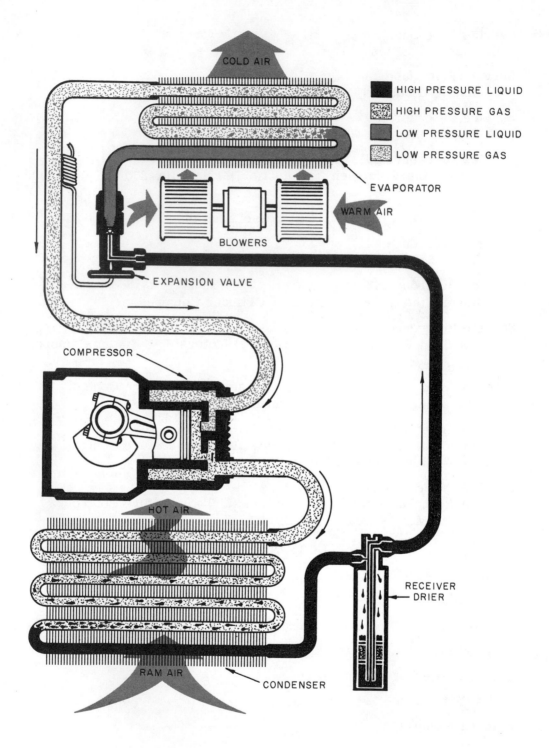

COLD AIR

HIGH PRESSURE LIQUID
HIGH PRESSURE GAS
LOW PRESSURE LIQUID
LOW PRESSURE GAS

EVAPORATOR

WARM AIR

BLOWERS

EXPANSION VALVE

COMPRESSOR

HOT AIR

RECEIVER DRIER

RAM AIR

CONDENSER

BASIC THEORY

Topic 1 INTRODUCTION

Recently a friend said to me, "When I bought my auto air conditioner, it was a luxury. It was not half paid for before it became a necessity."

Automotive air conditioning is fast becoming one of the most popular of all the auto accessories. Some manufacturers predict that in the next ten years about eighty percent of all new cars will be equipped with factory air conditioners.

In 1962, 11.31% of all cars were equipped with factory air conditioners, accounting for 756,781 units. In figures given by the Automotive Air Conditioning Association, close to three million units were sold the first half of 1966, surpassing all of 1965 sales. Just as my friend said, "Auto air conditioning has become a necessity."

Without air conditioning we would have no space program. Indeed, we could not produce many of the vital parts associated with the space program. Many precision parts, such as bearings and electrical components, are manufactured under very strict tolerances which require humidity and temperature control to within a few degrees change.

Before we briefly trace the development of air conditioning, and its application to automobiles, let us review its definition. Air conditioning is the process which cools, cleans and circulates air, and controls its moisture content. Ideally, it does all of these simultaneously. Since "cooling" refers to the removal of heat, another term for refrigeration, air conditioning obviously includes refrigeration.

HISTORICAL DEVELOPMENT OF AIR CONDITIONING

Although refrigeration, as we know it, is only about sixty years old, some of its principles were known as long ago as ten thousand years before Christ.

The Egyptians had a system to remove heat from Pharaoh's palace. The walls were constructed of huge stone block, weighing over a thousand tons, one side polished, the other side rough.

At night, 3,000 slaves would dismantle the walls and move the stones to the Sahara Desert. Since temperatures in the desert got very low at night the stones would be cooled. Actually, the heat absorbed during the day was dissipated in the cool air of the night. Before daybreak the slaves would then move the stones back to the palace site and cement them back into place.

COOLING WATER
BY EVAPORATING MOISTURE

It is guessed that the pharaoh enjoyed temperatures of about 80°F inside the palace while outside they soared to 130°F or more. It took 3,000 slaves all night to do a job that modern refrigeration can easily do today.

The early Egyptians also found that water could be cooled by placing it in porous jars on rooftops at sundown. The night breezes evaporated the moisture which seeped through the jars, making the water inside the jars cooler.

Much more recently, after the turn of the 20th century, a Mr. T.C. Northcott in Luray, Virginia was perhaps the first man in history to have a home with central heating and air conditioning.

A heating and ventilating engineer, Mr. Northcott had his house built on a hill above the famous Caverns of Luray. He and his family were hay fever sufferers, and he knew that air filtered through limestone was dust and pollen free.

Some distance behind the house he sank a five-foot shaft down into the ceiling of the cavern. He used a 42-inch fan to pull 8,000 cubic feet of air per minute through the shaft.

From the shed where the shaft was sunk, he built a passage or duct to the house. This was divided into two chambers, the upper one contained air that was heated by the sun, the lower one carried air from the cavern. The upper duct was used on chilly days; the lower duct, on warm days. Humidity was regulated in a chamber in his basement where air from both ducts could be mixed. The warmer air contained a higher amount of moisture, or humidity, than the cooler, as is the case of all air. From this mixing chamber, Mr. Northcott could direct air to any or all rooms of his house via a network of smaller pipes, or ducts. In the winter the air was heated by steam coils located in the base of each of the branch ducts.

Each year more than 350,000 people visit the Caverns of Luray where the temperature remains a constant, dust- and pollen-free 54° F. Many are impressed that this is the home of one inventor who enjoyed cool comfort, the first home known to have central heating and air conditioning.

Domestic refrigeration first made its appearance in 1910, although as early as 1820 ice was first made artificially. In 1913 the first manually-operated machine was produced by J. L. Larsen. In 1918 the Kelvinator Company produced the first automatic refrigerator. Acceptance was slow and by 1920 only about 200 units were sold.

In 1926 the first hermetic, or sealed refrigerator was introduced by General Electric. The following year, Electrolux introduced an automatic absorption unit. It was in 1927 that the first air conditioner appeared on the market.

Mobile air conditioning has made it possible for the space age to be upon us in the twentieth century. What was fiction just a few years ago is commonplace today. Atomic submarines are able to remain submerged indefinitely due, in part, to air conditioning.

Modern medicines and delicate machine components are perfected in scientifically controlled atmospheres. Computer brain centers are able to function because they are kept to within a specified range of temperature and humidity.

From the days of pharaoh, who had his palace torn down each night to keep cool, to Sir Francis Bacon, who, in 1626, stuffed a chicken with snow to freeze it and died as a result of eating the chicken, to the early 1900s, you can see that in the past sixty years the refrigeration industry has been growing at a rapid pace.

AUTOMOTIVE AIR CONDITIONING

Automotive air conditioning makes it possible to change the condition of the air in the car by controlling its moisture content (humidity) and heat content (temperature) simultaneously.

Air conditioning was available for automobiles in 1927-28; but for this era, the term meant the car was equipped with a heater, ventilation, and a means of filtering the air.

In 1938 a few passenger buses were air conditioned. Two years later, in 1940, Packard offered the first car cooling by means of refrigeration. These first automotive units were commercial units adapted for automotive use.

No accurate records were kept, but before the outbreak of World War II there were between 3,000 and 4,000 cooling units installed in Packards.

World War II prevented the improvement of auto air conditioning until the early 1950s when the demand for it began in the Southwest.

Many large firms have found that by installing air conditioning in the cars of their salesmen, sales have increased, and in some instances, doubled.

Taxicabs and truckcabs are being air conditioned. Taxicab business has increased because of air conditioning. Truckers have realized larger profits because drivers whose cabs are air conditioned cover more mileage than do those whose trucks are not air conditioned.

By 1967 all of the state police cars on the Florida Sunshine State Parkway had been air conditioned. More law enforcement agencies are following this practice, not only in Florida, but all over the country.

Today automobile air conditioning is no longer a luxury -- it is a necessity. Millions of Americans enjoy the benefits it produces. Businessmen and women are able to drive to their appointments in comfort and arrive fresh and alert. Those who suffer from allergies are able to travel without fear of coming in contact with excessive dust and airborne pollens. With all America on the move, automotive air conditioning is playing an important role in promoting the comfort, health, and safety of travelers throughout the land.

How does this affect you? As the popularity of automobile air conditioning in cars and trucks increases, it is obvious that there is an increased need for maintenance and service personnel. Many shops that just a few years ago took on air conditioning as a "fill-in" now find this service their primary "moneymaker."

All that is required to handle this, the most expensive of all automobile options, is a working knowledge and understanding of the operation and function of the controls and circuits of the automobile air conditioner, as well as a good knowledge of the equipment, special tools, techniques, and "tricks" of the trade.

There has been a rapid increase of automobiles equipped with air conditioning systems during the past twenty years or so. Only 40,600 automobiles were equipped with air conditioning in 1953, but the trend was fast growing. In 1957, just four years later, the figure was 405,404 — almost ten times as many. In 1962 the one million figure was reached, and in three years that figure was doubled. Over two million 1965 automobiles were equipped with air conditioning. In 1967 the figure was a staggering 3,546,255 units. In 1972 about 70% of all domestic automobiles were equipped with air conditioning. The figure is expected to "level off" at 80%. It is easy to understand how automotive air conditioning has become the cooling industry's most sought after product.

REVIEW QUESTIONS

1. Who was the first automobile manufacturer to offer true air conditioning?

   _____

2. How did moving the stones of Pharaoh's palace into the desert at night help in keeping the palace cool during the day? _____

   _____

3. What do you feel has been man's greatest accomplishment because of air conditioning? _____

   _____

4. What percentage of production cars are expected to be equipped with air conditioning in the next ten years? _____

5. What are some of the benefits of automotive air conditioning?_____

   _____

   _____

Topic 2 BODY COMFORT

The normal temperature of the adult human body is 98.6° F. This temperature is sometimes called "subsurface" or "deep-tissue" temperature as opposed to "surface" or "skin" temperature. An understanding of the manner by which the body maintains this temperature will help to understand the manner by which the air conditioning process helps to keep the body comfortable.

THE BODY PRODUCES HEAT

All food taken into the body contains heat in the form of calories. The 'large" or "great" calorie, which is used to express the heat value of food, is the amount of heat required to raise one kilogram of water one degree centigrade. To further express the calorie, 252 calories equal one British thermal unit. One British thermal unit (BTU) equals the amount of heat required to raise the temperature of one pound of water one degree Fahrenheit.

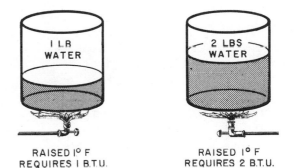

EFFECT OF WEIGHT ON B.T.U.

As calories are taken into the body, they are converted into energy and stored for future use. The conversion process generates heat and all body movements not only use up the stored energy, but also add to the heat generated by the conversion process.

For body comfort, all the heat produced must be given off by the body. Since the body consistently produces more heat than it requires, heat must be constantly given off or removed.

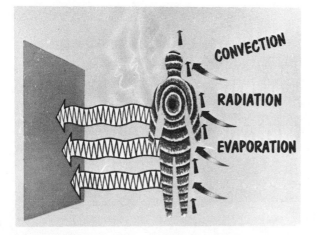

THE BODY REJECTS HEAT

The constant removal of body heat takes place through three natural processes which usually occur simultaneously. These processes are:

- convection

- radiation

- evaporation

Convection

The convection process of removing heat is based on two phenomena:

 Heat flows from a hot surface to a surface containing less heat. For example, heat will flow from the body to the surrounding air that is below the skin temperature.

 Heat rises. This is evident by observing the smoke from a burning cigarette, or the steam from a boiling pot.

When these two phenomena are applied to the body process of removing heat, the following occurs:

✓ The body gives off heat to the less hot surrounding air.

✓ The surrounding air becomes warmer and moves upward.

✓ As the warmer air moves upward, less warm air takes its place, and the convection cycle is completed.

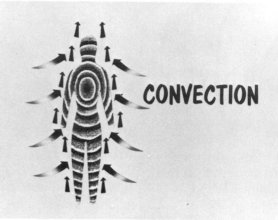

Radiation

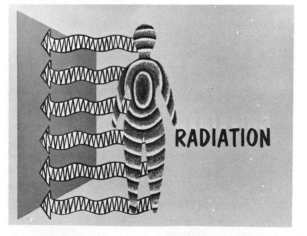

Radiation is the process which moves heat from a heat source to an object by means of heat rays. This principle is based on the phenomenon, noted previously, that heat moves from a hot surface to a less hot surface. Radiation takes place independent of convection, however, and does not require air movement to complete the heat transfer. It is not affected by air temperature although it is affected by the temperature of the surrounding surfaces.

The body quickly experiences the effects of sun radiation when it moves from a shady to a sunny area.

Evaporation

Evaporation is the process in which moisture becomes a vapor. As moisture evaporates from a warm surface, it removes heat and thus cools the surface. This

6

process takes place constantly on the body surface. Moisture is given off through the pores of the skin, and, as the moisture evaporates, it removes heat from the body.

Perspiration that appears as drops of moisture on the body, indicates the body is producing more heat than can be removed by convection, radiation, and normal evaporation.

CONDITIONS THAT AFFECT BODY HEAT

The three main factors that affect body heat are:

- temperature
- humidity
- air movement

Temperature

Cool air increases the rate of convection; warm air slows it down.

Cool air lowers the temperature of the surrounding surfaces and, therefore, increases the rate of radiation; warm air raises the surrounding surface temperature and, therefore, decreases the radiation rate. Cool air increases the rate of evaporation, warm air slows it down, depending upon the amount of moisture already in the air, and upon the amount of air movement.

Humidity

Moisture in the air is measured in terms of humidity. For example, 50 percent relative humidity means that the air contains one half of the amount of moisture that it is capable of holding at a given temperature. To better understand the measurement of humidity, a unit called a "grain of water vapor" is used. To give you an idea of the size of a "grain" a cup of water contains about 2,800 of them.

A low relative humidity permits heat to be given off from the body by evaporation. This occurs because the air at low humidity is relatively "dry" and thus can readily absorb moisture. A high relative humidity has the opposite effect; it slows down the evaporation process and thus decreases the speed at which heat can be removed by evaporation. An acceptable comfort range for the human body is 72-80°F. at 45-50% relative humidity.

Air Movement

Another factor which affects the ability of the body to give off heat is the movement of air around the body. As the air movement increases:

● The evaporation process of removing body heat speeds up since moisture in the air near the body is carried away at a faster rate.

● The convection process increases since the layer of warm air surrounding the body is carried away more rapidly.

● The radiation process tends to accelerate because the heat on the surrounding surfaces is removed at a faster rate, causing heat to radiate from the body at a faster rate.

As air movement decreases, the evaporation, convection and radiation processes decrease.

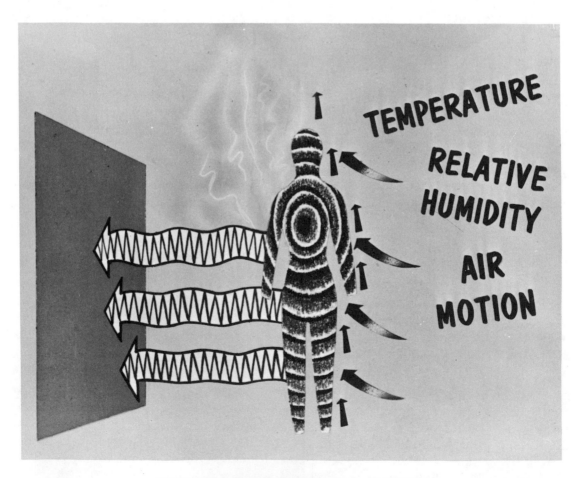

CONDITIONS WHICH AFFECT BODY COMFORT

REVIEW QUESTIONS

The following may be answered true (T) or false (F). (Questions 1 through 10)

_____ 1. Normal body temperature is 97.6° F.

_____ 2. The direction of heat flow is from a less warm to a warm surface.

_____ 3. Radiation and convection both depend on air movement for heat transfer.

_____ 4. Evaporation of perspiration is slower if the relative humidity of the air is low.

_____ 5. There are 252 calories in one BTU.

_____ 6. A large calorie is the amount of heat required to raise one pound of water one degree centigrade.

_____ 7. Relative humidity of 100% means that the air at a given temperature holds all of the moisture it is capable of holding.

_____ 8. The comfort range of the human body is 72–80° F.

_____ 9. The comfort range of the human body is 45–50% relative humidity.

_____ 10. The body continuously produces more heat than it needs.

11. Why do we perspire? _____

_____

12. Explain the three methods by which the body gives off heat.

a. _____ b. _____ c. _____

13. The body receives heat in two ways. Describe each.

a. _____

b. _____

14. A group of people in an enclosed room will raise the temperature of the room. Explain why this happens. _____

_____

Topic 3 MATTER

Since heat energy and the effect of heat within an air-conditioning system must be understood by the technician, the topics which follow deal with matter, heat, pressure, and the basic principles of refrigeration. These physical laws are fundamental to the understanding of air-conditioning systems. We will begin with a review of matter.

Matter is defined as anything that occupies space and has weight. All things around us are composed of matter and are found in one of three forms: solid, liquid, or gas. An easily understandable example of this is one of our more common elements, water. Water in its natural form is liquid. If some of its natural heat were removed it would turn to ice, a solid. If heat were added to water and the temperature raised enough, it would boil and vaporize, changing to gas (steam).

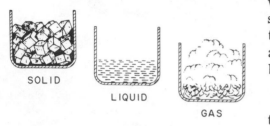

SOLID

LIQUID

GAS

THREE BASIC STATES OF MATTER

All things around us may be transferred to one of these three states of matter; however, we always think of them in their natural state.

Water, for instance, as a liquid will flow and will assume the shape of the container in which it is placed. As a liquid it cannot take a shape of its own, and in a container will exert a force out and downward. The greatest force will be toward the bottom, diminishing toward the top.

Steam or gas will dissipate into the surrounding air if not contained. Gas exerts pressure in all directions with equal force when in a sealed, or enclosed container.

Water in the solid state, or ice, will hold a certain shape and size. This shape will exert force in a downward direction only.

THE STRUCTURE OF MATTER

All matter, regardless of its state, is composed of small parts (particles) called "molecules." What happens to the speed freedom (or position) and number of these molecules determines:

● the state of the material

● its temperature

● its effect upon other parts or mechanisms of which it may be a part.

Each molecule of matter is actually the smallest particle of a material which retains all the properties

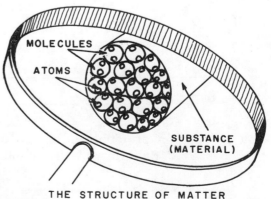

MOLECULES

ATOMS

SUBSTANCE (MATERIAL)

THE STRUCTURE OF MATTER

of the original material. For example, if a grain of salt were divided in two, and each subsequent particle again divided (and the process were continued as finely as possible) the smallest "stable" particle having all the properties of salt would be a molecule of salt. The word "stable" means that a molecule is satisfied to remain as it is.

As fine as the molecule may seem to be from this description, each molecule is in itself made up of even smaller particles of matter. These particles are known as "atoms." An atom is the smallest particle of matter having properties of the material of which it is composed. By contrast, the atoms within a molecule are not always stable. Instead, atoms have a tendency to join up with atoms of other substances forming new and different molecules and substances.

ARRANGEMENT AND MOVEMENT OF MOLECULES

The molecules in a given material are all alike. Different materials have different molecules. The characteristics and properties of different materials depend upon the nature and arrangement of the molecules. While millions upon millions of molecules form a material, the behavior of each molecule depends largely upon the material (substance) of which the molecule is composed.

NATURAL
GAS MOLECULE
(METHANE)

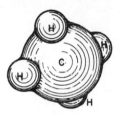

FOUR HYDROGEN ATOMS COMBINED WITH
ONE CARBON ATOM

WATER
MOLECULE

TWO HYDROGEN ATOMS COMBINED WITH
ONE OXYGEN ATOM

MOLECULES

Regardless of state, the molecules in a material are moving continuously. This movement or energy is called "kinetic" because it is an energy of motion. The addition of heat energy to a solid increases the kinetic energy of its molecules. In solids, this motion of the molecules is in the form of vibration where the particles never move far from a fixed position.

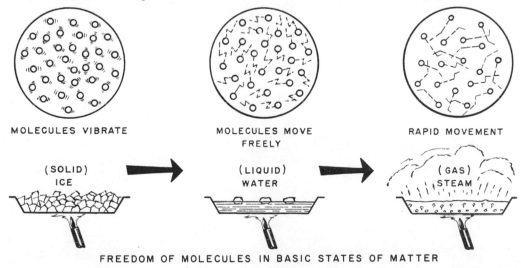

MOLECULES VIBRATE   MOLECULES MOVE   RAPID MOVEMENT
                               FREELY

(SOLID)   (LIQUID)   (GAS)
ICE   WATER   STEAM

FREEDOM OF MOLECULES IN BASIC STATES OF MATTER

We cause a change of state by taking away or adding heat energy. Heat, then, becomes the factor that governs the movement of the molecules making up the substance. In removing heat we cause the molecular action to slow down and this causes the liquids to solidify. By adding heat, the molecular action is speeded up and we can cause a liquid to boil.

REVIEW QUESTIONS

1. The three states of matter are _____ , _____ , and _____ .

2. When we remove heat from a liquid we cause a change of state to a _____ _____ .

3. In which direction will matter in the state of gas exert pressure? _____

4. Steam is water in the _____ state.

5. How may we effect a change of state from a liquid to a gas? _____ _____

6. How does the movement of the molecules differ between a liquid and a gas? _____

7. This movement of the molecules is known as _____ energy, because it is an energy of motion.

Topic 4 HEAT

As stated in Topic 2, heat may be transmitted in one of three ways; by conduction, convection, or radiation.

The term conduction means that a transfer of heat through a solid is taking place. An example of this is a piece of meat frying in a pan. Heat from the stove burner is conducted through the pan and cooks the meat.

The term convection means the transfer of heat by circulation of heated portions of a fluid. The automobile cooling system is a good example of convection cooling. The water, or coolant, in the cooling system carries off the heat created by the engine from the block to the radiator and then it is dissipated into the surrounding air.

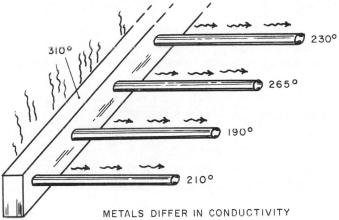

METALS DIFFER IN CONDUCTIVITY

Radiation is the term used when applied to the transmission of heat without heating the medium through which it is transmitted. About the best example of this is a good sunburn at the beach. The heat from the sun, or at least part of it, was transmitted to you through the air, or atmosphere.

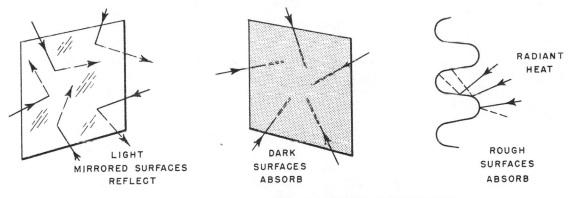

LIGHT
MIRRORED SURFACES
REFLECT

DARK
SURFACES
ABSORB

RADIANT
HEAT

ROUGH
SURFACES
ABSORB

REFLECTION, TRANSMISSION AND ABSORPTION OF HEAT RAYS

SENSIBLE HEAT

Sensible heat is any heat that we can measure on a thermometer. Sensible heat is heat that we can feel.

The temperature of the air that surrounds us, referred to as ambient temperature, is sensible heat. When the temperature of the air drops ten or fifteen degrees, we feel cool. An increase in the temperature causes us to feel warmer.

HEAT MEASURE

Heat energy is measured in terms of the calorie. The gram calorie is the smallest measure of heat energy. It takes one calorie to raise one gram of water from 15°C. to 16°C.

In our work, we will use the term British thermal unit, or BTU. There are 252 calories in one BTU. It takes one BTU to raise the temperature of one pound, or pint, of water one degree Fahrenheit.

Water, as we all know, is liquid between the temperatures of 32° F. and 212° F. This is a range of 180 degrees and is called subcooled liquid. For each BTU of heat we add to each pound of water in this range we will raise the temperature one degree.

If we were to take one pound of water at 32° F. and add 180 BTUs we could raise the temperature to 212° F.

To determine this, we must divide the BTUs being added by the number of pounds or pints, of water to which the BTUs are being added. This result is then added to the original temperature to obtain the new temperature.

$$BTUs \div lbs. = H \text{ (heat)}$$

$$H + temp. = new temp.$$

Let's add 180 BTUs to one pound of water at 32° F. and see what happens:

$$180 \text{ BTUs} \div 1 \text{ lb.} = 180 \text{ BTUs}$$

$$180 \text{ BTUs} + 32° F. = 212° F.$$

If we were to take ten pounds of water at 32° F. and add the same 180 BTUs we would only raise the temperature of the water to 50° F.

$$180 \text{ BTUs} \div 10 \text{ lbs.} = 18 \text{ BTUs}$$

$$18 \text{ BTUs} + 32° F. = 50° F.$$

We have added the same 180 BTUs in each case and have raised the temperature of both, but since we had ten times as much water in the second pan we only raised the temperature of the water one-tenth as much. It would take 1,800 BTUs to raise the temperature of ten pounds of water from 32° F. to 212° F.

$$1,800 \text{ BTUs} \div 10 \text{ lbs.} = 180 \text{ BTUs}$$

$$180 \text{ BTUs} + 32° F. = 212° F.$$

LATENT HEAT

Latent heat is the term applied to heat that is needed to cause a change of state of matter. This heat cannot be recorded on a thermometer, nor can it be felt.

Since we cannot use a thermometer to measure latent heat, we will use the British thermal unit, or BTU, as a standard of measure for the amount or quantity.

A change of state occurs when a solid changes to a liquid or a liquid changes to a gas or vice versa.

Water, for instance, at atmospheric pressure between 32° F. and 212° F. is called subcooled liquid. Water at exactly 212° F. is called saturated liquid; that is, it contains all of the heat possible to remain a liquid. Any addition of heat would cause it to boil, or vaporize.

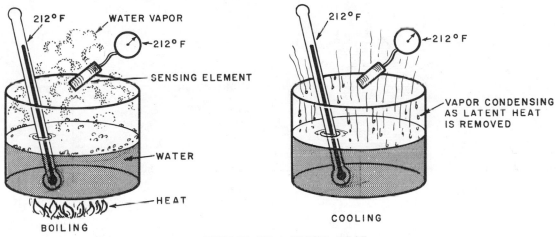

EFFECT OF LATENT HEAT

The amount of heat required to cause a change of state of one pound of water at 212° F. to one pound of steam at 212° F. is 970 BTUs. This is referred to as the latent heat of vaporization.

This is latent heat, which cannot be measured on a thermometer, and, you will note, does not cause a change of temperature.

Conversely, steam with an intensity of 212° F. will give up 970 BTUs of heat per pound as it condenses into water at 212° F. The heat released in this process is referred to as the latent heat of condensation.

The removal of an additional 180 BTUs per pound will lower the temperature of the water and can be measured on the thermometer until we reach 32° F.

At 32° F., the water has had all the heat removed that can be without causing a change of state. The amount of heat removal required to change one pound of water at 32° F. to one pound of ice at 32° F. is 144 BTUs. This is referred to as the latent heat of fusion.

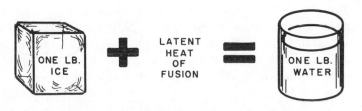

CHANGE FROM SOLID TO LIQUID STATE

This principle is the basis for air conditioning. A refrigerant is chosen for its ability to absorb and give up large quantities of heat rapidly.

It is by this process that we remove heat from the inside of the car and dissipate the heat in the outside air.

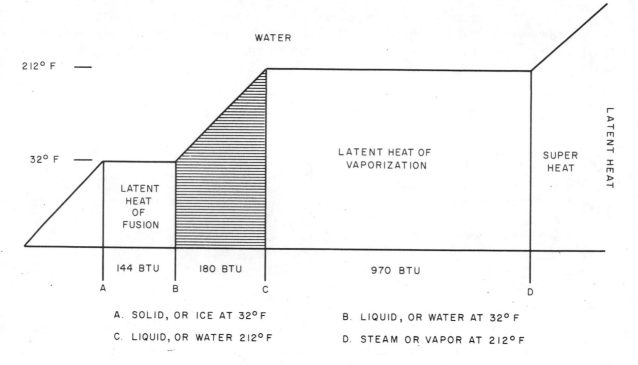

A. SOLID, OR ICE AT 32°F   B. LIQUID, OR WATER AT 32°F

C. LIQUID, OR WATER 212°F   D. STEAM OR VAPOR AT 212°F

SPECIFIC HEAT

Every element or compound which exists in nature or is manufactured has its own heat characteristics and the capacity to expel heat. Every substance has a different capacity for accepting or emitting heat. If we had a table full of miscellaneous items and, under laboratory conditions, measured the amount of heat we could remove from each, we would have as many heat values as there were items on the table.

The capacity to expel heat, or absorb heat, is known as "specific heat," or "thermal heat." It is defined as the amount of heat that can be absorbed by the material in order to undergo a temperature change of 1° F.

As an experiment, take three small balls, each made of a different substance, such as copper, steel and glass. Heat them in a container of hot oil until they have all reached the same temperature. Now place each of the three balls on a slab of paraffin and watch the results. Each ball will make a different depth in the paraffin, depending on the amount of heat emitted. This experiment points out that, at the same temperature, different materials absorb and emit different amounts of heat.

A scale has been devised to show the relation of various substances' ability to absorb or emit heat. Water, a common element, is used as a standard around which a specific heat scale has been devised. The value of water is given as 1. or 1.00. Most materials require less heat per pound to raise their temperature than does water. A couple of exceptions are ammonia, which has a specific heat of 1.10 and hydrogen, having a specific heat of 3.41.

For instance, it requires about 1/5 as many BTUs to raise the temperature of one pound of glass one degree Fahrenheit as compared with an equal amount of water. The specific heat of glass is .194. The specific heat of copper is .093, meaning that it takes only about 1/11th as many BTUs to raise the temperature of one pound of this material one degree Fahrenheit as it does one pound of water.

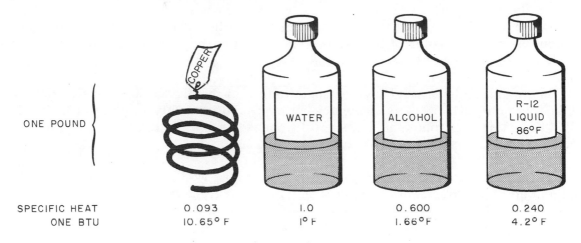

ONE POUND	COPPER	WATER	ALCOHOL	R-12 LIQUID 86°F
SPECIFIC HEAT	0.093	1.0	0.600	0.240
ONE BTU	10.65° F	1° F	1.66°F	4.2° F

When a comparison is made between glass and water and copper and water, it can be seen that it takes only .194 and .093 times as much heat to change the temperature of these materials one degree Fahrenheit. This condition exists because materials vary their ability to absorb and exchange heat. As with the experiment with the paraffin, if equal amounts of copper, steel, glass, or any other substance are heated through equal changes of temperature, each material will have absorbed a different amount of heat.

Knowing that the specific heat of water is 1.00, and that it requires one BTU to raise its temperature one degree Fahrenheit per pound, it is easy to determine how many degrees per pound other materials will be raised simply by dividing its specific heat value into 1.00.

OTHER SPECIFIC HEAT VALUES OF SOLIDS, LIQUIDS AND GASES ARE:			
Air	.240	Nitrogen	.240
Alcohol	.600	Oxygen	.220
Aluminum	.230	Rubber	.481
Brass	.086	Silver	.055
Carbon dioxide	.200	Steel	.118
Carbon tetrachloride	.200	Sulphuric acid	.336
Gasoline	.700	Tin	.045
Lead	.031	Water, sea	.940

For instance, the specific heat of aluminum is .230. We find that one BTU will raise the temperature of one pound of aluminum 4.35°F. This is determined as follows:

$$1.000 \div .230 = 4.347°F. \ (4.35°F.)$$

Values for other materials may be determined in the same manner. For example, the specific heat of lead is .031. One BTU will raise the temperature of one pound of lead 32.25° F., determined as follows:

$$1.000 \div .031 = 32.254°F. \ (32.25°F.)$$

Other specific heat that we may be concerned with is referred to as heat load. In an automobile, the color of the car is a factor, as is the amount of glass area and the number of passengers.

In a refrigerated truck body, the specific heat of the product being refrigerated is taken into consideration, as is the amount of insulation and type of material in the body. The number of times the doors will be opened as well as the length of time the product is to be refrigerated is also an important factor.

Specific heat of the product to be refrigerated as well as that of the materials used and other requirements are taken into consideration when estimating the size of the unit required. It is with the aid of these specific heat ratings that refrigeration requirements may be calculated to a given job.

More information may be found on this subject in Principles of Air Conditioning, section 3, and Principles of Refrigeration, unit 6. Both are published by Delmar Publishers.

COLD — THE ABSENCE OF HEAT

What is cold? What is meant by the term cold? We refer to an object as being cold and give no further thought to it. Cold is the absence of heat. To understand the term cold, we must first understand what heat is.

Heat is energy. Heat is ever present. We cannot contain it. The molecular structure of all things is changed into one of three forms by heat.

Heat is molecular movement. For instance, we have demonstrated in Topic 3 that water is liquid between 32° F. and 212° F. Add heat to water at 212° F. and we increase its molecular movement. It will vaporize, or turn to steam. Take heat away from water at 32° F. and we will decrease its molecular movement. It will solidify, or turn to ice.

With water we have demonstrated again the three states of matter: solid, liquid, and gas. We have changed them using heat as energy.

All matter generates heat, referred to as specific heat. The body generates heat that must be overcome for you to feel cool. The food in your refrigerator generates heat that must be overcome in order to keep the food at a safe temperature, or frozen in the freezer. We must overcome, or remove, the heat, or part of it, from all matter that is to be cooled.

Now, what is cold? It is beginning to look like cold is the absence of all heat. If this is true, at what point do we remove all the heat?

How about ice at 32° F.? Cold, but how about solid carbon dioxide, or dry ice, that is -109.3° F.? Dry ice is so cold that when you touch it you get the sensation of being burned. We cannot say that this is cold either, because it still contains many BTUs of heat.

Cold, then, is the absence of all heat. This does not occur until we reach the temperature of -459.67° F. All temperature above that contains heat. For instance, -459° F. still contains .67° F. of heat.

Even so, if you were exposed to temperatures this cold, for even a few minutes, you would become frozen so solidly that if someone were to touch you with a screwdriver blade you would shatter like marble being crushed by a hammer.

However, there is no danger that you will come into contact with temperatures so cold. Absolute cold has not been accomplished by man. Like all other things perfect, or absolute, it is believed that the complete removal of heat cannot be accomplished. A Dutch physicist, Wander de Haas, working at the University of Leiden, reached a temperature of .0044° C. above absolute zero. In 1957 Dr. Arthur Spohr, working at the Naval Research Laboratory, reached a temperature of less than one-millionth of a degree Kelvin above absolute zero.

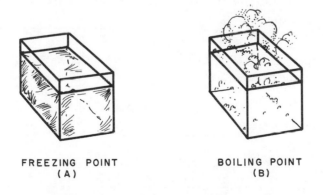

FREEZING POINT   BOILING POINT
     (A)   (B)

FIXED REFERENCE POINTS ON TEMPERATURE SCALES

Summarizing then, cold is the absence of heat energy. An absolute zero is the point at which all molecular movement stops. Since molecular movement causes heat energy, it follows that if there were no movement there would no longer be any heat. This condition has not yet been attained.

REVIEW QUESTIONS

1. Explain heat transfer by convection. _____
   _____
   _____
   _____

2. How is heat from the sun transmitted?
   _____
   _____
   _____

3. Define sensible heat. _____
   _____
   _____
   _____

4. What do we mean when we refer to ambient temperature? _____
   _____
   _____

5. What is the smallest measure of heat energy? _____

6. What is the boiling point of water at sea level? _____

7. If we were to add 160 BTUs to one pound of water at 35° F. what would the new temperature be? _____

8. If we were to add 180 BTUs to eight pounds of water at 35° F. what would the new temperature be? _____

9. If we were to add 180 BTUs to one pound of water at 32° F. what would the new temperature be? _____

10. What is latent heat? _____
    _____
    _____

11. What is specific heat? _____
    _____
    _____

12. What is absolute cold? _____

13. How many BTUs of heat energy must water at 40°.F. give up per pound to cause a change of state to a solid? _____

14. How many BTUs of heat energy must be added to water per pound at 40° F. to cause a change of state to a vapor? _____

15. Which of the following require less heat for a temperature change of 1°F.?
                              (water, gasoline, carbon tetrachloride)
_____

    Refer to the specific heat table at the bottom of page 17. If we add one BTU to one pound of the following matter, what will the increase in temperature be in degrees F.

16. Air   _____   19. Sulphuric acid   _____

17. Carbon tetrachloride _____   20. Rubber   _____

18. Silver   _____

Topic 5 PRESSURE

Understanding air conditioning necessitates understanding pressure. Webster's Dictionary defines pressure as a force acting against an opposing force.

The world we live in is surrounded by air, or gas. This is a form of matter in the gas state. As explained in Topic 3, gas exerts pressure in all directions with equal force.

The gas surrounding us is made up of 21% oxygen and 78% nitrogen. The remaining 1% is made up of other rare gases. This combination of gases is called atmosphere and extends some six hundred miles above the earth and is held there by gravity.

ATMOSPHERIC PRESSURE

This six-hundred mile belt of gas enveloping the earth exerts pressure that is measured in pounds per square inch, p.s.i.

In order to determine what the force of this pressure is, we take one square inch and find that the pressure exerted from the 600-mile column of gas is 14.69 p.s.i. This figure, rounded off to 14.7 p.s.i., is known as atmospheric pressure.

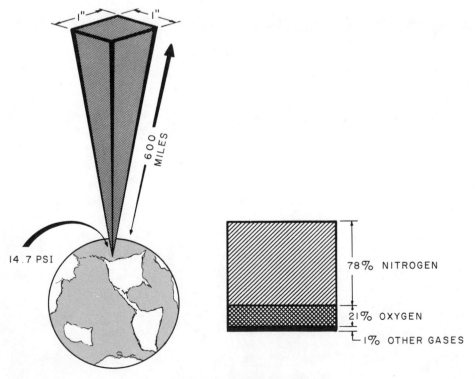

ATMOSPHERIC PRESSURE

TEMPERATURE AND PRESSURE

We refer to all pressures above atmospheric pressure as gage pressures, and all pressures below atmospheric pressure as a vacuum.

Zero gage pressure will remain zero regardless of what the altitude is. Pressures above atmospheric pressure will be recorded as pounds per square inch gage, or p.s.i.g. Pressure below atmospheric pressure will be recorded as inches of mercury or in. Hg (in. the abbreviation for inch and Hg the chemical symbol for mercury).

At sea level, atmospheric pressure (14.7 p.s.i.), the boiling point of water is 212° F. If we were at a point higher then sea level, the atmospheric pressure is lower and so is the boiling point of water. The point at which water boils decreases at about 1.1 degrees per thousand feet of altitude. To find the boiling point of water at any given altitude, simply multiply the altitude, in thousands of feet, by 1.1. The result of this should be subtracted from 212° F. for the new boiling point. For instance, if we were in an airplane flying at a height of 12,000 feet, water would boil at about 198.8° F.

$$12,000 \text{ ft.} \div 1,000 = 12$$

$$12 \times 1.1 = 13.2$$

$$212° \text{ F.} - 13.2 = 198.8° \text{ F.}$$

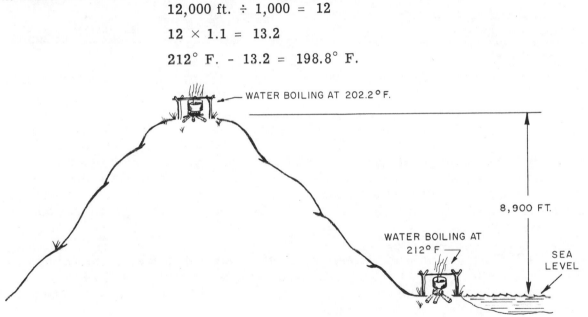

WATER BOILING AT 202.2° F.

WATER BOILING AT 212° F

8,900 FT.

SEA LEVEL

In Colorado water will boil at a lower temperature than it will in the flatlands or at sea level. An elevation there of 8,900 feet will work out as follows:

$$8,900 \text{ ft.} \div 1,000 = 8.9$$

$$8.9 \times 1.1 = 9.79 \text{ or } 9.8$$

$$212° \text{ F.} - 9.8° \text{ F.} = 202.2° \text{ F.}$$

The new boiling point for water for this particular part of Colorado is now about 202° F.

If the boiling point of water is affected by a pressure drop, then it is likely that a pressure increase will also affect the boiling point of water.

Our wives often take advantage of this principle when they prepare a meal with a pressure cooker. The boiling point of the water is increased because the pressure is increased. As the water changes from a liquid to a steam, or vapor, a pressure is created because the vapor cannot escape. This superheats the vapor to a higher temperature. The food is cooked much quicker because it is exposed to a greater temperature and pressure.

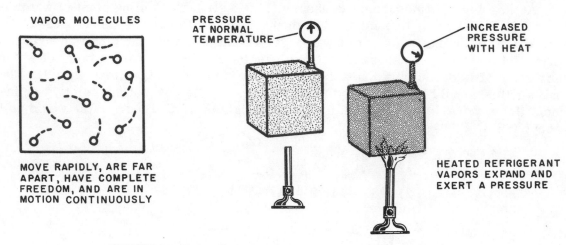

VAPOR MOLECULES

MOVE RAPIDLY, ARE FAR APART, HAVE COMPLETE FREEDOM, AND ARE IN MOTION CONTINUOUSLY

PRESSURE AT NORMAL TEMPERATURE

INCREASED PRESSURE WITH HEAT

HEATED REFRIGERANT VAPORS EXPAND AND EXERT A PRESSURE

TEMPERATURE RISE AFFECTS MOVEMENT AND PRESSURE

The automobile cooling system is another example of increasing temperature by increasing pressure. Some manufacturers have increased the working pressure of the cooling system to sixteen pounds pressure or more. With each increase per pound the boiling point of the water, or coolant, is increased about three degrees Fahrenheit.

A cooling system with a pressure cap of 7 p.s.i. will increase the boiling point of the coolant to about 233° F. To find the difference in boiling points of the coolant, multiply the rating of the cap in pounds by 3° F. The sum of this should be added to 212° F. to get the new boiling point.

$$7 \text{ p.s.i.} \times 3° \text{ F.} = 21° \text{ F.}$$

$$21° \text{ F.} + 212° \text{ F.} = 233° \text{ F.}$$

To find the boiling point of the coolant in a system with a 12-pound cap, follow the same procedure.

$$12 \text{ p.s.i.} \times 3° \text{ F.} = 36° \text{ F.}$$

$$36° \text{ F.} + 212° \text{ F.} = 248° \text{ F.}$$

Our new boiling point will now be 248° F.

If we had an apparatus that we knew would hold the temperature of the coolant at 260° F. and wanted to pressurize the system, we could determine the size of the cap to use by subtracting the normal boiling point of water from the desired temperature. We will divide the sum of that by 3° F. to get the size cap required in pounds. In this case we should require a 16-pound cap.

$$260° \text{ F. } - 212° \text{ F. } = 48° \text{ F.}$$
$$48° \text{ F. } \div 3° \text{ F. } = 16 \text{ p.s.i.}$$

If water boils at a higher temperature when pressure is applied to it and at a lower temperature when the pressure is low, it is easy to see how we can, to a greater degree of accuracy, control temperature if we control pressure.

REVIEW QUESTIONS

1. Define pressure. _____

_____

_____

_____

2. Define atmospheric pressure. _____

_____

_____

_____

3. What is atmospheric pressure at sea level?_____

4. What is the abbreviation p.s.i.g. ? _____

5. For what chemical is the symbol Hg used? _____

6. Where do we use the symbol Hg in refrigeration service? _____

_____

7. All pressures above atmospheric pressure are referred to as _____ pressures.

8. The boiling point of water at sea level is 212° F. What is the boiling point of water at 6,000'? at 8,500'? at 10,000'?

_____ , _____ , _____

9. What is the boiling point of water under a pressure of 3 p.s.i.? _____

10. What is the chief advantage of a pressurized cooling system? _____

_____

11. How does driving at high altitudes affect water in the cooling system of a nonpressurized system? _____

_____

12. How does driving at high altitudes affect water in the cooling system of a pressurized system? _____

_____

Topic 6 PRINCIPLES OF REFRIGERATION

AIR CONDITIONING

Usually when you hear the term "air conditioning," the first thing that comes to your mind is cold fresh air. Actually, a true air-conditioning system automatically controls the temperature, humidity, purity and circulation of air. In automotive language, air conditioning is any system that cools and dehumidifies the air inside of the passenger compartment of the automobile or truck.

THE MECHANICAL REFRIGERATION SYSTEM

In a mechanical refrigeration system, such as found in the modern automobile, a special refrigerant absorbs heat inside of the evaporator by changing from a liquid to a vapor. The evaporator is that part of the refrigeration system that is located inside the passenger compartment. Thus, air blown over the fins of the evaporator is directed to the passengers inside of the car for their comfort.

We say that the refrigerant absorbs heat inside the evaporator; we must dispose of this heat. We could just expel the heat-laden refrigerant vapor to the outside air, but this would be much too expensive. The refrigerant is reclaimed for reuse in the system and just the heat is removed and expelled to the outside air.

Reclaiming the refrigerant begins at the compressor. The compressor pressurizes the heat-laden vapor until its pressure and heat reach a point that is much hotter than the outside air. The compressor also pumps the vapor to the condenser, where it gives up its heat and changes once again to a liquid. The condenser is that part of the unit that is located outside the passenger compartment. Since the air passing over the condenser is much cooler than the vapor inside, the vapor gives up much of its heat and changes state to a liquid.

The refrigerant, now liquid, then passes to the receiver/drier where it is stored until needed again by the evaporator.

Here, in the mechanical refrigeration system, we demonstrate the three basic laws of refrigeration. These are the basis of all of the refrigeration in the world, natural or mechanical. The only exception is solar heat - the earth and sun relationship.

```
LAW I

To refrigerate is to remove heat.
The absence of heat is cold. Heat
is ever present.
```

As stated in Law I, we are removing the heat from the passenger compartment of the automobile. In so doing, we are lowering the temperature; the absence of heat is cold.

> ## LAW II
>
> Heat is ready to flow or pass to any-thing that has less heat. Nothing can stop the flow of heat; we can only slow it down. We cannot contain heat, no matter how much insulation we use.

As stated in Law II, heat is ready to flow to anything that contains less heat. Such is the case of the special refrigerant in the evaporator.

> ## LAW III
>
> For a liquid to change to a gas it has to take on heat. The heat is carried off in the gas vapor.

As stated in Law III, the liquid refrigerant in the evaporator takes on heat as it changes to a vapor. This heat is carried off to be expelled outside of the car.

TON OF REFRIGERATION

For years refrigeration units were advertised, and sold with the rating of horse-power or hp. The horsepower is a theoretical unit of energy. One horsepower is the amount of energy required to raise 33,000 pounds one foot in one minute.

Units were referred to as 1/4 hp., 1/2 hp., 3/4 hp., or 1 hp. This was a consider-ably inaccurate method of considering the output of an air-conditioning unit since the horsepower rating referred to the compressor size only.

A ton of refrigeration was generally considered as one horsepower. A half horsepower unit was considered a half ton of refrigeration.

To arrive at a ton of refrigeration we must know that the latent heat of fusion, the amount of heat required to cause a change of state of one pound of ice at 32° F. to one pound of water at 32° F., is 144 BTUs.

We use this as a basis, or formula, for obtaining a ton of refrigeration. In a short ton there are 2,000 pounds of matter, or in this case, solid water. We know that it requires 144 BTUs to change one pound of this solid water (ice) to liquid. Then for one ton we must multiply the amount of energy required to change one pound by the weight in pounds of a ton.

$$144 \text{ BTUs} \times 2{,}000 \text{ lbs.} = 288{,}000 \text{ BTUs}$$

This gives us the amount of BTUs required to cause a change of state of one ton of ice to one ton of liquid in twenty-four hours. In order to determine the BTU/hr. rating, we must divide this figure by 24.

$$144 \text{ BTUs} \times 2{,}000 \text{ lbs.} = 288{,}000 \text{ BTUs}$$

$$288{,}000 \text{ BTUs} \div 24 \text{ hrs.} = 12{,}000 \text{ BTU/hr.}$$

One ton of refrigeration now becomes 12,000 BTU/hr. Most air-conditioning units are sold now on a BTU rating rather than by ton or horsepower. When an advertiser lists his unit as a one-ton unit he must also list the BTU rating of the machine. The reason for this is that machines of a lesser BTU rating have been passed off as one-ton units. For example; a 3/4 ton unit should have a rating of 9,000 BTUs.

$$144 \text{ BTUs} \times 2{,}000 \text{ lbs.} = 288{,}000 \text{ BTUs}$$

$$288{,}000 \text{ BTUs} \times 3/4 \text{ ton} = 216{,}000 \text{ BTUs}$$

$$216{,}000 \text{ BTUs} \div 24 \text{ hrs.} = 9{,}000 \text{ BTU/hr.}$$

This gives us a figure of 3,000 BTUs for each quarter ton of refrigeration.

What then should 11,000 BTU/hr. be? From the standpoint of rating by ton or horsepower, since one is the closest, the machine becomes a 1-ton or 1-hp. unit. The same holds true with a 13,000 BTU/hr. unit.

To go a step further, suppose a machine (A) is rated at 10,525 BTU/hr. Another machine (B) is rated at 13,475 BTU/hr. Since both of these figures are closer to 1 hp. than they are to the next fraction, or quarter horsepower, they both must be rated as 1 hp. Actually, these two machines are almost a quarter horsepower apart in rating.

Machine A	10,525 BTU/hr.
Machine B	13,475 BTU/hr.
Difference	2,950 BTU/hr.

It is easy to see that in buying air conditioners on a hp. or ton rating, they may not always be what they seem to be.

Automotive air conditioners are rated at well over a ton of refrigeration. Because of the tremendous heat load on the car, a unit of 8,000 to 10,000 BTUs would do a very poor job of keeping the average car of today cool.

General Motors, for instance, rates their factory installed units at a full one and three-quarter tons, or about 21,000 BTUs. This is the amount of cooling that would be required to cool the average two-bedroom home. Of course, a house is well insulated and the problem of heat by radiation is not so great.

REVIEW QUESTIONS

1. What is a ton of refrigeration? _____

_____

_____

2. What is a horsepower of refrigeration? _____

_____

3. Why are units referred to in terms of BTU/hr. rating now instead of by the ton or horsepower? _____

_____

_____

4. What could the range BTU rating of a 1-ton unit be? _____

_____

5. What is the capacity of the air conditioner of the average car today?

_____

6. The absence of _____ is cold. We remove the _____ from the passenger compartment as it passes through the _____.

7. Heat is ready to flow to anything that has less _____ . Heat is readily absorbed by the less _____ refrigerant in the _____ .

8. As the liquid refrigerant takes on _____ it changes to a _____ .

9. Heat is dissipated in the outside air in the _____ .

10. As refrigerant gives up its heat, it changes from a _____ to a _____ .

Topic 7 REFRIGERANTS

The term, refrigerant, refers to the fluid used in a refrigerating system to produce "cold" by removing heat. Refrigerant 12 has been adopted for automotive use because it has the highest safety factor of any refrigerant available that is capable of withstanding high pressures and temperatures without deteriorating or decomposing.

Since nature did not provide a perfect refrigerant, it was necessary for man to devise a compound to meet his particular needs. A fluorinated hydrocarbon known as carbon tetrachloride met this requirement most closely with a few minor changes.

Carbon tetrachloride, referred to as "carbon-tet," is made up of one atom of carbon (C) and four atoms of chlorine (Cl). The chemical symbol for this element is CCl_4.

To improve this element to produce a more desirable refrigerant, two of the chlorine atoms are removed and two atoms of fluorine (F) are introduced in their place.

This new compound, known as dichlorodifluoromethane, is Refrigerant 12. It is used in automobile air conditioners and in many other applications. The chemical symbol for Refrigerant 12 is CCl_2F_2. This means that it contains one atom of carbon, two of chlorine and two atoms of fluorine.

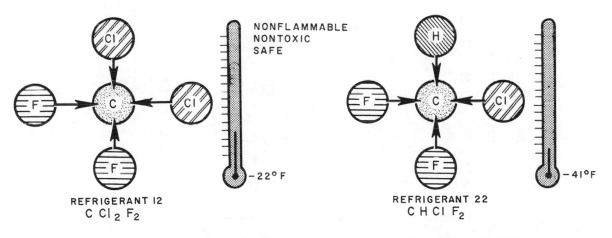

COMPOSITION, BOILING POINT AND PROPERTIES OF REFRIGERANTS

This refrigerant is ideal because of its stability at high, as well as low, operating temperatures. It does not react with most metals such as iron, aluminum, copper, and steel is soluble in oil and does not harm, or is not harmed by rubber. It is nonflammable and nonexplosive in either a gas or liquid form and is noninjurious to animal or plant life and has no effect on the taste, smell, or color of water or food.

Refrigerant 12 is odorless in concentrates of less than 20%. When detected by the smell, it has a slight odor of its original element, carbon tetrachloride.

31

TEMPERATURE AND PRESSURE RELATIONSHIP OF REFRIGERANT 12

One of the characteristics of R 12, and one that makes it a desirable automotive refrigerant, is its close proximity to temperature and pressure between the 20 to 80 pounds per square inch (p.s.i.) range.

TEMPERATURE-PRESSURE RELATION CHART
(FOR REFRIGERANT 12)

Temp. F.	Press. PSI	Temp. F.	Press. PSI	Temp. F.	Press. PSI	Temp. F.	Press. PSI	Temp. F.	Press. PSI
0	9.1	35	32.5	60	57.7	85	91.7	110	136.0
2	10.1	36	33.4	61	58.9	86	93.2	111	138.0
4	11.2	37	34.3	62	60.0	87	94.8	112	140.1
6	12.3	38	35.1	63	61.3	88	96.4	113	142.1
8	13.4	39	36.0	64	62.5	89	98.0	114	144.2
10	14.6	40	36.9	65	63.7	90	99.6	115	146.3
12	15.8	41	37.9	66	64.9	91	101.3	116	148.4
14	17.1	42	38.8	67	66.2	92	103.0	117	151.2
16	18.3	43	39.7	68	67.5	93	104.6	118	152.7
18	19.7	44	40.7	69	68.8	94	106.3	119	154.9
20	21.0	45	41.7	70	70.1	95	108.1	120	157.1
21	21.7	46	42.6	71	71.4	96	109.8	121	159.3
22	22.4	47	43.6	72	72.8	97	111.5	122	161.5
23	23.1	48	44.6	73	74.2	98	113.3	123	163.8
24	23.8	49	45.6	74	75.5	99	115.1	124	166.1
25	24.6	50	46.6	75	76.9	100	116.9	125	168.4
26	25.3	51	47.8	76	78.3	101	118.8	126	170.7
27	26.1	52	48.7	77	79.2	102	120.6	127	173.1
28	26.8	53	49.8	78	81.1	103	122.4	128	175.4
29	27.6	54	50.9	79	82.5	104	124.3	129	177.8
30	28.4	55	52.0	80	84.0	105	126.2	130	182.2
31	29.2	56	53.1	81	85.5	106	128.1	131	182.6
32	30.0	57	55.4	82	87.0	107	130.0	132	185.1
33	30.9	58	56.6	83	88.5	108	132.1	133	187.6
34	31.7	59	57.1	84	90.1	109	135.1	134	190.1

A glance at the temperature-pressure chart will indicate only a slight variation between the temperature and the pressure of the refrigerant in this range. Only a highly calibrated thermometer and pressure gage would detect the variation. It is safe to assume that in this range for every pound of pressure recorded, the temperature is the same. For instance, as indicated on the chart, a pressure of 23.1 p.s.i.g. has a temperature of 23. This is indicative of the temperature of the refrigerant itself and not of the outside surface of the container, nor of the air passing over it.

The objective in air conditioning in the automobile, is to allow the evaporator to reach its coldest point without icing up. Since ice will form at 32°F., the fins and cooling coils of the evaporator must not be allowed to drop below that point. Because of the temperature rise through the walls of the cooling fins and coils, the temperature of the refrigerant may be several degrees cooler than that of the air passing through the evaporator.

If the pressure gage reads 28 p.s.i.g., the temperature of the refrigerant in the evaporator is about 30°F. Due to the temperature rise, the air passing over the coil will be about 34 or 35°F.

A thermometer should be used with a manifold gage to properly service an air conditioner.

HANDLING REFRIGERANT

Liquid refrigerant, if allowed to strike the eye, can cause blindness. If allowed to strike the body it can cause frostbite.

If a refrigerant container is heated, or allowed to come into contact with a heating apparatus the refrigerant pressure inside will build up to such proportions that the container will explode.

If refrigerant is allowed to come into contact with an open flame, or heated metal, a poisonous gas will be created. Inhalation of this gas can cause you to become violently ill.

Remember -- refrigerant is not a toy. It should only be handled by a trained refrigeration serviceman.

It should be mentioned that the term "Freon" has become a common shop term when referring to Refrigerant 12. "Freon" and "Freon 12" are registered trademarks of the E. I. du Pont de Nemours and Company and should be used only when referring to refrigerant manufactured or packaged by them or a processing plant licensed to do so.

Refrigerant 12 is also packaged in the United States under several other brand names, such as Genatron 12, Isotron 12, Ucon 12, and others.

Refrigerant 12 has been abbreviated to R 12 and is accepted by the industry by this name.

R 12 is packaged by several vendors in 15-oz. cans, referred to as "pound" cans. It may also be obtained in two and two and a half pound cans. These cans use a special adapter as a means of transferring their contents. No attempt should be made to remove the contents by other means.

R 12 is also available in 10- and 12-pound disposable cylinders, in 25- and 145-pound deposit cylinders. It is also sold to manufacturers in 2,000-pound cylinders, tank trucks and tank cars.

Cylinders, or bulk, is the least expensive way of buying refrigerant in most cases, though the one-pound cans are the most popular because of their convenience and ease of measuring the proper amount of refrigerant into the system.

R 12 drums and cylinders are easily identified. They are painted white in color. Since there has been no complete standardization of refrigerant color codes it is suggested that care be exercised to be sure of the contents of a cylinder before introducing it into the system. Some manufacturers may use another color.

All refrigerant now used in automotive applications is R 12 though some earlier units used Refrigerant 22 (R 22).

R 22 has the same basic makeup as does R 12 with one exception. Another element of chlorine was removed and an atom of hydrogen introduced in its place.

This compound, known as monochlorodifluoromethane, chemical symbol $CHClF_2$, is popular as a refrigerant for window units and commercial air conditioning.

There has been much talk of a refrigerant designed to take the place of both R 12 and R 22. There has been no refrigerant designed to replace these two refrigerants, but with certain system changes R 502 could be used.

Refrigerant 502 is a combination of two refrigerants, one of them being R 22. The proper name for this refrigerant is monochlorodifluoromethane-pentafluoromethane. Its chemical symbol is $CHClF_2 - CClF_2Cf_3$.

The cost of R 502 is considerably higher than that of R 12 so we will not discuss this refrigerant as a replacement.

REVIEW QUESTIONS

1. Give three reasons why Refrigerant 12 is best suited for automotive air conditioning use.

   a. _____

   _____

   b. _____

   _____

   c. _____

   _____

2. What concentration of Refrigerant 12 may be detected by smell? What does it smell like? _____

_____

3. Name three situations in which handling Refrigerant 12 may be dangerous.

   a. _____

   b. _____

   c. _____

4. What color is a refrigerant container? _____ Always? _____

5. Name another refrigerant closely resembling Refrigerant 12.

   _____

6. Between _____ p.s.i. and _____ p.s.i., the temperature and pressure of Refrigerant 12 is in close proximity.

7. Temperature of the air passing over the coils will be _____ than that of the refrigerant, allowing for a temperature _____.

8. Using the chart found at the bottom of this page, give the refrigerant temperature for the following gage readings.

   a. 21 p.s.i. _____   b. 30 p.s.i. _____   c. 36 p.s.i. _____

9. Again, using the chart, what is the pressure of the following:

   a. 24°F. _____   b. 50°F. _____   c. 34°F. _____

10. To prevent ice from forming on the fins and coils, the temperature of the evaporator should never be allowed to go below_____°F, which is ___p.s.i.

Temperature-Pressure Relationship (For Refrigerant 12)					
Temp. F.	Press. p.s.i.	Temp. F	Press. p.s.i.	Temp. F.	Press. p.s.i.
0	9.1	25	24.6	40	36.9
2	10.1	26	25.3	41	37.9
4	11.2	27	26.1	42	38.8
6	12.3	28	26.8	43	39.7
8	13.4	29	27.6	44	40.7
10	14.6	30	28.4	45	41.7
12	15.8	31	29.2	46	42.6
14	17.1	32	30.0	47	43.6
16	18.3	33	30.9	48	44.6
18	19.7	34	31.7	49	45.6
20	21.0	35	32.5	50	46.6
21	21.7	36	33.4	51	47.8
22	22.4	37	34.3	52	48.7
23	23.1	38	35.1	53	49.8
24	23.8	39	36.0	54	50.9

Topic 8 SPECIAL SAFETY PRECAUTIONS

Although there are many refrigerants used in air conditioning and refrigeration systems, in automotive air conditioning only Refrigerant 12 is used.

The preceding topic discussed briefly some of the hazards associated with the use of R 12. Because of their importance, however, we shall repeat those hazards now and emphasize safe procedures in handling R 12.

Refrigerant 12 is odorless and cannot be detected in small quantities. It is colorless and will not stain.

There are, however, a few words of caution concerning the handling of Refrigerant 12 (R 12).

Suitable eye protection should be worn when handling R 12 because of its low evaporating temperature. R 12 evaporates at -21.6° F.

If liquid R 12 strikes the eye, the eyeball may be frozen. Freezing the eye can cause blindness. If liquid R 12 should strike the eye, do not rub it. Follow these instructions:

1. Do not rub the eye.

2. Splash large quantities of cool water into the eye to raise the temperature.

3. Tape on a sterile eye patch to avoid the possibility of dirt entering the eye.

4. Rush to a doctor or hospital for immediate professional aid.

5. Do not attempt to treat it yourself.

If liquid R 12 strikes the skin, frostbite may occur. Care must always be exercised when handling refrigerants. Should liquid R 12 strike you anywhere else on the body, follow the same procedures as outlined. Splash on cool water to raise the temperature.

Refrigerant 12 is harmless unless released in a confined space where it could cause drowsiness. We will not be concerned with this since the auto air conditioner capacity is not great enough to cause any problems.

If R 12 is allowed to come into contact with an open flame or a very hot metal, Phosgene gas will be formed. Phosgene gas is poisonous and can be very dangerous. This gas can make a person very sick when inhaled. Phosgene gas inhaled a little at a time over a period of time can be cumulative and may result in a toxic condition.

The following rules must be followed when handling R 12, or other similar refrigerants.

1. Above 130° F. liquid refrigerant will completely fill a container and hydrostatic pressure will build up rapidly with each degree of temperature rise. To provide for some margin of safety, never heat a refrigerant cylinder above 125° F.

2. Never apply a direct flame to a refrigerant cylinder or container. Never place an electric resistance heater near or in direct contact with a container of refrigerant.

3. Do not abuse a refrigerant cylinder or container. Use an approved valve wrench for opening and closing valves to avoid damage. Secure all cylinders in an upright position for storage and withdrawal of refrigerant.

4. Do not handle refrigerant without suitable eye protection.

5. Do not overheat the refrigerant container.

6. Do not discharge refrigerant into an enclosed area having an open flame.

7. When purging a system, discharge refrigerant slowly.

8. Do not introduce anything but pure Refrigerant 12 and refrigerant oil into the system.

REVIEW QUESTIONS

1. What does Refrigerant 12 smell like? _____

2. What may happen if Refrigerant 12 strikes the skin? _____

3. What may happen if Refrigerant 12 strikes the eye? _____

_____

4. What do you consider the most important safety measure to observe if liquid refrigerant strikes the eye? _____

_____

5. What gas is given off by Refrigerant 12 in contact with an open flame?

_____

_____

6. Why should you not overheat the refrigerant container? _____

_____

Topic 9 THE REFRIGERATION CIRCUIT

The following unit deals with the basic refrigeration circuit. The temperature of such a unit is maintained by a thermostatically controlled clutch. The clutch is cycled on and off as the thermostat may indicate and thus allows a proper cycle, or defrost period.

Each component will be discussed as will its purpose and placement in the air-conditioning circuit. Its function, troubleshooting and servicing, will be found in this book under the heading of the specific part.

Though different systems vary in size of hoses for a particular line, they will, in general, be as described here. The state of refrigerant will be given in each hose and component. This is the state of the refrigerant in a normal operating unit. It should again be pointed out that a suitable eye protection is suggested when servicing the air conditioner.

The following functional description of the refrigeration part of the air-conditioning system is intended to familiarize the serviceman with the general arrangement and function of the components in the system. A complete understanding of the overall operation of the system is necessary when working on air conditioning.

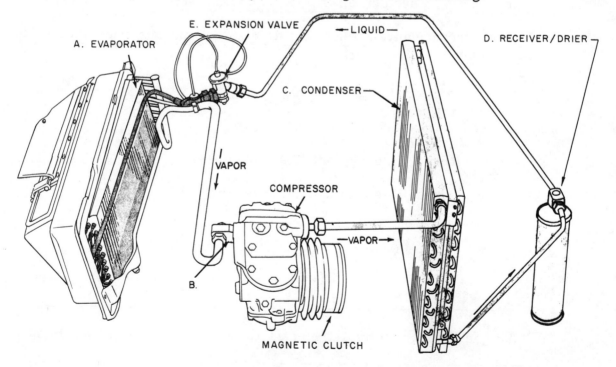

REFRIGERATION SYSTEM COMPONENTS (TYPICAL)

Note the schematic diagram of refrigeration components. The compressor (B) pumps heat-laden refrigerant vapor from the evaporator (A). It compresses the refrigerant and sends it, under high pressure, to the condenser (C) as a superheated vapor.

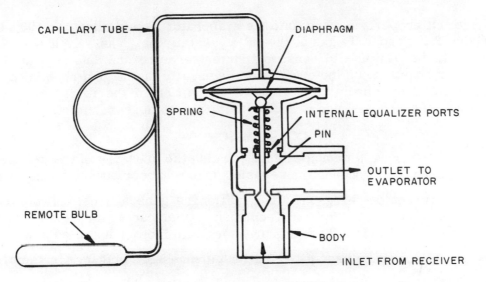

THERMOSTATIC EXPANSION VALVE

THERMOSTATIC EXPANSION VALVE AND EVAPORATOR

The thermostatic expansion valve, or TXV, is located at the inlet side of the evaporator. It is the controlling device for the system and separates the high side from the low side. A small restriction, or orifice, in the valve allows only a small amount of liquid refrigerant through, modulating according to evaporator temperature. The largest the orifice can become is about .008″ so it can easily be seen that only a small amount of refrigerant can pass even when the valve is wide open.

The state of the refrigerant inside of the TXV and immediately after it is 100% liquid. It is not all liquid long, however. As soon as the liquid pressure is dropped it starts to boil, and in so doing must absorb or take on BTUs of heat. This heat is removed from the air passing over the coils and fins of the evaporator and causes the air to feel cool. Remember, we are removing the heat from the air, not creating cold air.

It is the job of the TXV to meter just the proper amount of refrigerant into the evaporator so that the outlet of the evaporator will be 100% low-pressure vapor, or gas.

If too much refrigerant is metered, a flooding condition is the result and the unit will not cool. It will not cool because the pressure of the refrigerant will be higher and it will not boil away so easily. Also, the evaporator full of liquid refrigerant eliminates a place for the refrigerant to properly vaporize which is necessary in order for it to take on heat. A flooding condition of the evaporator will allow an excess of liquid refrigerant to leave the evaporator and may cause serious damage to the next component, the compressor.

If too little refrigerant is metered into the evaporator, we refer to the system as being starved. Again the unit will not cool because the refrigerant will vaporize, or boil off, long before it passes through the evaporator.

Refrigerant properly metered into the evaporator should allow for 100% liquid just after the TXV, and 100% gas at the outlet, or tailpipe. The TXV has a sensing tube attached to the tailpipe to sense outlet temperature and thus regulate itself. The tailpipe, or hose leaving the evaporator, is usually the largest hose in the system, 5/8", though it may be as large as 3/4". Condition of the refrigerant in the tailpipe is low-pressure gas, and is directed into the compressor inlet.

COMPRESSOR

The compressor is a pump designed to raise the pressure of the refrigerant. Thus the refrigerant will condense more rapidly in the next component, the condenser.

The aftermarket or "hang-on" air conditioners generally use a two-cylinder compressor manufactured by York or Tecumseh. American Motors and some Ford Motor Company cars also use these compressors with factory installed units.

Chrysler Corporation uses two-cylinder compressors (mfg. by Air-temp Div.).

General Motors factory installed units used a Frigidaire five-cylinder compressor until 1961. In 1962, General Motors began using a Frigidaire three-double-ended-piston, six-cylinder compressor. The six-cylinder compressor is also found in many late model Ford Motor Company cars.

A one-cylinder Tecumseh compressor is found on many aftermarket installations of air conditioners in compact cars.

Each piston is equipped with a set of suction and discharge valves and valve plates. While one piston is on the intake stroke, the other is on the compression stroke. The piston draws in refrigerant through the suction valve and forces it out through the discharge valve. While the piston is on the downstroke, or intake stroke, the discharge valve is held closed by action of the piston and the higher pressure above it. With the piston on the downstroke the suction reed valve is opened allowing low-pressure gas to enter. When the piston is on the upstroke, or compression stroke, refrigerant is forced through the discharge valve while the suction valve is held closed by the same pressure.

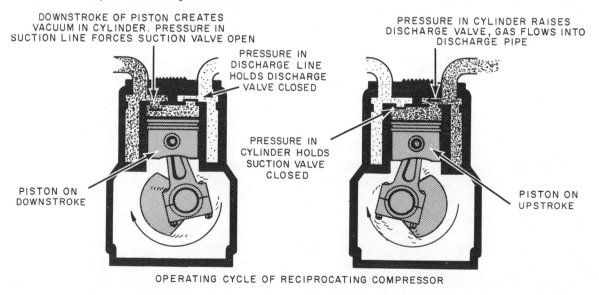

OPERATING CYCLE OF RECIPROCATING COMPRESSOR

The compressor is the device that separates the low side from the high side of the system. The state of the refrigerant on entering the compressor is low-pressure gas, and on leaving is high-pressure gas.

The compressor is equipped with service valves which are used as an aid in servicing the air-conditioning system. The manifold gage set is connected into the system at the service valve ports and all procedures such as evacuating and charging are carried on through the manifold and gage set.

The hose leaving the compressor contains high-pressure gas and is made of rubber, usually 1/2″ though some 5/8″ lines have been used. Referred to as the hot-gas discharge line, it connects to a condenser inlet, always on the top side of the condenser.

CONDENSER

The purpose of the condenser is just opposite to that of the evaporator. It is in the condenser that the refrigerant in the gas state is to liquefy, or condense. To do so it must give up its heat BTUs. Ram air, or air passing over the condenser, carries off heat and the gas condenses. This heat which is now removed to cause a change of state from a gas to a liquid is the same heat that was absorbed in the evaporator to cause a change of state from a liquid to a gas.

The state of the refrigerant will be almost 100% gas on entering the condenser. A very small amount of gas might turn to liquid in the hot-gas discharge line, but the amount would be so small that it wouldn't require considering.

We cannot consider that the refrigerant leaving the condenser is 100% liquid though. Since the condenser is capable of handling just so much heat at a given time, a small percentage of the refrigerant may leave the condenser in a gas state. This is of little consequence, however, since the next component is the receiver/drier.

As we mentioned earlier, the inlet of the condenser must be at the top. This will allow condensing refrigerant to drop to the bottom of the condenser where it will be forced, under pressure, to the drier through the liquid line.

Though we refer to the condition of the refrigerant in the condenser as liquid and gas, it is under high pressure and care must be exercised when servicing this part.

From the condenser we continue to the receiver/drier through the liquid line where the cycle starts over again. This liquid line, like the other, may be rubber or metal and in a variety of sizes.

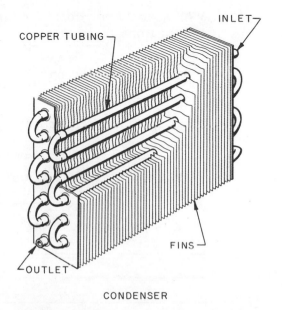

CONDENSER

So, in covering the refrigeration cycle we learn several things about refrigeration. When the pressure of the refrigerant is dropped in the evaporator it boils. In boiling it picks up BTUs of heat. The compressor raises the temperature and pressure of the refrigerant so that it will condense in the condenser where it will give up the same BTUs of heat that it picked up in the evaporator. We learn the direction of the refrigerant flow and the state of it in each part of the system.

We learn that the thermostatic expansion valve controls the flow of refrigerant into the evaporator thereby separating the high side from the low side   We learn that the compressor increases gas pressure, and that it is the device which separates the low side from the high side. This is the basic air-conditioning circuit from which all of the other automotive circuits are patterned. A good understanding of the simple circuit will make understanding the other circuits much easier.

REVIEW QUESTIONS

1. What is the purpose of the desiccant in the receiver/drier? _____

   _____

   _____

   _____

2. What would be the results if the receiver section of the drier were omitted?

   _____

   _____

3. What would be the results if the thermostatic expansion valve were omitted?

   _____

   _____

4. Which would you consider a more serious problem; a flooded or starved evaporator? _____

   Why? _____

   _____

5. What should the state of the refrigerant be immediately on entering the evaporator? _____

6. What should the state of the refrigerant be immediately on leaving the evaporator? _____

7. What is the purpose of the compressor service valves? _____

   _____

   _____

   _____

8. What is the purpose of the compressor suction reed valve? _____

_____

_____

9. What is the purpose of the compressor discharge reed valve? _____

_____

_____

10. Why should eyes be protected from refrigerant? _____

_____

_____

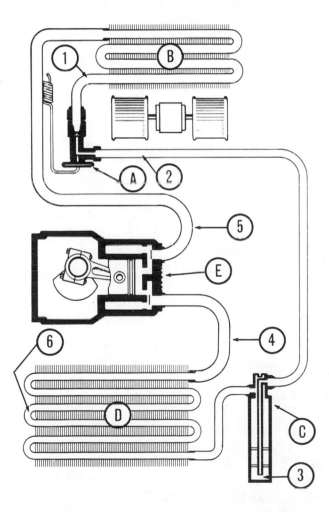

11. Refer to the diagram and tell what state the refrigerant is in (high pressure liquid, high pressure gas, low pressure liquid, low-pressure gas) at the following points as indicated on the diagram.

   1. _____

   2. _____

   3. _____

   4. _____

   5. _____

   6. _____

12. Refer to the diagram and name component parts as indicated.

   A. _____

   B. _____

   C. _____

   D. _____

   E. _____

13. Direction of refrigerant flow is from _____. (drier to expansion valve, expansion valve to drier)

14. The expansion valve is located at the _____ of the evaporator.

Topic 10 THE ELECTRICAL CIRCUIT

The following unit deals with the basic refrigeration electrical circuit and includes the rheostat or three-speed fan switch, and the thermostat as used for temperature control.

Each component will be discussed as will its purpose and placement in the electrical circuit. Its function, troubleshooting and servicing, will be found in this book under the heading of the specific part.

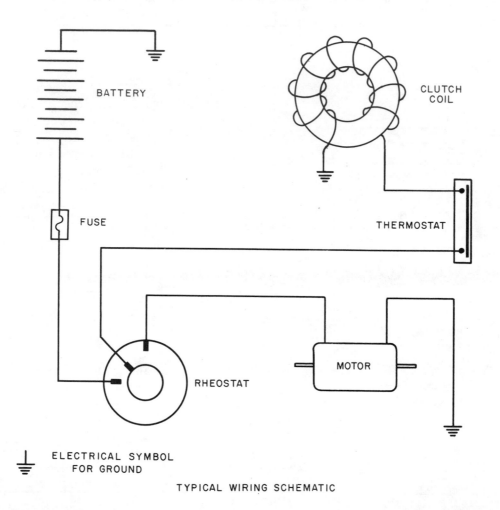

TYPICAL WIRING SCHEMATIC

The refrigeration electrical circuit should be fed from a separate accessory circuit from the fuse block or the ignition switch. This lead should be fused with a 20-ampere fuse or circuit breaker and should be a number 12 wire.

The blower control may be a rheostat, or may be a two- or three-speed switch. The rheostat-type control allows a full range of blower speeds from full fast to slow. The two- or three-speed switch only allows for blower speeds in steps such as "hi-lo" or "hi-med-lo."

In either case when the blower switch is energized on either speed, current is fed to the thermostat on most units. Once turned on, the blower speeds may be changed without affecting the thermostat supply. When turned off, however, the supply is cut and the complete unit is turned off.

The thermostat is a control device that reacts to changing temperatures which cause electrical contacts to make and break. The thermostat has a capillary, or sensing tube, extending into the evaporator core which acts as a monitor for evaporator temperature.

Closing of the points causes current to flow to the clutch field and energizes the clutch. This causes the compressor crankshaft to turn and starts the refrigeration cycle. When the temperature of the evaporator drops to a predetermined point, usually about 33° F., the points open and the clutch disengages. This allows for a defrost cycle in the evaporator and prevents ice from forming.

When the clutch disengages, the blowers remain at their predetermined speed. When the evaporator temperature rises, usually to about 45° F., or twelve degrees above the cutout point, the contacts in the thermostat again make contact and the clutch is engaged to resume the refrigeration cycle.

Some systems use a bimetallic thermostat for temperature control. This type of thermostat, having no capillary tube, relies on the temperature of the air that passes over it to cause the points to make and break. This type of thermostat is becoming more and more popular because it requires less space for installation and is considerably less expensive than the capillary tube type, though not so accurate.

REVIEW QUESTIONS

1. What effect does the closing of the electrical contacts in the rheostat have on the clutch? _____

2. What effect does the opening of the electrical contacts in the thermostat have on the clutch? _____

3. What is the normal temperature rise between the temperature when the thermostat cuts out until it cuts in? _____

4. In your opinion, which type of thermostat is the better one? _____

5. What is the rheostat used for? _____

Topic 11 REFRIGERATION OIL

Oil is needed to lubricate the seals, gaskets and other moving parts of the compressor. A small amount of oil is circulated through the system with the refrigerant and is an aid in keeping the thermostatic expansion valve in proper operating condition.

Only nonfoaming oil specifically formulated for use in designated air conditioners should be used in automotive air conditioners.

Refrigeration oil is highly refined. It is a mineral oil with all impurities, such as wax, moisture and sulphur, removed. It is considerably less expensive than some of the low-priced grades of motor oil. Under no circumstances should a motor oil, regardless of grade, be used in an air conditioner.

Refrigeration oil is available in several grades, or viscosities. Viscosity is determined by the time in seconds it takes a definite quantity of oil to flow through a certain size orifice at 100° F. The lower the viscosity number, the thinner the oil. Oils of 300, 525 and 1000 viscosity are the most commonly used oils in air conditioning.

The oil level of the compressor should be checked each time the air conditioner is serviced. Always check the compressor manufacturer's recommendations before adding oil to the refrigeration system. Procedures for adding oil to all compressors may be found in the Service Procedures, Section III, of this book.

Do not, at any time other than when pouring, allow the oil container to remain uncapped. Always be sure that the cap is in place and is tight. Oil absorbs moisture, and moisture is damaging to the air conditioner.

Here are a few simple rules to follow when handling refrigeration oil.

Use only approved refrigeration oil.

Do not transfer oil from one container to another.

Do not return oil from a system to a container. Always discard it.

Make sure the cap is tight on the container when not in use.

Replace old oil if there is any doubt about its condition.

Avoid contaminating the oil.

REVIEW QUESTIONS

1. What is the primary purpose of refrigeration oil? _____

   _____

   _____

2. List three ways this oil can become contaminated.

   a. _____

   b. _____

   c. _____

Topic 12 MOISTURE

For all practical purposes, refrigerant has had all of its moisture removed. The moisture content of new refrigerant should not exceed ten parts of moisture per million parts of refrigerant, or 10 p.p.m.

If new refrigerant and refrigeration oil is used in the system, any moisture introduced must come from outside sources, such as a break in a line or from improperly fastened hoses or fittings on the installation.

Whenever a unit is removed from the system for repair or replacement there is always a danger of moisture entering the unit. Air contains moisture. Refrigerant will absorb moisture readily when exposed to it. To keep the system as moisture free as possible, all air conditioners use a receiver/drier containing a bag of desiccant such as silica gel, which has the characteristic of absorbing and holding a small quantity of moisture.

One drop of water in excess of the amount that the desiccant can handle is free in the system; it cannot be controlled, and causes irreparable damage to the internal parts of the air conditioner.

Moisture in greater concentrates than 20 p.p.m. will cause serious damage. To give you an idea of how small an amount that is, one small drop of water in an air-conditioning system having a capacity of three pounds amounts to 40 p.p.m., or twice the amount that can be tolerated.

Refrigerant 12 reacts chemically with water to form hydrochloric acid. The heat generated in the system accelerates the process. The greater the concentration of water in the system, the more concentrated the corrosive acid.

This acid eats away at all metal parts, particularly steel. Iron, copper, and aluminum are damaged by these acids as well and oxides in the form of particles of metal are released into the refrigerant as sludge and cause further damage by plugging up screens in the thermostatic expansion valve, compressor inlet, or even the drier itself.

One manufacturer of automotive air conditioners indicates that alcohol, or methanol, should be added to the system. It is indicated that by adding 2 cc. of alcohol per pound of refrigerant a system freeze-up will be avoided. While this is true, adding alcohol to the system can cause even greater damage. The drier likes and seeks out moisture in the system, but prefers alcohol. It will release all of its moisture and absorb the alcohol. Now moisture is again free in the system to cause more damage.

Moisture content is the greatest enemy of the air-conditioning system. Once a system becomes saturated, irreparable damage is done inside the system. If neglected long enough, pinholes will be eaten through the evaporator and condenser coils, or any other metal tubing that is used. This will require their replacement.

Aluminum parts will be eaten away, making the compressor unserviceable. Its valves and fittings can become so corroded that they may no longer be usable.

Anytime there is evidence of moisture in a system, a thorough system cleanout is recommended, followed by the installation of a new drier and complete system pump-down using a vacuum pump. Topic 13 will discuss moisture removal in detail.

By following a few simple rules, the introduction of unwanted moisture and dirt can be eliminated.

- When servicing the air conditioner, always install the drier last.
- When servicing unit parts always cap open end of hoses and fittings immediately.
- Never work around water, or outside in the rain.
- Do not allow new refrigerant or refrigeration oil to become contaminated.
- Always keep refrigeration oil container capped.
- Develop clean habits. Allow no dirt to enter the system.
- Keep service tools free of grease and dirt.
- Never fill a unit without first insuring that air and moisture have been removed.

REVIEW QUESTIONS

1. What is the maximum moisture content allowable in new refrigerant?

   _____

2. List three ways that moisture can enter the system.

   a. _____

   b. _____

   c. _____

3. What component part of the system attracts the most moisture?

   _____

4. What does the effect of adding alcohol have on the system so far as freeze-up is concerned? _____

   _____

5. What adverse effect does the adding of alcohol have on the system?

   _____

   _____

   _____

6. What acid is formed by refrigerant and water? _____

7. What does this acid damage most? _____

8. How can this acid be eliminated? _____
_____
_____

9. How can this acid be prevented from forming? _____
_____
_____

10. What will the oxides, caused by the acid, do to the system? _____
_____
_____
_____

Topic 13 MOISTURE REMOVAL

In this unit we will discuss the reason for a unit pump-down, and explain how we are able to remove moisture in a vacuum. You will recall that we discussed earlier that we refer to a pressure below zero pounds gage pressure in terms of inches of mercury or "Hg."

Moisture removal from a system can cause serious problems for the serviceman who is not equipped with the proper tools. A vacuum pump is a must for the air-conditioning serviceman, and is the most efficient means of moisture removal, though other methods are used.

Moisture is removed in the air-conditioning system by creating a vacuum. In a vacuum, the moisture in the system boils, and the pumping action of the vacuum pump pulls the moisture out of the system in a vapor.

As soon as the pressure is raised, on the discharge side of the pump, the vapor again liquefies. This usually occurs inside of the pump.

Some recommend the use of the air-conditioning compressor as a means of evacuation. This is not a prescribed procedure since a minimum of thirty minutes is required for moisture removal at a compressor speed of about 1750 r.p.m. The compressor is lubricated by oil contained in the refrigerant and will run dry when operated as a vacuum pump. This, alone, can cause serious damage to the compressor. As previously explained, when the pressure is raised inside of the pump the vapor again liquefies, usually inside of the pump. This means that if the automotive compressor is used we are going to pull the moisture-laden vapor out of the system and deposit most of it inside of the compressor. What is gained? It is still inside of the system.

To understand how a vacuum pump effects moisture removal, review Topic 5. This topic covers temperature/pressure relationships and the boiling of water at a lower temperature at higher altitudes. A point to remember is that at higher altitudes the atmospheric pressure is less. A vacuum pump can simulate conditions at a higher altitude by mechanical means. A good vacuum pump is one capable of pulling down to 29.76″ Hg or better. At this pressure water will boil at 40° F. That means that if the ambient temperature is 40° F. or higher, water will boil out of the system.

If we were to start at 0″ Hg at sea level we know that water will boil at 212° F. To find the boiling point of water in a vacuum the following table may be used. It will be noted that the boiling point of water is not affected as much the first 28″ Hg as it is the last 2″ Hg. The boiling point of water is only lowered to 100° F. at 27.99″ Hg, a drop of 112° F. However, a drop of the boiling point by 120° is indicated in the next two inches.

Boiling Point of Water Under a Vacuum	
System Vacuum Inches Mercury	Temperature °F. Boiling Point
24.04	140
25.39	130
26.45	120
27.32	110
27.99	100
28.50	90
28.89	80
29.18	70
29.40	60
29.66	50
29.71	40
29.76	30
29.82	20
29.86	10
29.87	5
29.88	0
29.90	-10
29.91	-20

The amount of vacuum reached plus the amount of time the system is subjected to a vacuum will determine the amount of moisture removed from the system.

Minimum recommended pumping time is thirty minutes. If time allows, however, a four-hour pump-down is better.

The removal of moisture from a system may be thought of in terms of boiling away a saucepan of water. It is not enough to get the water to boil, time must be allowed for it to boil away.

REVIEW QUESTIONS

1. What chemical symbol is used to denote a vacuum? _____

2. What tool do we use to effect moisture removal? _____

3. What vacuum should a good vacuum pump pull down to? _____

4. What is the minimum length of time a vacuum pump should be used for moisture removal? _____

5. Why is the air-conditioner compressor a poor vacuum pump for removing moisture? _____

Topic 14 THERMOMETERS

About 1585, Galileo Galilei, a famous Italian scientist, constructed a crude water thermometer. Although extremely inaccurate, his principles paved the way for others.

Over a hundred years later, in 1714, Gabriel D. Fahrenheit, a German physicist, engaged in the manufacture of meteorological instruments in Holland, constructed a thermometer using a column of mercury.

Until this time, since the days of Galilei, tubes of alcohol were in use, as were various other types of temperature measuring devices.

Fahrenheit realized that even though many thermometers had been made, there was no standard scale for all of them. Seeing the need for a place to start, or a place on the glass tube to be a standard, he decided that a zero should be placed on the tube to indicate no heat, or the absence of heat. Then, he thought everything above zero would be relative and contain so many units of heat.

Fahrenheit set out to find the coldest place in the world so he could take his column of mercury there to be marked. He inquired of sailors along the waterfront and found that their idea of the coldest place in the world was Iceland.

Off to Iceland he went. Once there, he sought what was believed to be the coldest part of Iceland, there to wait for the coldest day.

When told, "This is the coldest day we have seen." he made a mark on his glass tube to indicate zero, the absence of heat. Then he waited until it got warmer and noted that when ice melted, his mercury column had expanded 32/1000th of its original volume. When the thermometer was placed again on melting ice it indicated the same mark. He designated that point as 32°.

He also noted that the normal body temperature was 98° and that when water boiled his column of mercury expanded to 212/1000th of its original volume.

Fahrenheit's thermometer has been accepted as standard and is the most widely used today, though there are three other scales in use.

About the same time that Fahrenheit was working on his thermometer, Anders Celsius, a Swedish astronomer, presented the first idea of the centigrade thermometer. He proposed the temperature of melting ice as 100° and the boiling point of water as 0°.

The following year, 1743, Christin, working independently of Celsius, proposed a centigrade scale. This was the same as the Celsius scale inverted, and is the one in use today.

In 1848, at the age of 24, W. T. Kelvin, known as Lord Kelvin, proposed the absolute scale of temperature, which still bears his name. The Kelvin scale is referred to as the "Absolute Centigrade Scale" and is used in scientific work.

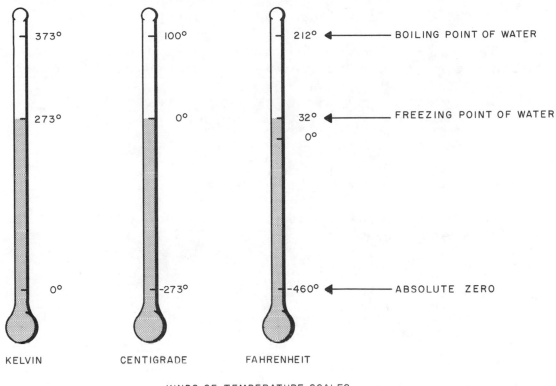

KINDS OF TEMPERATURE SCALES

Most of our work will deal with the Fahrenheit scale. However, it may be desirable to occasionally convert the centigrade scale to the Fahrenheit scale or vice versa.

To do so is quite simple.

> To change a centigrade reading to Fahrenheit:
>
> a. Multiply the reading by 9/5
>
> b. Add 32°

For example, suppose we were given a temperature of 115° C. and desire to know the temperature Fahrenheit.

$$\text{a. } 115° \text{ C.} \times 9/5 = 207$$
$$\text{b. } 207 + 32° = 239° \text{ F.}$$

Let's try that again. We know that the boiling point of water is 100° C. or 212° F. Suppose we were given a temperature of 100° C. Let's see if it works; again refer to the formula.

55

a. 100° C × 9.5 = 180

b. 180 + 32   = 212° F.

To change a Fahrenheit reading to centigrade, the formula is reversed. Instead of multiplying by 9/5, we multiply by 5/9. Before multiplying, subtract the 32°.

To change Fahrenheit to centigrade:

a. Subtract 32°

b. Multiply by 5/9

For example, suppose we were given a temperature of 221° F. and desire to know the temperature centigrade.

a. 221° F. - 32° = 189

b. 189 × 5/9   = 105° C.

Let's prove that formula just as we did before, knowing the boiling point of water on both scales. Let's convert 212° F. to centigrade.

a. 212° F. - 32° = 180

b. 180 × 5/9   = 100° C.

REVIEW QUESTIONS

1. Change 25° C. to Fahrenheit. _____

2. Change 40° C. to Fahrenheit. _____

3. Change 0° C. to Fahrenheit. _____

4. Change 59° F. to centigrade. _____

5. Change 113° F. to centigrade. _____

6. Change 32° F. to centigrade. _____

7. Change 100° C. to Fahrenheit. _____

8. Change 212° F. to centigrade. _____

9. Name three temperature scales in use today.

a. _____ c. _____

b. _____

10. Of the three scales in use today, which one do we use in our work?

_____

11. How did the Celsius scale differ from the Christin scale? _____

_____

_____

_____

12. How did the German physicist, who traveled to Iceland to perfect his thermometer, determine the freezing point of water as 32° on his scale?

_____

_____

_____

13. What is normal body temperature on this scale? _____

Topic 15 SERVICE VALVES

It is necessary, from time to time, for the serviceman to "enter" the air-conditioning system for certain diagnostic services and procedures which require the recording of pressures within the system. Topic 16 will deal with the gages and manifold used in this service. In this unit we will deal with the service valve, a device, usually located on the compressor, that enables the serviceman to enter the refrigeration system by mechanical means.

Most units are equipped with two service valves though some may have three. Since all valves are the same we will be concerned here with the operation of one valve in the system. The system, however, may be equipped with one of two types of valves. The two types of valves are the hand shutoff type and the Schrader valve.

The hand shutoff type of valve is a three-position valve that may be used for one of three functions.

A Shut off refrigerant flow. Gage port out of the system

B Normal refrigerant operation. Gage port out of the system

C Normal refrigerant operation. Gage port in the system

We will discuss each position and determine at what points refrigerant will be allowed to flow under each position.

1 — TO SERVICE PORT
2 — TO HOSE
3 — TO COMPRESSOR

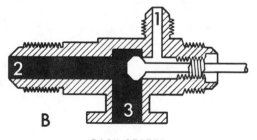

FRONT SEATED

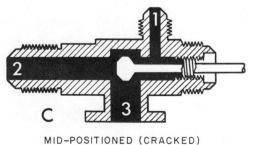

BACK SEATED

MID-POSITIONED (CRACKED)

SERVICE VALVES

SHUT OFF REFRIGERANT FLOW. GAGE PORT OUT OF SYSTEM

In this position we refer to the service valve as being in the front-seated position.

Refer to illustration A. You can see that the refrigerant is trapped in the hose end of the service valve. The gage port fitting is toward the atmosphere. By following the path through the valve you can see that the gage port only connects to the compressor. If the compressor were run with the service valve in this position and the gage port capped, serious damage would occur in the compressor. There would be no area to pump into.

Never operate a compressor with the service valves in this position unless to perform such tests as may be determined to be necessary.

NORMAL REFRIGERANT OPERATION — GAGE PORT OUT OF THE SYSTEM

The service valve in this position is referred to as in the back-seated position. As shown in Figure B , the compressor and hose outlet are connected and refrigerant is free to flow if the compressor is started. With the service valve in this position the gage port is closed off and pressure readings may not be taken. All of the service valves should be in this position when the system is operating normally.

NORMAL REFRIGERANT OPERATION — GAGE PORT IN THE SYSTEM

The service valve in this position is referred to as in the cracked, or mid position. It is in this position that the system can be operated and the pressures recorded through the gage port openings, Figure C.

It must be remembered, however, that the valves must always be back seated before attempting to remove the gage hose from the service valves. To fail to do so will result in a loss of refrigerant. Figure C illustrates the presence of refrigerant at all outlets of the service valve in the cracked position.

THE SCHRADER-TYPE VALVE

The Schrader-type service valve is becoming more popular in auto air conditioning. This type of valve may only be in one of two positions; cracked or back seated.

A special fitting is attached to the service hose. When this fitting is screwed onto the valve, a pin depresses the center of the Schrader valve to allow pressure readings on the gages. The removal of the fitting again closes the valve and it is again in the back-seated position. It should be remembered that the hose should never be

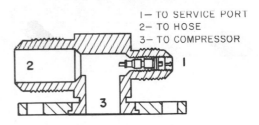

1— TO SERVICE PORT
2— TO HOSE
3— TO COMPRESSOR

SCHRADER COMPRESSOR VALVE

removed from the fitting while attached to the service valve. To do so will result in a loss of refrigerant.

This type of valve cannot be front seated, which is desirable in some cases when unit repair is indicated.

Service valves require very little repair. Occasionally one will be found to leak. If the leak is through the gage port opening, a cap with rubber insert may be used. If the leak is around the service stem or other part of the valve, complete replacement is usually recommended.

As mentioned earlier, most systems will have two service valves, but some may have three. When three valves are used, two of them will be low-side valves which are used for pressure or temperature control testing. Testing information is given in the Service Procedures (Section III) of this text.

It should be pointed out that the service valves are not always found on the compressor. The high-side service valve will be found anywhere from the outlet of the compressor to the inlet of the condenser. The low-side service valve will be found between the outlet of the evaporator and the inlet of the compressor.

REVIEW QUESTIONS

1. How many service valves are used on the compressor? _____
   What are they? _____

   _____

2. How many positions does the hand shutoff service valve have? _____
   What are they? _____

   _____

3. What position of the service valve(s) will cause damage to the compressor?

   _____

4. In what position are the service valve(s) under normal operation?

   _____

5. Describe the action of the Schrader-type valve. _____

   _____

   _____

Topic 16 TEST GAGES AND MANIFOLD SET

The proper testing and diagnosis of an air-conditioning system require that a serviceman have a manifold set with gages attached. The servicing of most air conditioners requires the use of two gages. However, some units require three.

One gage is used in the high (or discharge) side of the system while the other is used in the low (or suction) side of the system. Units requiring the use of three gages have another low side (or compound) gage added. It is used in the suction side of the air conditioner.

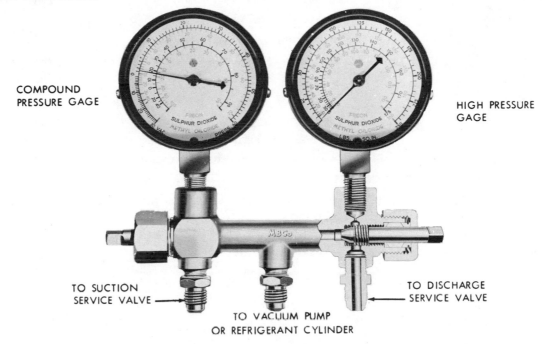

COMPOUND PRESSURE GAGE

HIGH PRESSURE GAGE

TO SUCTION SERVICE VALVE

TO VACUUM PUMP OR REFRIGERANT CYLINDER

TO DISCHARGE SERVICE VALVE

TESTING MANIFOLD (Courtesy of Mueller Brass)

THE LOW-SIDE GAGE

The low-side gage is a compound gage. This means that it will register both pressure and vacuum. This gage is connected to the low side of the system and registers pressures in that part of the air conditioner only.

The low side, as outlined in topic 9, is that part of the system from the thermostatic valve outlet to the compressor inlet and includes the evaporator and tail pipe.

The vacuum side of the gage must be calibrated to show from 0-30 inches of mercury (0"-30" Hg).

The pressure side of the gage must be calibrated to read a minimum of 80 pounds pressure, but should be constructed in such a manner that pressures as high as 250 pounds will not damage it.

COMPOUND GAGE

61

While pressures in this range do not normally occur in the low side of the system, they may be encountered if the manifold were hooked up backward by mistake.

Normally, eighty pounds per square inch pressure will be the maximum encountered in the low side of the system.

THE HIGH-SIDE GAGE

The high-side gage is used to determine pressures in the high side (or discharge side) of the air conditioner. Pressures seldom exceed 300 p.s.i.g. in this side. It is desirable that a minimum high-side scale be 300 p.s.i., though a top scale of 400 to 500 p.s.i. is preferred.

The high side, as outlined in topic 9, is that part of the system from the compressor outlet to the thermostatic expansion valve inlet and includes the condenser, receiver-drier, and connecting hoses or line.

THE MANIFOLD

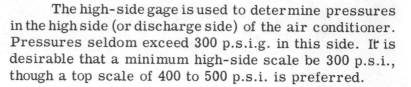

PRESSURE GAGE

The gages are connected into the air-conditioning system through a manifold. The manifold is a device having fittings for gages and hoses with provisions for controlling the flow of refrigerant through the manifold.

The gages are attached to the manifold by 1/8″ pipe connections. The manifold is connected to the compressor service valves by rubber hoses about 36″ long with 1/4″ female flare fittings on each end. The hoses are connected to the manifold by 1/8″ male pipe connections with 1/4″ male flare adapters.

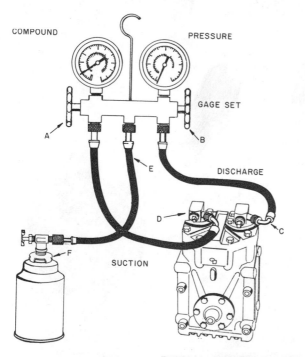

A — LOW-SIDE MANIFOLD HAND VALVE
B — HIGH-SIDE MANIFOLD HAND VALVE
C — HIGH-SIDE COMPRESSOR SERVICE VALVE
D — LOW-SIDE COMPRESSOR SERVICE VALVE
E — CHARGING HOSE
F — CAN TAP

TYPICAL MANIFOLD HOOKUP WITH REFRIGERANT

The low side hose and fitting is fastened directly below the low side gage; the high side hose and fitting below the high side gage.

The center port of the manifold set is used for charging or evacuation procedures, or any other service that may be necessary.

Both the high and low side of the manifold have hand shutoff valves. When the hand valve is turned all the way in, in a clockwise direction, the manifold is closed. The pressures on that side of the system will, however, be recorded on the gage above the hose.

Cracking the hand valve, in the counterclockwise direction, opens the system to the middle service port of the manifold set. This is desirable only when it is necessary to let refrigerant out or into the system.

If the hand valve on the low side of the manifold is cracked, the action takes place between the low side and the center port only. The low side gage is recording low side pressure only. The high side remains closed; pressures read on the high side indicate high side pressures only.

The manifold gage set is used to perform nearly all air-conditioning test and service procedures.

The illustration below shows manifold hand valves in the closed, or off position. Pressure can still be recorded on each gage.

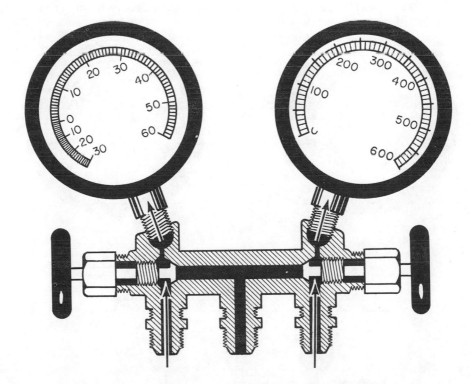

The illustration below shows the manifold hand valve in suction side cracked, while high side remains closed. Pressure is recorded on both gages even though one hand valve is cracked.

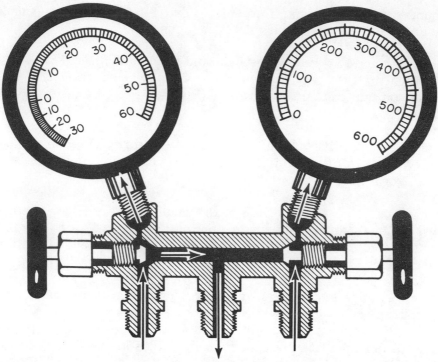

The illustration below shows manifold hand valve in discharge side cracked, while the low side remains closed. Pressure is recorded on both gages, though one hand valve is cracked.

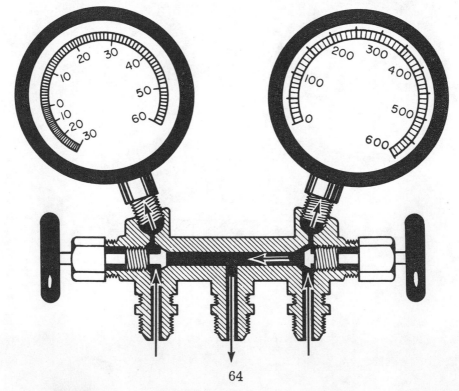

The illustration below shows both manifold hand valves cracked. They will both be cracked when discharging or evacuating the system. Pressures recorded on both gages will not be correct during this operation. Some high-side pressures may be fed to the low-side gage as well.

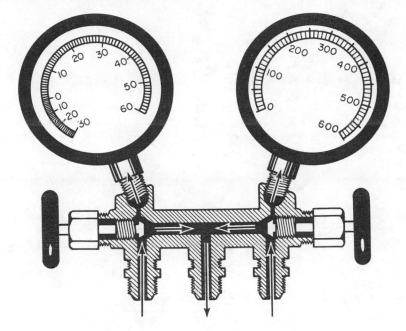

The manifold illustrated is the straight side-wheel (hand valve) type. The manifold is also available with offset side-wheel or front-wheel types of hand valves.

HOSES

Charging hoses are available in a variety of colors, such as blue, white, red, and yellow. Lengths of 36″ are usually standard, although hoses may be purchased in 12″, 18″, 60″, or 72″ lengths.

When color-coded hoses are used, blue is used for the low side, red is used for the high side, and white or yellow is used for the center port.

Standard hose ends are for 1/4″ flare fittings and have replaceable nylon, neoprene, or rubber gaskets. Hoses are available for use with Schrader-type service valves. Hoses not having the Schrader-type adaptor may be used with an accessory adaptor.

THE THIRD GAGE

Some conditioning units require the use of a third gage. Some of these units may use an evaporator pressure regulator of some type as a means of temperature control. The third gage is used to measure the pressure drop across this control device. The third gage port may be found at the evaporator or on the compressor head. Not all units with an evaporator pressure regulator have the third gage port, however. If no third port is found, a two-gage manifold set is used.

The third gage may be a separate compound gage-hose set-up, or it may be an integral part of a three-gage manifold. The third gage, if fastened to the manifold, has no physical internal connection but is held in place with a solid bar.

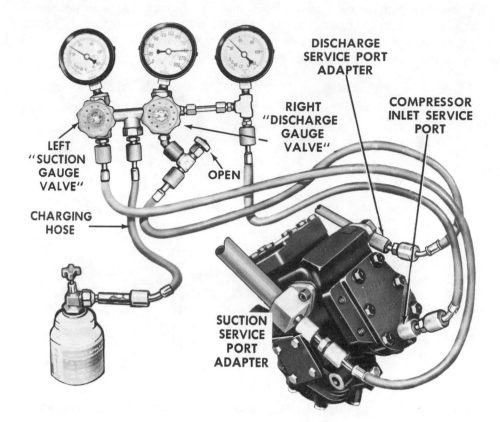

DISCHARGE
SERVICE PORT
ADAPTER

RIGHT
"DISCHARGE
GAUGE
VALVE"

COMPRESSOR
INLET SERVICE
PORT

LEFT
"SUCTION
GAUGE
VALVE"

OPEN

CHARGING
HOSE

SUCTION
SERVICE
PORT
ADAPTER

ADDING A PARTIAL CHARGE TO THE CHRYSLER COMPRESSOR, SHOWING THIRD GAGE AND NEEDLE
VALVE WITH THE MANIFOLD GAGE SET

THE NEEDLE VALVE

It may be desirable to install a needle valve in the high side manifold hose when testing some General Motors and Chrysler air conditioners. These, and other units that use a Schrader-type valve, cannot be adjusted. The high side gage will sometimes oscillate to the point that the needle on the gage cannot be read. The needle valve is simply a device in the high side charging hose that can be used to damp out oscillations of the needle in the gage.

REVIEW QUESTIONS

1. How low should the compound gage read? _____

2. How could the compound gage be damaged by accidental use? _____

   _____

   _____

3. What should the minimum scale reading of the high side gage be?

   _____

4. What is the purpose of the manifold? _____

   _____

   _____

5. What connection does the third gage have with the manifold and gage set?

   _____

   _____

6. Is the third gage a compound, or pressure, gage? _____

7. What is the purpose of the needle valve? _____

   _____

   _____

8. Why is the needle valve needed? _____

   _____

   _____

Topic 17 LEAK DETECTORS

There are several methods of detecting leaks in an air-conditioning system, from using a soap solution to an expensive self-contained electronic instrument.

The most popular instrument is the halide gas torch. Its initial low cost, ease of handling, and simplicity of construction and operation make it most desirable.

The halide gas torch is capable of detecting a leak as slight as one pound in ten years, though a bit of practice is required to be able to recognize a leak so slight.

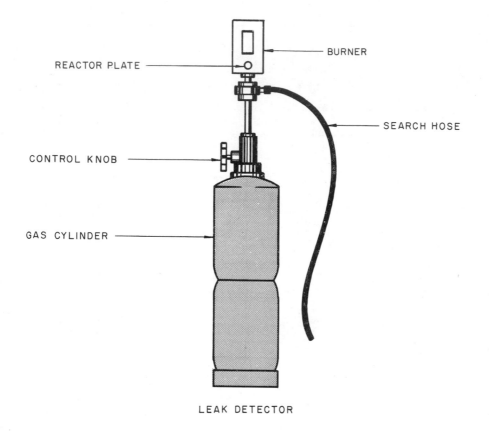

LEAK DETECTOR

This leak detector consists of two major parts: the detector unit and the gas cylinder. The gas cylinder is a nonrefillable pressure tank containing a gas such as propane. The detector unit consists of a valve, a device for controlling the flow of gas; the burner, a chamber where gas and air are mixed; and the search hose, a rubber tube through which air passes to the chamber.

Relatively little maintenance is required of the halide leak detector. Occasionally the reactor plate, a part of the burner, must be replaced to insure proper operation.

Improper operation of the leak detector may sometimes be traced to an obstructed or collapsed search hose. Dirt in the orifice or burner will also cause improper operation of the unit.

Air is drawn into the burner through the search hose and into the reaction plate. The copper reaction plate should be heated red hot by the flame which should be burning about a quarter inch above the plate opening.

When the search hose comes into contact with refrigerant, the refrigerant is drawn into the search tube and into the reaction plate. This will cause the flame to turn violet, and in some cases, if the leak is severe enough, will put the flame out.

Proper use of this detector will be covered elsewhere in this book; however, the following precautions should be observed when using this unit.

> A halide leak detector must only be used in well-ventilated spaces. It must never be used in a place where explosives, such as gases, dust, or vapors may be present. Never inhale the vapors or fumes from the halide leak detector: they may be poisonous.

As mentioned earlier, a soap solution is sometimes more desirable for the location of small leaks. Many times a leak will be in a confined space and a halide or electronic leak detector cannot pinpoint it.

Mix about a half cup of soap powder with water to form a thick solution, just light enough to make suds with a small paintbrush. When applying this solution to the suspected area, soap bubbles will reveal a leak.

Many times a leak will be a "cold" or "pressure" leak. A cold leak is one that is believed to leak only when the unit is not at operating temperature, such as the period that the car is parked overnight. On the other hand, a pressure leak is one that is believed to be occurring at periods of high pressure within the system, such as when the automobile is slowly moving in heavy traffic on a very warm day.

With these two types of leak it is sometimes desirable to introduce a dye solution into the system. This dye is available in yellow or red, and is manufactured for use in air-conditioning systems without affecting their operation.

Generally, when a leak cannot be detected in the shop, a dye solution is added, the car driven a few days, and the leak can be detected by the dye trace.

Once a dye is introduced into the system, it must remain there unless the complete system is cleaned out, oil changed, and drier replaced. The method of introducing dye into the system is covered in section III, procedure 21.

Electronic leak detectors are the most sensitive of all. They are, of course, more expensive initially and upkeep is a bit higher than the halide detector.

Referred to as the halogen leak detector, an electronic detector is capable of detecting Refrigerant 12 loss at a rate as slow as one-half ounce per year. That is one hundred parts of refrigerant in one million parts of air, 100 p.p.m.

Two such models are the General Electric Type H-10 and Cordless Type H-11 Halogen Leak Detectors. The H-10 operates on 120 volts, 60 cycles, and the H-11 is a portable, cordless model that operates from a rechargeable battery. Both units are simple and easy to operate and maintain.

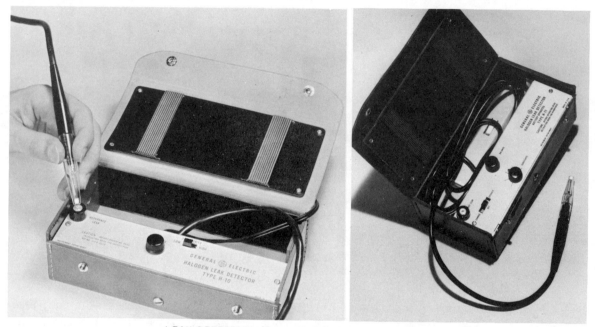

LEAK DETECTORS (Courtesy of General Electric Co.)

A more portable halogen leak detector is the model 508 TIF by Thermal Industries. It is powered by two ordinary flashlight batteries and weighs just 23 ounces. Being battery-operated, it has no warmup period and no element to wear out.

LEAK DETECTOR (Courtesy of Thermal Industries)

Space does not permit our listing all of the fine leak detectors available for the refrigeration serviceman. Contact your local refrigeration supplier for further information on these instruments.

REVIEW QUESTIONS

1. What method of leak detection is most popular? _____

2. Name at least two precautions to observe when handling a leak detector.

   a. _____

   b. _____

3. What type leak will warrant the use of a dye solution?

   _____

4. How is a soap solution added to the system?

   _____

   _____

5. What is the sensitivity of an electronic leak detector? _____

6. What is one type of electronic leak detector? _____

   _____

   _____

Topic 18   THE RECEIVER/DEHYDRATOR

The receiver/dehydrator is perhaps one of the most important parts of the air-conditioning system. Since the load on the evaporator varies because of added heat or humidity and refrigerant losses occur through small leaks, there should be a tank where extra refrigerant is stored until needed by the evaporator. It is the receiver section of the tank that is designed to serve in this capacity.

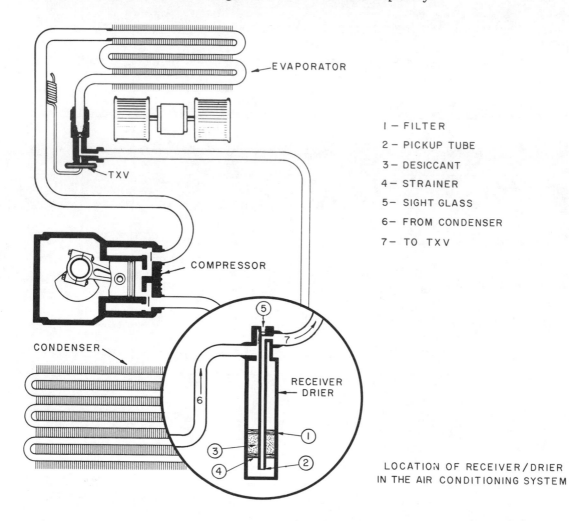

EVAPORATOR

TXV

COMPRESSOR

CONDENSER

1 — FILTER
2 — PICKUP TUBE
3 — DESICCANT
4 — STRAINER
5 — SIGHT GLASS
6 — FROM CONDENSER
7 — TO TXV

RECEIVER
DRIER

LOCATION OF RECEIVER/DRIER
IN THE AIR CONDITIONING SYSTEM

Some early air conditioner models used a separate tank as a receiver. In addition to storing liquid refrigerant, the use of a receiver lessens the necessity of precisely measuring the charge of refrigerant into the system. A couple of ounces over or under the recommended charge will make little difference in system operation.

A separate dehydrator, or drier, is used in systems having a receiver tank. The drier is usually an in-line type containing a filter and desiccant or drying material. A sight glass is usually added to the outlet of the drier to allow a means to observe refrigerant flow in the system.

THE DESICCANT

A desiccant is a solid substance capable of removing moisture from a gas, liquid or solid. The drier desiccant used is usually silica gel, molecular sieve, or Mobil-Gel. It may be held in place within the receiver between two screens, which also act as strainers, or they may be placed in a metal mesh bag and held in place with a metal spring. In some cases the bag is simply placed into the tank and not held in place. It is not uncommon to shake a drier tank and hear the desiccant move from end to end. This does not mean that the receiver/drier is damaged.

A desiccant's capacity for absorbing moisture depends, of course, on the volume and type of material used. For instance, five cubic inches of silical gel has the capacity of absorbing and holding about 100 drops of water at 150°F.

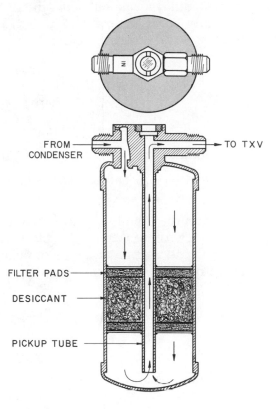

RECEIVER / DRIER

THE FILTER

The filter is usually a packing of material through which the refrigerant must pass before it can leave the tank. Its purpose is to prevent the desiccant dust and other solids from being carried through with the refrigerant. Some driers have two filters, one on each side of the desiccant. The refrigerant must pass through both filters and the desiccant before leaving the receiver tank. Some driers do not have a filter and rely on the strainer to catch all foreign particles that may pass into the receiver/drier.

THE PICKUP TUBE

The pickup tube is a device to insure that 100% liquid refrigerant is fed to the thermostatic expansion valve. Since the refrigerant entering the tank may have some gases with the liquid, the tank also acts as a separator. The liquid drops to the bottom of the tank and the gas remains on top. The pickup tube is extended to the bottom of the tank where a constant supply of gas-free liquid is insured.

THE STRAINER

The strainer is made of fine wire mesh and is placed in the tank as an aid in removing particles of impurities passing through the receiver/drier. Some tanks have two strainers, one on each side of the desiccant, which also serve to hold it in place. While some driers may not have a filter, all should have a strainer. Refrigerant has to pass through the strainer(s) before leaving the receiver tank.

THE SIGHT GLASS

The sight glass serves to indicate:

1. whether there is enough refrigerant in the system.
2. whether the refrigerant is dry within safe limits.

It is placed in the liquid, or outlet side of the receiver/drier. This provides a means for the serviceman to observe the state of the refrigerant within the system. A steady stream of liquid will be one free of bubbles as observed in the glass. The presence of bubbles or foam indicates a system malfunction or a loss of refrigerant.

SUMMARY

The location of the receiver/drier has a direct bearing on its ability to absorb and hold moisture. As pointed out earlier five cubic inches of silica gel desiccant holds 100 drops of moisture at 150°F. As the temperature increases, the ability of the desiccant to hold moisture decreases. The ability of a desiccant to hold moisture is in direct proportion to the surrounding temperature.

The addition of alcohol to the air-conditioning system, as recommended by one manufacturer, also decreases the drier's capacity to hold moisture. While the addition of alcohol will prevent any moisture in the system from freezing, it will prove detrimental in the long run. Moisture in the system in contact with Refrigerant 12 forms hydrochloric acid which attacks all metal parts. Damage will occur to parts such as the thermostatic expansion valve, compressor valve plates, and service valves.

When the air-conditioning system is operating in late evening and early morning with lower outside temperatures, the drier holds its moisture and prevents it from circulating in the system. Increased temperature during the heat of the day raises the temperature of the desiccant, and if it has reached its saturation point, it releases some of its moisture into the system.

These droplets of moisture, and it only takes one, collect inside the thermostatic expansion valve and change to ice in the valve orifice. This ice blocks the flow of refrigerant and cooling will stop.

Evidence of moisture in the system is not so easy to detect in the shop procedures because it takes some time for the droplets to form and turn to ice. Diagnosis will be made easier if the customer has the following complaint:

"The air conditioner works fine for about fifteen minutes or
so but then it just quits. It even puts out hot air. I can turn
it off for a few minutes, then turn it on, and it will work fine
for another ten to fifteen minutes."

This complaint is a common one. It is caused by servicemen who are not careful in their installation or servicing of the air conditioner, and who allow moisture or
moisture-laden air to enter the system. This condition can also be caused by improper pumpdown for moisture removal before charging. The only remedy for such
a situation is to install a new drier and pump the system for as long as possible to
remove excess moisture before recharging.

The receiver/drier is usually located under the hood of the car in front of the
radiator. The drier should be located where it will be kept as cool as possible. Late
model General Motors driers are located on the engine side of the fan shroud. At
least one independent manufacturer mounts the drier in the evaporator where it is
always surrounded by the cool air of the evaporator.

Most fittings on the driers are 3/8" male flares for inlet and outlet. There
are a few 1/4" male flare fittings and some 3/8" female flare fittings used. Most
General Motors driers and late model Chrysler products have fittings of 3/8" o-ring
design, male or female, depending on the year and model of the car.

Driers are also equipped with
5/16" barb-type fittings that the hose
slips over. The hose is then held in
place with hose clamps. This drier
is popular with independent manufacturers because it helps lower the cost
price of the unit by eliminating two
fittings that are otherwise necessary.

Manufacturers' recommendations
should be followed when mounting a
drier. For proper operation, the ver-
tical-type drier must not be mounted
on an incline of more than 15°. The
inlet of the drier must be connected
to the condenser outlet.

Usually, "IN" is stamped on the
inlet side of the drier. If not, an arrow
indicating direction of refrigerant flow

RECEIVER / DRIERS

should be visible. It is important to remember that the flow of refrigerant is out of
the condenser bottom and toward the thermostatic expansion valve inlet. Reversing
the drier may result in insufficient cooling.

Occasionally, due to improper handling or shipping, the internal parts of the drier may become dislodged resulting in a partial restriction within the drier. This condition will be evident by a marked temperature change between the inlet and outlet of the tank. If the restriction is great enough, frosting may occur at the drier outlet.

Should the pickup tube be broken away due to rough handling, the result will be abnormal flashing of the gas in the liquid line, the same as would be the indication of a low charge of refrigerant. In either case, a new drier should be installed.

When installing or servicing an air-conditioning system, the drier should be the last part connected to the system and all care should be exercised to prevent moisture and moisture-laden air from entering the system and drier. Do not uncap the drier until the unit is ready for its installation. Remember: the desiccant will attract moisture from the surrounding air.

A complete evacuation of the system with an approved vacuum pump is essential for moisture removal. This procedure is covered by Service Procedure 4, Section III of this text.

Any time a refrigeration system is opened for service it is possible for foreign matter to enter. Matter such as dirt and moisture or other noncondensibles have a deteriorating effect on refrigerant.

As has been discussed, moisture and refrigerant form hydrochloric acid, which in turn causes corrosion of all metal parts. This corrosion will, in time, slough off into the system in small particles which can stop the flow of refrigerant by clogging screens that are placed in the system to catch them.

A screen is located in the inlet of the thermostatic expansion valve, the inlet of the compressor and in the receiver/drier. All but the screen in the drier may be cleaned or replaced. If the screen in the drier becomes clogged, unit replacement is required.

REVIEW QUESTIONS

1. What is Mobil-Gel and molecular sieve?

   _____

   _____

2. What is the purpose of silica gel in the dehydrator? _____

   _____

3. What is the holding capacity of five cubic inches of desiccant at 150°F.?

   _____

4. What is the purpose of the filter? _____

_____

5. What is the purpose of the pickup tube? _____

_____

_____

6. On which side of the drier is the sight glass placed? _____

7. When should alcohol be added to the air conditioner? _____

_____

8. What effect does alcohol have on the holding capacity of the desiccant?

_____

9. What acid will form in a system not free of moisture? _____

10. At what angle of incline may the drier be mounted? _____

11. Do we always connect the drier into the system as the last part to be fastened?

_____

12. Can the drier be installed backward? _____

_____

Topic 19 THE THERMOSTATIC EXPANSION VALVE

The control of the quantity, or amount, of refrigerant entering the evaporator core is the job of the thermostatic expansion valve. Of the two types of valves in use, the internally equalized and externally equalized valves, the internally equalized valve is the most popular. Some manufacturers, however, to meet the requirements of certain controls, use an externally equalized expansion valve.

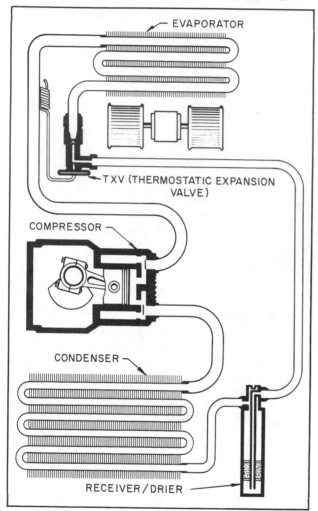

LOCATION OF THE THERMOSTATIC EXPANSION VALVE IN THE AIR CONDITIONING SYSTEM

The control device that meters or regulates flow of refrigerant entering the evaporator is the thermostatic expansion valve. It is located at or near the inlet of the evaporator. The valve has three main functions: throttling action, modulating action and controlling action.

THROTTLING ACTION OF THE EXPANSION VALVE H+LSide

The expansion valve separates the high side of the system from the low side and since there is a pressure drop across the valve, the flow of refrigerant is restricted, or throttled. The state of the refrigerant entering the valve is high-pressure liquid. The state of the refrigerant leaving the valve is low-pressure liquid. A drop in pressure takes place without causing a change of state.

MODULATING ACTION OF THE EXPANSION VALVE meter

The expansion valve is designed to meter just the proper amount of liquid refrigerant into the evaporator as may be required for proper cooling. The amount of refrigerant required for proper cooling will vary with different heat loads. The valve will modulate from the wide open position to the closed position and seek a point between for the proper metering of the refrigerant.

Heat + load — opening + closing of valve controls temp.

CONTROLLING ACTION OF THE EXPANSION VALVE

The expansion valve is designed to change the amount of liquid refrigerant metered into the evaporator in response to load or heat changes. As the load increases, more refrigerant is required to be metered into the evaporator. As the load is decreased, the valve closes and meters less refrigerant into the evaporator. It is this controlling action of the valve that allows proper temperature control.

EXPANSION VALVE SUPERHEAT

The liquid refrigerant admitted to the evaporator coil will usually completely vaporize, or evaporate, before reaching the coil outlet. Knowing that the liquid vaporizes at a low temperature, at about -21.6°F., it can be seen that the vapor remains cold, even though the liquid is completely evaporated.

The cold vapor flowing through the remainder of the coil continues to absorb heat, becoming superheated. This means that the temperature of the refrigerant has been raised above the point at which it evaporated, or vaporized.

For example; an evaporator operating at a suction pressure of 28.5 p.s.i.g. would have a saturated liquid temperature of 30°F., according to the temperature-pressure chart. As the refrigerant vaporizes through absorption of the heat in the evaporator, the temperature of the vapor rises until the vapor temperature at the coil outlet, or tailpipe, reaches 35°F., a difference of 5°F. between inlet and outlet refrigerant temperature.

This difference in temperature is known as superheat. All expansion valves are adjusted at the factory to operate under the superheat conditions present in the particular type of unit for which they are designed. It is important, when replacing an expansion valve, to use one of the proper superheat range as well as the proper size. Though valves may look the same, they differ a great deal in application.

THE THERMOSTATIC EXPANSION VALVE, A CONTROL DEVICE

The expansion valve consists of seven major parts, which include:

valve body	push rod
valve stem and needle	superheat spring and adjuster
valve seat	capillary tube with remote bulb
valve diaphragm	

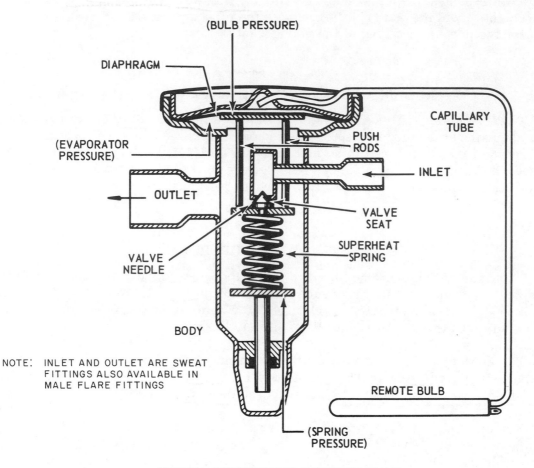

(BULB PRESSURE)

DIAPHRAGM

CAPILLARY
TUBE

PUSH
RODS

(EVAPORATOR
PRESSURE)

INLET

OUTLET

VALVE
SEAT

SUPERHEAT
SPRING

VALVE
NEEDLE

BODY

NOTE: INLET AND OUTLET ARE SWEAT
FITTINGS ALSO AVAILABLE IN
MALE FLARE FITTINGS

REMOTE BULB

(SPRING
PRESSURE)

TYPICAL THERMOSTATIC EXPANSION VALVE

The remote bulb is fastened to the outlet, or tailpipe, of the evaporator. It senses tailpipe temperatures and activates the diaphragm in the valve through the capillary tube and causes the proper amount of refrigerant to flow into the evaporator case.

For example, when the temperature of the tailpipe is high it is because the evaporator is starved of refrigerant. This is evidenced by an increase in superheated vapor leaving the evaporator.

This heat causes pressure to be exerted on the diaphragm by the expanding gases in the remote bulb through the capillary tube. The diaphragm, in turn, forces the push rods down against the valve stem and needle and pushes it off its seat. In so doing, more refrigerant is fed into the evaporator.

Conversely, a low temperature will allow less force on the capillary tube and diaphragm and will seat the needle which will restrict the flow of refrigerant into the evaporator.

It is the balance of pressure between the superheat spring and diaphragm that regulates the flow of refrigerant into the evaporator.

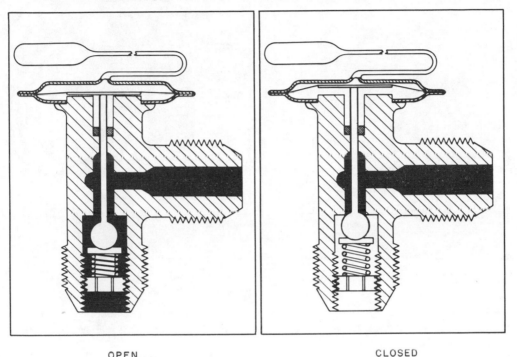

OPEN   CLOSED

THERMOSTATIC EXPANSION VALVE

Starving the evaporator of refrigerant is the result of too little refrigerant being metered by the expansion valve. This condition may be caused by an improper valve being installed into the system, a partially clogged strainer or valve, or a warped or defective push rod or other internal parts.

The evaporator is flooded when too much refrigerant is metered into the core by the expansion valve. This condition may be caused by improper placement of the remote bulb, poor contact of the bulb on the tailpipe, or damaged and binding internal parts of the valve.

THE EXTERNAL EQUALIZER

To overcome the effect of a pressure drop in the larger evaporators, the externally equalized expansion valve is used. The external equalizer tube is connected to the tailpipe of the evaporator and runs to the underside of the diaphragm in the expansion valve.

This balances the pressure of the tailpipe through the expansion valve remote bulb taken from the tailpipe. The use of an external equalizer eliminates the effect of the pressure drop across the evaporator coil and the superheat settings now depend only on the adjustment of the spring tension.

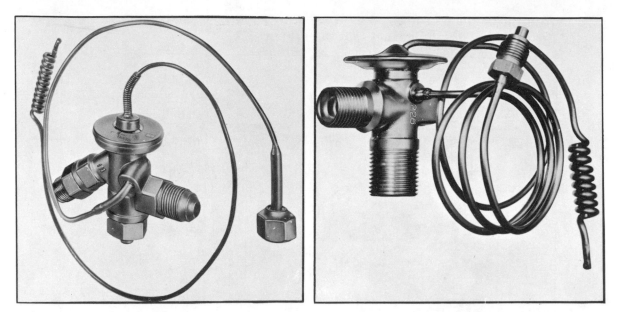

FLARE TYPE   O-RING TYPE
EXTERNALLY EQUALIZED THERMOSTATIC EXPANSION VALVE

All evaporators having a pressure drop of greater than two pounds have an external equalizer. Most factory units by Chrysler and General Motors use an externally-equalized thermostatic expansion valve.

SUMMARY

The thermostatic expansion valve is equipped with a screen in the inlet side of the valve that may be cleaned if plugged or clogged. Should the screen require cleaning, the receiver/dehydrator should be replaced. If the screen is plugged to the point that cleaning is not practical, a new one should be installed. Never leave the screen out of a system.

If the expansion valve has been removed from the car for cleaning or other service, it may be bench checked before reinstalling. Bench checking an expansion valve for efficiency is covered in Service Procedure 32, Section III of this text. This procedure may save time and refrigerant that otherwise may be lost if the valve were proved to be defective.

From this description of the thermostatic expansion valve, it can be seen that the valve is more sensitive to foreign materials than any other part of the air-conditioning system.

To prevent the vital parts of the valve from sticking, or becoming corroded, the air conditioner should be operated for short periods during the months that normal operation is not practical.

In so doing, the internal parts of the expansion valve as well as the compressor are kept lubricated and operating freely.

REVIEW QUESTIONS

1. Name two types of expansion valves.
   a. _internal_　　　b. _external_

2. What are the expansion valve's three main functions?
   a. _throttle_
   b. _modulate_
   c. _control_

3. What do we mean by superheat range of the TXV? _temp of refrig has been raised above pt. at which it evaporated or vaporized._

4. When the evaporator is starved of refrigerant, what is the state of the refrigerant leaving the tailpipe? _Too little refrig, temp is high at tailpipe_

5. Where is the equalizer tube fastened? _Tailpipe of evaporator_

6. Where is the remote bulb fastened? _capillary tube + low side evap + comp'r._

7. Where is the screen located? _inlet side of valve_

8. Is the screen serviceable? _yes._

9. How may we prevent the TXV from becoming stuck when the air conditioner is not in normal use? _use system_

10. Who uses an externally equalized TXV in most cases?
    Chrysler & G.m.

Topic 20 THE THERMOSTAT

An electric clutch is used on the compressor of most aftermarket units and some factory installed units to provide a means of constant temperature control in the automobile air conditioner. This clutch is controlled by a thermostat in the evaporator. The thermostat is set initially by the driver to a predetermined point and is then held constant by the temperature of the unit itself.

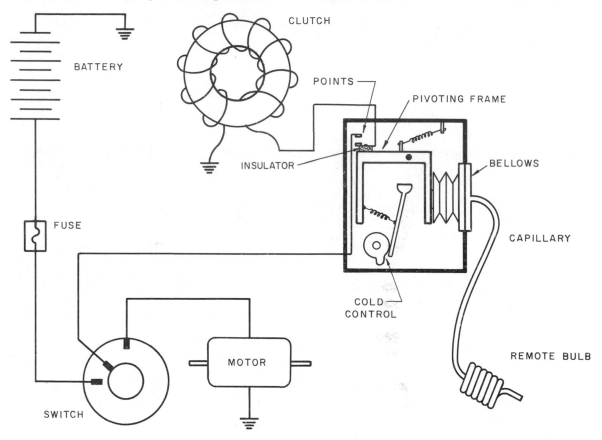

THE BELLOWS TYPE THERMOSTAT

The thermostat is nothing more than a thermal device which controls an electrical switch. When warm, the switch is closed, and when cold, it is open. Most thermostats have a positive off position to provide a means of turning the clutch off regardless of temperature. This allows the use of the fans without having refrigerated air, if so desired.

Two types of thermostats are used, mostly found on hang-on units. They are the bellows type and the bimetallic type.

The bellows-type thermostat has a capillary tube connected to it which is filled with Refrigerant 12 or CO_2. The capillary is attached to the bellows inside of the thermostat, which is attached to a swinging frame assembly. One point is fastened to this frame and the other point is fastened to the body of the unit. However, both points are insulated from the rest of the thermostat.

Expansion of the gases inside the capillary tube exerts pressure on the bellows, which in turn closes the points at a prescribed temperature. Manual temperature control is accomplished by a shaft connected to the swinging frame, controlled by an external knob.   Turning the knob in a clockwise direction increases spring tension. against the bellows. More pressure is required to overcome an increased spring tension.   More pressure, of course, means more heat. Since it is heat that we are removing from the evaporator, this means that a lower temperature will be required to OPEN the points.   On a temperature rise the heat will again exert pressure on the bellows to CLOSE the points and allow for cooling.

Another spring inside of the thermostat regulates the interval that the points are open.   This interval is usually about 12°F. temperature rise to give sufficient time for the evaporator to defrost.

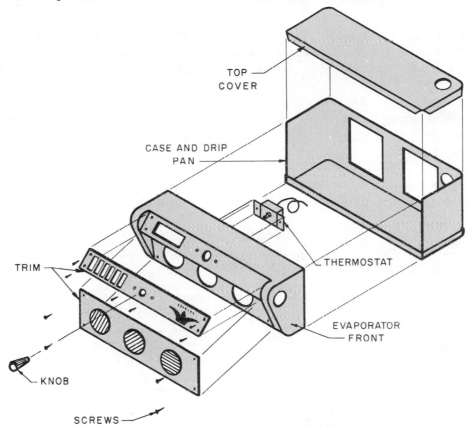

TYPICAL EVAPORATOR CASE SHOWING THE LOCATION OF THE THERMOSTAT
AT THE FRONT OF THE EVAPORATOR COIL.

Care must be exercised when handling the capillary tube thermostat. Sharp bends and kinks should be avoided in the capillary. When it is necessary to bend a capillary, make a bend no sharper than one formed around the finger.

For best results the end of the capillary should be inserted into the evaporator core between the fins about one inch. Do not attempt to insert the capillary all the way through the fins since the blowers are usually behind the core.

A thermostat that has lost its charge in the capillary for any reason must be replaced. A lost charge will result in a unit that has no ON (cooling) cycle. Recharging the capillary with standard tools is not possible.

The bimetallic-type thermostat is desirable as a replacement part because of its lower cost. This type does not have a capillary tube, and depends on air passing over it for its proper operation.

Manual temperature control is accomplished by the driver the same as with the bellows type. Cold air passing over the bimetallic leaf in the rear of the thermostat causes it to retract. In so doing it bows enough to open a set of points. As it warms up, the other leaf, reacting to heat, pulls the points back together. The off cycle of this thermostat is also about 12°F. allowing for sufficient defrost time.

The bimetallic thermostat is limited in application because it has to be mounted inside of the evaporator itself. Many times the bellows-type thermostat has to be used. The long capillary tube allows its placement some distance from the evaporator core.

Most thermostats are adjustable. They have a provision for regulating the range between the opening and closing of the points as well. Some thermostats have the adjustment under the control knob in the shaft; others under a fiber cover on the body of the unit.

If a setscrew cannot be found on the thermostat it may be considered a nonadjustable type. Malfunction of this type of thermostat requires complete unit replacement.

REVIEW QUESTIONS

1. What is the purpose of the thermostat? _____

_____

2. What is the capillary tube filled with? _____

3. What is the result if the capillary tube has lost its charge of inert gas?

_____

4. Do all thermostats have a capillary tube? _____

5. Are most thermostats adjustable by the serviceman? _____

6. What is the off (defrost) cycle of the thermostat if it is operating properly?

_____

7. Are all thermostats adjustable by the driver? _____

8. What is a good rule to follow when bending the capillary tube?

_____

Topic 21 THE MAGNETIC CLUTCH

The manufacturers of all automotive air conditioners today use a magnetic clutch as a means of disengaging the compressor when it is not needed. This may be the case when a defrost cycle is indicated in the evaporator, or at other times when the air conditioner is not being used.

Basically, all clutches operate on the same principle, that of magnetic attraction. They may be designated in two general types; the stationary field and the rotating field clutches.

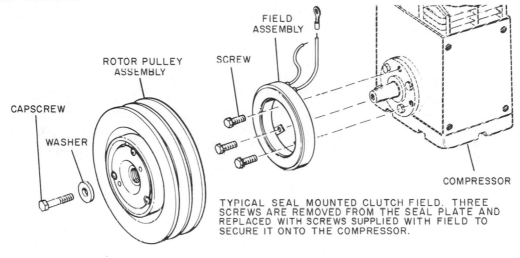

TYPICAL SEAL MOUNTED CLUTCH FIELD. THREE SCREWS ARE REMOVED FROM THE SEAL PLATE AND REPLACED WITH SCREWS SUPPLIED WITH FIELD TO SECURE IT ON TO THE COMPRESSOR.

THE STATIONARY FIELD CLUTCH

The stationary field clutch is perhaps the most desirable with fewer parts to wear out.

The field is mounted to the compressor by mechanical means depending on the type field and compressor. The rotor is held on the armature by means of a bearing and snap rings. The armature is mounted on the compressor crankshaft.

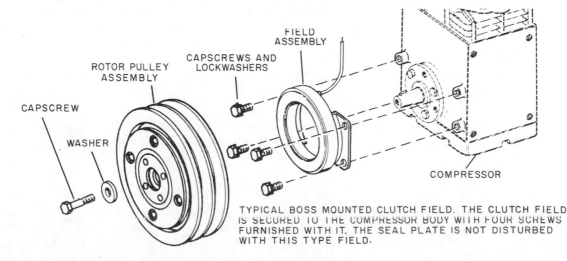

TYPICAL BOSS MOUNTED CLUTCH FIELD. THE CLUTCH FIELD IS SECURED TO THE COMPRESSOR BODY WITH FOUR SCREWS FURNISHED WITH IT. THE SEAL PLATE IS NOT DISTURBED WITH THIS TYPE FIELD.

When no current is fed to the field there is no magnetic force applied to the clutch and the rotor is free to turn on the armature, which remains stationary on the crankshaft.

When the thermostat or switch is closed, current is fed to the field. This sets up a magnetic force between the field and armature, pulling it into the rotor. When the armature becomes engaged with the rotor, it becomes as one piece and the complete unit turns while the field remains stationary. This causes the compressor crankshaft to turn, starting the refrigeration cycle.

When the switch or thermostat is opened, current is cut off. The armature snaps back out and stops while the rotor continues to turn. Pumping action of the compressor is stopped until current is again applied to the field.

THE ROTATING FIELD CLUTCH

The rotating field-type clutch is the same in operation with the exception of the field placement. The field is a part of the rotor and turns with the rotor. Current is fed into the field by means of brushes which are mounted on the compressor.

Current fed to the field through the brushes sets up a magnetic field which pulls the armature into contact with the rotor. Now the complete unit turns, field included, causing the compressor to turn.

In both type clutches, slots are machined in the armature and rotor to aid in concentrating the magnetic field and increase attraction between them.

Since the clutch will engage and disengage at high speeds as required for proper temperature control, it is understandable that considerable scoring will occur between the armature and rotor. Scoring of the two surfaces is allowable and should not be cause for concern.

Clutch coils of the proper voltage should be used. A coil rated at twelve volts, used on a six-volt system, will not allow for a full buildup of magnetic flux and armature slippage will result. This will result in a shortened clutch life as well as poor cooling. Conversely, a six-volt field used on a twelve-volt system will result in a short field life because the voltage applied to it may cause serious damage. When it is necessary to use six-volt equipment in a car equipped with a twelve-volt system, a suitable dropping resistor should be used.

Spacing between the coil and pulley is important. The pulley should be as close as possible for better magnetic flux travel, but not so close that the rotor will drag the coil housing.

Spacing between the rotor and armature is also important. If spacing is too close, the armature will drag on the rotor when the unit is turned off. If spacing is too far apart, the result will be poor contact between the armature and rotor when the unit is turned on. Either situation will result in serious clutch malfunctions.

Spacing should be so that when the clutch is off, no drag is evidenced; when turned on no slippage occurs with the exception of the moment when the clutch is first engaged.

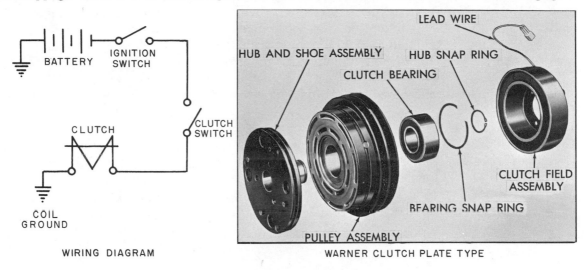

WIRING DIAGRAM   WARNER CLUTCH PLATE TYPE

THE BALL AND RAMP CLUTCH

General Motors used a different type clutch on their units through 1960. Starting with 1961 they use a ball and ramp clutch which is similar to the armature, rotor type, using a stationary field.

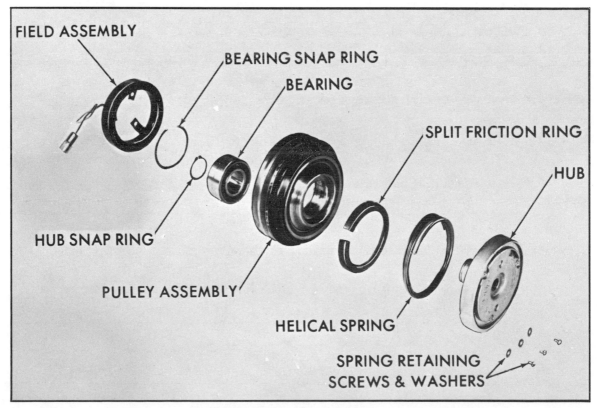

WARNER HELI — GRIP CLUTCH

The six-cylinder Frigidaire compressor uses a stationary magnetic field. However, this field is mounted on the front compressor head. The rotor likewise is mounted on the front head of the compressor. The armature is mounted on the crankshaft. When no current is applied, the rotor turns freely while the armature is stationary. When current is applied the armature is pulled into the rotor and both pieces turn as one thereby turning the compressor crankshaft.

Clutch repair and service diagnosis is covered in Service Procedures (Section III) of this text.

Frigidaire and Chrysler Air-temp units do not use a magnetic clutch as a means of temperature control. They use, instead, a different type of control device, which controls the flow of refrigerant within the system. Magnetic clutches are used in these units just to turn them on when they are to be used and off when they are no longer wanted.

REVIEW QUESTIONS

1. Name two types of magnetic clutch.

   a. _____

   b. _____

2. What feeds current to the field of the clutch in both types? _____

   _____

3. What type of clutch uses a brush set? _____

4. What type of clutch does not have a rotating field? _____

5. Who uses a ball and ramp-type clutch? _____

   _____

6. What type of field does the ball and ramp-type clutch use? _____

7. Are cycling clutches used on all air conditioning? _____

   _____

Topic 22 TEMPERATURE CONTROL DEVICES

Controlling evaporator temperature by controlling its pressure is a method that has been used successfully for years with factory air conditioners. This type of control does not use a cycling clutch as a method of temperature control.

From time to time independent manufacturers attempt to market units using this method of temperature control, but all go back to the cycling clutch for one of several reasons, perhaps cost being the main factor.

SUCTION THROTTLING REGULATORS

The suction throttling regulated system includes all types of controls used to regulate the pressure of the evaporator by regulating the amount of refrigerant vapor that is allowed to leave the evaporator. This system may be mounted in the tailpipe of the evaporator, in the suction line, or in the inlet of the compressor.

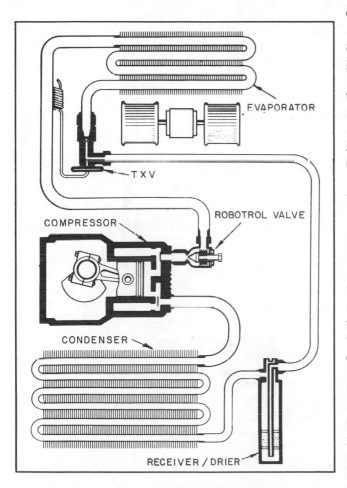

LOCATION OF ROBOTROL VALVE IN THE
AIR CONDITIONING SYSTEM

If an inspection of the system does not reveal a control device, it may be assumed that the system uses a cycling clutch as a means of temperature control. Some independent manufacturers used a suction throttling regulator which was located inside the evaporator and adjusted manually by the driver. This device has been discontinued in favor of the thermostat, however.

THE ROBOTROL VALVE

The Robotrol valve used by Mark IV is designed to work automatically and is preset by the serviceman. No provisions are made for the driver to change the temperature settings. The Robotrol valve is regulated at the factory to close the valve when the suction line pressure drops to a point that would allow the evaporator to freeze up. An adjusting screw is provided to allow the serviceman to change spring tension, thereby changing its setting in the field if humidity conditions indicate its necessity. Turning the adjusting screw in, or in a clockwise direction, increases spring tension and provides a higher pressure setting for the evaporator.

Conversely, turning the screw out, or in a counterclockwise direction, lessens spring tension and lowers evaporator operating pressure.

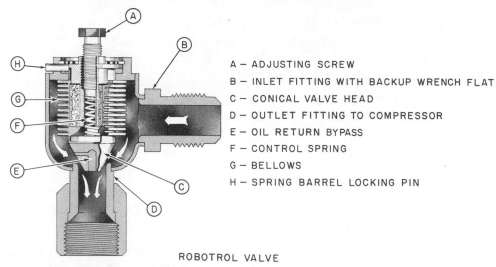

A — ADJUSTING SCREW
B — INLET FITTING WITH BACKUP WRENCH FLAT
C — CONICAL VALVE HEAD
D — OUTLET FITTING TO COMPRESSOR
E — OIL RETURN BYPASS
F — CONTROL SPRING
G — BELLOWS
H — SPRING BARREL LOCKING PIN

ROBOTROL VALVE

A correct setting of the RoboTrol valve will maintain about 26 p.s.i.g. in the evaporator coil. This should allow for temperatures above 32°F. in the evaporator and thus prevent condensate freezeup.

THE SELECTROL VALVE

The SelecTrol valve, used by Mark IV, is a metering device situated in the evaporator in the tailpipe. Located on the right side of the case, a manual control allows the driver to control evaporator temperature as desired for comfort.

The SelecTrol valve has a positive action: moving the valve plunger inward by rotating the control knob clockwise brings the plunger closer to the seat and restricts the flow of refrigerant. Restricting the flow of refrigerant leaving the evaporator causes pressure to build up. Higher pressure means higher temperature.

Spring tension is relieved by rotating the knob in the counterclockwise direction. The plunger moves farther away from the seat and allows more refrigerant to leave the evaporator. Therefore, since the thermostatic expansion valve is a metering device at the evaporator inlet, evaporator pressure is lowered. Lower pressure means lower temperature.

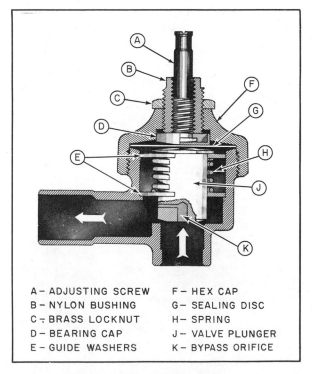

A — ADJUSTING SCREW   F — HEX CAP
B — NYLON BUSHING   G — SEALING DISC
C — BRASS LOCKNUT   H — SPRING
D — BEARING CAP   J — VALVE PLUNGER
E — GUIDE WASHERS   K — BYPASS ORIFICE

TYPICAL SELECTROL VALVE

92

Flow cannot be completely shut off because of a small bypass hole in the body which allows a small amount of refrigerant and refrigeration oil to circulate past the valve. This is necessary to insure proper lubrication.

THE EVAPORATOR PRESSURE REGULATOR*

The evaporator pressure regulator valve, or EPR valve is a suction control device used on Chrysler Motors Airtemp units.

The EPR valve is a fully automatic control device located under the suction service valve internally. The EPR valve maintains evaporator pressure and temperature to a point above freezing to prevent evaporator freezeup during normal operation.

It is necessary to use a third gage when checking the operation of the EPR valve. An air conditioner operating correctly will result in an evaporator pressure of 22-26 p.s.i.g. to maintain temperatures above freezing in the evaporator. The compressor inlet pressure should be about 15 p.s.i.g. depending on evaporator load.

The external EPR valve has an oil return fitting with a small line running to the oil check plug, which has been replaced with a fitting to accept the line. This allows for positive crankcase lubrication at all times.

A balance is maintained between control spring pressure and evaporator pressure. A diaphragm is used to seal the chamber and prevent leaking refrigerant. An increase of evaporator pressure against the diaphragm will overcome the spring tension and move the valve away from the seat to increase refrigerant flow out of the evaporator.

A decrease in evaporator pressure will allow the spring to move the valve toward the seat, cutting down refrigerant flow from the evaporator. This opening and closing, like a bouncing ball, will continue until a balance is reached between evaporator pressure and spring tension, at which time the valve will remain constant until evaporator load or compressor speed changes, requiring a new balance of pressure.

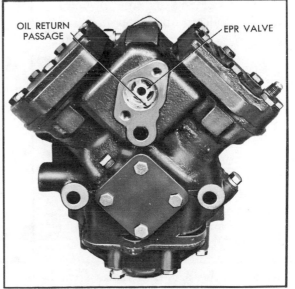

EPR VALVE AND OIL RETURN PASSAGE

The EPR valve is located in the suction side of the compressor between the evaporator and compressor. This EPR valve is an internal part of the compressor, though it may be serviced separately.

*Parts of this text and illustration are by courtesy of Chrysler Motors Corporation.

This valve cannot be adjusted. Any malfunction requires complete replacement.

An oil passage inside of the compressor and through the EPR valve provides a passage between the suction line and compressor crankcase. This allows oil carried out of the compressor by the refrigerant vapor to return to the compressor crankcase.

Another function of the oil return passage is to pressurize the crankcase, which prevents the pressure from dropping below atmospheric pressure. If pressure of the crankcase dropped into a vacuum, atmospheric pressure could enter the system through the compressor shaft seal.

EVAPORATOR TEMPERATURE REGULATOR

The Evaporator Temperature Regulator (ETR) is used on Chrysler products having an automatic temperature control unit. It replaces the standard Evaporator Pressure Regulator (EPR) used on the standard air conditioning unit.

The operation of the ETR valve is controlled by an ETR switch which is located on, or near, the evaporator case. The switch, an electrical device, has a temperature-sensing bulb which is inserted into the evaporator fins. The switch closes if the evaporator temperature goes lower than about 38°F., and sends a current to the ETR valve in the compressor. This closes the ETR valve, shutting off the flow of refrigerant, thus warming up the evaporator.

The ETR valve and EPR valve differ in that the ETR valve is either open or closed, while the EPR valve operates in varying degrees of being open or closed, not stopping, but slowing down the flow of refrigerant.

THE SUCTION THROTTLING VALVE*

The suction throttling valve, STV, is located at the outlet or tailpipe of the evaporator or nearby, between the compressor inlet and evaporator outlet. This valve is used in General Motors cars for the years 1962 through 1965 as an evaporator pressure control device to prevent condensate from freezing on the evaporator core, and to adjust the temperature of the air that flows from the evaporator.

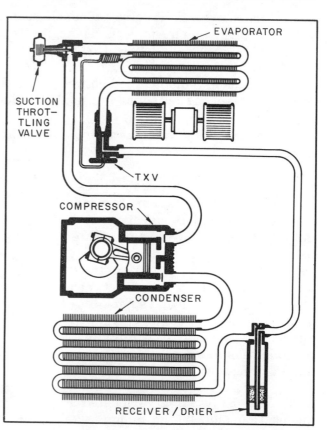

LOCATION OF THE SUCTION THROTTLING VALVE IN THE AIR CONDITIONING SYSTEM

* Parts of this text and illustrations are by courtesy of Harrison Radiator Division, General Motors Corporation.

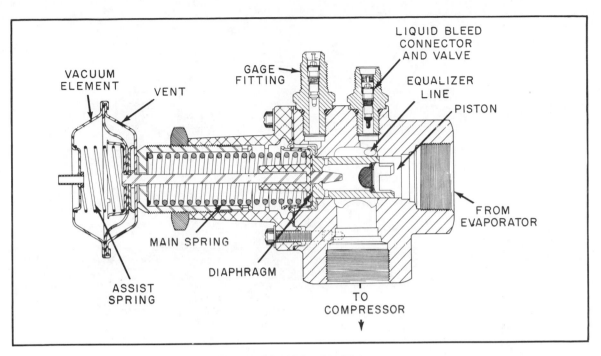

VACUUM CONTROLLED STV

The main function of the valve is to maintain the evaporator pressure at a pre-determined pressure setting. A setting of 29-30 p.s.i.g. will maintain the temperature of the evaporator core surface above 32°F. This will prevent condensate from freezing on the core.

The opposing forces, spring pressure and atmospheric pressure on the one side of the valve diaphragm, and evaporator pressure on the opposite side of the diaphragm, constitute a balanced valve and control its operation.

When the evaporator pressure rises above the predetermined setting, this increase in evaporator pressure is exerted against the valve piston on through the bleed holes in the piston to the underside of the diaphragm. The pressures under the diaphragm overcome the spring pressure causing the valve piston to move in an opening direction. As the piston opens, it reaches a balanced position and the evaporator pressure returns to its original setting, 29-30 p.s.i.g.

When the evaporator pressure drops below the predetermined setting, the spring pressure overcomes the opposing evaporator pressure and forces the piston in a closing direction until the predetermined pressure setting is once again achieved.

The minimum operating pressure of the suction throttling valve is preset by an adjustment screw in both the mechanically- and vacuum-operated valves. Maximum operating pressure may be obtained on the mechanically-operated valve by means of a Bowden cable running from the instrument panel to the lever arm on the valve. When reduced load conditions require elevated control pressures, the lever arm actuates the inner spring assembly causing the piston to throttle in a closing direction. This results in a higher evaporator pressure and the desired increase in discharge air temperature.

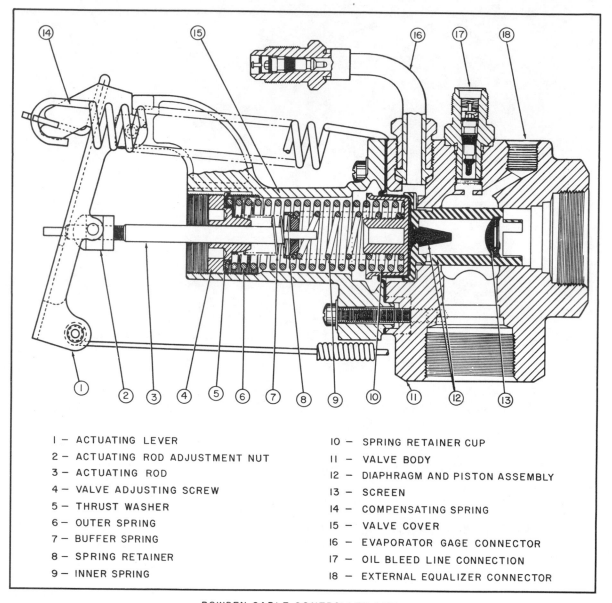

1 — ACTUATING LEVER
2 — ACTUATING ROD ADJUSTMENT NUT
3 — ACTUATING ROD
4 — VALVE ADJUSTING SCREW
5 — THRUST WASHER
6 — OUTER SPRING
7 — BUFFER SPRING
8 — SPRING RETAINER
9 — INNER SPRING

10 — SPRING RETAINER CUP
11 — VALVE BODY
12 — DIAPHRAGM AND PISTON ASSEMBLY
13 — SCREEN
14 — COMPENSATING SPRING
15 — VALVE COVER
16 — EVAPORATOR GAGE CONNECTOR
17 — OIL BLEED LINE CONNECTION
18 — EXTERNAL EQUALIZER CONNECTOR

BOWDEN-CABLE CONTROLLED STV

Control spring pressure is used to balance evaporator pressure. The vacuum-controlled STV has one spring which may be adjusted by rotating the vacuum diaphragm chamber, thus increasing and decreasing spring pressure to raise or lower evaporator pressure.

The cable-operated unit has three springs in the end of the STV housing. The large spring is adjusted by rotating an adjustment screw in the end cap. A smaller inner spring has one end attached to the actuating rod. Movement of the actuating lever will increase or decrease the tension to this spring. The third and smallest of the three is a buffer spring, the sole purpose of which is to hold the inner parts of the valve in their proper positions.

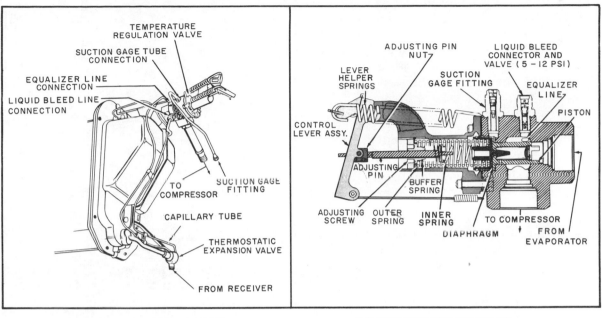

EVAPORATOR CUSTOM SYSTEM   SUCTION THROTTLING VALVE

Both types of STVs have a diaphragm firmly secured between the two sections of the valve. This diaphragm seals the valve chamber off from the spring chamber. A piston is secured to the diaphragm by a rubber tab which is a part of the diaphragm.

The most common problems with this valve are a leaking diaphragm or a sticking piston. Diagnosis and repair procedures are covered in Section III of this text.

An oil bypass line connects the STV with the evaporator. A partial refrigerant charge can result in unequal pressures between the two, with oil flooding the evaporator as a result. A check valve in the STV fitting will open from 5-12 pounds pressure to clear the evaporator of excess oil.

PILOT-OPERATED ABSOLUTE VALVE *

The function of the pilot-operated absolute suction throttling valve (POA) is to control the evaporator pressure. This is accomplished by throttling, or restricting, the outlet of the evaporator so that the pressure within the evaporator is maintained at a predetermined value to prevent the freezing of atmospheric moisture on the evaporator core.

The valve design eliminates any fabric-type diaphragm that is exposed to atmospheric or engine vacuum. As its name implies, it contains a pilot valve that has an evacuated bronze bellows which serves as the "operating force." Since the bellows contain a nearly perfect vacuum, the valve is referred to this absolute zero pressure.

---

* Text and illustrations covering the pilot-operated absolute valve are used through the courtesy of the Oldsmobile and Pontiac Divisions of General Motors Corporation.

The inlet end of the valve has a test port containing a valve core. The service test gage is connected to this fitting to determine the evaporator pressure. The other two fittings on the POA valve are the oil bleed line and expansion valve external equalizer line.

The valve cannot be repaired or adjusted and is to be replaced as an assembly once it has been determined that it is malfunctioning.

BASIC OPERATION

A bronze bellows is used to control a small needle valve which, in turn, controls a large piston. The bellows is constructed so that it has a tendency to expand when the pressure surrounding it goes below 28.5 p.s.i., or contract when the pressure goes above 28.5 p.s.i. Each time the bellows expands or closes, the needle valve-pressure surrounding the bellows increases. When the pressure increases sufficiently, the bellows contracts and opens the needle valve; then pressure surrounding the bellows drops. When the pressure drops sufficiently, the bellows expands.

Because the compressor draws action (suction) on the outlet end of the POA valve (compressor inlet), a lower pressure exists at the outlet of the POA valve than at the inlet of the POA valve. When the bellows expands and the pressure around the bellows starts to increase, simultaneously the lower pressure on the top side of the piston approaches the pressure on the underside. The closer the two pressures become equal, the more the spring pushes the piston closed. The more the two pressures become unequal, the more the bottom (higher) pressure pushes the piston open.

Procedures for checking the POA valve will be found in Service Procedure 28, Section III of this text.

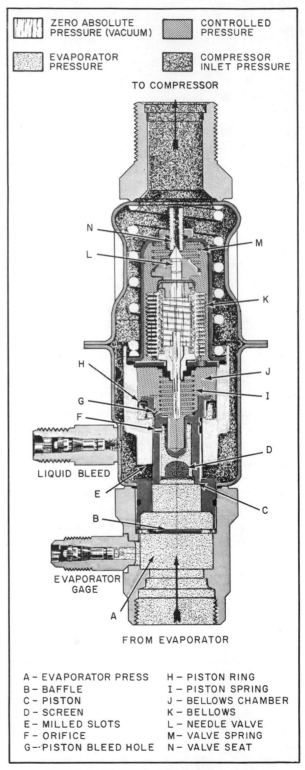

CUTAWAY DRAWING OF THE POA SUCTION THROTTLING VALVE SHOWING CONDITION OF REFRIGERANT PRESSURE WITHIN THE VALVE AS WELL AS VARIOUS PARTS

SUMMARY

When the bellows expands, the pressure increases on top of the piston to nearly equal the pressure below the piston with the result that the spring pushes the piston closed. When the bellows contracts and the pressure drops on top of the piston, the higher pressure below the piston pushes it open.

1ST STAGE EXISTING CONDITIONS

SYSTEM IS OFF, PRESSURE EQUAL ON BOTH INLET AND OUTLET AND PRESSURE IS APPROXIMATELY 70 P.S.I. (NORMAL DAY OF 70 – 80° F.).

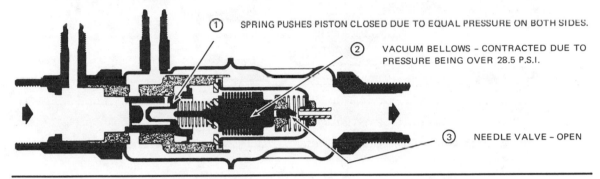

① SPRING PUSHES PISTON CLOSED DUE TO EQUAL PRESSURE ON BOTH SIDES.

② VACUUM BELLOWS – CONTRACTED DUE TO PRESSURE BEING OVER 28.5 P.S.I.

③ NEEDLE VALVE – OPEN

2ND STAGE EXISTING CONDITIONS – PISTON OPENS

SYSTEM IS ON, COMPRESSOR IS PULLING DOWN PRESSURE, THEREFORE, OUTLET SIDE (COMPRESSOR SIDE) HAS LOWER MEASURE THAN INLET SIDE.

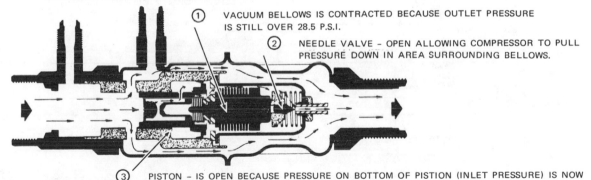

① VACUUM BELLOWS IS CONTRACTED BECAUSE OUTLET PRESSURE IS STILL OVER 28.5 P.S.I.

② NEEDLE VALVE – OPEN ALLOWING COMPRESSOR TO PULL PRESSURE DOWN IN AREA SURROUNDING BELLOWS.

③ PISTON – IS OPEN BECAUSE PRESSURE ON BOTTOM OF PISTON (INLET PRESSURE) IS NOW GREATER THAN PRESSURE ON TOP OF PISTON (OUTLET PRESSURE).

3RD STAGE EXISTING CONDITIONS – BELLOWS CLOSES

COMPRESSOR HAS PULLED OUTLET PRESSURE DOWN TO 28.5 P.S.I., THEREFORE:

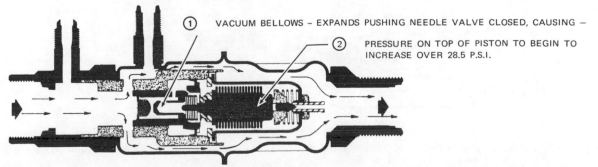

① VACUUM BELLOWS – EXPANDS PUSHING NEEDLE VALVE CLOSED, CAUSING –

② PRESSURE ON TOP OF PISTON TO BEGIN TO INCREASE OVER 28.5 P.S.I.

4TH STAGE EXISTING CONDITIONS - PISTON CLOSES

THE PRESSURE SURROUNDING BELLOWS AND ON TOP OF PISTON HAS NOW INCREASED SUFFICIENTLY OVER 28.5 P.S.I. TO BECOME NEARLY EQUAL (WITHIN 1.3 P.S.I.) OF INLET PRESSURE. SINCE —

① PRESSURE ON BOTH SIDES OF PISTON NEARLY EQUAL – SPRING TAKES OVER AND PUSHES THE PISTON CLOSED

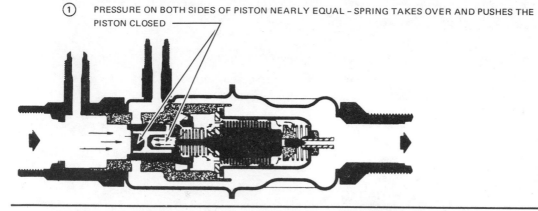

5TH STAGE EXISTING CONDITIONS - BELLOWS OPENS

THE PRESSURE SURROUNDING BELLOWS AND ON TOP OF PISTON IS NOW SUFFICIENTLY OVER 28.5 P.S.I. — THE RESULT IS THAT —

① VACUUM BELLOWS – HAS CONTRACTED DUE TO INCREASE IN PRESSURE.

② NEEDLE VALVE – OPENS AGAIN ALLOWING COMPRESSOR TO PULL PRESSURE DOWN IN AREA SURROUNDING BELLOWS.

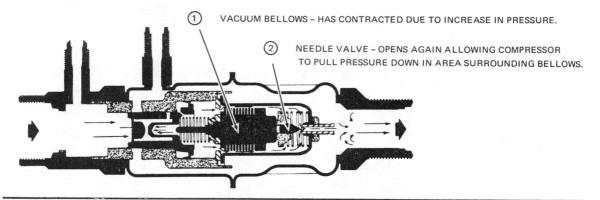

6TH STAGE EXISTING CONDITIONS - PISTON OPENS

AN UNEQUAL PRESSURE OCCURS BECAUSE COMPRESSOR IS IN THE PROCESS OF PULLING OUTLET PRESSURE DOWN.

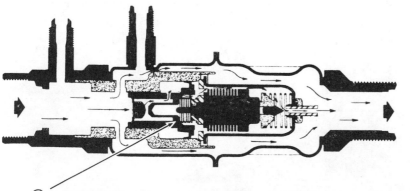

① PISTON – OPENS BECAUSE PRESSURE ON BOTTOM (INLET SIDE) IS GREATER THAN PRESSURE ON TOP OF PISTON.

REVIEW QUESTIONS

1. Are suction throttling regulators used on factory air conditioners only?

   _____

2. Where is the RoboTrol valve located in the system? _____

   _____

3. What is the normal setting for the RoboTrol valve? _____

4. Where is the SelecTrol valve located in the system? _____

   _____

5. What automobile manufacturer uses the evaporator pressure regulator (EPR) valve? _____

6. Are any of the EPR valves adjustable? _____

7. On what system do we use the third gage? _____

   _____

8. Where is the EPR valve located? _____

   _____

9. What two types of control are used with the suction throttling valve?

   _____

10. Are all suction throttling valves (STV) repairable? _____

11. What is the normal pressure setting of the STV at maximum cooling?

   _____

12. What is the pilot-operated absolute valve and how does it differ from the suction throttling valve? _____

   _____

   _____

Topic 23 AUTOMATIC TEMPERATURE CONTROLS

The automatic temperature heater-air conditioner as used in the modern automobile operates on an electro-pneumatic, electro-servo, or electro-thermo hydraulic-pneumatic principle.

If this sounds too complicated, we'll just "kick out" the "shop manual terms" and say the control is an electrical and vacuum operated device, designed to control the automobile heater and air conditioner automatically to hold the passenger compartment temperature to a preset, desired level.

The automatic control system is found in many luxury automobiles as well as in some of the so-called "low priced" models. Briefly, this system is designed so that it will maintain the in-car temperature level as set (within system capabilities) regardless of outside temperature conditions. Its function also is to hold in-car relative humidity to a healthful level and for preventing window fogging.

If, for instance, the temperature selected is 75° F., the control system will maintain an in-car condition of 75° F. at 45 to 55 percent humidity regardless of outside weather conditions.

In even the hottest weather, the system should rapidly cool the automobile interior to the predetermined temperature (75° F.). It should then modulate the degree of cooling to whatever is required in order to maintain the desired temperature level. In mild weather and climate conditions, the passenger compartment is held to this same predetermined temperature (75° F.) without having to reset or change the control.

In cold weather, the system should rapidly heat the passenger compartment to the predetermined 75° F. level, and then automatically maintain this condition.

The purpose of this topic is to give a basic understanding of the theory of operation of this system and its components. Diagnosis and repair procedures are given in the service procedures section of this book.

Basically there are two types of control system, electro-pneumatic (or electro-servo) and thermo-hydraulic-pneumatic. The electro-pneumatic (or electro-servo) unit may be broken into four groups: the sensor circuit, the amplifier, the transducer, and the servo.

The thermo-hydraulic-pneumatic unit can also be divided into four groups: the sensors and power element assembly, the vacuum regulator and restrictor assembly, the power element lever and bracket assembly, and the temperature door actuators, levers, and control group.

An explanation of each of these systems follows.

ELECTRO-PNEUMATIC TEMPERATURE CONTROL

The electro-pneumatic system, as its name implies, operates on electricity and air. In this case, "electro" refers to the direct current (d.c.) of the automobile electrical system and "pneumatic" to the vacuum of the engine.

SENSORS

There are usually three sensors located in the system and are identified as: in-car sensor, duct sensor, and ambient sensor. The in-car sensor will be found in the passenger compartment in such a location that it will sense "average" in-car temperature. The duct sensor is located in the heater case or duct in such a position that it will sense "average" duct temperature of the air coming from the evaporator or heater core. The ambient sensor is located in such a position that it will be able to sense ambient temperatures (temperature of the air entering the unit).

Each of the sensors, though they may vary in appearance, have the same general operating characteristics; that is, they are extremely sensitive to slight changes in temperature. Their resistance values change inversely to temperature change. For example, when sensing temperature decreases, the resistance of the sensor increases. Conversely, when temperature increases, the value of the sensor decreases.

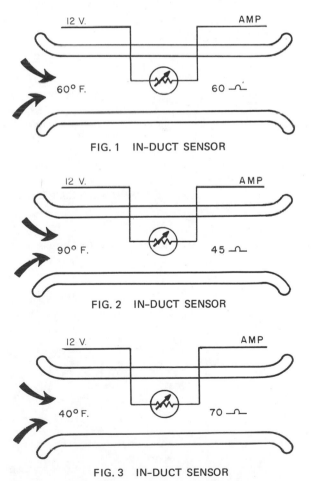

FIG. 1   IN-DUCT SENSOR

FIG. 2   IN-DUCT SENSOR

FIG. 3   IN-DUCT SENSOR

The sensor is actually a resistor whose resistance value is determined by its temperature. This type of resistor is called a thermistor. Without studying thermistor operation, the above description of sensors and Figures 1 through 3 should provide a basic understanding of thermistors.

If we were to have one thermistor in a duct, with air passing through it having a temperature of 60° F., as shown in Figure 1, the resistance value would be 60 ohms. This is shown in the thermistor value chart, Figure 9. If the temperature in this duct were 90° F., the resistance will decrease to about 45 ohms, as shown in Figure 2. If, however, the temperature were decreased to 40° F., the resistance would be increased to 70 ohms, as indicated in Figure 3.

Figure 9 gives individual sensor values at various temperatures. Compare the chart with the examples given here. Note that each sensor has different values for a particular temperature.

Before proceeding, it should be stated that the operation of the temperature control device is dependent on several things; one of them is the amount of voltage that is supplied to the amplifier after passing through the temperature control and three sensors. Other determinations for proper operation will be discussed later.

Proper sensor wiring, in its simplest form, is shown in Figure 4. It is easily seen that a temperature variation in either, or all, of the sensors will affect output voltage and so control temperature.

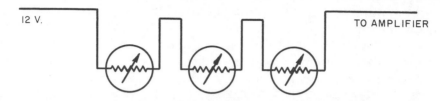

FIG. 4   IN-CAR, DUCT AND AMBIENT SENSOR WIRING

Examples given here show a 12-volt battery input voltage to the sensor string. This would mean that the temperature control would rely entirely on sensor values. If this were the actual case, the driver would have no control over the temperature except as it may be preset from the factory. To give a driver control over the circuit, a variable resistor is added. This variable resistor is directly connected to the temperature knob.

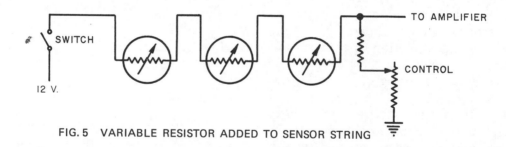

FIG. 5   VARIABLE RESISTOR ADDED TO SENSOR STRING

This arrangement will vary the input voltage of the amplifier by adding resistance to the circuit. For example, with the same conditions, the sensor output is varied by varying control resistance. The following are given as examples: the sensors have the same values in each figure. Figure 6 shows maximum variable resistance; Figure 7, minimum variable resistance; and Figure 8 is about midway. This would be equal to setting the temperature control for about 85° F., 65° F., and 75° F. in that order.

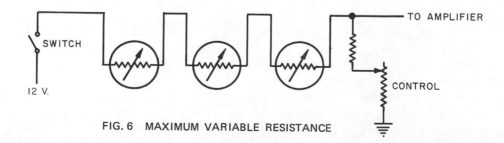

FIG. 6   MAXIMUM VARIABLE RESISTANCE

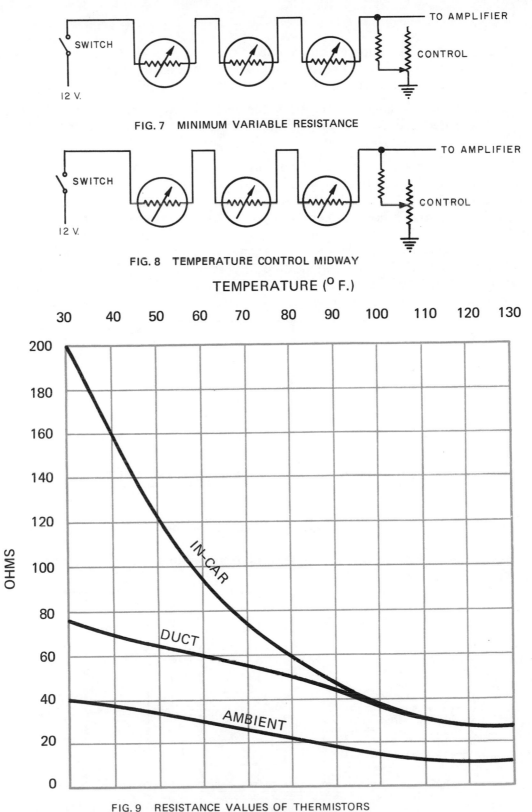

FIG. 7   MINIMUM VARIABLE RESISTANCE

FIG. 8   TEMPERATURE CONTROL MIDWAY

FIG. 9   RESISTANCE VALUES OF THERMISTORS
AT VARIOUS TEMPERATURES

AMPLIFIER

The amplifier provides a voltage output that is proportional to its input voltage from the sensors. Particular operation and theory of the amplifier circuit will not be discussed except to give a circuit diagram (Figure 10) and a brief description.

The amplifier is usually mounted on the rear or bottom of the control panel, and has a diode, transistors, a capacitor, and several fixed resistors mounted in breadboard fashion.

Unit repair of the amplifier assembly is not suggested for the layman. If the amplifier should prove to be defective, it should be replaced as a unit. If, however, the serviceman has a knowledge of checking resistors, diodes, capacitors, and transistors, in many cases he may repair the amplifier. Manufacturers' shop manuals should be consulted for individual component values. Repair will not be discussed in this text because a good knowledge of electron theory is necessary. Books are listed in the bibliography that aid in the study of electron theory and basic direct current fundamentals, if it is desired.

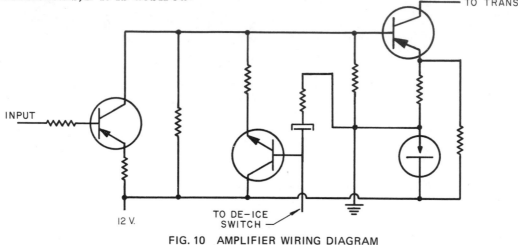

FIG. 10   AMPLIFIER WIRING DIAGRAM

The proper wiring to connect these two circuits, the sensor string and amplifier, is shown in Figure 11.

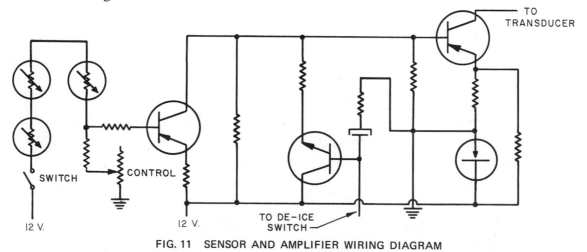

FIG. 11   SENSOR AND AMPLIFIER WIRING DIAGRAM

TRANSDUCER

The purpose of the transducer (Figure 12) is to transfer the <u>electrical</u> signal from the amplifier into a vacuum signal. This <u>vacuum</u> signal is used to regulate the power-servo unit.

The current output of the amplifier causes contraction and expansion of the wire element of the transducer. This contraction or expansion regulates the value of the vacuum which, in turn, is used to regulate the power servo.

The transducer is a production device and has no provisions for field repair. If, for any reason, the transducer does not pass performance procedures, it must be replaced as a complete unit.

FIG. 12   TRANSDUCER ASSEMBLY

Vacuum at the "source" fitting is full manifold vacuum. Vacuum at the "servo" fitting depends inversely on the power supplied to it from the amplifier at the electrical connection. The complete electrical circuit is shown in Figure 13.

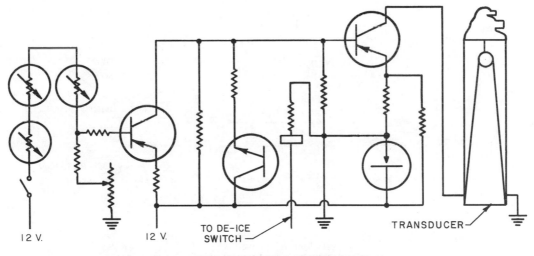

FIG. 13   ELECTRO-PNEUMATIC WIRING DIAGRAM

POWER SERVO

The power servo, or "servo," performs most of the functions that control the heating and air conditioning components. A servo unit is shown on the following page, Figure 14.

The servo unit is comprised of four basic parts: the vacuum power unit, the blower circuit board, the rotary vacuum valve, and the override door link that attaches to the temperature door.

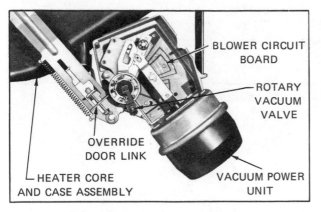

FIG. 14   POWER SERVO ASSEMBLY

The vacuum unit can be considered a positioning device that is connected to a pivot arm, which positions the temperature door correctly and also the rotary vacuum valve which, in turn, positions the other doors and the blower contacts that determine the proper blower speeds.

A vacuum schematic, with power servo and door actuators, is shown in Figure 15. An electrical schematic of this unit is shown in Figure 45-1 (Service Procedure 45).

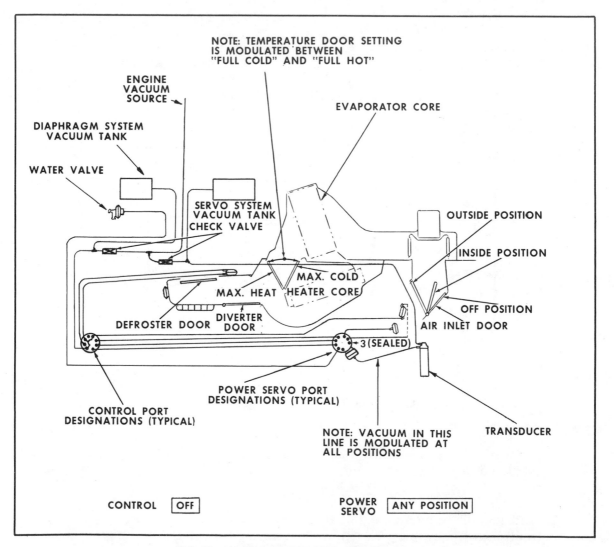

FIG. 15   VACUUM SCHEMATIC (SYSTEM OFF)

ELECTRO-THERMO-HYDRAULIC-PNEUMATIC TEMPERATURE CONTROL

The automatic temperature control, using thermo-hydraulic-pneumatic means for maintaining proper temperatures, operates basically the same as the electro-pneumatic system. It differs, however, in control design and function.

Figure 16 is a diagram of this type of system. It should be noted that the power element (hydraulic) assembly is the controlling factor of this system. The temperature may be set from 65° F. to 85° F., depending on driver and passenger requirements.

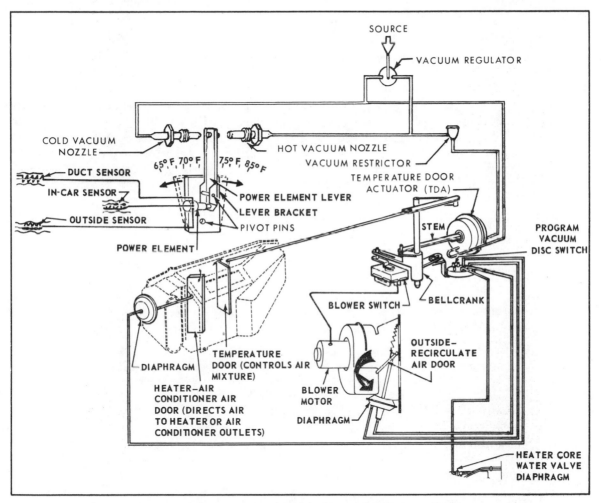

FIG. 16   THERMO-HYDRAULIC-PNEUMATIC SYSTEM DIAGRAM

SENSORS AND POWER ELEMENT

The sensors are a part of the power element assembly. There are three sensors identified as: in-car sensor, duct sensor, and ambient sensor. The in-car sensor is located inside a duct, placed so that air of "average" in-car temperature will cross it. The duct sensor is located in the duct of the evaporator-heater case in such a position that it will sense "average" duct temperature. The ambient sensor is positioned so that it will sense ambient temperatures or the temperature of outside air entering the unit.

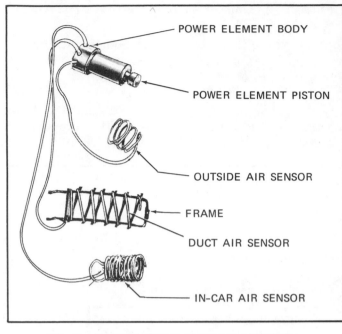

FIG. 17   SENSOR-POWER ELEMENT ASSEMBLY

Each sensor consists of a hollow copper line connected to a cylinder to which a piston is fitted to one end. The other end of the tube is sealed. The tubes are filled with a liquid that expands or contracts with temperature change.

A sensor-power element assembly is shown in Figure 17.

Temperature sensing of each of the three sensor tubes causes expansion or contraction of fluid. Expansion causes the piston of the power element assembly to be pushed outward. Contraction of liquid causes the piston to move inward in a specific amount.

The power element is no more than a device, having a piston which transmits a hydro-signal to actuate the power element lever mechanism.

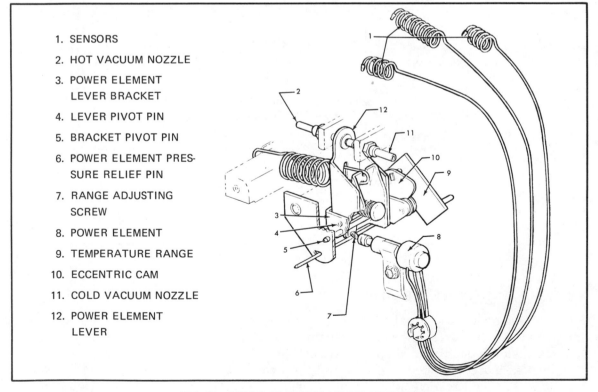

1. SENSORS
2. HOT VACUUM NOZZLE
3. POWER ELEMENT LEVER BRACKET
4. LEVER PIVOT PIN
5. BRACKET PIVOT PIN
6. POWER ELEMENT PRESSURE RELIEF PIN
7. RANGE ADJUSTING SCREW
8. POWER ELEMENT
9. TEMPERATURE RANGE
10. ECCENTRIC CAM
11. COLD VACUUM NOZZLE
12. POWER ELEMENT LEVER

FIG. 18   POWER ELEMENT LEVER MECHANISM

POWER ELEMENT ASSEMBLY

The power lever mechanism (Figure 18) completes the power element assembly. The power lever is hinged to a movable bracket to permit the end of the lever (between hot and cold nozzles) to be moved against either of the nozzles, creating a vacuum at the temperature door actuator while at the same time maintaining the opposite end in contact with the piston of the power element body.

The temperature door actuator (TDA) will be covered in Topic 24, Electric and Vacuum Control Devices, under the heading of "Double Action Vacuum Motors."

TEMPERATURE DOOR

The temperature door regulates the air mixture. The position of this door, determined by the power element assembly, regulates duct output temperature. See "Mode Doors" in Topic 24 for more information on temperature door operation.

PROGRAM VACUUM SWITCH

The program vacuum switch is actuated by the temperature door actuator (TDA) lever, controlling the coolant (water) valve, thermostatic valve, master switch diaphragm, inside-outside air diaphragm, and all other components that are pneumatically (vacuum) controlled in the system.

The program vacuum switch also activates the blower switch and electrical selector switch, and controls blower speeds as determined, in part, by the system mode. The selector switch determines high or low automatic setting, high or low defog, or low de-ice settings.

REVIEW QUESTIONS

Part 1 — Electro-Pneumatic Temperature Control

1. What is the purpose of the transducer? _____

_____

2. What is the purpose of the amplifier? _____

_____

3. What air does the in-car sensor sense? _____

_____

4. What is a thermistor? _____

_____

5. How is the transducer adjusted? _____

_____

6. How is the amplifier repaired? _____

_____

7. What controls the output voltage of the amplifier? _____

_____

8. Draw a diagram of the thermistor.

9. Draw a diagram of the resistor.

10. Where does the transducer receive its vacuum power? _____

_____

Part 2 — Electro-Thermo-Hydraulic-Pneumatic Temperature Control

1. Name the three sensors used in this system. _____

_____

_____

2. What is the purpose of the power element lever? _____

_____

3. What is the purpose of the temperature door? _____

_____

Topic 24 ELECTRIC AND VACUUM CONTROL DEVICES

There are a good many control devices used on the modern automobile that are vacuum (pneumatic) or electrically controlled, such as actuators for door and trunk locks and headlight covers. However, this topic will be concerned only with those control devices used in the automatic temperature control system.

HEATER CONTROL

The heater control valve may be located on the engine or fender well; it may also be mounted near the heater core or inside the heater case. In some applications the control may be actuated by cable; however, the control in the automatic temperature system is vacuum actuated. Its operation is governed by varying vacuum values. A typical vacuum-operated hot water heater control valve is shown in Figure 1.

It may be noted in Figure 2-A that with no vacuum applied, the control valve will be closed. This is its normal operating position.

FIG. 1

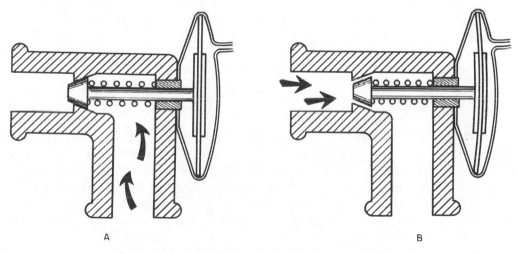

A   B

FIG. 2   WATER VALVE   (A) NORMAL   (B) REVERSED

The combination of water and spring pressure aids in keeping the valve in the closed position. Most valves are indexed or have other provisions to prevent them from being installed backwards. On some applications, however, accidental reversing of the hoses may occur. Figure 2-B shows what effect reversing the hoses may have on water circulation.

Assuming that the control valve in Figure 2-B has no vacuum applied, it may be noted that the pressure of the water will affect spring pressure, causing the valve to open and allowing hot water to flow in the heater core. Actually, a pulsation condition is more apt to occur at speeds in excess of 50 m.p.h. when water pressure is high. This condition would greatly affect temperature control operation.

The normal operation of the valve allows for varying degrees of opening to control water flow. Figure 3-A shows no vacuum; 3-B, a partial vacuum; and 3-C, a full vacuum.

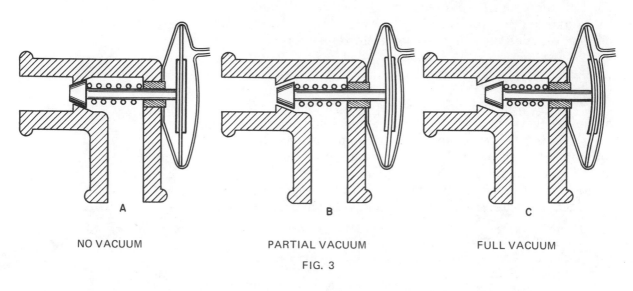

NO VACUUM   PARTIAL VACUUM   FULL VACUUM

FIG. 3

Since part of the operation of the control system is to provide for an in-car relative humidity of about 50 percent, the hot water valve is often "cracked" to allow a little heat into the system. This hot water will create a condition containing a great deal of humidity and will be mixed with the cooler air in the passenger compartment area to maintain the desired temperature and humidity level.

REFRIGERANT PRESSURE CONTROLS

The refrigerant pressure control devices on General Motors automobiles, starting in 1962, were changed, in most cases, to vacuum controlled. Although some G.M. pressure control devices are still cable controlled, those used in the temperature control system are vacuum controlled. Large model units have a self-contained vacuum source and do not depend on the demands of the control system for their operation. This control device, the pilot-operated absolute suction throttling valve (POASTV), is covered in Topic 22. Other devices, such as the vacuum- and cable-controlled suction throttling valve (STV), as well as the Chrysler evaporator pressure regulator (EPR) and evaporator temperature regulator (ETR), are also covered in Topic 22.

MODE DOORS

Vacuum-operated mode doors include the temperature deflector, diverter, defroster, outside-inside inlet, and heater-air conditioner outlet doors.

There are a number of combinations of positions for the various doors in any one of many conditions. For example, in the air conditioning cycle alone there may be six different arrangements for the mode doors. There is a different arrangement for "normal" or "de-fog" in each of three conditions: "full outside," "full recirculate," and "modulated air conditioning."

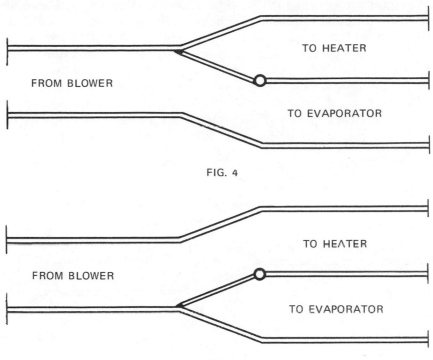

TO HEATER

FROM BLOWER

TO EVAPORATOR

FIG. 4

TO HEATER

FROM BLOWER

TO EVAPORATOR

FIG. 5

Most mode doors are used to divert the passage of air from one passage to another as shown in Figures 4 and 5. In Figure 4, the air is deflected into the air conditioning core. In Figure 5, the ductwork shows that the air is diverted into the heater core.

To affect a change in conditions, the door must be operated either manually or remotely. A cable could be used for this purpose, as it often is, but with the automatic temperature controls, a device known as a vacuum motor is used. Of course, it isn't a motor in the sense that you are used to the term. It is a motor, however, in the sense that it imparts motion. The vacuum motor is referred to by many as a vacuum "pot."

Figure 6 shows a vacuum motor as used to operate the mode doors. It is shown in Figure 6-A as being in the relaxed position, and in Figure 6-B, it is in the applied position.

In the relaxed position, the spring will hold the arm in the extended position. In the applied position, vacuum overcomes the spring pressure to pull the arm into the IN position. The normal, or OFF, position of this vacuum motor is in the relaxed position.

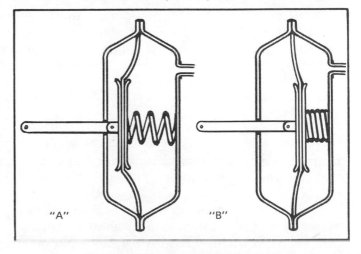

"A"   "B"

FIG. 6 VACUUM MOTOR OR "POT"

Most vacuum motors are of the type shown in Figure 6. Some, however, may have two vacuum hose attachments. These may serve as a tee fitting for another vacuum motor, or may be double action, such as the one used for temperature control on automatic temperature units. This control is known as a double-action vacuum motor. If both vacuum hose ports are on the same side, it is not a double-acting vacuum motor. Fittings on both sides indicate double action.

Figure 7 shows diagrams of the duct arrangement previously described, but now with the inclusion of the vacuum motors.

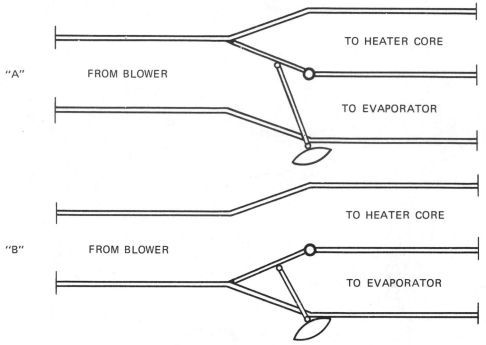

"A"   FROM BLOWER   TO HEATER CORE   TO EVAPORATOR

"B"   FROM BLOWER   TO HEATER CORE   TO EVAPORATOR

FIG. 7   AIR DIVERTER DOOR WITH VACUUM MOTOR

TEMPERATURE DOOR

As outlined in "Mode Doors," the temperature door functions to regulate the air mixture. The position of the temperature mode door determines temperature of the duct air in an automatic temperature control system. The temperature door is regulated by the vacuum motor, a temperature door actuator, or by a servo.

DOUBLE-ACTION VACUUM MOTORS

The vacuum motor has a double-action diaphragm which allows a vacuum to be applied to either side, thus causing the control arm attached to the rubber diaphragm to be extended.

This type of vacuum control is found in some automatic temperature control units and is called a temperature door actuator, or TDA.

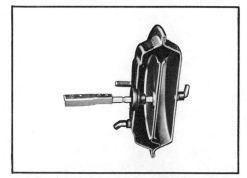

FIG. 8   DOUBLE-ACTION VACUUM MOTOR

BLOWER CONTROL

The blower control permits the selection of a "high" or "low" range of air flow. While the low range will result in less air noise due to reduced air flow, it may cost additionally in terms of comfort. The high range is preferred for maximum operation. In either range, however, air flow will vary automatically due to the demand placed on the system by varying weather conditions. The high blower speed is in operation only when the servo is in the maximum air conditioning position. This part of the operation is electrically controlled, however, and not vacuum controlled. The vacuum-controlled servo has electric contacts to complete various circuits as does the vacuum switch section of the servo.

TIME DELAY RELAY

The time delay control unit is designed to prevent the heat cycle from coming on in the automatic unit until the engine coolant has reached a temperature of 110° F. The unit consists of two resistors, condensers, and transistors. Figure 9 shows the time delay circuit of the wiring diagram.

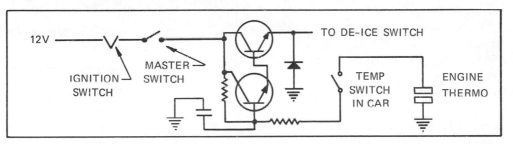

FIG. 9   TIME DELAY RELAY SCHEMATIC

AMBIENT SWITCH

The ambient switch, not to be confused with an ambient sensor, is an electrical switch actuated by changing ambient temperature. The ambient switch has been used in many custom and automatic systems since 1966.

This switch is located outside the engine area where it can sense ambient temperature only. Its location depends on design. It is not, however, in a position that will allow sensing of engine heat.

At 35° F., the ambient switch, by pressing the master switch, will turn the air conditioning compressor ON. It turns the compressor OFF if ambient temperatures fall 25° F.

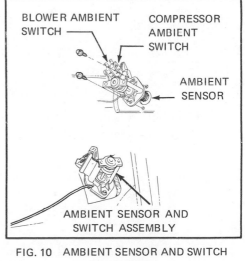

FIG. 10   AMBIENT SENSOR AND SWITCH
ASSEMBLY

Whenever ambient temperature is between 64° F. and 55° F., the switch, bypassing the master control and time delay relay, allows the blowers to run regardless of engine coolant temperature.

Operating the air conditioning compressor or blower at low ambient temperatures reduces humidity of incoming air by condensing the moisture out of it. This helps prevent fogging of windows when an automobile is being operated during rainy, damp, and cool weather conditions.

THERMOSTATIC VACUUM VALVE

The thermostatic vacuum valve (TVV) is a vacuum control valve which is sensitive to temperature. It is mounted on the side of the heater core or where it may sense coolant temperature. It consists of a power element cylinder, with piston, vacuum parts, and spring. The power element is filled with a temperature-sensitive compound so that when the engine is cold and the coolant is not warm, the inlet part of the TVV is blocked and the outlet part is vented. When coolant temperature reaches a specified range, usually 100° to 125° F., the sensitive compound in the cylinder expands and pushes the piston to a point permitting vacuum flow.

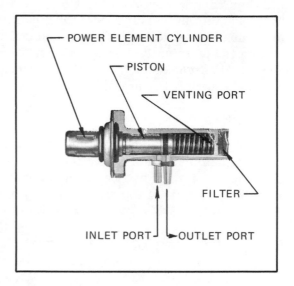

FIG. 11   THERMOSTATIC VACUUM VALVE (TVV)

In the automatic temperature control system, vacuum flow is from the selector vacuum disc switch and to the program vacuum disc switch, master switch, vacuum diaphragm, and outside-recirculate air-cooled diaphragm.

The TVV only serves as a time delay on cold days and is used on late model automatic systems.

REVIEW QUESTIONS

1. What is most likely to occur when the heater hoses are connected backward to the heater control valve? _____

   _____

2. What position is the heater control valve in with no vacuum applied? _____

   _____

3. How is the operation of the POASTV controlled in the General Motors units?

   _____

4. What is the purpose of the mode door? _____

   _____

5. What is a vacuum "pot"? _____

_____

6. No vacuum applied to a vacuum motor will leave it in the _____ position.

7. What controls the air flow in "high" range so far as blower speed is concerned? _____

8. What is the purpose of the time delay switch in the heat mode?

_____

9. How is the humidity raised in the passenger compartment?

_____

10. Where is the heater control located? _____

_____

SYSTEM DIAGNOSIS

Section II

INTRODUCTION

The diagnosis of system malfunction largely depends on the mechanic's ability to interpret the gage pressure readings into system problems. A system operating normally will have a low side gage pressure reading that will correspond with the temperature of the refrigerant evaporating in the evaporator, allowing for a few degrees temperature rise due to loss in the tube walls and fins. The high side will have a gage pressure that will correspond with the temperature of the refrigerant condensing in the condenser, allowing for a few degrees temperature drop due to loss in the tube walls and fins.

Any deviation from that which is normal indicates a malfunction within the system due to a faulty control device, obstruction, defective part, or improper installation.

Diagnosis of system malfunction is made easier with the knowledge that the temperature and pressure of Refrigerant 12 is in close proximity between the pressures of twenty and eighty pounds per square inch (p.s.i.). A glance at the temperature-pressure chart on the following page will show that there is only a slight variation between the temperature and pressure of the refrigerant in the lower range.

It is correct to assume that for every pound of pressure added to the low side, a temperature increase of about one degree Fahrenheit takes place. For instance, a pressure of 23.8 on the chart indicates a temperature of 24°F. A change of pressure of almost one pound to 24.6 p.s.i. gives us a temperature increase to 25°F.

It must be pointed out that the actual temperature of the air passing over the coils of the evaporator will be several degrees warmer allowing for a temperature rise caused by the loss in the fins and tubing of the evaporator.

The temperature-pressure chart on the following page may be used with the problems in this section. It may be necessary to refer to the text in Section I, or to the Service Procedures in Section III in order to solve these problems.

TEMPERATURE PRESSURE CHART

Evaporator Pressure Gage Reading p.s.i.	Evaporator Temperature °F.	High Pressure Gage Reading p.s.i.	Ambient Temperature °F.
0	-21	72	40
2.4	-15	86	50
4.5	-10	105	60
10.1	2	109	62
11.2	4	113	64
12.3	6	117	66
13.4	8	122	68
14.6	10	126	70
15.8	12	129	71
17.1	14	132	72
18.3	16	134	73
19.7	18	137	74
21	20	140	75
22.4	22	144	76
23.1	23	148	77
23.8	24	152	78
24.6	25	156	79
25.3	26	160	80
26.1	27	162	81
26.8	28	165	82
27.6	29	167	83
28.4	30	170	84
29.2	31	172	85
30	32	175	86
30.9	33	177	87
31.7	34	180	88
32.5	35	182	89
33.4	36	185	90
34.3	37	187	91
35.1	38	189	92
36	39	191	93
36.9	40	193	94
37.9	41	195	95
38.8	42	200	96
39.7	43	205	97
41.7	45	210	98
43.6	47	215	99
45.6	49	220	100
48.7	52	228	102
49.8	53	236	104
55.4	57	260	110
60	62	275	115
64.9	66	290	120

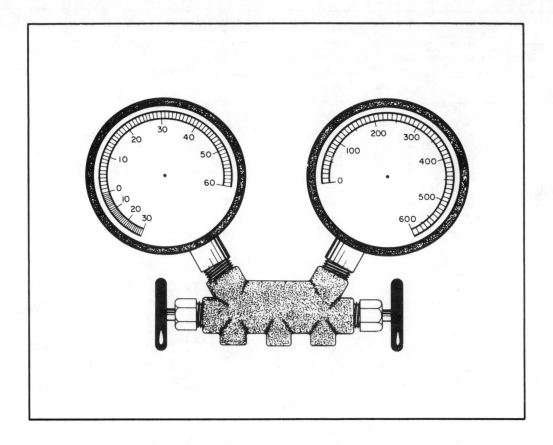

TEMPERATURE-PRESSURE RELATIONSHIP - 1

Consider all conditions normal in this problem. It is designed to familiarize you with the similarities of temperature and pressure.

1. With an ambient temperature of 95°F., what is the normal head pressure? _____ Show it on the gage above.

2. With an evaporator temperature of 33°F., what is the normal suction pressure? _____ Show it on the gage above.

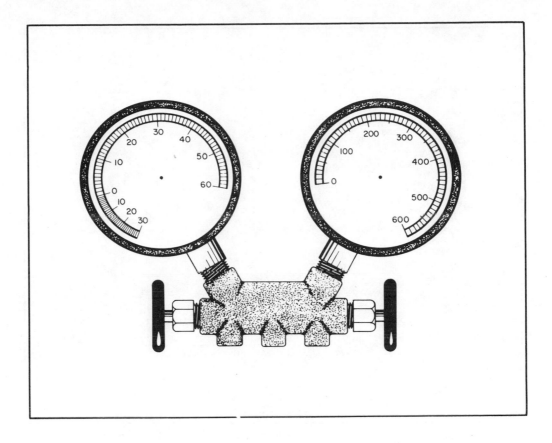

TEMPERATURE-PRESSURE RELATIONSHIP - 2

Consider all conditions normal in this problem, designed to familiarize you with the similarities of temperature and pressure.

1. A head pressure of 185 p.s.i. is normal if the ambient temperature is _____°F. Show this pressure reading on the high side gage above.

2. An evaporator temperature of 31°F. results in a low-side gage reading of _____ p.s.i. Show this gage reading on the low-side gage above.

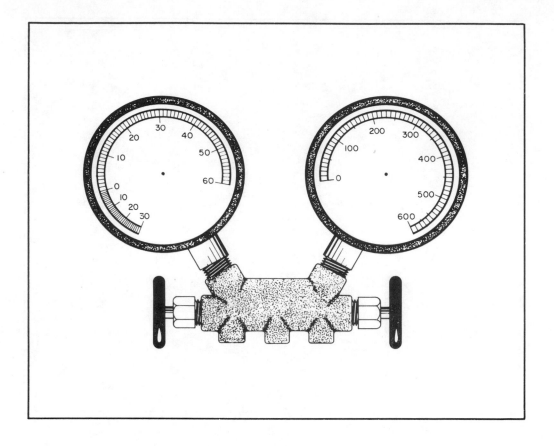

TEMPERATURE-PRESSURE RELATIONSHIP - 3

All conditions may be considered normal in this problem. It is designed to familiarize you with the similarities of temperature and pressure.

1. Ambient temperature is 100°F. What is the normal high-side pressure?
    _____ Show it on the gage above.

2. The low-side gage reads 26 p.s.i. What is the temperature of the refrigerant in the evaporator?_____ Show this gage reading on the low-side gage above.

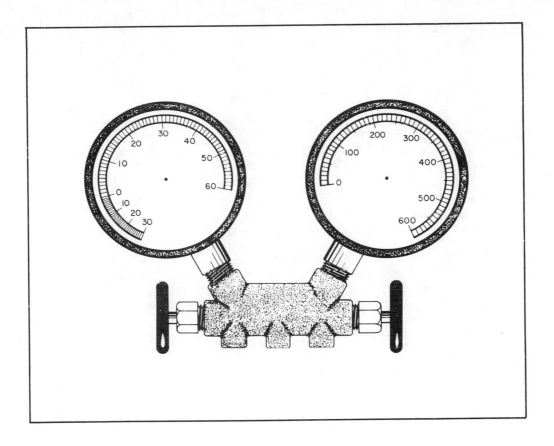

TEMPERATURE-PRESSURE RELATIONSHIP - 4

All conditions are normal. This problem is designed to familiarize you with the similarities of temperature and pressure.

1. The high-side gage reads 195 p.s.i. Show this reading on the high-side gage above. What is the ambient temperature in this problem?_____°F.

2. The low-side gage reads 30 p.s.i. Show this reading on the low-side gage above. What is the evaporator temperature in this problem?_____°F.

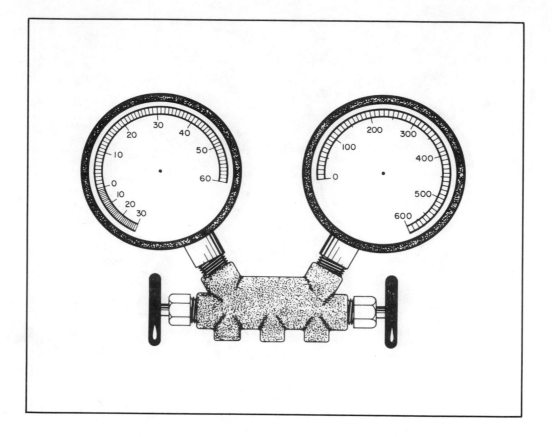

SYSTEM DIAGNOSIS - 1 (The Compressor)

CONDITIONS: Ambient temperature 90°F.
             Low-side gage   50 p.s.i.
             High-side gage   120 p.s.i.

DIAGNOSIS: 1. Show the high- and low-side readings on the gages above.

2. What should the normal high-side reading be? _____ p.s.i.

3. What is the evaporator temperature in this problem? _____ °F.

4. A low-side reading of 50 p.s.i. is _____ . (high, low)

5. A high-side reading of 120 p.s.i. is _____ . (high, low)

6. This condition would result in _____ (good, poor, no) cooling from the evaporator.

7. An internal _____ of the compressor is indicated by the above conditions.

8. To correct the above condition, a new _____ and/or _____ must be installed.

9. The above condition is generally caused by excessive _____ _____ .

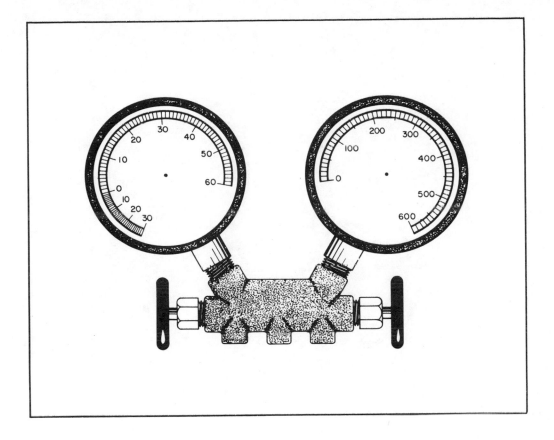

SYSTEM DIAGNOSIS - 2 (The Condenser)

CONDITIONS: Ambient temperature 95°F.
Low-side gage   55 p.s.i.
High-side gage   300 p.s.i.

DIAGNOSIS:
1. Show the high- and low-side gage readings on the gages above.

2. What should the normal high-side gage reading be? _____ p.s.i.

3. What is the evaporator temperature in this problem? _____°F.

4. A low-side reading of 55 p.s.i. is _____ . (high, low)

5. A high-side pressure reading of 300 p.s.i. is _____. (high,low)

6. This condition will result in _____ (good, poor, no) cooling from the evaporator.

7. Give two conditions outside of the air-conditioning system that can cause this pressure.

8. Give two conditions inside of the air-conditioning system that can cause this pressure.

9. Give one type of damage that may occur by operating the air conditioner with this head pressure.

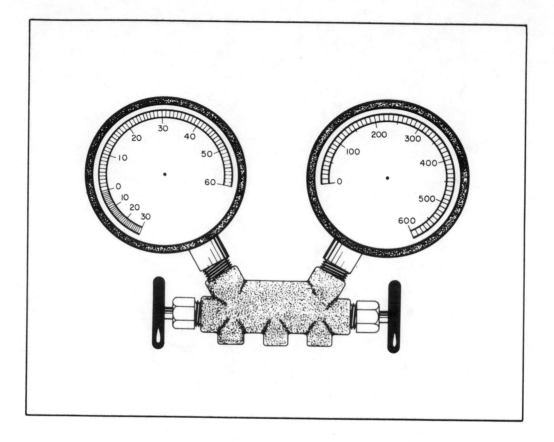

SYSTEM DIAGNOSIS - 3 (The Dehydrator)

CONDITIONS: Ambient temperature 100°F.
             Low-side gage   5 p.s.i.
             High-side gage   305 p.s.i.

DIAGNOSIS: 1. Show the high- and low-side gage readings on the gages above.

2. What should the normal high-side reading be? _____ p.s.i.

3. What is the evaporator temperature in this problem?   Explain.

4. A low-side reading of 5 p.s.i. is _____ . (high, low)

5. A high-side reading of 305 p.s.i. is _____ . (high, low)

6. This condition would result in _____(good, poor, no) cool-
    ing from the evaporator.

7. A restriction at the _____ is indicated by the above readings.

8. Frosting is likely to occur at the point of _____

9. How may this system be repaired? _____

    _____

    _____

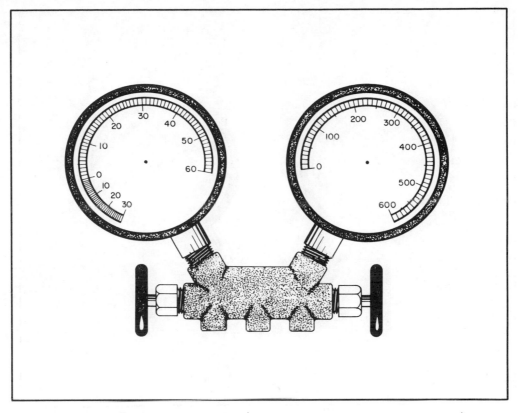

SYSTEM DIAGNOSIS - 4   (Thermostatic Expansion Valve)

CONDITIONS: Ambient temperature 95°F.
             Low-side gage   2 p.s.i.
             High-side gage   170 p.s.i.

DIAGNOSIS: 1. Show the high-and-low side manifold readings on the gages above.

             2. What should the normal high-side reading be?_____ p.s.i.

             3. What is the evaporator temperature in this problem?   Explain.

             4. A low-side reading of 2 p.s.i. is _____ . (high, normal, low)

             5. A high-side reading of 170 is _____. (high, normal, low)

             6. This condition will result in _____. (good, poor, no) cool-
                 ing from the evaporator.

             7. This condition indicates a _____(starved, flooded) evapor-
                 ator due to a defective _____.

             8. This condition will usually be accompanied by frosting at the valve
                 _____ .

             9. How may this condition be corrected? _____

                 _____

129

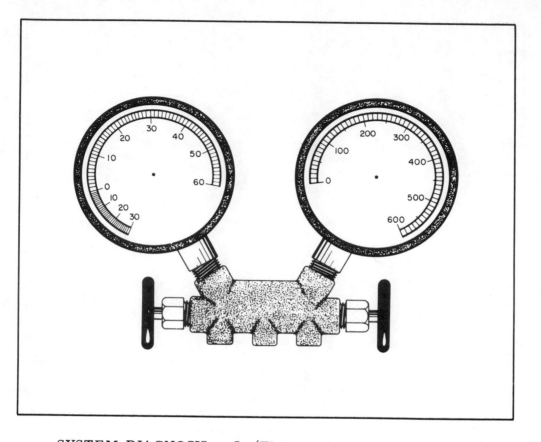

SYSTEM DIAGNOSIS - 5 (Thermostatic Expansion Valve)

CONDITIONS: Ambient temperature 95°F.
Low-side gage   55 p.s.i.
High-side gage   160 p.s.i.

DIAGNOSIS:
1. Show the high-and-low side manifold readings on the gages above.

2. What should the normal high side reading be? _____ p.s.i.

3. What is the evaporator temperature in this problem? _____°F.

4. A low-side reading of 55 p.s.i. is _____ . (high, normal, low)

5. A high-side reading of 160 is _____ . (high, normal, low)

6. This condition will result in _____ (good, poor, no) cooling from the evaporator.

7. This condition indicates a _____ (starved, flooded) evaporator due to a malfunctioning _____ .

8. List two possible causes for this malfunctioning.

9. May moisture in the system cause the above system malfunction? Explain.

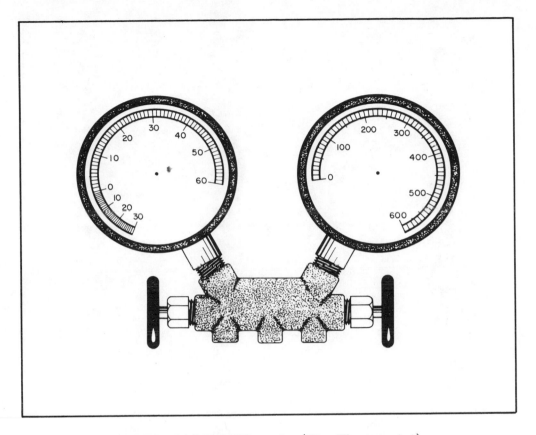

SYSTEM DIAGNOSIS - 6   (The Thermostat)

CONDITIONS: Ambient temp. 97°F.; Low-side gage 10 p.s.i.; High-side gage 205 p.s.i.

DIAGNOSIS: 1. Show the high-and-low side gage readings on the gages above.

2. A high-side pressure of 205 p.s.i. in this problem is _____ .
    (high, normal, low)

3. A low-side pressure of 10 p.s.i. in this problem is _____ .
    (high, normal, low)

4. What is the evaporator temperature in this problem? _____°F.

5. This condition would result in _____ (good, poor, no)
    cooling from the evaporator.

6. This condition may be accompanied by frosting of the _____ ,
    which will block off air flow and result in poor _____ .

7. List two possible causes of a malfunctioning thermostat that may
    cause this problem. _____ and _____

8. How may the customer cause the above problem by unintentional
    means?

9. List two types of thermostats.

10. Are all thermostats adjustable? _____

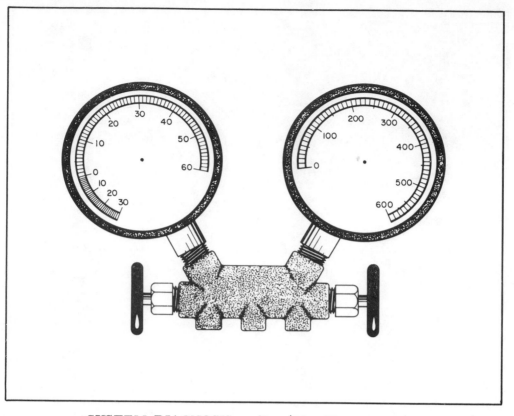

SYSTEM DIAGNOSIS - 7   (The Thermostat)

CONDITIONS: Ambient temp. 98°F.; Low side gage 60 p.s.i.; High side gage 210 p.s.i.

DIAGNOSIS: 1.   Show the high-and-low side gage readings on the gages above.

2.   A high-side pressure of 210 p.s.i. in this problem is _____ .
(high, normal, low)

3.   A low-side pressure of 60 p.s.i. in this problem is _____ .
(high, normal, low)

4.   What is the evaporator temperature? _____°F.

5.   This condition would result in _____ (good, poor, no) cooling from the evaporator.

6.   Give two possible causes for this malfunction.

7.   How may the customer cause the above problem by unintentional means?

8.   May all thermostats be adjusted? Explain.

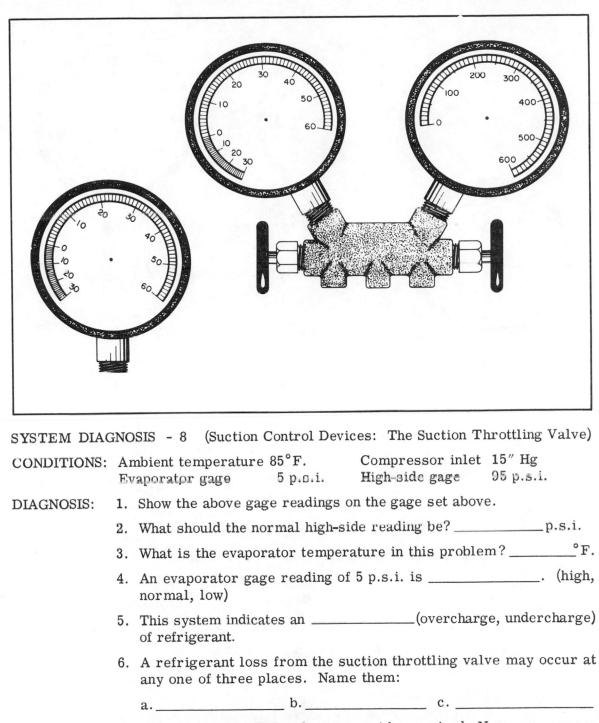

SYSTEM DIAGNOSIS - 8   (Suction Control Devices: The Suction Throttling Valve)

CONDITIONS: Ambient temperature 85°F.   Compressor inlet 15″ Hg
                  Evaporator gage   5 p.s.i.   High-side gage   95 p.s.i.

DIAGNOSIS: 1. Show the above gage readings on the gage set above.

2. What should the normal high-side reading be? _____p.s.i.

3. What is the evaporator temperature in this problem? _____°F.

4. An evaporator gage reading of 5 p.s.i. is _____. (high, normal, low)

5. This system indicates an _____(overcharge, undercharge) of refrigerant.

6. A refrigerant loss from the suction throttling valve may occur at any one of three places. Name them:

    a. _____ b. _____ c. _____

7. All suction throttling valves may not be repaired. Name one reason for this. _____

8. May the screen in the STV be removed for cleaning? _____ Is this screen in the system before or after the screen in the thermostatic expansion valve? _____

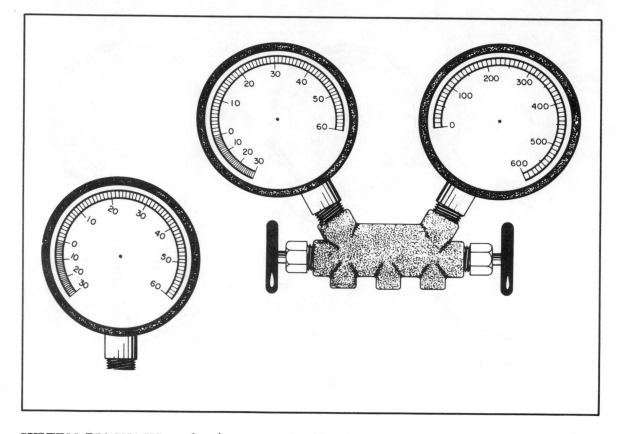

SYSTEM DIAGNOSIS - 9   (Suction Control Devices: The Suction Throttling Valve)

CONDITIONS: Ambient temperature 96°F.   Compressor inlet   36 p.s.i.
             Evaporator gage   38 p.s.i.   High-side gage   195 p.s.i.

DIAGNOSIS: 1. Show the above gage readings on the gage set above.

2. What should the normal high-side reading be? _____ p.s.i.

3. What is the evaporator temperature in this problem? _____ °F.

4. Is the suction throttling valve causing the malfunction in this
    problem? _____ Explain. _____
    _____

5. Can this system problem be corrected by an adjustment of the
    suction throttling valve? _____ Explain. _____
    _____

6. What would you do to correct the problem in this situation?
    _____
    _____

7. What should the correct evaporator pressure be? _____ p.s.i.

8. What should the correct compressor inlet pressure be? Explain.

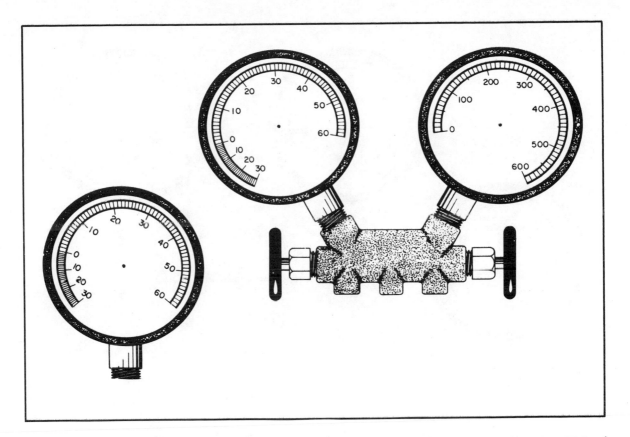

SYSTEM DIAGNOSIS - 10   (Suction Control Devices: The Suction Throttling Valve)

CONDITIONS: Ambient temperature 98°F.   Compressor inlet   15 p.s.i.
                Evaporator gage   38 p.s.i.   High-side gage   200 p.s.i.

DIAGNOSIS: 1. Show the gage pressures on the gage set above.

                2. What should the normal high-side pressure be? _____ p.s.i.

                3. What is the evaporator temperature in this problem? _____°F.

                4. This condition will result in _____ (good, poor, no) cooling from the evaporator.

                5. Is the STV causing the malfunction in this problem? _____ Explain.

                6. Can the problem be corrected by adjusting the STV? _____ Explain.

                7. In this problem a pressure _____ is indicated across the STV.

                8. What would you do to correct the problem in this situation?

                _____

                _____

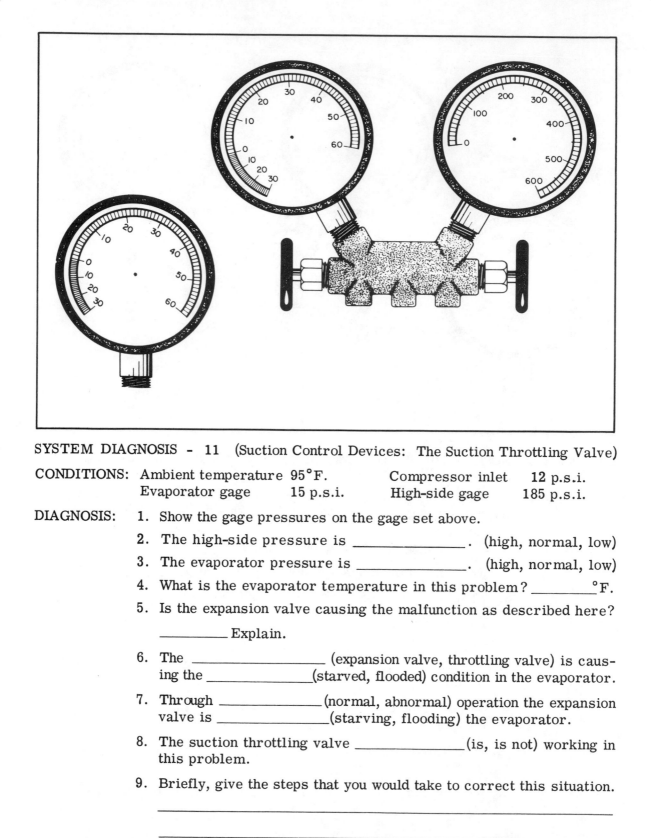

SYSTEM DIAGNOSIS - 11   (Suction Control Devices: The Suction Throttling Valve)

CONDITIONS: Ambient temperature 95°F.   Compressor inlet   12 p.s.i.
             Evaporator gage   15 p.s.i.   High-side gage   185 p.s.i.

DIAGNOSIS: 1. Show the gage pressures on the gage set above.

2. The high-side pressure is _____. (high, normal, low)

3. The evaporator pressure is _____. (high, normal, low)

4. What is the evaporator temperature in this problem? _____°F.

5. Is the expansion valve causing the malfunction as described here?

    _____ Explain.

6. The _____ (expansion valve, throttling valve) is caus-
    ing the _____(starved, flooded) condition in the evaporator.

7. Through _____(normal, abnormal) operation the expansion
    valve is _____(starving, flooding) the evaporator.

8. The suction throttling valve _____(is, is not) working in
    this problem.

9. Briefly, give the steps that you would take to correct this situation.

    _____

    _____

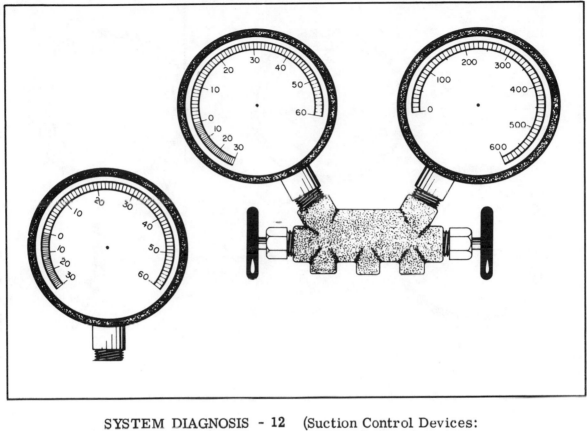

SYSTEM DIAGNOSIS - 12   (Suction Control Devices:
The Evaporator Pressure Regulator)

CONDITIONS: Ambient temperature 96°F.   Compressor inlet   38 p.s.i.
            Evaporator gage   39 p.s.i.   High-side gage   190 p.s.i.

DIAGNOSIS: 1. Show the pressures on the gage set above.

            2. The evaporator and compressor inlet pressures are _____ .
               (high, normal, low)

            3. A malfunctioning _____ (expansion valve, pressure
               regulator) is causing the _____(high, normal,low) low-
               side pressure.

            4. This condition will result in _____(good, poor, no) cooling.

            5. May the EPR valve be adjusted to correct the malfunction? _____
               Explain. _____

               _____

            6. Is the EPR valve at fault? _____

            7. Briefly explain procedures taken to correct this malfunction.

               _____

               _____

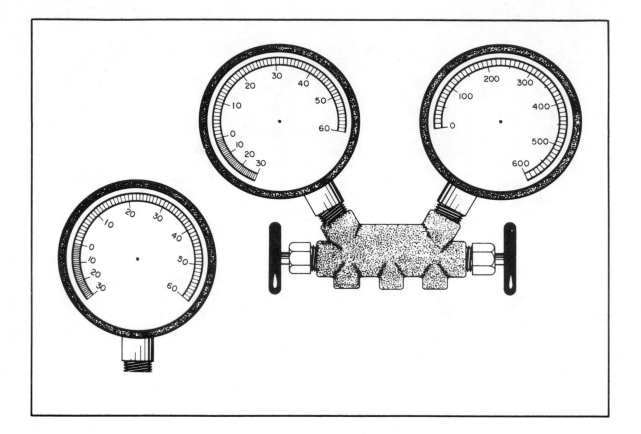

SYSTEM DIAGNOSIS - 13   (Suction Control Devices:
The Evaporator Pressure Regulator)

CONDITIONS: Ambient temperature 100°F.
             Evaporator gage   38 p.s.i.
             Compressor inlet   14 p.s.i.
             High-side gage   212 p.s.i.

DIAGNOSIS: 1. Show gage pressures on the gage set above.

             2. What is the evaporator temperature in this problem? _____°F.

             3. The evaporator pressure is _____ . (high, normal, low)

             4. The compressor inlet pressure is _____ . (high, low, normal)

             5. A malfunction of the _____
                is indicated in this problem.

             6. Give the procedure for correcting the above problem.

             _____

             _____

             _____

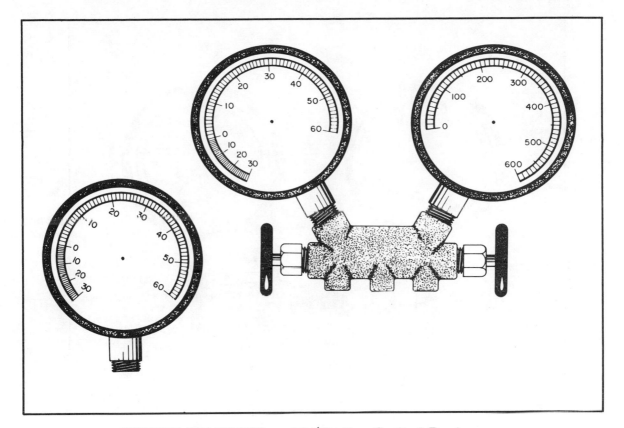

SYSTEM DIAGNOSIS - 14 (Suction Control Devices:
The Evaporator Pressure Regulator)

CONDITIONS: Ambient temperature 99°F.   Compressor inlet   14 p.s.i.
             Evaporator gage   16 p.s.i.   High-side gage   207 p.s.i.

DIAGNOSIS: 1. Show the gage readings above to correspond to conditions given.

2. The evaporator temperature in this problem is _____°F.

3. The EPR valve _____ (is, is not) operating in this problem.

4. Can the EPR valve be adjusted for more efficient operation? _____
    Explain your answer. _____

    _____

5. The expansion valve _____ (may, may not) be at fault in
    this problem. Explain. _____

    _____

6. The thermostat _____ (may, may not) be at fault in the
    above problem. Explain. _____

    _____

7. What should the evaporator temperature be if the system is to oper-
    ate properly? _____°F.; and this would be a pressure of _____ p.s.i.

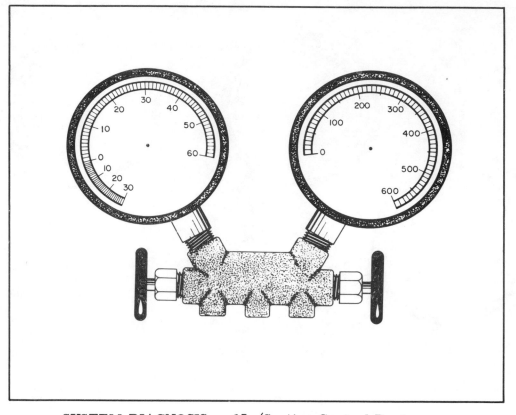

SYSTEM DIAGNOSIS - 15 (Suction Control Devices:
The Pilot Operated Absolute Valve)

CONDITIONS: Ambient temp. 105°F.; Evaporator gage 22 p.s.i., High-side gage 222 p.s.i.

DIAGNOSIS:

1. Show the gage readings on the above gage set.

2. An evaporator pressure of **22** p.s.i. indicates a temperature of _____°F. This is _____ (too high, too low, normal) for normal system cooling.

3. A high-side gage pressure of **222** p.s.i. is _____ (high, normal, low) with an ambient temperature of **105°F**.

4. The POA valve _____ (may, may not) be adjusted for more efficient operation.

5. List one of the advantages of the POA valve. _____
_____

6. List one of the disadvantages of the POA valve. _____
_____

7. How would you correct the condition as described above?
_____
_____

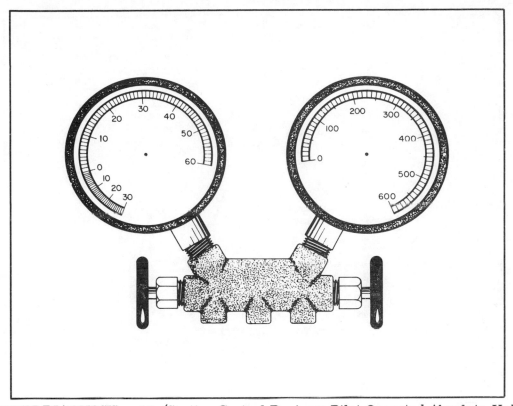

SYSTEM DIAGNOSIS - 16 (Suction Control Devices: Pilot Operated Absolute Valve)

CONDITIONS: Ambient temp. 110°F.; Evaporator gage 42 p.s.i.; High-side gage 240 p.s.i.

DIAGNOSIS:
1. Show the gage readings on the gage set above.

2. An evaporator pressure of 42 p.s.i. indicates a temperature of
_____.___°F. For system cooling this is considered _____.
(low, normal, high)

3. For good cooling, what should the system low-side pressure be?
_____ p.s.i.

4. With an ambient temperature of 110°F., what should the normal high-side pressure be? _____ p.s.i.

5. In this particular problem, may the POA valve be adjusted for more efficient operation? _____ Explain. _____
_____

6. Under what conditions may the POA valve be adjusted for more efficient operation? _____

Explain. _____

7. Who uses the POA valve? _____

8. A leak may occur at the POA valve in one of two places. Name one.
_____

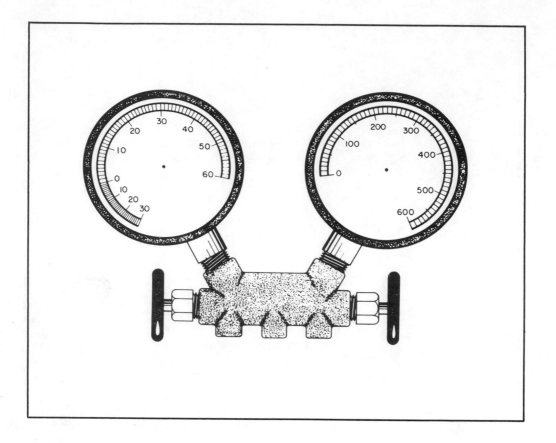

SYSTEM DIAGNOSIS - 17   (The System)

CONDITIONS: Ambient temperature 90°F.

                       Low-side gage   80 p.s.i.

                       High-side gage   80 p.s.i.

DIAGNOSIS: 1. Show the high- and low-side gage readings on the gages above.

                       2. What should the normal high-side reading be? _____ p.s.i.

                       3. The high side is _____. (high, normal, low)

                       4. The low side is _____. (high, normal, low)

                       5. List three possible problems with the above system:

                              a. _____

                              b. _____

                              c. _____

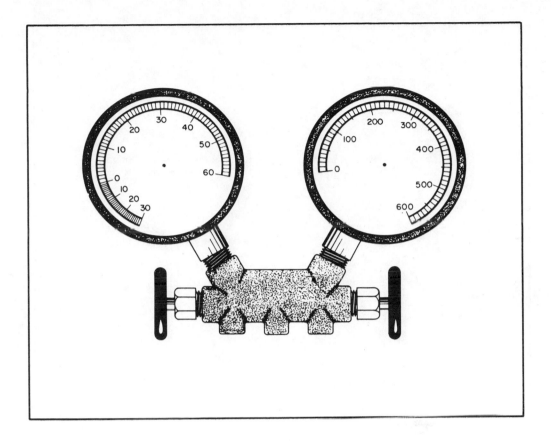

SYSTEM DIAGNOSIS - 18 (The System)

CONDITIONS: Ambient temperature 80°F.

Low-side gage   20 p.s.i.

High-side gage   155 p.s.i.

DIAGNOSIS: 1. Show the high- and low-side gage readings on the gage set above.

2. The low-side gage is _____ . (low, normal, high)

3. List four possible problems with the above system.

a. _____

b. _____

c. _____

d. _____

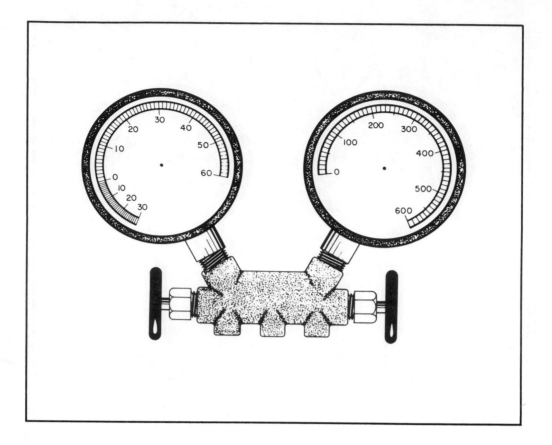

SYSTEM DIAGNOSIS - 19 (The System)

CONDITIONS: Ambient temperature 83°F.

Low-side gage   37 p.s.i.

High-side gage   160 p.s.i.

DIAGNOSIS: 1. Show the gage readings on the set above.

2. The evaporator temperature is about _____°F. in this problem. This is _____. (low, normal, high)

3. List four possible causes of the above malfunction.

a. _____

b. _____

c. _____

d. _____

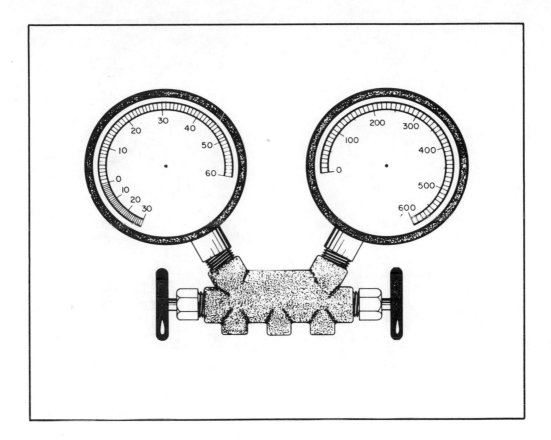

SYSTEM DIAGNOSIS -20 (The System)

CONDITIONS: Ambient temperature 90°F.

Low-side gage   50 p.s.i.

High-side gage   170 p.s.i.

DIAGNOSIS: 1. Show the gage readings on the set above.

                2. The high-side pressure is _____. (high, normal, low)

                3. List four possible causes of the above malfunction.

                    a. _____

                    b. _____

                    c. _____

                    d. _____

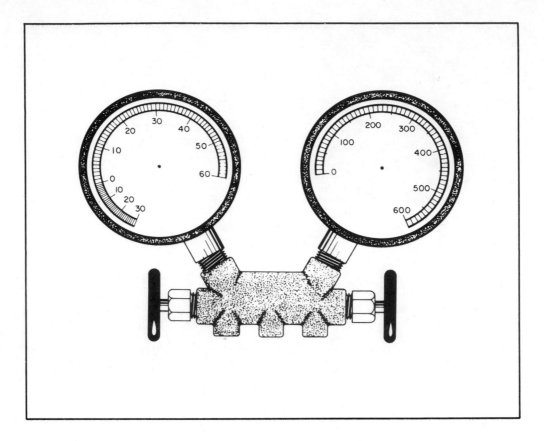

SYSTEM DIAGNOSIS - 21 (The System)

CONDITIONS: Ambient temperature 95°F.

Low-side gage   37 p.s.i.

High-side gage   250 p.s.i.

DIAGNOSIS: 1. Show the gage readings on the set above.

2. The low-side gage is _____. (high, normal, low)

3. The high-side gage is _____. (high, normal, low)

4. List two possible causes of the above malfunction.

a. _____

b. _____

5. An _____ (undercharge, overcharge) of refrigerant may cause this problem.

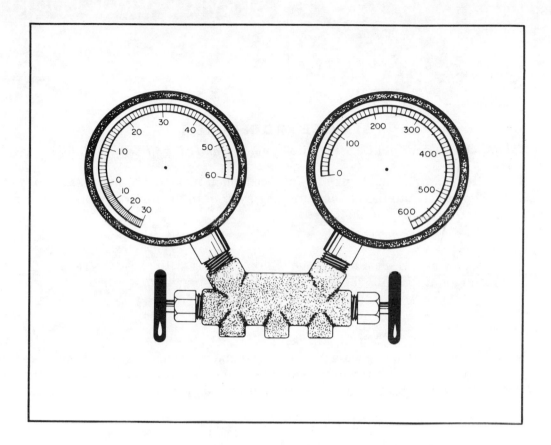

SYSTEM DIAGNOSIS - **22** (The System)

CONDITIONS: Ambient temperature 96°F.

Low-side gage   39 p.s.i.

High-side gage   325 p.s.i.

DIAGNOSIS: 1. Show the gage readings on the set above.

2. List six possible causes of excessive head pressure:

a. _____

b. _____

c. _____

d. _____

e. _____

f. _____

3. High head pressure is _____(always, not always) accompanied by high suction pressure.

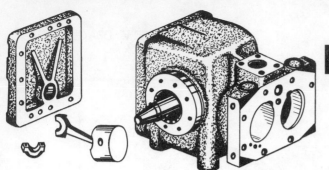

SERVICE PROCEDURE 1

To Connect Manifold Gage Set Into System *(Hand Shutoff Service Valves)*

The following procedure may be followed when it becomes necessary to install the manifold gage set into the air conditioning system to perform any one of the many operational tests that may be indicated.

> Safety glasses should be worn while working with a refrigerant. Remember, liquid refrigerant in the eyes can cause blindness.

TOOLS

Manifold gage set equipped with compound and pressure gage and three service hoses, service valve wrench, suitable wrenches to remove protective caps from service ports, suitable eye protection, fender covers

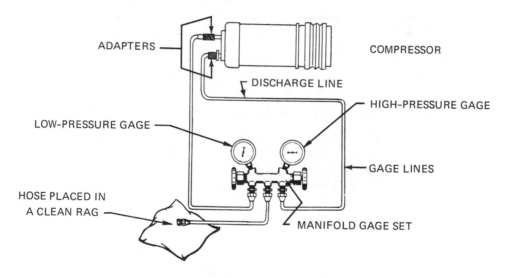

FIG. 1-1   TYPICAL MANIFOLD SET HOOKUP

PROCEDURE

BASIC PREPARATION

1. Place fender cover on the car to avoid damage to the car finish.

2. Use a wrench of the correct size to remove protective caps from service valve stems. Some caps are made of light metal and may be removed by hand.

3. Using a correct wrench, remove protective acorn caps from service ports. CAUTION: Remove caps slowly to insure that no refrigerant is leaking past the service valve.

CONNECT MANIFOLD GAGE SERVICE HOSES TO COMPRESSOR

1. Connect low side manifold hose to suction side of compressor; connect high side manifold hose to the discharge side of the compressor, fingertight.

2. Make sure hand shutoff valves are closed on manifold set before next step.

PURGE SERVICE HOSES

1. Use service valve wrench and rotate suction side service valve stem two or three turns clockwise; repeat with discharge service valve stem.

2. Purge air from the low side hose by cracking the low side hand valve for a few seconds, then close.

3. Repeat with high side hand valve to purge air from the high side hose.

PREPARE SYSTEM FOR OPERATIONAL TESTS

1. Start the motor and adjust speed to about 1250 r.p.m. by adjusting the idle speed screw or setting on high cam.

2. Turn on air conditioner and adjust all controls for maximum cold, with blower on high speed.

3. If motor is cold, allow time for sufficient warmup, five or ten minutes.

4. Perform operational tests as may be indicated.

REVIEW QUESTIONS

1. If refrigerant is leaking past the service valve because of a poor seat, where will it leak out of the system? _____

2. How is the suction side of the compressor valve identified? _____

_____

3. How tight should the manifold hoses be fastened to the service valve ports?

_____

4. How do we mid-position the service valves? _____

_____

5. How do we crack the manifold hand valves? _____

_____

SERVICE PROCEDURE 2
To Connect Manifold Gage Set Into System *(Schrader Valve Fittings)*

The following procedure may be followed when it becomes necessary to install the manifold gage set into the air conditioning system equipped with Schrader-type service valves to perform any one of the many operational tests that may be indicated.

> Safety glasses should be worn while working with a refrigerant. Remember, liquid refrigerant in the eyes can result in blindness.

TOOLS

Manifold gage set equipped with compound and pressure gage and three service hoses equipped with a Schrader adapter, service valve wrench, suitable eye protection, suitable wrench to remove port caps, fender covers

PROCEDURE

BASIC PREPARATION

1. Place a fender cover on the car to avoid damage to the finish.

2. Using a wrench of correct size to avoid damage, remove protective acorn caps from compressor high- and low-side service ports.

    CAUTION: Remove caps slowly to insure that no refrigerant is leaking past a defective Schrader valve.

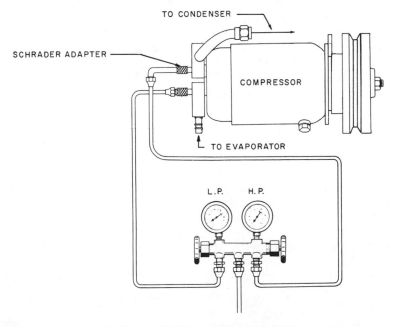

FIG. 2-1   MANIFOLD HOOKUP USING SCHRADER ADAPTERS

CONNECT MANIFOLD GAGE SERVICE HOSES TO COMPRESSOR

1. Service hoses must be equipped with a Schrader valve depressing pin; if not, a suitable adapter such as the Kent Moore J-5420 must be used.

2. Make sure the manifold hand shutoff valves are closed before the next step.

3. Connect low side manifold hose to the suction side of the compressor; connect high side manifold hose to the discharge side of the compressor, fingertight.

PURGE SERVICE HOSES

1. Purge the air from the low side hose by cracking the low side service valve on the manifold for a few seconds, then close.

2. Repeat with the high side manifold hand valve to purge air from the high side hose.

PREPARE SYSTEM FOR OPERATIONAL TESTS

1. Start the engine and adjust speed to about 1250 r.p.m. by adjusting the idle speed screw or setting on high cam.

2. Turn on air conditioner and adjust all controls for maximum cooling with blower on high speed.

3. If engine is cold, allow time for sufficient warmup, five or ten minutes.

4. Perform operational tests as may be indicated.

REVIEW QUESTIONS

1. Why is it important to wear safety glasses? _____

_____

2. Describe a compound gage. _____

_____

3. What is meant by purging air? _____

_____

4. Are the Schrader-type fittings equipped with service valves? _____

5. Is it necessary to have manifold hand shutoff valves with the Schrader-type fittings? _____

_____

SERVICE PROCEDURE 3
To Purge the Air Conditioning System

To purge the air conditioning system is to remove all of the refrigerant in the system. This may be necessary in order to replace component parts that have failed during normal operation.

> Adequate ventilation should be maintained during this operation. Do not discharge Refrigerant 12 near an open flame as phosgene gas, a toxic gas, may result.

TOOLS

Complete manifold gage set, service valve wrench, protective covers, suitable hand wrenches, eye goggles

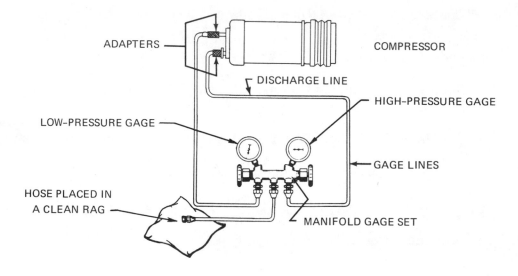

FIG. 3-1   MANIFOLD HOOKUP TO PURGE SYSTEM

PROCEDURE

PREPARE SYSTEM

1. Connect manifold gage set into system and set all controls to maximum cold position.

2. Set engine speed to 1000-1200 r.p.m. and operate for 10-15 minutes.

3. This procedure should be followed whenever possible to stabilize the system; however, certain system malfunctions may make this procedure impossible.

PURGE REFRIGERANT FROM SYSTEM

1. Return engine speed to normal to prevent dieseling and shut off engine.

2. Open low and high side manifold hand valves slowly to allow refrigerant to bleed off through the center hose.

3. Open hand valves only enough to bleed off refrigerant. Purging rapidly will draw excessive oil from the system.

4. The center hose may be placed in a clean rag. If any refrigeration oil is pulled out of the system, it will show up on the rag.

SYSTEM PURGED OF REFRIGERANT

1. Both manifold gages will read zero when the system is purged.

2. Close hand manifold valves when refrigerant ceases to bleed off.

3. The system is now purged of refrigerant and may be opened for service as may be required.

4. Cap all openings and hoses to avoid the possibility of dirt or foreign matter entering the system.

REVIEW QUESTIONS

1. What is meant by purging the air conditioning system? _____

2. What happens if Refrigerant 12 is discharged near an open flame? _____

3. After stabilizing a system, why do we return the engine to normal speed before shutting it off? _____

4. What will be the result if a hand valve is opened all the way while purging?

5. How do you know when the system is purged of refrigerant? _____

SERVICE PROCEDURE 4
To Evacuate the System Using a Vacuum Pump or Charging Station

It is necessary to evacuate the air conditioning system any time the system has been serviced to the extent that it has been purged of refrigerant. Evacuation is necessary to rid the system of all air and moisture that may have been allowed to enter the unit. At or near sea level, a good vacuum pump is one that is capable of pulling 29″ Hg or better. For each 1000 feet of elevation, the reading will be about 1 inch higher.

As we lower the pressure in the air conditioning system, we lower the boiling temperature of the water (moisture) that may be present. Then we are able to pull this water, in the form of vapor, out of the system. The following table demonstrates the effectiveness of moisture removal under a given vacuum.

System Vacuum	Temperature °F.
27.99	100
28.89	80
29.40	60
29.71	40
29.82	20
29.88	0

TOOLS

Service valve wrench; hand wrenches fender covers; manifold and gage set; vacuum pump, or charging station

PROCEDURE

PREPARE SYSTEM

1. Connect manifold gage set into the system.

2. Place high-and low-side compressor service valves in the cracked position.

3. Place high-and low-manifold hand valves in the closed position.

4. Remove protective caps from the inlet and exhaust of the vacuum pump. Make sure the port cap is removed from the exhaust port to avoid damage to the vacuum pump.

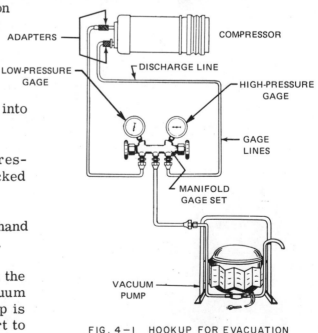

FIG. 4-1   HOOKUP FOR EVACUATION OF SYSTEM

5. Connect the center manifold hose to the inlet of the vacuum pump.

EVACUATE SYSTEM

1. Start vacuum pump.

2. Open low-side manifold hand valve and observe compound gage needle. It should pull down into a slight vacuum.

3. After about 5 minutes the compound gage should be below 20″ Hg and the high-side gage should be slightly below the zero index of the gage.

4. If the high-side needle does not drop below zero, unless restricted by a stop, system blockage is indicated.

5. If system is blocked, discontinue evacuation. Repair or remove obstruction. If system is clear, continue.

6. Operate for 15 minutes and observe gages. The system should now be at about 24-26″ Hg minimum if there is no leak.

7. If the system is not down to 24-26″ Hg, close low-side hand valve and observe the compound gage.

8. If the compound gage rises, indicating a loss of vacuum, there is a leak which must be repaired before continuing with evacuation. Leak check as outlined in Service Procedures 6 or 7.

9. If no leak is evident, continue pumpdown.

COMPLETE EVACUATION

1. Pump for a minimum of 30 minutes, longer if time permits.

2. After pumpdown, close high- and low-side manifold hand valves. (High-side valve may be opened after checking for system blockage.)

3. Shut off vacuum pump, disconnect manifold hose and replace protective caps.

CHECK SYSTEM FOR IRREGULARITIES

1. Note the compound gage. It should read about 29″ Hg.

2. The compound gage should not rise at a rate faster than 1″ in five minutes.

3. If the system fails to meet this requirement, although not indicated previously, a partial charge must be installed and the system must be leak checked as outlined in Service Procedures 6 or 7.

4. After the leak is detected and repaired, the system must be purged of refrigerant and completely evacuated.

5. If the system holds vacuum as specified, continue with the charging procedure, or other procedures as indicated.

REVIEW QUESTIONS

1. What is the recommended minimum pumping requirement for a vacuum pump at sea level? _____

2. How is moisture removed from the system in a vacuum? _____

    _____

3. Can we normally remove moisture from a system under 27″ Hg vacuum?

    _____

4. What is indicated if a pumpdown of 25″ Hg is not accomplished in 15 minutes?

    _____

    _____

5. What is the recommended minimum pumpdown time? _____

6. If the system has no leak, the vacuum rise after pumpdown should be no greater than 1″ Hg per _____ minutes.

SERVICE PROCEDURE 5

To Evacuate the System Using the Unit Compressor as a Vacuum Pump

The following is not a recommended procedure and should be used only when no other choice is available. Moisture is boiled off and removed under a vacuum. Only that part of the compressor on the low side will be under a vacuum, so most of the moisture removed from the system in this manner will be deposited on the valve plates of the compressor. Air is the only noncondensible that will effectively be removed from the system. The practice of using the unit compressor as a vacuum pump will prove detrimental to the compressor and failure resulting from this practice will void the manufacturer's warranty. A vacuum of greater than 25″ Hg can seldom be pulled. In this vacuum, water boils at about 125°F.

TOOLS

Service valve wrench, suitable hand wrenches, fender covers, manifold gage set

PROCEDURE

PREPARE SYSTEM

1. Connect manifold gage set into system

2. Place low side service valve in the cracked position; front seat high side service valve.

3. Place high and low side manifold hand valves in the closed position.

EVACUATE SYSTEM

1. Start car engine and operate at idle speed, about 500 r.p.m.

2. Open high side manifold hand valve.

3. Turn on air conditioner or engage compressor clutch to start compressor operation.

4. Observe compound gage. When vacuum reaches 25″ Hg, close high side manifold gage.

NOTE: A vacuum of below 25″ Hg is Seldom Attained With This Procedure. Continued Operation of the Compressor After Reaching this Vacuum Will Increase Wear and Cause Possible Damage to the Compressor as it is Operating Without Sufficient Lubrication. Compressor Failure Due to Lack of Oil Will Void the Manufacturer's Warranty. There is No Substitute for a Vacuum Pump.

5. Disengage clutch or shut off car engine.

CHECK FOR SYSTEM IRREGULARITIES

1. The compound gage should not rise at a rate faster than 1" Hg in 5 minutes.

2. If the system fails to meet this requirement, a partial charge must be installed and the system leak checked as outlined in Leak Test, Procedure 6 or 7.

3. After the leak is located and corrected, the system must be purged and evacuation procedures repeated.

REVIEW QUESTIONS

1. Do you feel that the use of the unit compressor is effective as a vacuum pump? Explain. _____

   _____

2. What vacuum will the unit compressor pull down? _____

3. How fast should the compressor be operated while using it as a vacuum pump?

   _____

4. What position should the manifold high side hand valve be in for this test?

   _____

5. What will happen if the high side hand valve is not in the proper position?

   _____

   _____

SERVICE PROCEDURE 6

To Leak Test the System Using Halide Leak Detector

The halide leak detector, a propane torch, is the most popular leak detector with the refrigeration serviceman because of its low initial cost and low cost upkeep. About the only maintenance required, other than propellant replacement, is an occasional reactor plate replacement.

To check the sensitivity of the reactor plate, pass the pickup hose over a recently opened and empty can of refrigerant, or crack open a service valve. The flame should have a violet reaction. If little or no color change occurs, replace the reactor plate.

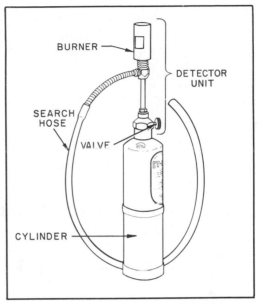

FIG. 6-1 LEAK DETECTOR (TORCH)

When leak testing, all joints and fittings should be free of oil to eliminate the possibility of a false reading caused by refrigerant absorption in the oil. Cigarette smoke, purging of another unit nearby, as well as vapors in the surrounding air may also give a false reading on the detector.

> A halide leak detector must only be used in a well-ventilated area. It must never be used in spaces where explosive gases are present. When refrigerant comes into contact with an open flame, phosgene gas is formed. Never inhale the vapors or fumes from the halide leak detector, they may be poisonous.

TOOLS

Service valve wrench, suitable hand wrenches, eye protection, fender covers, manifold gage set, halide leak detector

PROCEDURE

PREPARE SYSTEM

1. Connect manifold gage set into the system.

2. Place high-and low-side compressor service valves in the cracked position.

3. Place high-and low-side manifold hand valves in the closed position.

4. Determine presence of refrigerant in the system. A minimum of 50 p.s.i.g. is needed for leak detection.

5. If there is insufficient charge of refrigerant in the system, continue with the next step, "Add Refrigerant for Leak Test Pressure." If sufficient, skip the next step and proceed with "Prepare Leak Detector."

ADD REFRIGERANT FOR LEAK TEST PRESSURE

1. Open high and low side hand valves to purge hoses of air, and then close.

2. Attach center manifold hose to refrigerant container.

3. Open refrigerant container service valve.

4. Open high side manifold hand valve until a pressure of 50 p.s.i. is reached on the low side gage, then close high side hand valve.

5. Close refrigerant container service valve and remove hose.

PREPARE LEAK DETECTOR

1. Open valve and light the gas. Adjust for low flame which burns about 1/2″ above the reactor plate.

2. Let it burn until the reactor plate, a copper element, turns to a cherry red color.

3. Lower flame until it is about 1/4″ above or even with the reactor plate.

FIG. 6-2   LEAK TESTING THE CONDENSER

CHECK FOR LEAKS IN THE AIR CONDITIONING SYSTEM

1. Move the search hose under all joints and connections in the system. Seals and control devices must not be overlooked.

2. Disconnect any vacuum hoses connected to the system and check their ports for refrigerant vapors.

REACTION OF HALIDE LEAK DETECTOR IN PRESENCE OF REFRIGERANT

Watch for a color change in the flame above the reactor plate.

- Pale blue - no refrigerant loss
- Pale yellow at edges of flame - very small refrigerant loss
- Yellow - small amount of refrigerant loss
- Purplish-blue - large amount of refrigerant loss
- Violet - heavy amount of refrigerant loss, may be great enough to extinguish flame

REPAIR SYSTEM

1. After leak is located, purge system of refrigerant.

2. Repair as indicated and check compressor oil as outlined in Service Procedure 19.

3. Add oil if required; add refrigerant and recheck for leaks.

4. If no leaks are found, the system may be evacuated and charged.

5. Perform other service procedures as indicated.

REVIEW QUESTIONS

1. What gas is formed when Refrigerant 12 comes into contact with an open flame? _____

2. What pressure is normally required to detect a leak? _____

3. How high should the flame burn in the leak detector? _____

4. What color is the flame to indicate a small refrigerant loss? _____

5. What part of the leak detector is used to search for leaks? _____

SERVICE PROCEDURE 7
To Leak Test the System Using an Electronic Leak Detector

The electronic leak detector is by far the most sensitive of all the leak detectors. Some are capable of detecting the presence of refrigerant as fine as half an ounce per year. Initial cost and upkeep are the controlling factors. If your shop does a lot of air conditioning work, the electronic leak detector may prove to be of great value in detecting those otherwise "impossible" leaks.

> An electronic leak detector must only be used in a well-ventilated area. It must never be used in spaces where explosive gases are present.

TOOLS

Service valve wrench, hand tools, fender covers, manifold gage set, electronic leak detector

PROCEDURE

PREPARE SYSTEM

1. Follow procedure as outlined in Service Procedure 6.

ADD REFRIGERANT FOR LEAK TEST PRESSURE

1. Again, follow procedure as outlined in Service Procedure 6.

PREPARE LEAK DETECTOR

NOTE: Follow procedure as outlined in manufacturer's instructions with the leak detector since models may vary considerably. The following, however, may be used as a guide.

1. Turn controls and sensitivity knobs to off or zero.

2. Plug leak detector into approved voltage and turn switch on; allow to warm up for about five minutes.

3. After warmup, place the probe at the reference leak and adjust the controls and sensitivity knob until the detector reacts; remove probe; reaction should stop. If it continues, the adjustment is too high. If it stops, the adjustment is adequate.

CHECK SYSTEM FOR LEAKS

1. Move the search hose under all joints and connections. Do not overlook seals and control devices.

2. Disconnect any vacuum hoses connected to the system and check their ports for refrigerant vapor indicating a control leak.

3. When a leak is located, the detector will react as it does when placed by the reference leak.

4. Do not keep the probe in contact with refrigerant any longer than necessary to locate the leak.

> Never place the probe in a stream of refrigerant, or where a severe leak is known to exist. This will damage the sensitive parts of the leak detector.

REPAIR SYSTEM

1. After the leak is located, purge system of refrigerant.

2. Repair as indicated and check compressor oil as outlined in Service Procedure 19.

3. Add oil and refrigerant and recheck for leaks.

4. If no leaks are found, purge the system, evacuate and charge as outlined in Service Procedures 3, 4 and 8.

5. Perform other service procedures as may be indicated.

REVIEW QUESTIONS

1. What is the sensitivity of the electronic leak detector? _____

2. What is the greatest advantage of the electronic leak detector? _____

_____

_____

_____

3. What disadvantage might there be in the use of an electronic leak detector?

_____

_____

SERVICE PROCEDURE 8

To Charge System Using Pound Cans *(System Off)*

Although commonly referred to as "pound cans," these containers actually hold 15 ounces of refrigerant. Gaining rapidly in popularity, pound cans are now found in most shops: in those doing a large volume of business as well as in the small shop.

Care should be taken that only R12 is introduced into the air conditioning system. These containers are, for the most part, painted white, though for positive identification the chemical name and symbol is dichlorodifluoromethane, or CCl_2F_2.

CAUTION

Above 130°F., liquid refrigerant will completely fill a container and hydrostatic pressure will build up rapidly with each degree of temperature added. Never heat a refrigerant container above 125°F. It should never be necessary to heat a refrigerant container. Never apply a direct flame or an electric resistance heater to a refrigerant container. Do not abuse a refrigerant container. Use only approved wrenches to open and close valves. Store in an upright position.

> Do not handle refrigerant without suitable eye protection and do not discharge refrigerant into an enclosed area having an open flame.

TOOLS

Service valve wrench, suitable hand wrenches, eye protection, fender covers, manifold gage set, can tap

MATERIAL

Refrigerant 12

PROCEDURE

PREPARE SYSTEM

1. Connect manifold gage set into the system.

2. Place high and low side compressor service valve in the cracked position.

3. Place high and low side manifold hand valve in the closed position.

4. Place system under a vacuum after adequate pump-down.

INSTALL CAN TAP VALVE TO CONTAINER OF REFRIGERANT

1. The valve stem should be in the out, or counterclockwise, position.

2. Attach valve to can and secure locking nut if so equipped.

3. Connect center manifold hose to can tap port.

4. Pierce can by closing can tap shutoff valve. Turn all the way in the clockwise direction.

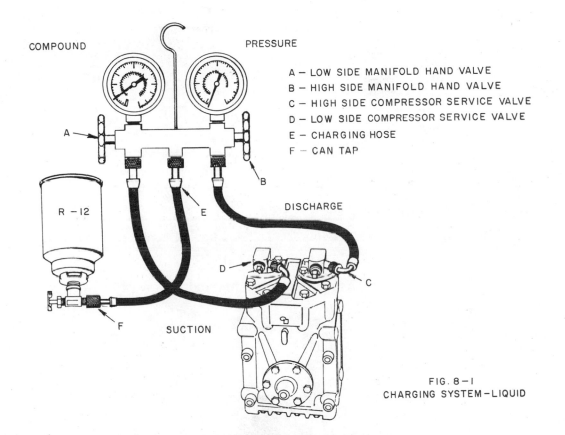

A — LOW SIDE MANIFOLD HAND VALVE
B — HIGH SIDE MANIFOLD HAND VALVE
C — HIGH SIDE COMPRESSOR SERVICE VALVE
D — LOW SIDE COMPRESSOR SERVICE VALVE
E — CHARGING HOSE
F — CAN TAP

FIG. 8—1
CHARGING SYSTEM—LIQUID

PURGE LINE OF AIR

1. With can pierced, back can tap valve out all the way in a counterclockwise position.

2. Center hose is now charged with refrigerant. Do not crack high or low side hand valve.

3. Loosen center hose connected at manifold set until a hiss can be heard. Allow gases to escape for a few seconds, then tighten.

4. The system is now purged and under a vacuum.

CHARGE SYSTEM

1. Open high side gage manifold hand valve.

2. Observe low side gage pressure. If gage does not come out of a vacuum and into a pressure, system blockage is indicated.

3. If the system is blocked, correct condition, evacuate and proceed.

4. Invert container and allow liquid refrigerant to enter the system.

5. To determine when the can is empty, tap it on the bottom. A hollow ring should be heard when empty.

6. Repeat with additional cans of refrigerant as required to completely charge the air conditioner. Refer to manufacturer's recommendations for system capacity.

COMPLETE SYSTEM CHARGE

1. Close high side manifold hand valve.

2. Remove can tap from center hose.

3. Rotate compressor clutch by hand through two or three revolutions to insure that no liquid refrigerant has entered the low side of the compressor.

4. Start the engine and set to fast idle.

5. Engage clutch to start compressor and set all controls to maximum cooling.

6. Perform performance test if indicated.

7. Back seat compressor service valves and remove manifold gage set from system.

8. Replace all protective caps and covers.

REVIEW QUESTIONS

1. What are the net contents of a pound can? _____

2. What is the proper name for Refrigerant 12? Circle one of the following:

   a. Dichlorodifluoromethane   b. Monochlorodifluoromethane

3. What is the chemical symbol for Refrigerant 12? Circle one of the following:

   a. $CHClF_2$ b. CCl_2F_2 c. CH_2Cl_2

4. Why is it important to be able to recognize the chemical name and symbol for Refrigerant 12? _____

   _____

5. When charging liquid with the system off, through which side of the compressor do you charge? _____

SERVICE PROCEDURE 9

To Charge System Using Pound Cans *(System Running)*

Read the introduction and caution outlined in Service Procedure 8, "To Charge System Using Pound Cans (System Off) ."

CAUTION

With the refrigerant can or tank inverted, vapor will rise to the top of the container and liquid refrigerant will be forced into the charging hoses. Do not invert the refrigerant container with low side pressures in excess of 40 p.s.i.g. Regulating the valve on the container or the manifold hand valve will insure a pressure of 40 p.s.i.g., or below. Liquid refrigerant entering the compressor low side can cause serious damage to internal parts such as pistons, reed valves, head and head gaskets.

> If ambient temperature is lower than 80°F. do not invert the refrigerant container. Car engine and air conditioning system should be at operating temperature.

TOOLS

Service valve wrench, hand wrenches, eye protection, fender covers, manifold gage set, can tap

MATERIAL

Refrigerant 12

PROCEDURE

PREPARE SYSTEM

1. Connect manifold gage set into the system. Set both hand valves in the closed position.

2. Set compressor high and low side service valves in the cracked position.

3. Place system under a vacuum after adequate pump-down.

INSTALL CAN TAP TO CAN OF REFRIGERANT

1. Set can tap in the counterclockwise position.

2. Attach valve to refrigerant container and secure locking nut if so equipped.

3. Connect center manifold hose to can tap port.

4. Pierce can by turning shutoff valve in the clockwise position.

167

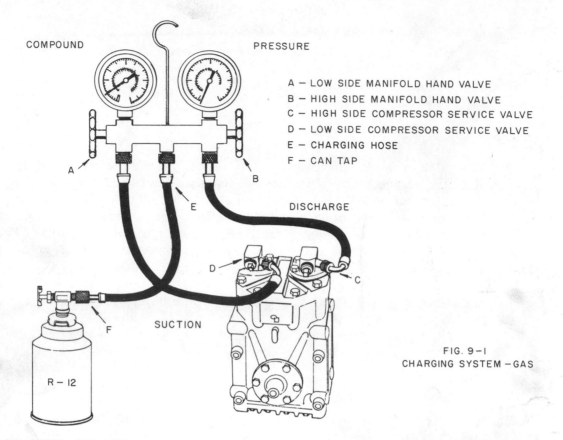

COMPOUND   PRESSURE

A – LOW SIDE MANIFOLD HAND VALVE
B – HIGH SIDE MANIFOLD HAND VALVE
C – HIGH SIDE COMPRESSOR SERVICE VALVE
D – LOW SIDE COMPRESSOR SERVICE VALVE
E – CHARGING HOSE
F – CAN TAP

DISCHARGE

SUCTION

R – 12

FIG. 9–1
CHARGING SYSTEM – GAS

PURGE LINE OF AIR

1. With can pierced, back can tap valve out in a counterclockwise position.

2. Center hose is now charged with refrigerant and air. Do not crack high or low side manifold hand valve.

3. Loosen center hose connector at manifold set until a hiss can be heard. Allow gas to escape for a few seconds, and then tighten fingertight.

4. The system is now purged and under a vacuum.

CHECK SYSTEM FOR BLOCKAGE

1. Open high side gage manifold hand valve; observe low side gage pressure. Close high side hand valve.

2. If low side gage does not come out of a vacuum and into a pressure, system blockage is indicated.

3. Correct blockage, if indicated, evacuate and proceed with the following step.

CHARGE SYSTEM

1. Start engine and adjust speed to about 1250 r.p.m. by turning idle screw or setting on high cam.

2. Insure that both manifold hand valves are closed.

3. Adjust controls for maximum cooling, blower on high speed.

4. Open low side gage manifold hand valve to allow refrigerant, in the gas state, to enter the system.

5. After pressure on the low side has dropped below 40 p.s.i.g., the can may be inverted for more rapid removal of refrigerant.

6. To determine when can is empty, tap it on the bottom. A hollow ring should be heard when empty.

7. Repeat with additional cans of refrigerant as required to completely charge the system. Refer to manufacturer's recommendations for system capacity. NOTE: If system capacity is not known, charge unit until the sight glass is clear, then add 1/4 pound.

COMPLETE SYSTEM CHARGE

1. Close low side manifold hand valve.

2. Remove can tap from center hose.

3. Hold performance test if indicated.

4. Back seat the compressor service valves and remove the manifold gage set.

5. Replace all protective caps and covers.

REVIEW QUESTIONS

1. What rule is followed in inverting the refrigerant container? _____

_____

_____

2. When the system is running, through which side is refrigerant fed?

_____

3. What will be the result if the refrigerant is fed into the system through the other side? _____

_____

4. How may you determine if the refrigerant can is empty? _____

_____

5. Are both compressor service valves in the mid-position for system charging?

_____

SERVICE PROCEDURE 10
To Charge System from a Bulk Source

Bulk refrigerant containers are available in 25-pound and 145-pound cylinders for the shop that does a large volume of air conditioning service. In using the bulk container, a set of scales, or other approved measuring device, should be used to determine when proper system charge is reached.

Read again the service caution outlined in Service Procedure 8. The importance of careful handling of refrigerant and refrigerant containers cannot be over-emphasized. All cases of injury stem from carelessness and improper handling.

Remember, accidents do not happen. They are caused by an act of carelessness.

TOOLS

Service valve wrench, hand wrenches, eye protection, fender covers, manifold gage set, scales

MATERIAL

Refrigerant 12 as indicated

PROCEDURE

PREPARE SYSTEM

1. Connect manifold gage set into the system.

2. Set high and low side compressor service valves in the cracked position.

3. Set high and low side manifold hand valves in the closed position.

4. Place system under a vacuum after prescribed pump-down.

CONNECT REFRIGERANT CONTAINER; PURGE

1. Connect center manifold gage hose to refrigerant cylinder adapter.

2. Open refrigerant cylinder hand valve.

3. Crack center hose at manifold gage set for a few seconds to purge hose of air.

4. The system is now purged and under a vacuum.

CHECK SYSTEM FOR BLOCKAGE

1. Do not start engine at this time. Do not turn air conditioner on.

2. Open high side manifold hand valve; observe low side gage. Close high side hand valve.

3. System blockage is indicated if low side gage does not come out of a vacuum and into a pressure.

4. If blocked, correct blockage, re-evacuate and proceed with the following step.

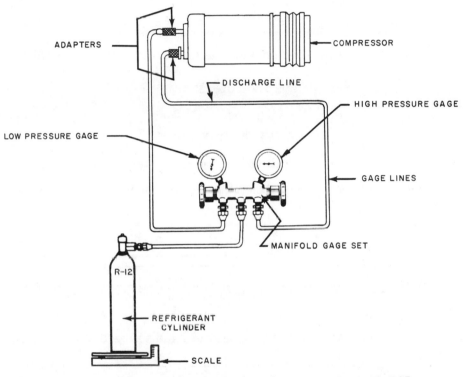

FIG. 10-1 SYSTEM HOOK-UP FOR CHARGING FROM A BULK SOURCE

CHARGE SYSTEM

1. Insure that both high and low side manifold hand valves are closed.

2. Start engine and adjust speed to about 1250 r.p.m.

3. Adjust air conditioning controls for maximum cooling, blower on high speed.

4. Keep refrigerant cylinder in the upright position. A slug of liquid refrigerant allowed to enter the compressor could cause serious damage.

5. Open low side manifold hand valve and allow refrigerant in the gas state to enter the system.

6. Place cylinder on a scale to insure proper measurement of the refrigerant. If system capacity is not known, clear the sight glass and add four ounces. Then the amount of refrigerant used can be determined by the scale.

COMPLETE SYSTEM CHARGE

1. When full, close low side manifold hand valve.

2. Close cylinder service valve and remove hose from adapter.

3. Hold performance or other test as indicated.

4. Return car to normal idle speed. Shut off engine.

5. Back seat the compressor service valves and remove the manifold gage set.

6. Replace all protective caps and covers.

REVIEW QUESTIONS

1. While charging system with engine running, determine the following:

    a. What is the position of the compressor low side service valve?

    _____

    b. What is the position of the compressor high side service valve?

    _____

    c. What is the position of the manifold hand valve on the low side?

    _____

    d. What is the position of the manifold hand valve on the high side?

    _____

2. What is the position of the refrigerant cylinder? _____

3. How can you insure the proper amount of refrigerant charge? _____

    _____

    _____

SERVICE PROCEDURE 11
To Isolate Compressor from the System

With systems having high-and low-side compressor service valves, the compressor may be isolated from the system. The refrigerant will be retained in the system while service is being performed on the compressor. With systems using a Schrader-type service port, the compressor cannot be isolated, and must be purged of refrigerant to perform these services.

TOOLS

Service valve wrench, hand wrenches, eye protection, fender covers, manifold gage set

PROCEDURE

PREPARE SYSTEM

1. With manifold gage set connected into the system, set both hand valves in the closed position.

2. Set both compressor service valves in the cracked position.

3. Stabilize system by running car engine at about 1200 r.p.m. with air conditioner controls turned on maximum cooling for about 10 minutes.

ISOLATE THE COMPRESSOR

1. Return car engine to idle speed, about 500 r.p.m.

2. Close low-side service valve until low-side gage reads 10″ Hg.

3. Turn off car motor. Completely close (front seat) low-side service valve.

4. Close high-side service valve.

5. Open low-side manifold hand valve and allow trapped refrigerant to escape.

6. Repeat with high-side hand valve. Close both valves when gages read zero.

7. Compressor is isolated and may be removed from the car if necessary.

Service valves must be removed from the compressor. Do not attempt to remove hoses.

RETURN COMPRESSOR TO SYSTEM

1. If compressor was removed from car, replace service valve gaskets with new ones.

2. Purge air from compressor as follows:

   a. Open high-side manifold hand valve.

   b. Crack low-side compressor service valve off front-seated position.

   c. Low-side refrigerant pressure will force air out of compressor through high-side manifold set.

   d. After a few seconds of purging, close high-side manifold hand valve.

3. Mid-position the low-side compressor service valve.

4. Mid-position the high-side compressor service valve.

CONTINUE PERFORMANCE TEST

1. With manifold gage set hooked up, check refrigerant charge.

2. Add refrigerant as necessary.

RETURN SYSTEM TO SERVICE

1. Back seat high- and low-side compressor service valves.

2. Remove service hoses and replace protective caps.

REVIEW QUESTIONS

1. Why would it be desirable to isolate the compressor from the system?

   _____

   _____

2. May all compressors be isolated? _____

   Why? _____

3. When isolating the compressor, what should the compressor speed be?

   _____

4. What is the pressure in the compressor after it is isolated? _____

5. Can a compressor equipped with Schrader valves be isolated?   Explain.

   _____

   _____

SERVICE PROCEDURE 12
To Performance-Test the Air Conditioner

Humidity has an important bearing on the temperature of the air delivered to the interior of the car. It is important to understand the effect humidity has on the performance of the system. When humidity is high, the evaporator has to perform a double duty. It must lower the air temperature as well as the temperature of the moisture carried in the air. Condensing the moisture in the air transfers a great deal of the heat energy into the evaporator. This reduces the amount of heat the evaporator can absorb from the air.

Evaporator capacity used to reduce the amount of moisture in the air is not wasted, however. Lowering the moisture content of the air entering the vehicle adds to the comfort of the passengers.

The following will serve as a guide to the service procedures relating to holding a performance test of the automobile air conditioner. Reference should be made to the manufacturer's service manuals for accurate data.

TOOLS

Service valve wrench, hand wrenches, eye protection, fender covers, manifold gage set, thermometer

PROCEDURE

PREPARE SYSTEM

1. With manifold gage set connected into the system, set both hand valves in the closed position.

2. Set compressor high- and low-side service valves in the cracked position.

3. Have car engine running on high cam or idle screw run into about 1500-1700 r.p.m.

4. Place fan in front of radiator to assist ram air flow.

5. Turn on air conditioner; set all controls to maximum cooling.

6. Insert thermometer in air conditioning duct closest to evaporator core. Set blower on medium or low speed.

VISUAL CHECK OF AIR CONDITIONER

a. Low-pressure gage within specified range, 20-30 p.s.i.g.

b. High-side gage within specified range, 160-220 p.s.i.g.

c. Discharge air temperature within specified range, 40°F. - 50°F.

175

INSPECT HIGH AND LOW SIDE OF SYSTEM FOR EVEN TEMPERATURES

1. Feel hoses and components in high side of system for even heat.

   CAUTION: Certain system malfunctions will cause high-side components to become superheated to the point that a serious burn can result if care is not taken when handling high-side components.

2. Note the inlet and outlet temperatures of the drier assembly. Any change of temperature indicates a clogged or defective drier.

3. All lines and components on the high side should be warm to the touch.

4. All lines and components on the low side of the system should be cool to the touch.

5. Note the thermostatic expansion valve. If frosted or cold on the inlet side, a defective valve may be indicated.

TEST THERMOSTATS AND CONTROL DEVICES

1. Refer to the service manual for performance testing of the particular type of control device used.

2. Insure that thermostat will engage and disengage clutch. There should be about a 12°F. temperature rise between the cutout and cut-in point of the thermostat.

3. The following is a guide for determining the proper gage readings and temperatures.

Ambient Air Temperature, °F	70	80	90	100	110
Average Compressor Head Pressure p.s.i.g	150-190	170-220	190-250	220-300	270-370
Average Evaporator Temperature, °F	38-45	39-47	40-50	42-55	45-60

4. The relative humidity at a particular temperature has a bearing on the quality of the air as indicated by the following chart, which should be used as a guide only.

Ambient Temperature,°F	70	80	90	100
Relative Humidity, %	50 60 90	50 60 90	40 50 60	20 40 50
Discharge Air Temp.,°F	40 41 42	42 43 47	41 44 49	43 49 55

5. Complete performance test as outlined in manufacturer's service manual.

RETURN SYSTEM TO SERVICE

1. Return engine speed to normal idle.

2. Back seat high- and low-side compressor service valves.

3. Remove service hoses and replace protective caps.

REVIEW QUESTIONS

1. What is the purpose of the performance test? _____

_____

_____

2. Does high humidity have an effect on the air conditioning system? _____
Explain. _____

_____

_____

3. At what speed should the engine run to perform the air conditioning performance test? _____

4. What will a temperature change at the inlet and outlet of the drier indicate?

_____

_____

_____

5. What will a temperature change at the inlet and outlet of the expansion valve
indicate? _____

_____

_____

SERVICE PROCEDURE 13
To Make a Volumetric Test of the Air Conditioning Compressor

The volumetric test or compressor capacity test may be held to determine the condition of the discharge reed valves and the piston rings.

TOOLS

Manifold gage set, 1/4" test caps, 1/2" test cap, 5/8" or 3/4" test cap (as applicable), service valve wrench, hand wrenches

MATERIAL

Refrigerant for recharging the system if necessary.

PROCEDURE

PREPARE SYSTEM FOR VOLUMETRIC TEST

1. Attach the gage manifold set to the compressor.

2. Start the engine and adjust speed to 1000–1200 r.p.m.

3. Adjust controls for maximum cooling. Operate for about 10–15 minutes.

4. After 10–15 minutes shut off all air conditioning controls.

5. Return car speed to idle to prevent dieseling, and shut off car engine.

6. If compressor is equipped with high-and low-side service valves, compressor may be isolated, the valves removed and substituted with another set of valves for this test. If so equipped, follow procedure as outlined in Service Procedure 11.

7. If compressor is equipped with service Schrader-type valves, the system will have to be purged of refrigerant. Follow procedure as outlined in Service Procedure 3.

8. With system purged of refrigerant, disconnect high-side hose from compressor outlet. Cap hose end to prevent dirt and moisture entrance while holding compressor check. Repeat with low-side hose.

9. If compressor is isolated, remove high-and low-side service valves and substitute other valves for this test. DO NOT REMOVE HIGH-AND LOW-SIDE COMPRESSOR HOSES IF COMPRESSOR IS ISOLATED!

10. Seal the compressor inlet fitting with the correct size flare cap.

11. Connect the high-side gage hose to the high-side compressor service valve and open the high-side manifold hand valve.

12. Disconnect the low-side gage hose from the compressor and manifold.

13. Remove the center hose on manifold and install a 1/4" test cap on the manifold fitting. The test cap is made by drilling a 1/4" acorn cap with a #71 drill. This will give an orifice of 0.026".

14. If a Schrader-type valve is used, install an adapter to open low side of compressor to the atmosphere. If service valves are used, BOTH SIDES MUST BE CRACKED OR FRONT SEATED. The acorn nut must be removed from the low side valve.

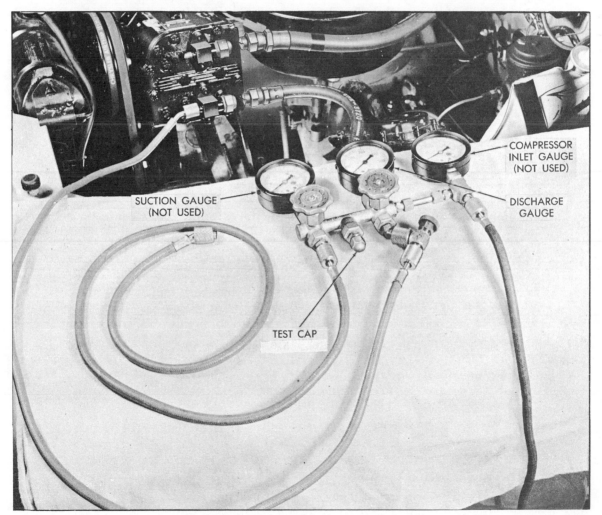

FIG. 14—1 VOLUMETRIC TEST HOOKUP

HOLD VOLUMETRIC, OR CAPACITY TEST

1. Start engine and idle at exactly 500 r.p.m.

2. Engage clutch and operate the compressor as an air pump.

> NOTE: Never operate the air conditioning compressor as an air pump for over 15 seconds at a time. To do so may seriously damage the compressor due to improper lubrication. Manufacturer's warranty is void if failure is due to lack of lubrication.

Air is drawn in at the compressor inlet and pressurized to the center of the gage manifold and high-side gage.

3. As soon as maximum pressure is reached, turn off compressor.

CONCLUSIONS

a. Read high-side manifold gage. High-side gage should read 180-200 p.s.i.

b. If the reading is low, faulty reed valves or valve plate gasket is indicated.

c. Repair as indicated. Follow procedure outlined in this book.

RECHECK SYSTEM

1. If repairs are necessary and made, the compressor should be rechecked. Follow the procedure outlined above.

RETURN COMPRESSOR TO SERVICE

1. Remove all caps and plugs; reconnect all lines and service valves.

2. If system was purged, evacuate and charge as outlined previously.

3. If compressor was isolated, purge compressor of air as follows:

a. Open high-side manifold hand valve.

b. Crack the compressor low-side service valve off the front-seated position.

c. After a few seconds of purging, close the high-side manifold hand valve.

d. Mid-position low- and high-side compressor service valves.

CONTINUE PERFORMANCE TEST

1. With the manifold gage set hooked up, check refrigerant charge.

2. Add refrigerant if necessary.

RETURN SYSTEM TO SERVICE

1. Back seat high-and low-side compressor service valves.

2. Remove service hoses and replace protective caps.

REVIEW QUESTIONS

1. What is the purpose of the volumetric test? _____

_____

_____

2. What specific parts of the air conditioner does the volumetric test apply to?

_____

_____

3. At what speed should the compressor be run to hold the test? _____

4. What should the high-side gage read if proper? _____

5. If the high-side gage is low, what malfunction is indicated? _____

_____

SERVICE PROCEDURE 14
To Replace the Compressor Shaft Oil Seal *(York and Tecumseh)*

The following procedure may be followed when it is necessary to replace the compressor shaft oil seal. If the seal area can properly be serviced on the car, it will not be necessary to remove the compressor from the mount. If engine fan or radiator clearance makes it impossible to remove the clutch for seal service, the compressor must be removed from the car.

TOOLS

1/4″ drive handle with 3/8″, 7/16″ and 1/2″ sockets; 3/4″ open end wrench; 5/8″ × 2″ N.C. bolt; screwdriver; razor blade

MATERIAL

Ample supply of clean refrigeration oil; seal assembly, which includes the seal plate, seal nose, and gasket(s)

PROCEDURE

PREPARE COMPRESSOR FOR SERVICE

1. Isolate the compressor. Follow procedure as outlined in Service Procedure 11.

2. If seal cannot be properly serviced with the compressor mounted in the car, it must be removed.

3. With a 1/2″ socket, remove the 7/16″ Nyloc bolt from the compressor crankshaft at the clutch hub.

4. Using a 5/8″ NC bolt, remove the clutch rotor. This bolt is inserted into the clutch hub at the point the 7/16″ Nyloc bolt was removed.

5. If a stationary field type and fields are mounted to seal plate, remove the three bolts holding it in place and remove fields.

6. If rotating fields and brushes are mounted on the seal plate, remove the brushes. Take care not to break the soft carbon brush.

7. Clean the seal plate and all adjoining surfaces.

REMOVE SEAL ASSEMBLY

1. Remove the six (or remaining three) capscrews from the seal plate.

2. Gently pry the seal plate loose. Be careful not to nick or mar the crankcase mating surface or the compressor crankshaft.

3. Remove the seal nose assembly from the crankshaft by prying behind the seal. Be careful not to nick or mar the crankshaft.

4. With a razor blade, remove all gasket material from the crankcase mating surface.

5. Clean all foreign matter from the crankcase, crankshaft and all adjacent surfaces.

INSTALL NEW SEAL ASSEMBLY

1. The Woodruff key must be removed from crankshaft before attempting to install the new seal.

2. Soak new seal and all gaskets in clean refrigeration oil for a few minutes. Apply ample oil to crankshaft and mating parts.

3. Remove carbon nose end from shaft seal and slide shaft seal onto crankshaft. If drive pins are located in shaft shoulder, line up notches in shaft seal springholder to engage. If the new seal does not have notches, remove the drive pins.

4. Install seal nose; flush with clean refrigeration oil.

INSTALL NEW SEAL PLATE

1. Flush seal plate and seal nose with clean refrigeration oil to insure no foreign particles.

2. YORK: Place new seal plate and gasket(s) over crankshaft and move seal back to final operating position. Insert original three (or six) capscrews fingertight.

    TECUMSEH: Place new seal plate and O-ring over crankshaft and move seal back to final operating position. Insert the original three (or six) capscrews and tighten fingertight.

3. Rotate the compressor crankshaft to make sure there is no binding due to misalignment.

4. Make sure of even clearance between crankshaft and seal plate all around.

5. Tighten all capscrews evenly to a torque of 10-12 ft.-lbs. Tighten in diagonally opposite sequence.

RETURN COMPRESSOR TO SERVICE

1. Replace clutch field or brush assembly.

2. Replace Woodruff key to crankshaft.

3. Replace clutch rotor and 5/16" Nyloc bolt.

4. If compressor was removed from the car, replace and install service valves with new service valve gaskets.

5. Purge air from the compressor as follows:

   a. Open high-side manifold hand valve.

   b. Crack low-side compressor service valve from front-seated position.

   c. Low-side refrigerant pressure will force air out of the compressor through the high-side manifold hose.

   d. After a few seconds of purging, close the high-side manifold hand valve.

6. Mid-position the high- and low-side compressor service valves.

CONTINUE PERFORMANCE TEST

1. Check refrigerant charge. Add refrigerant if necessary.

2. Check manifold gage readings. Correct abnormal conditions if indicated.

RETURN SYSTEM TO SERVICE

1. Back seat high- and low-side compressor service valves.

2. Remove service hoses and replace protective caps.

REVIEW QUESTIONS

1. Why is it necessary to isolate the compressor when servicing the compressor shaft seal? _____

2. What tool is used to remove the clutch rotor? _____

3. Why is the Woodruff key removed before replacing the new seal? _____

4. Which seal assembly uses the O-ring only? _____

5. What is the torque of the seal plate? _____

SERVICE PROCEDURE 15

To Replace the Compressor Shaft Oil Seal *(Chrysler Air-Temp)*

The following procedure may be used when it is necessary to replace compressor shaft oil seal. The seal can usually be replaced with the compressor on the vehicle. This procedure deals with the Chrysler Air-Temp compressor only. The MoPar unit, using the York or Tecumseh compressor, is covered in Service Procedure 14.

TOOLS

Quarter-inch drive handle with 7/16" and 1/2" sockets, 3/4" open end wrench, 5/8" × 2" NC or NF bolt, screwdriver

MATERIAL

Ample supply of clean refrigeration oil; seal assembly, which consists of an O-ring gasket for the bearing housing, stationary seat and gasket assembly, and the rotating seal assembly

PROCEDURE

PREPARE COMPRESSOR FOR SERVICE

1. If the compressor is equipped with both high- and low-side service valves, the compressor may be isolated. Follow procedure as outlined in Service Procedure 11.

2. If compressor is not equipped with a high-and-low side service valve, the system must be purged of refrigerant. Follow procedure as outlined in Service Procedure 3.

3. With a 1/2" socket, remove 7/16" bolt from the crankshaft located at clutch hub.

4. Using a 5/8" NF or NC bolt, remove clutch rotor. This bolt is inserted into clutch hub at the point the 7/16" bolt was removed.

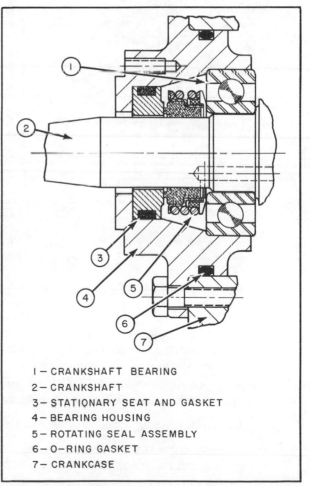

1 — CRANKSHAFT BEARING
2 — CRANKSHAFT
3 — STATIONARY SEAT AND GASKET
4 — BEARING HOUSING
5 — ROTATING SEAL ASSEMBLY
6 — O-RING GASKET
7 — CRANKCASE

FIG. 15-1 CUTAWAY OF CHRYSLER SHAFT OIL SEAL

185

5. If equipped with stationary fields, locate the three screws holding it to the seal housing and remove it. If equipped with rotating fields, carefully remove the brush set by removing the two screws holding it to the seal housing.

6. Clean the seal plate and all adjacent surfaces.

REMOVE OLD SEAL ASSEMBLY

1. Remove the Woodruff key from the crankshaft.

2. Remove the bearing housing bolts.

3. Remove the bearing housing. This is accomplished by using two screw-drivers in slots provided to pry the housing from the crankcase, Figure 15-2.

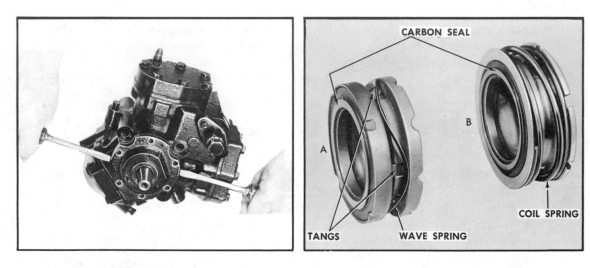

FIG. 15-2 REMOVING THE CRANKSHAFT BEARING HOUSING

FIG. 15-3 GAS SEAL IDENTIFICATION (A) CARTRIDGE-TYPE (B) UNITIZED-TYPE

4. Remove the bearing housing O-ring gasket and discard it.

5. Remove the stationary seat and gasket assembly from the bearing housing and discard it.

6. Remove and discard the gas, or shaft seal assembly from the crankshaft, using a small screwdriver. Take care not to nick or scratch the crankshaft. Either of two types of gas seals (cartridge or unitized) may be used since they are interchangeable. For identification, the unitized type has a coil spring while the cartridge type has a wave spring, Fig. 15-3.

7. Clean all foreign material from the bearing housing and crankshaft.

8. It may sometimes be necessary to polish these surfaces to remove small nicks, burrs or scratches. After polishing, flush all surfaces liberally with clean refrigeration oil.

INSTALL NEW SEAL ASSEMBLY

1. Lubricate the crankshaft, bearing housing and all adjacent parts with clean refrigeration oil.

2. Dip the stationary seat and gasket assembly into clean refrigeration oil for a few minutes.

3. Install the stationary seat and gasket assembly into the bearing housing. Insure that it is fully seated and avoid damage to the seal surface.

4. Install the bearing housing O-ring into the groove provided.

5. Dip the gas seal assembly into clean refrigeration oil for a few minutes.

6. Slide the gas seal assembly onto the compressor crankshaft. Make sure that the carbon nose of the seal assembly is facing outward.

7. Install the crankshaft bearing housing, with seal and O-ring in place, onto the crankcase body. Replace capscrews and draw in uniformly.

8. Tighten the bearing housing capscrews to a torque of 10-13 ft.-lbs.

RETURN COMPRESSOR TO SERVICE

1. Replace Woodruff key. Replace brush or field assembly.

2. Replace clutch assembly and 5/16" retaining bolt.

3. If equipped with service valves, purge air from the compressor as follows:

    a. Open high-side manifold hand valve.

    b. Crack low-side compressor service valve from the front-seated position.

    c. Low-side refrigerant pressure will force air out of the compressor through the high-side manifold hose.

    d. After a few seconds of purging, close the high-side manifold hand valve.

    e. Mid-position high- and low-side compressor service valves.

4. If equipped with Schrader-type service valves, the unit must be evacuated. Follow procedures as outlined in Service Procedure 4.

CONTINUE PERFORMANCE TEST

1. If system is equipped with compressor service valves, check for proper refrigerant charge. Add refrigerant if necessary.

2. Check manifold gage readings. Correct abnormal conditions if indicated.

RETURN SYSTEM TO SERVICE

1. Back seat high- and low-side compressor service valves.

2. Remove service hoses and replace protective caps.

REVIEW QUESTIONS

1. What compressor does a Chrysler MoPar use? _____

2. What size wrench is used to remove the center bolt from the crankshaft?

   _____

3. Name two type fields:

   a. _____   b. _____

4. Which type field does not use brushes? _____

5. What is the recommended torque of the bearing housing? _____

SERVICE PROCEDURE 16

To Replace Seal on General Motors' Compressors *(6 Cylinder)*

Seal replacement on the General Motors' six-cylinder compressor requires a different procedure than do other types of compressors, or, for that matter, than the General Motors' five-cylinder compressor.

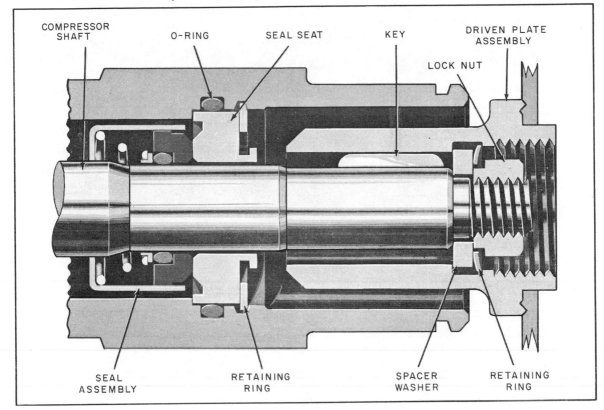

FIG. 16-1 COMPRESSOR SHAFT AND SEAL

Careful handling of all seal parts is important. If the fingers are allowed to come into direct contact with the carbon seal face or the steel seal seat, they may become etched by acid from the fingers.

Since all six-cylinder compressors are equipped with Schrader-type service valves, it will be necessary to purge the system of refrigerant in order to service the seal. This is true even if the sealing can be accomplished with the compressor mounted in the car.

TOOLS

Manifold gage set, hand wrenches, snap ring pliers, seal seat remover, shaft seal remover, pulley puller, thinwall 9/16" socket with handle, hub and drive plate puller, hub and drive plate installer, can tap, and (if compressor is removed from the car) test fitting, O-ring installer, O-ring remover

MATERIAL

Clean refrigeration oil, compressor shaft seal kit, refrigerant

NOTE: The compressor shaft seal kit should consist of: shaft seal seat retainer ring, shaft seal seat, shaft seal, shaft seal seat O-ring.

PROCEDURE

PREPARE COMPRESSOR FOR SERVICE

1. Compressor and system must be purged of refrigerant. Follow Service Procedure 3.

2. If unable to gain clearance to service compressor seal with the compressor in the car, remove it from the car. The service valves should be removed from the rear of the compressor as a unit. Plug all hose and service valve openings when removed. Affix test fitting to rear of compressor.

REMOVE OLD SEAL

1. Using a 9/16″ thinwall socket, remove the shaft nut.

2. With a pair of snap ring pliers, remove the clutch hub retainer ring.

3. Remove the spacer found under the ring.

4. Using a clutch hub and drive plate puller, remove this part.

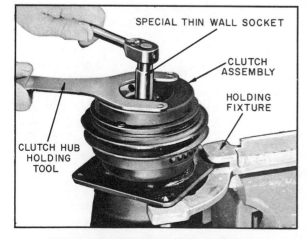

FIG. 16-2 REMOVING SHAFT LOCKNUT

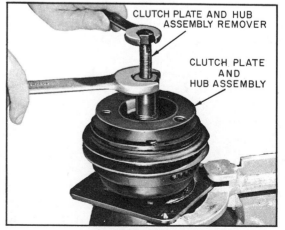

FIG. 16-3 REMOVING HUB AND DRIVE PLATE ASSEMBLY

FIG. 16-4 REMOVING SHAFT SEAL RETAINER

FIG. 16-5 REMOVING SEAL SEAT

5. Next, with a set of snap ring pliers, remove the shaft seal seat retainer ring.

6. Using a shaft seal seat remover, remove this part.

7. Using a shaft seal remover, remove the shaft seal.

8. Using a wire with a hook on the end, remove the shaft seal seat O-ring. Take care not to scratch the internal mating surfaces.

FIG. 16-6 REMOVING SHAFT SEAL ASSEMBLY

FIG. 16-7 REMOVING SEAL SEAT O-RING

INSTALL NEW SEAL

1. Perform the following procedure step-by-step to avoid damage to the new seal assembly.

2. Insure that the inner bore of the compressor is free of all foreign material. Clean out with clean refrigeration oil.

3. Place the seal seat O-ring on the installer tool and slide the O-ring into place. Remove the tool.

4. Coat shaft seal liberally with oil and place it on the shaft seal installer tool. Slide into place in the bore. Rotate clockwise until it, is felt to seat on compressor crankshaft "flat" provided for it. Remove the tool.

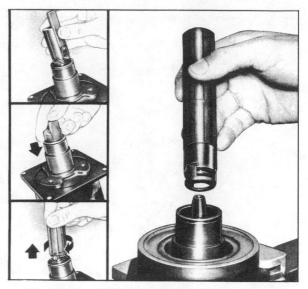

FIG. 16-8 INSTALL SEAL SEAT O-RING AND SHAFT SEAL

FIG. 16-9 DRIVE PLATE KEY INSTALLED IN KEYWAY

5. Place the shaft seal seat on the remover/installer tool.

NOTE: This part may be replaced without the use of this tool. However, it is recommended that this tool be used to prevent its accidentally being installed upside-down. If this occurs, the compressor will have to be completely dismantled in order to get it back out of the well.

6. Next, install the shaft seal seat snap ring. Note that the beveled edge of the snap ring must face the outside of the compressor.

SPECIAL TOOLS

FIG. 16-10 INSTALLING DRIVEN PLATE

CLEARANCE .030"

FIG. 16-11 CHECKING AIR GAP

7. Before replacing clutch hub and drive plate, the seal should be leak checked.

LEAK TEST SHAFT SEAL

1. With the test fitting in place, connect the manifold gage set to the test ports.

2. Tap a can of refrigerant and purge lines of air. Open high- and low-side manifold hand valves to allow refrigerant pressure to enter compressor.

3. With a leak detector, check the shaft seal area for escaping refrigerant.

4. If a small leak is detected, rotate the crankshaft a few turns to "seat" the seal; then recheck.

REPLACE CLUTCH HUB AND DRIVE PLATE ASSEMBLY

1. Place the crankshaft drive key into the keyway provided. Allow about 3/16" to stick out of the end of the keyway.

2. Align the keyway in hub and drive plate with the key and slide into position. NOTE: Take care not to force the drive key into the shaft seal. Periodic rotation of the drive plate will insure proper seating. If key is driven into seal, it will hang on the snap ring and make rotation of the drive plate difficult or impossible.

3. Using a hub and drive plate installer, press this part onto the crankshaft.

4. There should be about .030" clearance between the drive plate and rotor.

5. Replace spacer and clutch hub retainer ring.

6. Replace the shaft nut.

RETURN COMPRESSOR TO SERVICE

1. If removed, return compressor to car. Remove test fitting and replace service valves.

2. Evacuate and charge as outlined in this manual.

3. Continue performance tests as may be necessary.

REVIEW QUESTIONS

1. Are the same service tools used on the five- and six-cylinder compressors?

_____

2. Is the rotor removed on the six-cylinder compressor the same as the five-cylinder compressor? _____

3. In sequence, list the REMOVAL order of the following.
   a. Retaining ring   c. Seal assembly
   b. Seal seat O-ring   d. Seal seat

4. What wrench is used to remove the crankshaft nut? _____

5. Proper sequence for INSTALLATION must be followed to avoid damage, when replacing the seal seat O-ring, to the _____.

SERVICE PROCEDURE 17

To Service the Magnetic Clutch

Regardless of the type of field, clutch bearings and brushes may be replaced, and brush races may be cleaned. In most cases, however, only the stationary field assembly may be replaced if proved to be defective.

The following is a brief outline dealing with all clutches in general and may be used as a guide in servicing them.

TOOLS

Snap ring pliers, screwdriver, 5/8" NC bolt, 5/8" NF bolt, hand wrenches, small arbor press, ammeter

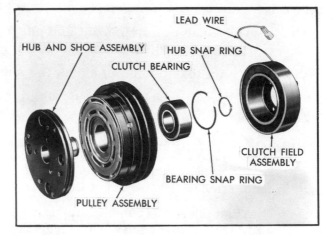

FIG. 17—1, MAGNETIC CLUTCH—STATIONARY FIELD TYPE

MATERIAL

Field, bearing, or brush set as may be indicated

PROCEDURE

TEST CLUTCH FIELD COIL

1. Disconnect the field coil wire from the body wiring.

2. Connect an ammeter to the positive side of the battery.

3. Connect the other side of the ammeter to the clutch coil field lead.

4. Check draw. At twelve volts, field draw should be **2.5** to **3.5** amperes.

   a. A reading of zero indicates an open field coil or bad brushes.

   b. A reading of less than **2.5** amps. indicates defective brushes, or added resistance due to the accumulation of dirt and foreign material, perhaps causing a poor ground.

   c. A reading in excess of **3.5** amps. indicates shorted field coil windings or a shorted field coil.

   d. If the coil does not fall to within the **2.5** to **3.5** amp. specifications, it must be replaced or corrected as indicated.

REMOVAL OF CLUTCH ASSEMBLY

1. Loosen and remove the belts from the compressor.

2. Remove the capscrew from the center of the compressor crankshaft.

3. Insert a 5/8″ NC or NF (as indicated) capscrew into the threaded portion of the clutch rotor.

4. Tighten capscrew against the crankshaft of the compressor until the rotor slips from the shaft.

5. Remove the field coil attaching screws and lift the coil from the compressor OR remove the screws holding the brush set in place and remove brushes. Take care not to break them.

FIG. 17-2 REMOVING HUB AND SHOE ASSEMBLY   FIG. 17-3 REMOVING BEARING FROM PULLEY ASSEMBLY

DISASSEMBLE CLUTCH PULLEY ASSEMBLY

1. Remove the snap ring from the rear of the clutch hub.

2. Using the proper puller or arbor press, press the hub from the clutch rotor.

3. Remove the bearing snap ring from the rotor.

4. Place the rotor in an arbor and press the bearing out.

   NOTE: Press the bearing out only if it is to be replaced. Pressing the bearing on the inner race will damage it.

ASSEMBLE CLUTCH PULLEY

1. Inspect all parts. The clutch hub and rotor may have scoring, which is to be expected; however, excessive scoring indicates that the clutch may need replacing.

2. Replace all parts that prove to be defective.

3. To assemble the clutch, follow the preceding procedure in reverse.

   NOTE: Remove the 5/8" bolt before replacing the rotor. Take care not to damage the brush set when replacing the rotor.

REVIEW QUESTIONS

Indicate whether each of the following statements is true or false by writing T (true) or F (false) in the space provided.

_____   1. If a rotating field is found to be defective, the entire clutch must be replaced in most cases.

_____   2. A clutch field draw of ten amps. indicates a direct short.

_____   3. Clutch draw should be 2.5 to 3.5 amps.

_____   4. Clutch brushes may be replaced without removing the rotor.

_____   5. Bearings should be removed and inspected each time the clutch is serviced.

_____   6. Clutch field draw is taken by connecting a voltmeter between the clutch field and ground.

_____   7. Clutch field draw is taken by connecting a voltmeter into the circuit by disconnecting the field lead.

_____   8. If the clutch hub or rotor is scored, they must be replaced.

_____   9. A 5/8" bolt is used to remove the clutch rotor.

_____   10. A field draw of .5 amperes indicates a shorted clutch coil.

SERVICE PROCEDURE 18
To Repair the Heli-Grip Clutch

The Heli-Grip clutch is used by several independent manufacturers and on late model Chrysler units. Instead of a clutch plate, the Heli-Grip clutch uses a split friction ring and helical spring to engage the clutch hub with the pulley assembly.

This clutch uses a stationary field coil assembly, either seal-plate mounted with three capscrews, or crankcase-boss mounted with four capscrews.

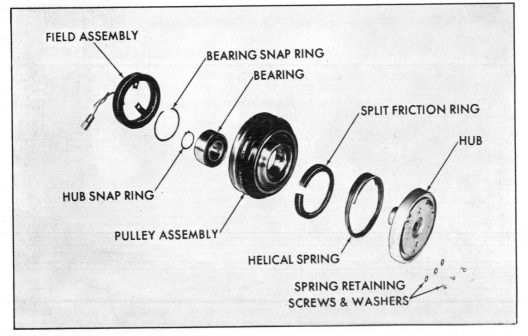

FIG. 18–1 HELI–GRIP CLUTCH

TOOLS

Snap ring pliers, screwdriver, 5/8″ NC bolt, small arbor press or puller

MATERIAL

Field, bearing, friction ring, or helical spring as may be indicated

PROCEDURE

TEST CLUTCH FIELD COIL

1. Disconnect the field coil wire from the body wiring.

2. Connect an ammeter to the positive side of the battery.

3. Connect the other side of the ammeter to clutch field lead. Check field draw.

197

a. At 12 volts the field draw should be 2.7 - 3.1 amperes.

b. A reading of 0 amperes indicates an open field coil circuit.

c. A reading in excess of 3.1 indicates shorted field windings or a shorted field coil.

d. If the coil does not fall within the above specifications it must be replaced.

REMOVAL OF CLUTCH ASSEMBLY

1. Loosen and remove the belts from the compressor pulley.

2. Remove the Nylok capscrew and washer from the crankshaft.

3. Insert a 5/8″ NC capscrew into threaded portion of the clutch rotor. Tighten against the crankshaft of the compressor until the rotor slips from the shaft.

4. Remove the field coil attaching screws and lift the coil from the compressor crankcase.

DISASSEMBLE CLUTCH PULLEY ASSEMBLY

1. Remove the snap ring from the rear of the clutch hub.

2. With hub facing downward, place the pulley assembly on an arbor press, or use puller.

3. Press the hub from the pulley.

4. From the front of the hub, remove the three screws securing the helical spring.

5. With a screwdriver, gently pry out the tanged end of the spring. Turn the spring counterclockwise to remove it from the hub.

FIG. 18-2 REMOVING HUB ASSEMBLY

6. Remove the split friction ring from the rotor.

7. Remove the bearing snap ring from the rotor.

8. Place the pulley assembly on an arbor press, with the pulley side down. Pressing on the inner race of the bearing, remove it from the rotor.

   NOTE: Remove the bearing only if it is to be replaced. Pressing on the inner race may damage the bearing.

ASSEMBLE CLUTCH PULLEY

1. Inspect all parts for wear and replace as necessary.

2. To assemble the clutch pulley assembly, follow the preceding procedure in reverse.

   NOTE: The tip of the helical spring should be flat and approximately level with the rear face of the hub.

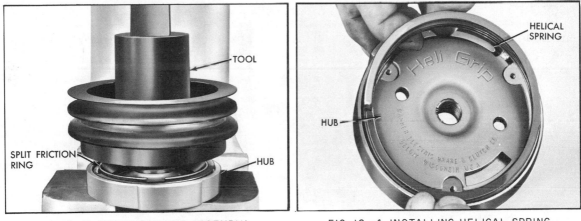

FIG. 18-3 INSTALLING HUB ASSEMBLY   FIG. 18-4 INSTALLING HELICAL SPRING

REVIEW QUESTIONS

Indicate whether each of the following statements is true or false by writing T (true) or F (false) in the space provided.

_____ 1. The Heli-Grip clutch uses a rotating field.

_____ 2. No ampere reading indicates a shorted field.

_____ 3. The tool used to remove the rotor is a 5/8" NC capscrew.

_____ 4. An open coil will result in a clutch that will not shut off.

_____ 5. Correct field draw is 2.7 to 3.1 volts.

_____ 6. The Heli-Grip clutch uses a rotor and clutch plate.

_____ 7. The Heli-Grip clutch is used on Chrysler products only.

_____ 8. A loose connection may result in a low field draw and an inoperative clutch.

SERVICE PROCEDURE 19
To Check Compressor Oil Level *(Air-Temp, Tecumseh, York)*

The following procedure may be followed when it becomes necessary to check the oil level in the Air-Temp, Tecumseh and York compressors having high- and low-compressor service valves. Those with Schrader-type valves require that refrigerant be purged from the system to check the oil level.

TOOLS

Service valve wrench, hand wrenches, eye protection, fender covers, manifold gage set, oil dipstick

MATERIAL

Refrigeration oil

PROCEDURE

PREPARE SYSTEM

1. Compressor must be isolated from the system. Follow procedure outlined in this manual.

CHECK OIL LEVEL

1. Remove plug from compressor body to gain access to compressor crankcase.

2. Use correct dipstick and measure oil.

3. Compare with chart below to determine proper oil level.

	York	Tecumseh	Air-Temp
Vertical	1 1/4″	7/8″	
Inclined	2″	1 1/4″	
Horizontal	7/8″	1 1/8″	
R. H. Mount			2 3/4″
L. C. Mount			3 1/8″

4. Fill with refrigeration oil as necessary to bring level to proper height.

RETURN COMPRESSOR TO SYSTEM

1. Replace oil check plug.

2. If oil check plug was removed from compressor for more than five minutes, purge air from compressor as follows:

   a. Open high-side manifold hand valve.

   b. Crack low-side compressor service valve off front-seated position.

   c. Low-side refrigerant pressure will force air out of compressor through high-side manifold set.

   d. After five seconds of purging, close high-side manifold hand valve.

3. Mid-position low- and high-side compressor service valves.

CONTINUE PERFORMANCE TEST

1. With manifold gage set hooked up, check refrigerant charge.

2. Add refrigerant if necessary.

3. Continue performance testing as indicated, or return to service.

RETURN SYSTEM TO SERVICE

1. Backseat high-and low-side compressor service valves.

2. Remove service hoses and re-place protective caps.

NOTE: An oil dipstick, such as the one shown here, may be made from a piece of medium soft wire, such as a black coat hanger. A black wire should be used so the refrigeration oil level can be more easily seen on the stick.

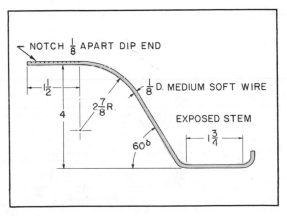

FIG. 19 – 1 OIL DIPSTICK

REVIEW QUESTIONS

1. Why must the compressor be isolated from the system? _____

_____

2. What tool is used to measure the oil level? _____

3. Should air be purged from the compressor after checking the oil? _____

4. Which compressor may not be mounted inclined or horizontal? _____

5. May any good, clean refrigeration oil be used in the compressors? _____

SERVICE PROCEDURE 20
To Check and Add Oil *(General Motors' Compressors, 6 Cylinder)*

Six-cylinder General Motors' compressors are fully charged originally, with ten ounces of 525 viscosity refrigeration oil. Design and configuration of the six-cylinder compressor require a radical departure from the oil checking procedure used on the five-cylinder compressors.

In a six-cylinder compressor, it is not recommended that the oil level be checked as a matter of course. Generally, compressor oil level should be checked only where there is evidence of a major loss, such as may be caused by a broken refrigeration line, a serious seal leak, or a collision.

To check the compressor oil charge, it is necessary to remove the compressor from the car, drain and measure the oil. In all instances requiring an oil check, it is suggested that the oil drained from the compressor be discarded after a note is made of the measure.

We must assume that the compressor has been isolated or purged of refrigerant and removed from the car for the following procedure. It is not possible in all cases, however, to stabilize the system, which allows the system oil to return to the compressor. The following procedure will be broken into two parts: Part I deals with the compressor removed from a system that could not be stabilized, and Part II deals with the compressor from a system that was stabilized.

TOOLS

Graduated container(s)

MATERIAL

Refrigeration oil as required

PART I - PROCEDURE

DRAIN COMPRESSOR

1. Remove the oil drain plug located in the compressor oil sump.

2. Place compressor in a horizontal position, with the drain hole downward, over a graduated container.

3. Drain compressor, measure amount of oil removed and discard.

NOTE AMOUNT OF OIL DRAINED; SECURE NEW OIL FOR REPLACEMENT

1. If the amount of oil removed is more than 1 1/2 fluid ounces and the system shows no signs of a great loss, replace the same amount of oil.

2. If the amount of oil removed is less than 1 1/2 fluid ounces and the system shows signs of greater loss, add six fluid ounces of clean refrigeration oil.

3. In the case of a replacement compressor, follow the procedures outlined in steps 1 and 2.

4. In the case of a rebuilt compressor, add one ounce to the amount outlined in steps 1 and 2.

PART II - PROCEDURE

DRAIN COMPRESSOR

1. Follow steps as outlined in Part I.

NOTE AMOUNT OF OIL DRAINED; SECURE NEW OIL FOR REPLACEMENT

1. If the quantity drained was four fluid ounces or more, add the same amount of new refrigeration oil to the compressor.

2. If the quantity of oil drained was less than four fluid ounces, add six fluid ounces of new refrigeration oil to the compressor.

SERVICE NOTES

If the compressor, removed and drained, shows signs of a foreign material or if the oil contains chips or other foreign matter, replace the receiver-dehydrator and flush or replace all component parts as necessary.

If a system is flushed, add a full ten ounces of clean refrigeration oil to the new or replacement compressor.

Except for a system that has been flushed, add the additional amounts of oil to any system that has had the following components replaced.

Evaporator . . . . 3 fluid ounces
Condenser . . . . 1 fluid ounce
Receiver-dehydrator . . . . . . 1 fluid ounce

Disregard any loss of oil due to the changing of a line or muffler, unless such part has a measurable amount in it, in which case the same amount of clean refrigeration oil must be replaced.

REVIEW QUESTIONS

1. What is the normal charge and grade of oil in the General Motors' six-cylinder compressor? _____

2. Should the compressor oil level be checked each time the unit is serviced?

_____

3. How much oil must be added for the replacement of the following parts:

   a. Evaporator   b. Condenser   c. Receiver-dehydrator

   _____   _____   _____

4. If it is impossible to stabilize the system and less than 1 1/2 ounce of oil is removed, how much should be replaced? _____

5. If the system has been stabilized and four ounces of oil is removed, how much should be replaced? _____

SERVICE PROCEDURE 21
To Add Dye or Trace to the Air Conditioning System

A dye or trace solution may be introduced into an air conditioning system as an aid in pinpointing a small leak. It will show the exact location of a leak with a telltale orange-red or yellow film, depending on the color used. Once introduced into the air conditioning system, however, it will remain until removed, which will require system cleaning. The trace solution is formulated for use in air conditioning systems and will not affect system operation in any way.

TOOLS

Manifold gage set, 1/4″ × 1′ copper tubing, 1/4″ flare nuts, service valve wrench or Schrader adapter, hand wrenches, oil filler, can tap

MATERIAL

Dye or trace solution as required, Refrigerant 12

PROCEDURE

PREPARE SYSTEM

1. Connect manifold gage set into the system. Purge all lines of air.

2. Fasten center manifold hose to oil filler tube, filled with **8-12** ounces of dye material.

3. Make up a charging line using one-foot piece of copper tube and female flare nuts. Secure to refrigerant can tap and oil filler tube.

4. Attach can tap to can of Refrigerant **12** and pierce the can.

5. Purge copper line of air.

ADD DYE TO SYSTEM

1. Start engine and operate at idle speeds. Set controls for maximum cooling.

2. Open the low-side manifold hand valve slowly and allow the **8-12** ounces of trace dye to enter the system.

3. Allow little or no refrigerant to enter the system. Shut off manifold hand valve.

4. Shut off air conditioner and car engine.

CONCLUSION

1. Observe hoses and fittings for signs of dye solution. If nothing is observed, make arrangements to have car the following day for diagnosis and repair.

2. If one or more leaks is detected, repair as indicated. The dye solution may remain in the system without causing harm to the system.

RETURN SYSTEM TO NORMAL OPERATION

1. Remove manifold and gage set.

2. Replace protective caps.

REVIEW QUESTIONS

Indicate whether each of the following statements is true or false by writing T (true) or F (false) in the space provided.

_____   1. Dye trace solution will eventually fade out of the system.

_____   2. Dye should not be used unless absolutely necessary since it does not mix well with refrigerants and refrigeration oil.

_____   3. Dye trace helps pinpoint a leak by leaving a telltale blue film.

_____   4. A leak can be pinpointed almost immediately using this solution.

_____   5. To remove the dye solution, it is necessary to evacuate and recharge the unit.

SERVICE PROCEDURE 22
To Adjust Thermostat *(Cycling Clutch Units)*

The thermostat, which controls evaporator temperature by cycling the clutch, is preset at the factory. Different altitudes and humidity conditions may require that the thermostat be checked and occasionally adjusted to local conditions. The following procedure will deal with the thermostat adjustment. It should be noted that some thermostats have no provisions for adjustment.

TOOLS

Service thermometer, manifold and gage set, hand wrenches, service valve wrench, small screwdriver

PROCEDURE

PREPARE SYSTEM FOR SERVICE

1. Connect manifold and gage set into the system.

2. Start engine and set to 1200-1500 r.p.m. Set air conditioning controls for maximum cooling.

3. Operate for 5-10 minutes with core thermometer inserted into the evaporator at or near the thermostatic expansion valve. MAKE SURE EVAPORATOR DOES NOT HAVE BLOWERS MOUNTED IN THE FRONT OF THE UNIT.

4. Check the sight glass to insure a full charge of refrigerant.

CHECK THERMOSTAT OPERATION

1. Turn thermostat to the full on, or clockwise, position.

2. Turn blowers to low or medium speeds.

3. Observe manifold compound gage: it should read from 14 p.s.i.g. to 26 p.s.i.g. after the system has been operated for 5-10 minutes.

4. Observe manifold pressure or high-side gage. High-side pressure should compare approximately with the temperature-pressure chart.

5. Compare low pressure gage readings with the core thermometer readings against the temperature-pressure relationship chart. The thermometer should read from 15°F. to 35°F., allowing for a temperature rise due to wall loss in the evaporator coil tubing.

| Temperature-Pressure Relationship Chart | | | |
| Low Side | | High Side | |
Evap. Temp.	Evap. Pres.	Cond. Pres.	Ambient Temp.
5°	11.8	72	40°
10°	14.7	86	50°
15°	17.1	105	60°
20°	21.1	126	70°
22°	22.5	140	75°
24°	23.9	160	80°
26°	25.4	185	90°
28°	26.9	195	95°
30°	28.4	220	100°
32°	30.0	240	105°
34°	31.7	260	110°
36°	33.4	275	115°
38°	35.1	290	120°
40°	36.9	305	125°

CHECK THERMOSTAT CUTOUT AND CUT-IN POINT

NOTE: For proper thermostat operation, dealer service manual should be consulted; however, the following may be used as a guide.

1. The thermostat should cut out when the thermometer indicates 24-26°F.

2. The thermostat should cut back in when the thermometer indicates 36-38°F.

3. The manifold compound gage should show a pressure rise of about 26-32 p.s.i.g. between cutout and cut-in.

4. Check the thermostat operation three or four times to insure consistent operation.

ADJUST THERMOSTAT

1. Remove the evaporator front or out outlets as necessary to make the thermostat accessible.

2. Locate the adjustment screw (found behind an access door on some models).

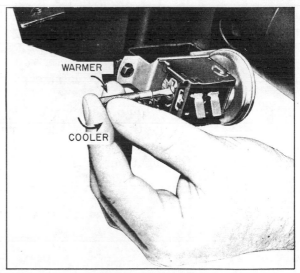

FIG. 22-1 THERMOSTATIC SWITCH ADJUSTMENT

NOTE: The design of some evaporators requires the thermostat to be removed from the case in order to gain access to the adjusting screw.

3. Rotate the adjusting screw in a counterclockwise direction to lower the temperature by delaying the point opening. Conversely, a clockwise rotation of the screw will increase the temperature.

4. Check the operation of the thermostat for the newly-adjusted cycle of operation. If determined to be correct, check three or four times to insure consistent operation.

5. If the cycle of operation is inconsistent or cannot be adjusted, the thermostat must be replaced.

RETURN SYSTEM TO SERVICE

1. Return engine to normal idle speed and turn off.

2. Replace thermostat access door and replace thermostat into evaporator case. Replace other parts that may have been removed to allow access.

3. REMOVE THE THERMOMETER.

4. Back seat the compressor service valves and remove manifold gage set. Replace protective covers and caps.

REVIEW QUESTIONS

Indicate whether each of the following statements is true or false by writing T (true) or F (false) in the space provided.

_____   1. All thermostats may be adjusted.

_____   2. The unit should be stabilized before attempting to adjust the thermostat.

_____   3. A full charge of refrigerant is unimportant in checking the thermostat.

_____   4. The thermostat should cut out the clutch when it reaches 35°F. to insure that the unit does not freeze up.

_____   5. A temperature rise of six degrees is sufficient to allow proper defrost time.

SERVICE PROCEDURE 23
To Test Operation of the Evaporator Pressure Regulator Valve

The evaporator pressure regulator valve (EPR), used by Chrysler, is calibrated to produce maximum cooling without causing frost or ice to form on the evaporator fins. If, for any reason, the factory calibration is disturbed, the EPR valve will not function properly. A restriction of the EPR will result in high evaporator temperatures and poor cooling. An EPR valve not restricting properly will result in an evaporator running too cold and freezing up.

The evaporator pressure regulator test will determine if the valve is functioning properly or not.

FIG. 23-1 SERVICE VALVE REMOVED TO SHOW EPR VALVE

TOOLS

Manifold gage set consisting of two compound gages, one pressure gage, service valve wrench, hand tools

MATERIAL

EPR valve and service valve gasket if indicated.

PROCEDURE

PREPARE SYSTEM FOR TEST

1. Connect compound manifold gage to suction service port at the rear of the compressor.

2. Connect second compound manifold gage to compressor inlet port located on right head of the compressor (located on the EPR valve on 1960 models).

3. Connect the high-side gage hose to the discharge service valve located at the front of the compressor.

4. Purge air from manifold gage hoses by cracking hoses at manifold for a few seconds each.

5. Adjust engine speed to about 1250 r.p.m.

6. Insure that hoses are clear of belts and pulleys and close car hood. Open all windows.

7. Set air conditioning controls for maximum cooling and operate for 10-15 minutes to stabilize the system.

READ BOTH COMPOUND GAGES

1. With the EPR valve operating properly, the evaporator pressure gage and the compressor inlet gage should read about the same, or within 1 or 2 pounds. Both gages should read 26-28 p.s.i.g.

FORCE OPERATION OF EPR VALVE

1. Set blower switch to the lowest position and depress the FRESH COOL button or lever.

2. Check evaporator outlet for increased cooling with windows now closed.

3. Evaporator pressure should settle at about 22-26 p.s.i.g.

4. Compressor inlet pressure should drop to about 15-17 p.s.i.g. If the inlet pressure does not drop to this point, increase engine speed to approximately 2000 r.p.m.

CONCLUSION

1. Repeat steps above to insure constant operation of the EPR valve.

2. Replace the EPR valve if pressures are not within prescribed limits.

RETURN SYSTEM TO SERVICE

1. Return engine to normal idle speed to prevent dieseling.

2. Turn off air conditioner. Shut off engine.

3. Remove manifold gage set and replace protective caps.

REVIEW QUESTIONS

Indicate whether each of the following statements is true or false by writing T (true) or F (False) in the space provided.

_____ 1. EPR valve test should be made with the engine operating at 1250 r.p.m.

_____ 2. EPR valves are used on General Motors' air conditioners.

_____ 3. No cycling clutch is used with the EPR valve.

_____ 4. The EPR maintains evaporator temperature by controlling its pressure.

_____ 5. The compressor inlet fitting is found on the right head.

SERVICE PROCEDURE 24

To Test Operation of the Evaporator Temperature Regulator

The evaporator temperature regulator (ETR) valve, used by Chrysler, replaces the standard evaporator pressure regulator (EPR) valve in the automatic temperature control systems.

Used to keep the fins on the evaporator from icing, the ETR valve is an electrical device operated by an ETR switch which has a sensing tube inserted into the evaporator fins. The switch closes if the evaporator temperature goes lower than about 38° F. When this switch closes, it sends current to the ETR valve in the compressor. The ETR valve shuts off refrigerant flow until the evaporator warms up. Both the EPR and ETR valve accomplish the same thing, but the ETR valve controls refrigerant flow electrically, while the EPR valve controls flow by pressure differential.

The ETR and EPR valves are located under the suction service valve, as shown in Figure 23-1, page 209.

TOOLS

Manifold gage set, hand tools

MATERIAL

ETR valve and gasket or ETR switch, if indicated.

PROCEDURE

PREPARE SYSTEM FOR TEST

1. Connect compound manifold gage to suction service port at the rear of the compressor.

2. Connect second compound manifold gage to compressor inlet port, located on right head of compressor.

3. Connect the high-side gage hose to the discharge service valve.

4. Purge air from manifold gage hoses by cracking hoses at manifold for a few seconds each.

5. Start engine and adjust speed to 1000 r.p.m.

6. Close all windows and doors after depressing the AUTO button and setting control dial at 65.

7. Connect test light to ETR valve lead.

HOLD TEST

1. Observe compressor inlet pressure. NOTE: Pressure should be normal.

2. Observe test light. NOTE: Light should be off.

3. Watch for test light to come on, indicating the ETR switch is sending current to the ETR valve. NOTE: If ETR switch is defective, light may not be off as indicated in step 2, or may not come on as indicated in step 3.

4. When test light comes on, observe compressor inlet pressure. Pressure should drop to zero pressure. If it does not, a defective ETR is indicated. NOTE: Head pressure will vary 25 to 35 pounds as the ETR valve opens and closes.

RETURN SYSTEM TO SERVICE

1. Return engine to normal idle to prevent dieseling.

2. Turn off air conditioner. Shut off engine.

3 Remove manifold gage set and replace protective caps.

4. Remove test light.

REVIEW QUESTIONS

1. Briefly, what is the purpose of the ETR valve? _____

_____

2. How is the ETR valve different from the EPR valve? _____

_____

3. What is the "normal" compressor inlet reading for the ETR/EPR system?

_____

SERVICE PROCEDURE 25
To Check and Adjust the Suction Throttling Valve

The suction throttling valve (STV) is adjusted to regulate evaporator pressure so that it will not fall below 29-31 p.s.i.g. Below 29 p.s.i.g. the evaporator will be too cold. It will freeze up by allowing condensate to ice over the evaporator fins and coils. If the pressure is higher than 31 p.s.i.g., the discharge air temperature will be warmer than normal.

The following procedure may be used to check STV operation and to adjust if necessary. If at any time during the test, head pressure exceeds 375 p.s.i.g., discontinue the test and check for the following problems:

1. Engine cooling system leak or system blocked
2. Restricted liquid line or receiver
3. Air in refrigeration system
4. Overcharge of refrigerant or oil
5. Insufficient ram air

The following procedure will be given in two parts: Part I will deal with the Bowden cable-controlled STV and Part II will deal with the vacuum-controlled STV.

TOOLS

Manifold gage set, service valve wrench or Schrader adapters, hand tools, screwdriver, STV adjustment tool

PART I - PROCEDURE

PREPARE SYSTEM FOR TEST AND/OR ADJUSTMENT

1. Attach the gage manifold set to the compressor and STV. Use a third gage if three fittings are found.

2. Start the engine and adjust to 1000-1200 r.p.m. Adjust all air-conditioning controls for maximum cooling.

3. Move temperature control back and forth 10 to 15 times to normalize the diaphragm in the STV.

4. Visually check the Bowden cable and control as well as the control lever to insure that there is free movement through the full sweep of operation.

ADJUST CABLE

1. Position the temperature lever fully to the cold position and loosen cable clamp on the valve.

2. Position cable in the clamp to force the valve lever to seat against its stop.

3. Tighten cable clamp screw. Check for free operation.

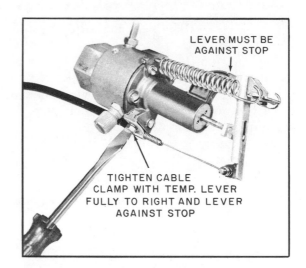

FIG. 25-1 ADJUSTING BOWDEN CABLE

VALVE ADJUSTMENT

1. Make sure Bowden cable is properly adjusted before making STV adjustments.

2. Raise engine speed to about 1600 r.p.m. and depress high blower button or lever. Operate 5-10 minutes.

3. Evaporator pressure should now read 29-31 p.s.i.g.

4. Adjust STV until evaporator pressure is within these limits.

   a. Engage the pins of the adjusting tool in holes in valve adjusting screw.

   b. **Turn to adjust. Clockwise rotation will increase spring tension and will raise evaporator pressure.**

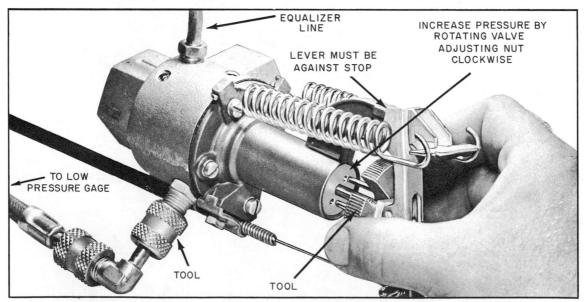

FIG. 25-2. ADJUSTING SUCTION THROTTLING VALVE

5. After obtaining a pressure of 29-31 p.s.i.g., operate the control lever a few times to insure constant operation.

RETURN TO SERVICE

1. Drop engine speed back to normal idle to prevent dieseling when shut off. Shut off engine; shut off air conditioner.

2. Remove manifold and gage set and replace all protective caps and covers.

PART II - PROCEDURE

PREPARE SYSTEM FOR TEST AND/OR ADJUSTMENT

1. Follow procedure as outlined in Part I.

   NOTE: The vacuum-controlled STV does not use a Bowden cable. Therefore, no check must be made.

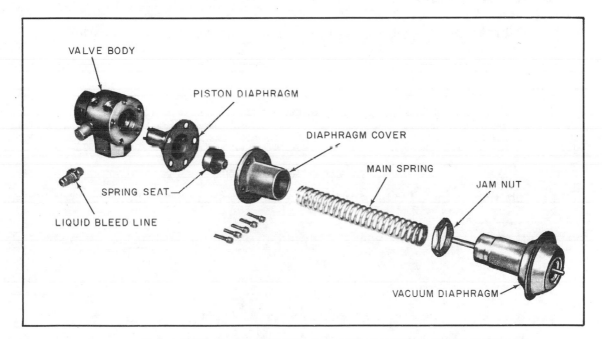

FIG. 25-3 EXPLODED VIEW OF A VACUUM-OPERATED SUCTION THROTTLING VALVE

VALVE ADJUSTMENT

1. Raise engine speed to 1500-1600 r.p.m.

2. Turn blower on high and set controls for maximum cooling. Operate for 5-10 minutes.

3. Evaporator pressure should now read **29-31** p.s.i.g.

4. Adjust STV until the evaporator pressure is within these limits.

   a. Disconnect vacuum hose from vacuum valve on STV.

   b. Loosen locknut on vacuum control.

   c. Rotate vacuum control clockwise to increase spring tension and raise evaporator pressure.

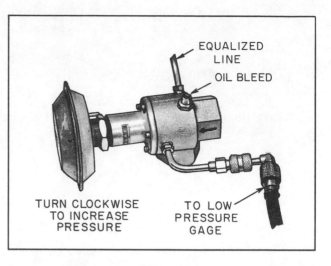

FIG. 25-4 SUCTION THROTTLING VALVE ADJUSTMENT

5. After obtaining a pressure of **29-30** p.s.i.g., tighten the locknut and reconnect the vacuum hose.

6. Operate the control lever a few times to insure constant operation.

RETURN TO SERVICE

1. Follow procedure as outlined in Part I.

REVIEW QUESTIONS

1. The job of the STV is to maintain evaporator pressure between _____ and _____ p.s.i.g.

2. If head pressure exceeds _____ p.s.i.g., air in the system may be indicated.

3. How may you normalize the STV? _____

   _____

4. What should the engine speed be for the STV test? _____

5. May an improperly adjusted Bowden cable cause poor cooling? _____
   Explain. _____

6. What should the engine speed be for STV adjustment? _____

7. Evaporator pressure is read at the _____.

8. Pressures below _____ p.s.i.g. will allow the evaporator to freeze up.

9. Evaporator pressure may be increased by adjusting STV adjustment _____.

10. Increased evaporator pressure means higher _____.

SERVICE PROCEDURE 26
To Rebuild the Suction Throttling Valve

The suction throttling valve (STV) has been used on General Motors' cars since 1962. Valves produced after 1965 cannot be serviced. This unit deals with the service procedure to be followed in rebuilding the early STV

The following procedure will be given in two parts: Part I deals with the cable-controlled STV and Part II deals with the vacuum-controlled valve.

The proper cleaning and servicing of the valve requires its removal from the car. This unit deals with the suction throttling valve out of the car.

TOOLS

Pliers, Phillips #2 screwdriver

MATERIAL

Clean refrigeration oil, diaphragm and/or piston assembly as required

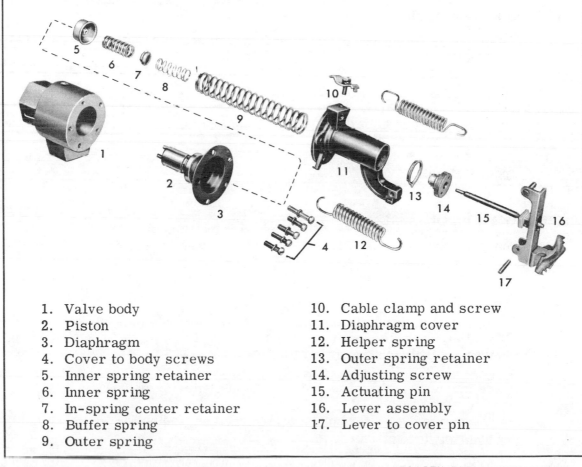

1. Valve body	10. Cable clamp and screw
2. Piston	11. Diaphragm cover
3. Diaphragm	12. Helper spring
4. Cover to body screws	13. Outer spring retainer
5. Inner spring retainer	14. Adjusting screw
6. Inner spring	15. Actuating pin
7. In-spring center retainer	16. Lever assembly
8. Buffer spring	17. Lever to cover pin
9. Outer spring	

FIG. 26-1   EXPLODED VIEW OF THE SUCTION THROTTLING VALVE – BOWDEN CABLE-CONTROLLED

PART I - PROCEDURE

DISMANTLE VALVE

1. Clean external surfaces of valve with clean mineral spirits.

2. Remove two helper springs located between the lever assembly and diaphragm cover.

3. Mark relationship of diaphragm cover and valve body to insure proper alignment on reassembly.

4. Remove five cover-to-body screws.

   CAUTION: Diaphragm cover is under heavy spring tension.

5. Remove diaphragm cover, outer spring, buffer spring, inner spring center retainer and inner spring.

6. Check inside diaphragm cover barrel and remove outer spring retainer.

7. Remove inner spring retainer, diaphragm and piston from valve body. Separate inner spring retainer from diaphragm.

   NOTE: It is not necessary to remove the adjusting screw, lever assembly or actuating pin.

8. Place all parts in clean mineral spirits for 10-15 minutes.

9. Remove parts and blow dry. Inspect all parts for damage.

10. Check inner spring retainer for rough spots or sharp edges. Clean with crocus cloth.

DIAPHRAGM-PISTON ASSEMBLY

1. Replace with a new assembly, or rebuild as outlined in Service Procedure 27.

ASSEMBLE VALVE

1. Place a new (or rebuilt) diaphragm-piston assembly into the bore of the valve body. Use an ample coating of clean refrigeration oil on all surfaces and insure that they are free of all foreign matter.

2. Place inner spring retainer into cavity at center of diaphragm.

3. Stack inner spring, inner spring center retainer and buffer spring on top of the inner spring retainer.

4. Carefully slide the outer spring over this assembly.

5. Replace the outer spring retainer in the diaphragm cover. Refrigeration oil will aid in holding it in place.

6. Slide diaphragm cover into position and line up all holes. Make sure that index mark made earlier is in line.

7. Press diaphragm cover in place and insert the five screws. Tighten hand tight.

8. Check all five screws to insure that they are tight.

PART II - PROCEDURE

DISASSEMBLE VALVE

1. Clean all external surfaces of the valve with clean mineral spirits.

2. Mark jam nut and back off one complete turn.

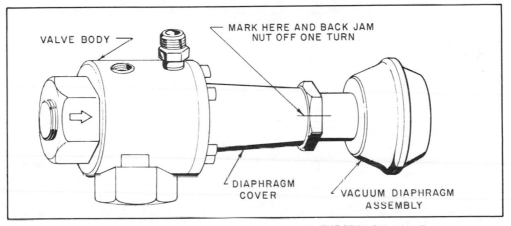

FIG. 26-2 VACUUM-CONTROLLED SUCTION THROTTLING VALVE

3. Remove vacuum control diaphragm assembly.

   CAUTION: **Vacuum control assembly is under heavy spring pressure.**

4. Remove five diaphragm-to-valve body screws and lift off diaphragm cover.

5. Remove spring retainer, diaphragm and piston from valve body. Separate spring retainer from diaphragm.

6. Place all parts in clean mineral spirits for 10-15 minutes.

7. Remove parts and blow dry. Inspect all parts for damage. Check spring retainer for rough spots or sharp edges. Clean with a crocus cloth.

DIAPHRAGM-PISTON ASSEMBLY

1. Replace with a new assembly, or rebuild as outlined in Service Procedure 27.

ASSEMBLE VALVE

1. Place the new (or rebuilt) diaphragm-piston assembly into the bore of the valve body, using an ample coating of clean refrigeration oil on all surfaces to insure they are free of all foreign matter.

2. Place spring retainer into the cavity at center of the diaphragm.

3. With the diaphragm cover in position, replace the five screws. Tighten hand tight. Check all five screws to be sure that they are tight.

4. Place outer spring into the diaphragm cover and carefully replace the vacuum diaphragm assembly.

   CAUTION: Take care not to cross the threads.

5. Tighten until the diaphragm jam nut touches the diaphragm cover, then back off one full turn. Now tighten the jam nut against the diaphragm cover. No further adjustment in the car should be necessary.

REVIEW QUESTIONS

1. May all suction throttling valves be rebuilt? _____
   Explain. _____

   _____

2. What is the most common fault with the STV? _____

   _____

   _____

3. Name two main parts of the STV.

   a. _____   b. _____

4. What cleaner should be used on the STV? _____

5. Must a piston and diaphragm assembly always be replaced? _____
   Explain. _____

   _____

   _____

SERVICE PROCEDURE 27

To Rebuild the Diaphragm-Piston Assembly for the STV

When rebuilding the suction throttling valve, the diaphragm-piston assembly can be replaced as an assembly or only the diaphragm may be replaced. The following procedure may be followed when it is necessary to rebuild the assembly.

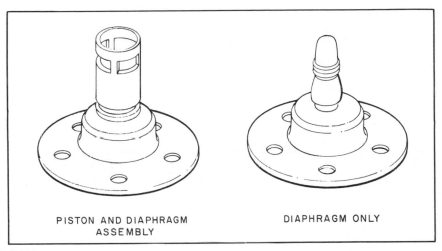

PISTON AND DIAPHRAGM ASSEMBLY

DIAPHRAGM ONLY

FIG. 27-1 SUCTION THROTTLING VALVE REPAIR PACKAGES

TOOLS

Small screwdriver, electric drill or hand drill, a letter "I" drill bit

MATERIAL

Clean refrigeration oil and diaphragm

PROCEDURE

REMOVE OLD DIAPHRAGM

1. At the opposite end of the diaphragm in the piston, remove a star-shaped retainer holding in a screen.

2. Remove the screen. Then remove nylon pilot from the end of the diaphragm.

3. Now pull the diaphragm from the piston.

INSTALL NEW DIAPHRAGM

1. Inspect the piston to insure that it is free of all scratches and burrs. Make no attempt to clean it. If it appears to be damaged, it must be discarded.

2. If hole in piston is too small for new diaphragm, a letter "I" drill may be used to enlarge it. After drilling, make sure that all foreign material is cleaned from the piston. CAUTION: <u>Make sure that none of the chips from the drilled hole scratch the piston.</u>

3. Remove the nylon pilot from the new diaphragm and coat with a liberal supply of clean refrigeration oil.

4. With a forceful twisting motion, insert new diaphragm into piston assembly.

5. From the other end of the piston, reinstall the screen and screen retainer after replacing the nylon pilot.

REVIEW QUESTIONS

1. What drill is used if it is necessary to enlarge the piston hole? _____

2. Why is it necessary to remove the star-shaped retainer and strainer?

   _____

   _____

3. How are scratches and burrs removed from the piston?

   _____

   _____

   _____

4. What is used as an aid in inserting the new diaphragm into the piston?

   _____

   _____

   _____

SERVICE PROCEDURE 28

To Test the Performance of the Pilot-Operated Absolute Valve

The pilot-operated absolute valve (POA) is an evaporator pressure regulator used to control the pressure and temperature of the evaporator. This valve is sealed and no repair is possible. If proved to be defective by the following test, it must be replaced with a new valve.

TOOLS

Manifold gage set with Schrader-type adapters; hand tools; can tap

MATERIAL

POA valve and refrigerant if indicated.

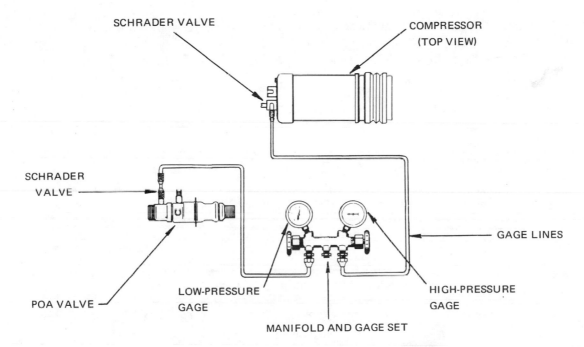

FIG. 28-1   GAGE HOOKUP TO SYSTEM WITH POA VALVE

PROCEDURE

PREPARE SYSTEM FOR TEST

1. Attach the gage manifold set into the system. The low-side manifold connects to the POA valve.

2. Start the engine and adjust to 1000-1200 r.p.m.

3. Adjust all air conditioning controls for maximum cooling.

4. Operate for 10-15 minutes.

CHECK POA VALVE

1. Read compound gage pressure. Pressure should be 27.5-29.5 p.s.i.g. at sea level. Refer to the chart below for proper reading at various altitudes.

2. If valve does not pass this test, replace the valve.

REPLACE POA VALVE

1. Purge system of refrigerant, Service Procedure 3.

2. Remove oil bleed line from POA valve.

3. Remove thermostatic valve external equalizer line from POA valve.

4. Remove inlet and outlet fitting from POA valve. Remove clamp which holds assembly in place and lift from the car.

5. Install a new valve and new O-rings by reversing the above procedure.

6. Evacuate and charge air conditioning system as outlined in Service Procedure 4.

7. Resume performance test if indicated.

RETURN SYSTEM TO SERVICE

1. Drop engine speed back to normal idle to prevent dieseling.

2. Turn off air conditioner and remove manifold gage set.

3. Replace protective caps and covers.

POA Valve Pressure Chart		
Altitude (Elevation)	Gage Pressure (Minimum)	Gage Pressure (Maximum)
0	27.5	29.5
1,000	28.0	30.0
2,000	28.5	30.5
3,000	29.0	31.0
4,000	29.5	31.5
5,000	30.0	32.0
6,000	30.4	32.4
7,000	30.8	32.8
8,000	31.3	33.3
9,000	31.7	33.7
10,000	32.2	34.2

REVIEW QUESTIONS

1. What is the main difference between the pilot-operated absolute valve and the suction throttling valve? _____

_____

2. What is the pressure of the POA valve if it is operating properly at sea level? _____

3. What is the pressure of the POA valve if it is operating properly at 10,000 feet? _____

4. Is the valve itself affected by altitude? _____

_____

_____

5. If the valve does not check out to specifications, may it be adjusted?_____

_____

SERVICE PROCEDURE 29
To Test the General Motors' Automatic Temperature Control *

Known as the Comfort Control or Comfortron system, the automatic temperature control system used by General Motors requires special testing tools and procedures. One such testing tool is the Kent Moore J-22368 which is used to isolate an electrical malfunction in the control system. The tester serves as a substitute for component parts of the system.

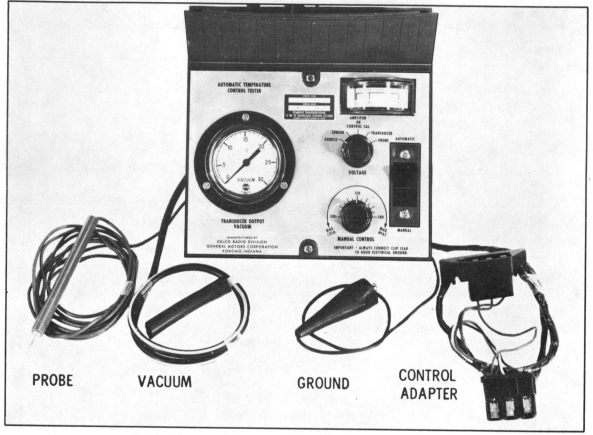

FIG.29—1 AUTOMATIC TEMPERATURE CONTROL TESTER

The following is an outline of procedures to follow in testing the automatic temperature control. It is advised that the equipment manufacturer's service manual be consulted for specifics and procedures on particular models.

TOOLS

Testing tool, such as Kent Moore J-22368 or J-21512; ohmmeter; hand tools; screwdriver

---

* Parts of this material are used by permission of Cadillac Motor Car Division and Oldsmobile Division of General Motors Corporation.

PROCEDURE

SENSOR STRING TEST

1. Place control system lever in automatic position and set the temperature dial to 75°F.

2. Start engine and set to fast idle.

3. Place amplifier switch on tester in SENSOR position.

4. Place sensor switch in A/C position. System and tester meter should go to full air conditioning.

5. Place sensor switch in the HTR position. System and tester meter should go to full heater.

6. If steps 2 and 3 fail to correct, proceed to Amplifier Check. If steps 2 and 3 are correct, proceed.

7. Check for loose connectors at each sensor.

8. With an ohmmeter, measure the resistance values of the in-car sensor, ambient sensor and duct sensor. Sensor resistance values will be given in the shop manual of the particular vehicle you are working on.

9. Replace any sensor that may be found to be defective.

10. If no sensors are found to be defective, carefully check all wiring and correct as necessary.

AMPLIFIER CHECK

1. Place amplifier switch on tester in AMPLIFIER position.

2. Turn amplifier control counterclockwise to the stop position. System and tester meter should go to full air conditioning.

3. Turn amplifier control to the stop in full clockwise position. System and meter should go to full heater position.

4. If test meter does not vary with variation in amplifier control, replace the transducer.

5. If steps 2 and 3 do not correct system operation, proceed to Vacuum Test. If steps 2 and 3 show correct system operation, proceed.

6. Disconnect lead from temperature dial rheostat. Connect an ohmmeter to the rheostat and to control panel ground.

7. Measure the resistance of the rheostat. It should be 1350-1650 ohms at 75°F. setting.

8. If rheostat value is correct, replace amplifier circuit board.

9. If rheostat value is incorrect, replace rheostat.

VACUUM TEST

1. Locate and gain access to transducer.

2. Place amplifier switch in AMPLIFIER position.

3. Turn amplifier control counterclockwise to the stop. Power servo unit should go to full air conditioning position.

4. Turn amplifier control clockwise to the stop position. The power servo should go to the full heater position.

5. Connect vacuum gage to transducer input. Gage should read about 13″ Hg.

6. Connect vacuum gage to the output of the transducer. Rotate tester amplifier control from stop to stop. The output of the transducer should vary.

7. If vacuum output does not vary, replace the transducer.

8. If output does vary, check power servo unit for mechanical interference.

9. If system still does not operate properly, replace the power servo unit.

REVIEW QUESTIONS

1. Briefly, what is the purpose of the automatic temperature control? _____
   _____
   _____

2. What should dial temperature be set at for most tests? _____

3. What should the dial rheostat register on the ohmmeter during the amplifier check? _____ _____

4. In performing the vacuum test, what should the vacuum be at the transducer input? _____

5. What should engine speed be when making checks of the automatic temperature control units? _____

SERVICE PROCEDURE 30
To Perform the Temperature Dial Test of the General Motors' Automatic Temperature Control *

The procedure for holding the temperature dial test will be given in two parts. Part I deals with the dial test using the special testing tool, and Part II deals with the dial test using two thermometers. While test II is less efficient, it allows for the tailoring of a system to meet the individual requirements of the owner.

TOOLS

Part I - control tester; Part II - auxiliary electric fan, two thermometers, masking tape

PART I - PROCEDURE
TEMPERATURE DIAL TEST WITH TESTING TOOL

1. Insure that system is operating properly. If not, correct as outlined in Service Procedure 29. Connect tester into system.

2. Place amplifier switch in SENSOR position.

3. Place sensor switch in MID position.

4. Adjust temperature dial until tester meter reads on centerline. Temperature dial should read 75°F.

5. If temperature dial does not read 75°F., adjust as outlined in Service Procedure 31.

6. If operating properly, shut off engine, remove tester from system and reconnect car wiring harness to amplifier.

PART II - PROCEDURE
TEMPERATURE DIAL TEST WITHOUT TESTING TOOL

1. Insure that system is operating properly. If not, correct as outlined in Service Procedure 29.

2. Using masking tape, suspend a thermometer from the headliner so that the bulb hangs at breath level over the driver's seat.

3. With masking tape, suspend second thermometer over front passenger's seat.

---

* This material is used by permission of Cadillac Motor Car Division, General Motors Corporation.

5. Close all windows and doors.

6. Place temperature control lever to the AUTOMATIC position and set temperature dial to 75°F.

7. Start engine and operate at 900 r.p.m.

8. Make certain that all air conditioning outlets are open. Adjust all outlets so that none are directed toward the thermometers.

9. Operate system for 25-30 minutes for stabilization. Then record readings from the two suspended thermometers.

10. If thermometer readings vary from 75°F., adjust temperature control as outlined in Service Procedure 31.

11. If operating properly, return car to normal idle to prevent dieseling and shut off engine. Remove thermometers.

REVIEW QUESTIONS

1. Why are two thermometers used in this test? _____

_____

_____

2. What should the dial be set at for comfort? _____

3. At what speed should the engine be running for this test?

4. How long should the system be operated before checking the thermometers?

_____

5. What temperature is desired on the thermometers? _____

SERVICE PROCEDURE 31

To Adjust Temperature Dial, General Motors' Automatic Temperature Control *

The temperature dial may or may not be operating properly. This unit will be broken down into two parts: Part I covers the temperature dial operating properly, and Part II, the temperature dial operating improperly. In some cases it is necessary to change the temperature dial setting for customer satisfaction on a properly operating dial. If this is the case, the owner will indicate the temperature dial setting at which he is most comfortable.

TOOLS

Automotic temperature control tester and temperature dial adjuster

PART I - PROCEDURE

ADJUSTING TEMPERATURE DIAL FOR CUSTOMER SATISFACTION

1. Set temperature dial to the setting indicated by the owner as being most comfortable.

2. Insert temperature dial adjuster between the temperature dial and casting.

3. Turn dial to 75°F. setting.

PART II - PROCEDURE

TEMPERATURE CONTROL DIAL ADJUSTMENT

1. Connect tester to control amplifier.

2. Set manual control on tester as outlined in car manufacturer's service manual.

3. Insert dial adjusting tool between temperature dial and casting.

4. While holding temperature dial on 75°F., rotate the adjusting tool until the voltmeter on tester reads 6.5 volts.

    NOTE: Check manufacturer's service manual for correct reading for each individual car.

5. Disconnect tester and reconnect wiring harness to amplifier.

---

* Parts of this material are used by permission of Cadillac Motor Car Division and Oldsmobile Division, General Motors Corporation.

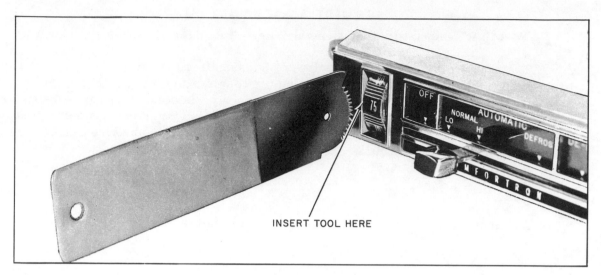

FIG. 31 – 1 ADJUSTING CONTROL DIAL

REVIEW QUESTIONS

1. When is it necessary to change the temperature dial on a unit operating satisfactorily? _____

   _____

2. What voltage should the tester read at 75°F? _____

SERVICE PROCEDURE 32
To Bench Test the Thermostatic Expansion Valve for Efficiency

This test must be made with the expansion valve out of the unit. Make sure that the strainer screen at the inlet of the valve is clean. A partially clogged screen will give incorrect readings.

TOOLS

Manifold and gage set, can tap, 1/4″ female flare coupler, 1/4″ male flare tee, 1/4″ test cap (drilled to .026″), 1/2″F × 1/4″M adapter, 3/8″F × 1/4″M adapter

MATERIAL

Refrigerant 12, pan of ice water and ice, salt, pan of hot water at 125°F.

NOTE

A constant source of pressure at 70 p.s.i.g. or higher is required to perform this test. This pressure may be attained from any suitable material such as dry air, carbon dioxide, dry nitrogen, Refrigerant 22, or Refrigerant 12. A cylinder of high-pressure material such as nitrogen must have a suitable pressure regulating valve.

PROCEDURE

PREPARE THERMOSTATIC EXPANSION VALVE FOR TEST

1. Close high- and low-side manifold hand valves.

2. Remove low-side service hose at manifold.

3. Install 1/4″ female flare coupler to low-side manifold.

4. Install 1/4″ male flare tee to flare coupler at low side.

5. Reinstall low-side manifold hose to 1/4″ flare tee.

6. Install 1/4″ test cap (drilled to .026) to 1/4″ tee.

7. Install 3/8″F × 1/4″M fitting to inlet of expansion valve.

8. Install 1/2″F × 1/4″M fitting to outlet of expansion valve.

9. Fasten low-side manifold hose to expansion valve outlet.

10. Fasten high-side manifold hose to expansion valve inlet.

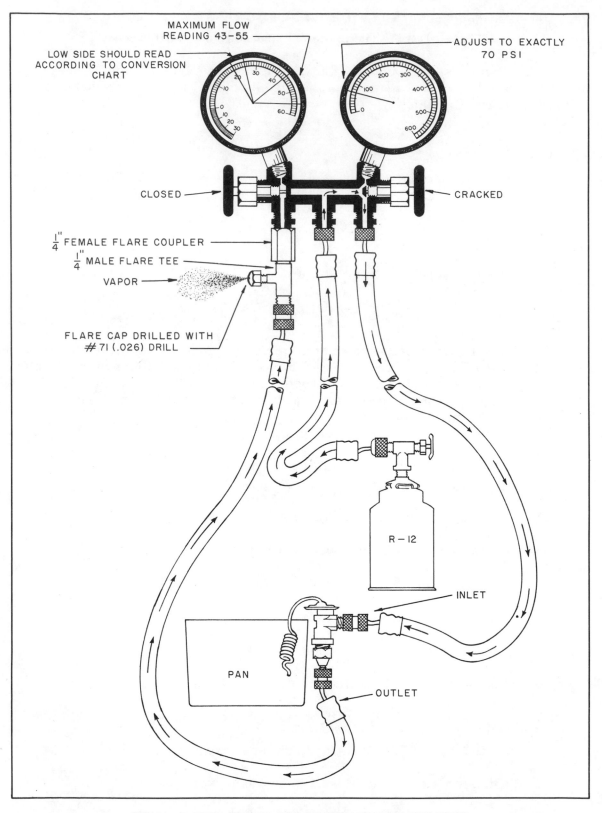

FIG. 32-1 TEST HOOKUP FOR INTERNALLY-EQUALIZED VALVE

11. Install can tap on can of R 12.

12. Pierce can and back piercing tap out to release pressure to manifold.

13. Fill an insulated container with cracked ice. Add water. Use a thermometer to obtain exactly 32°F. If necessary, add salt and stir mixture.

14. Heat water in a second container until it reaches 125°F.

NOTE: The diagram for the thermostatic expansion valve test hookup is for an internally-equalized thermostatic expansion valve only. If an externally-equalized expansion valve is to be tested, another fitting must be added BE-FORE the test cap. The external equalizer is connected to this fitting.

The following tools have to be added to check the externally-equalized expansion valve: 1 - 1/4″ female flare coupler and 1 - 1/4″ male flare tee.

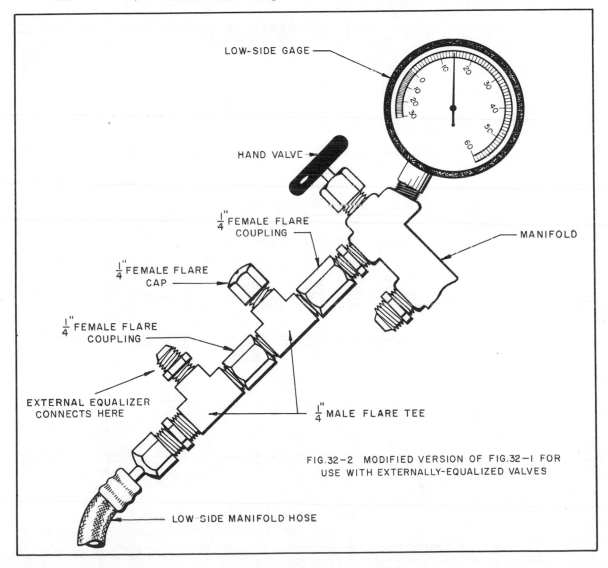

LOW-SIDE GAGE

HAND VALVE

$\frac{1}{4}$″ FEMALE FLARE COUPLING

$\frac{1}{4}$″ FEMALE FLARE CAP

MANIFOLD

$\frac{1}{4}$″ FEMALE FLARE COUPLING

EXTERNAL EQUALIZER CONNECTS HERE

$\frac{1}{4}$″ MALE FLARE TEE

FIG. 32-2 MODIFIED VERSION OF FIG. 32-1 FOR USE WITH EXTERNALLY-EQUALIZED VALVES

LOW-SIDE MANIFOLD HOSE

TEST EXPANSION VALVE FOR MAXIMUM FLOW

1. Invert refrigerant container.

2. Place remote bulb of thermostatic expansion valve into container of water heated to 125°F.

3. Open high-side gage manifold hand valve and adjust to exactly 70 p.s.i.g.

4. Read low-side gage. Maximum flow test should be 43-55 p.s.i.g. Readings over 55 p.s.i.g. indicate a flooding valve. A reading under 43 p.s.i.g. indicates a starving valve.

TEST EXPANSION VALVE FOR MINIMUM FLOW

1. Place thermal bulb into container of 32°F. liquid.

2. Open high-side gage manifold hand valve and adjust to exactly 70 p.s.i.g.

3. Read low-side gage. Refer to conversion chart for proper low-side reading. The low-side gage must be within the limits as specified in the conversion chart if the valve is to pass the minimum flow test.

NOTE: On the conversion chart, the valve superheat settings corresponding to valve outlet pressure readings are for Refrigerant 12 expansion valves only. Another set of pressure readings for the various superheats would be required for systems charged with a refrigerant other than R 12.

Conversion Chart	
Superheat Setting °F.	Pounds per Square Inch Gage Refrigerant 12 Pressure
5	23 lb. to 26 lb.
6	22 1/4 lb. to 25 1/4 lb.
7	21 1/2 lb. to 24 1/2 lb.
8	21 lb. to 24 lb.
9	20 1/4 lb. to 23 1/4 lb.
10	19 1/2 lb. to 22 1/2 lb.
11	19 lb. to 22 lb.
12	18 lb. to 21 lb.
13	17 1/2 lb. to 20 1/2 lb.
14	17 lb. to 20 lb.
15	15 1/2 lb. to 18 1/2 lb.

CLEANING THE EXPANSION VALVE

NOTE: If the expansion valve fails to pass either or both of the tests on page **236**, cleaning may be attempted. Otherwise, a new valve must be used. Though each valve will be different in structure, the following may be used as a guide:

1. Remove the diaphragm, capillary and remote bulb assembly.

2. Remove the superheat adjusting screw: count the number of turns required to remove the screw. This will aid in relocating the proper position when reassembling the valve.

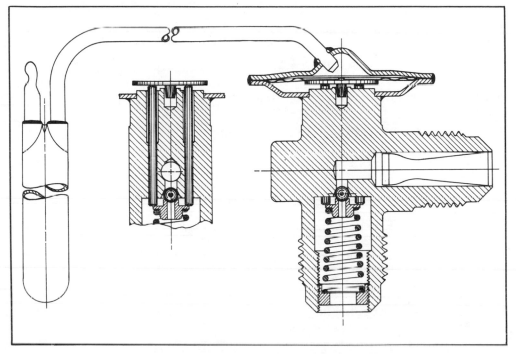

FIG. 32-3 CROSS SECTION OF THE THERMOSTATIC EXPANSION VALVE

3. Remove superheat spring and valve seat. Remove the valve and push rod(s).

4. Clean the valve and all parts in CLEAN mineral spirits. Let drain and blow dry.

5. Reverse the above order and reassemble the valve.

6. Check the expansion valve for maximum and minimum flow as outlined in this unit.

7. If valve fails to pass maximum/minimum flow test, attempt to adjust the superheat spring setting.

8. If valve fails test repeatedly a new one must be installed. No further repair is possible.

REVIEW QUESTIONS

1. What pressure source must be available for this test? _____
   _____

2. Why do we hold a minimum flow test? _____
   _____

3. Why do we hold a maximum flow test? _____
   _____

4. What should the minimum flow be? _____

5. What should the maximum flow be? _____

6. May all expansion valves be cleaned? _____

7. Name two types of thermostatic expansion valves.

   a. _____   b. _____

8. What should be used as a cleaning agent? _____

9. What size test cap is used in this test? _____

10. How may we test an externally-equalized valve? _____
    _____

11. In the diagram below, name as many of the component parts of the thermo-
    static expansion valve as you can.

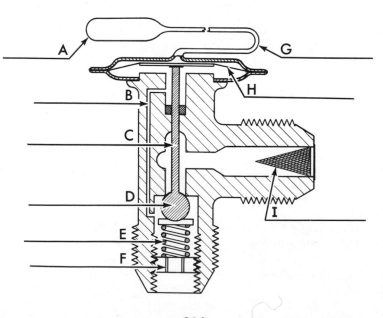

SERVICE PROCEDURE 33
To Test the Manifold Gage and Thermometer

The various tests of the refrigeration system depend on accurate pressure and temperature readings. If the gages are even a few pounds per square inch off, you may be replacing parts such as expansion valves and suction regulators when there is nothing wrong with them.

With an inaccurate thermometer, thermostats cannot be set properly. You will have units freezing up or not getting cold enough.

Be sure that your gages and thermometer are accurate by testing them regularly. No special equipment is needed to test them ..... just a can of refrigerant and a place to leave them overnight where the temperature is stable.

There is a definite temperature-pressure relationship for liquid refrigerant. Connect the gage set to be tested to a can of Refrigerant 12; a full can should be used. Tape a thermometer to the side of the can so that sensing element is below the liquid level in the can.

Put this rig where the temperature will be fairly constant overnight, such as in a corner or under a bench. The next morning read the thermometer and pressure gages. Use the temperature-pressure chart to see if the gages and/or thermometer are correct.

It should be pointed out that if the low-side gage is to be checked, the low-side hose must be fastened to the can tap. Conversely, if the high-side hose is connected to the can tap, the high-side gage may be checked.

If the manifold set has a hose hanger, a provision for hanging up the hose ends, both gages may be checked. To do this:

TEMPERATURE-PRESSURE RELATIONSHIP CHART (REFRIGERANT)

Temp. F.	Press. PSI	Temp. F.	Press. PSI	Temp. F.	Press. PSI
65	63.7	80	84.0	95	108.1
66	64.9	81	85.5	96	109.8
67	66.2	82	87.0	97	111.5
68	67.5	83	88.5	98	113.3
69	68.8	84	90.1	99	115.1
70	70.1	85	91.7	100	116.9
71	71.4	86	93.2	101	118.8
72	72.8	87	94.8	102	120.6
73	74.2	88	96.4	103	122.4
74	75.5	89	98.0	104	124.3
75	76.9	90	99.6	105	126.2
76	78.3	91	101.3	106	128.1
77	79.2	92	103.0	107	130.0
78	81.1	93	104.6	108	132.1
79	82.5	94	106.3	109	135.1

1. Connect the center hose to the can tap.

2. Crack the can tap.

3. Hang the high- and low-side manifold hoses up on the hose hangers.

4. Open high- and low-side manifold hand valves.

5. Check entire rig for leaks. If no leaks, rig may be left overnight to determine if gages and thermometer are correct.

REVIEW QUESTIONS

Indicate whether each of the following statements is true or false by writing T (true) or F (false) in the space provided (questions 1, 2 and 3).

_____   1. The thermometer and gage may be checked one against the other to determine accuracy.

_____   2. A defective gage may cause replacement of parts that are not bad.

_____   3. A defective thermometer may cause thermostat adjustment that will result in evaporator freeze-up.

4. Refer to the temperature-pressure chart on page 219. If the thermometer reads 78°F., the low-side gage reads 81 p.s.i.g., and the high side reads 84 p.s.i.g., what would you determine the trouble to be?

_____

_____

_____

5. Again, refer to the chart. Both high- and low-side gages read 77 p.s.i.g.; the thermometer reads 80°F. What would you determine the trouble to be?

_____

_____

_____

6. If the thermometer reads 74°F., what should the low-side manifold gage read if correct? _____

    What should the high-side manifold gage read if correct? _____

7. Explain your answer to question two above. _____

_____

_____

_____

8. Explain your answer to question three above. _____

_____

_____

_____

_____

SERVICE PROCEDURE 34
To Splice Refrigerant Hose and Insert Fittings

This procedure will deal with the proper handling of rubber refrigeration hose and insert fittings. In many cases a break in the hose, caused by rubbing or chafing against another part, may be successfully repaired using an insert splicer.

TOOLS

Razor blades, screwdriver

MATERIAL

Hose, fittings, refrigeration oil as may be required, clamp

PROCEDURE

PREPARE HOSE

1. Locate and mark proper length and location of hose.

2. With a razor blade, cut hose.
   NOTE: A single edge razor blade should be used. Single edge industrial blades are available at all cleaning supply houses.

3. Apply clean refrigeration oil to the inside of the hose to be used. Seal off other hose.

INSERT FITTING

1. Insure that fitting is free of all nicks and burrs.

2. Coat fitting liberally with clean refrigeration oil.

3. Slip insert fitting inside refrigeration hose in one constant, deliberate motion.

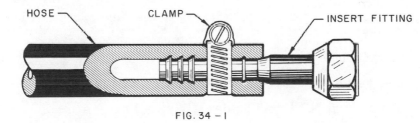

HOSE — CLAMP — — INSERT FITTING

FIG. 34 - 1

4. Affix hose clamp and tighten to approximately thirty foot-pounds.
   NOTE: Hose clamp should go on the approximate location of the fitting barb closest to the nut end of the fitting.

REVIEW QUESTIONS

1. How may an insert fitting be used to repair a damaged hose? _____

   _____

2. What torque should the hose clamp be tightened to? _____

3. What lubricant is used to insure easier installation of fitting into the hose?

_____

SERVICE PROCEDURE 35
To Join Flare Adapters to Copper Tubing

Flare adapters may be fastened to copper tubing with solder in automotive air conditioning applications. While it is generally advised to use silver solder for a leak-proof joint with maximum strength, a 50-50 or 95-5 solder may be used for low temperature applications. 50-50 solder may be used for temperatures to 250°F; however 95-5 must be used when temperatures to 350°F. are anticipated.

50-50 solder denotes a combination of 50% lead and 50% tin. An alloy of 95% tin and 5% antimony is known as 95-5 solder. 50-50 solder melts at 415°F., while 95-5 solder melts at 460°F. Silver solder, containing from 35-45% silver melts at 1120°F. Many of the same steps and procedures hold true for silver solder as for soft solder, but this procedure is not recommended for the unskilled. The following procedure will apply to soft solder. Procedures for silver soldering may be found in the book Basic Oxyacetylene Welding, published by Delmar Publishers, Albany, N.Y.

TOOLS

Portable torch with pressure regulator, tube cutter or hacksaw, file or inside-outside reamer

MATERIAL

Tube and fittings as may be required, solder and torch propellant, flux

PROCEDURE

PREPARE TUBE

1. Locate and mark the proper length of the tube and cut it with a tube cutter or hacksaw.

2. Insert tube in a vise or holding fixture. Dress off the end with file or reamer.

3. Insure that all surfaces to be joined are free of all dirt, oil or oxides.

4. Heat tube and "tin" with solder. Wipe off excess.

PREPARE FITTING

1. Insert fitting in a vise or holding fixture and insure that joining surfaces are free of all foreign material or oxides.

2. Heat fitting and "tin" inside with solder. Wipe out or shake out excess.

JOIN FITTING AND TUBE

1. Apply heat to fitting and tube, both pieces tinned.

2. As soon as hot enough, both pieces will slide into place. Apply heat for a few more minutes, then remove heat.

3. Apply solder. It should be drawn into the fitting by capillary action.

4. Reapply heat and more solder if not enough is pulled in during first application.

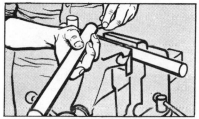

FIG. 35 –I DRESS OFF CUT END
WITH FILE OR REAMER

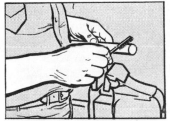

FIG. 35 –2 WIPE OFF EXCESS
SOLDER AFTER TINNING

FIG. 35 –3 MAKE SURE FITTING
IS FREE OF FOREIGN MATERIAL

FIG. 35 –4 AFTER TINNING
WIPE OUT EXCESS

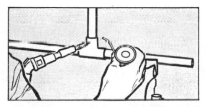

FIG. 35 –5 SOLDER IS DRAWN IN BY
CAPILLARY ACTION

REVIEW QUESTIONS

1. What is the composition of 50-50 solder? _____

   _____

2. What is the composition of 95-5 solder? _____

   _____

3. What is the melting point of 50-50 solder? _____

4. What do we mean by capillary action? _____

   _____

   _____

SERVICE PROCEDURE 36
To Affix Flare Nuts to Copper Tubing

The following unit will deal with the proper preparation of copper tubing to affix a flare nut, either a single- or a double-flare type. This unit will be broken into two parts: Part I dealing with the single-flare nut and Part II with the double-flare nut.

TOOLS

Tube cutter or hacksaw, file or inside-outside reamer, flaring tool

MATERIAL

Copper or aluminum tube and nut(s) as may be required

PART I - PROCEDURE

PREPARE TUBE

1. Locate and mark proper length and location of tube.

2. With a hacksaw or tube cutter, cut the tube.

3. Slide nut onto the tube and place tube in the flaring block of the flaring tool.

4. Insure that the proper length of tube is sticking out on top of the tool. Follow recommendations of the manufacturer; do not guess.

5. Dress off end of the tube with a file. Clean inside of tube of all burrs.

FLARE TUBE

1. Install the cone flare tool and tighten the cone down into the open tube end.

   NOTE: Do not tighten full force. Overtightening will thin the wall of the flare and weaken it.

2. Remove cone flare tool and inspect flare. It should be even and free from cracks.

   NOTE: If flare is uneven, split or cracked, make no attempt to correct it. Cut off the defective flare and repeat procedures outlined.

PART II - PROCEDURE

PREPARE TUBE

1. Locate and mark proper length of tube.

2. Cut the tube with a hacksaw or tube cutter.

3. Slide a nut onto the tube and place it in the flaring block of the flaring tool.

4. Select the proper double flare adapter, and, using the adapter as a guide, insure that the proper amount of tube is sticking out of the flaring block.

5. Dress off the end of the tube with a file, and clean the inside of the tube of all burrs.

FLARE TUBE

1. Install the adapter inside the tube.

2. Install the cone flare tool and tighten the cone down against the adapter.

   NOTE: Do not tighten full force. Tighten only until the tubing is bell shaped.

3. Loosen cone and remove adapter.

4. Tighten cone down into the tube until a double flare is formed.

   NOTE: Do not tighten full force. Overtightening will thin the wall of the flare and weaken it.

5. Remove cone. Remove tube from fixture and inspect for cracks.

   NOTE: If flare is not even and free of cracks, make no attempt to correct it. Cut off the defective flare and repeat the procedures as outlined.

REVIEW QUESTIONS

Indicate whether each of the following statements is true or false by writing T (true) or F (false) in the space provided.

_____   1. The cone must be drawn down into the tube tightly when forming a single flare.

_____   2. If a flare is uneven it may be dressed off with a file.

_____   3. A double flare is more desirable than a single flare.

_____   4. When making the fold of the double flare, exert pressure on the cone to insure a tight fold in the tube.

SERVICE PROCEDURE 37
To Gage Ball Shoes

When the internal assembly of the General Motors' six-cylinder compressor is rebuilt, it is necessary to discard or lay aside six ball shoes. If the shoes are not damaged, they may be gaged for reuse.

TOOLS

Micrometer

PROCEDURE

GAGE BALL SHOES

1. Check a ball with the micrometer. The ball should read .625″.

2. Slip a ball shoe between the ball and anvil of the micrometer.

3. Check micrometer reading.

4. Subtract ball reading, as obtained in step 1. Answer is ball shoe thickness. Index and lay aside for future use.

BALL SHOE IDENTIFICATION

a. ZERO ball shoes should be .017″ and are available under General Motors' part number 6557000.

b. Ball shoes found to be .017″ as outlined above may be identified as 6557000R, to indicate regaged.

c. Ball shoes are available in half thousands through .022″ as follows:

PART NUMBER	THICKNESS
6556175	.0175
6556180	.018
6556185	.0185
6556190	.019
6556195	.0195
6556200	.020
6556205	.0205
6556210	.021
6556215	.0215
6556220	.022

d. It is easy to see by the above chart that the last three numbers in the part number indicate the shoe thickness in thousandths.

REVIEW QUESTIONS

GAGING BALL SHOES

1. What should the ball of the internal assembly measure? _____

2. What is the shoe thickness of a reading of .6435"? _____

3. What is the shoe thickness of a reading of .645"? _____

4. What should the reading be if the shoe thickness is .018"? _____

5. What should the reading be if the shoe thickness is .0195"? _____

SERVICE PROCEDURE 38
To Install Mount and Drive Assemblies

This particular mount and drive assembly is designed for some models of Chrysler product automobiles, slant six-cylinder, with or without power steering.

No attempt should be made to install this mount and drive kit on another year or model car. Each kit is designed for a particular engine. Installation instructions are included with each kit and must be followed very closely to avoid costly mistakes. Measure all bolts to insure that they are as specified. Check all hoses to insure that they do not rub moving parts, such as pulleys and accelerator linkage.

The following are installation procedures for a typical mount and drive package.

TOOLS

Complete set of mechanic's hand tools, pullers, screwdrivers, hose clamp pliers, etc.

MATERIAL

Mount and drive kit as indicated, permatex, any belts or hoses that may be defective

PROCEDURE

1. Drain the radiator, then disconnect the water hoses and transmission fluid cooling lines. Unfasten the radiator mounting screws, then carefully remove the radiator from engine compartment.

2. Remove the engine fan, fan spacer, and water pump pulley. Discard the original fan spacer.

3. Always clean the face of the crankshaft pulley thoroughly before installing the drive pulley. Remove the bolts retaining the crankshaft pulley, and if the car is equipped with power steering, remove and discard the power steering pulley only. Install the drive pulley, using three 5/16" × 1"NC bolts with lockwashers, and one 3/4" × 2 1/4" NF bolt with lockwasher.

4. IMPORTANT. The following fuel filter line modification is optional on 1961 and 1962 models, but required on 1963 models. Unfasten the fuel filter line clamp from the water pump housing, then remove the original fuel line tubing, with union fitting, located between the carburetor and filter bowl. Cut the tubing so that the original union fitting can be removed and reinstalled against the flanged end of the 5/16" × 6 1/2" copper fuel line. Fasten the new tubing with union to the carburetor, then bend the long fuel line, with filter bowl, up and over the valve cover (as shown on engine schematic). Bend the new copper line to suit, then insert tubing into the filter bowl hose and tighten securely, reusing original clamp.

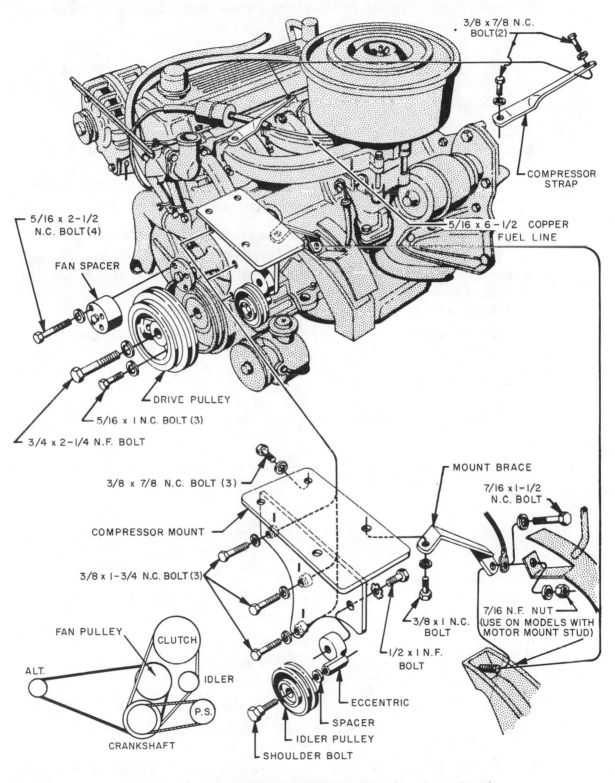

3/8 x 7/8 N.C. BOLT(2)

COMPRESSOR STRAP

5/16 x 6 – 1/2 COPPER FUEL LINE

5/16 x 2-1/2 N.C. BOLT(4)

FAN SPACER

DRIVE PULLEY

5/16 x 1 N.C. BOLT (3)

3/4 x 2-1/4 N.F. BOLT

3/8 x 7/8 N.C. BOLT (3)

COMPRESSOR MOUNT

3/8 x 1-3/4 N.C. BOLT(3)

MOUNT BRACE

7/16 x 1-1/2 N.C. BOLT

3/8 x 1 N.C. BOLT

7/16 N.F. NUT (USE ON MODELS WITH MOTOR MOUNT STUD)

1/2 x 1 N.F. BOLT

FAN PULLEY

CLUTCH

ALT.

IDLER

P.S.

CRANKSHAFT

ECCENTRIC

SPACER

IDLER PULLEY

SHOULDER BOLT

FIG. 38 – 1 TYPICAL MOUNT AND DRIVE ASSEMBLY (Courtesy of Mapco)

5. Remove the bolts from the engine as indicated by the schematic. Holding the mount in approximate position to the engine will help identify the proper bolts to be removed.

6. Loosely install the compressor mount to the engine, using three 3/8" × 1 3/4" NC bolts with lockwashers through the three front vertical mounting holes and welded spacers into the water pump housing.

7. Install the clutch coil and clutch to the compressor. Loosely install the compressor and clutch to the mount, using three 3/8" × 7/8" NC bolts with lockwashers through two forward and left rear top plate holes, into compressor.

8. Loosely install the compressor strap and mount brace as follows:

   a. -4 Compressor Strap- Insert 3/8" × 7/8" NC bolt with lockwasher through the flat strap end, into the engine head. A second 3/8" × 7/8" NC bolt with lockwasher is inserted through the opposite strap end into the compressor side.

   b. -5 Mount Brace- Insert a 7/16" × 1 1/2" NC bolt with lockwasher through the battery ground wire (power steering models only), the welder ear of brace and the motor mount bracket, into the engine block. On models equipped with motor mount stud, fasten the brace with a 7/16" NF nut and lockwasher. Now insert a 3/8" × 1" NC bolt with lockwasher through the upper brace and remaining top plate hole, into the compressor.

9. All assembly bolts and/or nuts should now be uniformly tightened so as not to cause strain or misalignment.

10. Install the eccentric and idler assembly to the front vertical, using a 1/2" × 1" NF bolt with starwasher.

11. Insert a 1 5/8" fan spacer between the original fan and pulley, then install this assembly, using four 5/16" × 2 1/2" NC bolts. Tighten securely.

12. Thread all drive belts as shown on the schematic. Adjust and tighten each belt as required for proper belt tension.

13. Replace the radiator, connect the water hoses and transmission fluid cooling lines. Add coolant.

    NOTE: Both the mount and drive pulley must be furnished by the same company to guarantee alignment.

REVIEW QUESTIONS

1. List three precautions to observe when installing a mount and drive assembly.

   a. _____

   _____

   b. _____

   _____

   c. _____

   _____

2. Are mount and drive assemblies interchangeable? _____

3. Why is it necessary to remove the radiator? _____

   _____

   _____

4. Why should the drive pulley and compressor mount be furnished by the same company? _____

   _____

5. What might be the results if the idler pulley were not in line with the compressor clutch and drive pulley? _____

   _____

6. What, in your opinion, is the purpose of the fan spacer? _____

   _____

   _____

   _____

7. Explain your answer for question 2 above. _____

   _____

   _____

   _____

8. How is the compressor driven off the engine? _____

   _____

   _____

   _____

SERVICE PROCEDURE 39
To Rebuild the York Compressor, All Models *

The following outline may be followed when it is necessary to completely tear down a York compressor for repair; some models will vary slightly from this procedure.

All York compressors are similar in appearance but must be identified as to the year and model; this is important when it is necessary to replace parts. Refer to York Compressor Identification in the Reference Section.

The procedure for rebuilding the York compressor will be given in five steps, as follows:

1. Shaft seal assembly servicing

2. Head and valve plate servicing

3. Pistons and connecting rods

4. Crankshaft and main bearings

5. Oil pump assembly

TOOLS

Set of quarter-inch drive sockets to 9/16", hard rubber hammer, small screwdriver, needle nose pliers, snap ring pliers, single edge razor blades, piston ring compressor, Allen wrench set, torque wrench (ft.-lb. and in-lb.)

MATERIAL

Ample supply of clean refrigeration oil, gasket set, seal assembly, and any other part(s) that may be found to be defective.

OIL CHARGE

Positions (See Note)		Oil Level					
		Minimum		Normal Running		Initial Charge	
Mounts	Range	Dip Stick Depth	Fractional Pints	Dip Stick Depth	Fractional Pints	Dip Stick Depth	Fractional Pints
Vertical	90° - 70°	7/8"	3/8 Pt.	1-1/4"	1/2 Pt.	1-3/8"	5/8 Pt.
Inclined	50° - 15°	1-5/8"	1/3 Pt.	2"	3/8 Pt.	2-3/4"	5/8 Pt.
Horizontal	10° - 0°	3/4"	1/4 Pt.	7/8"	1/4 Pt.	1-5/8"	5/8 Pt.

Type Oil - "Suniso" #5, "Texaco" Capella E, or equivalent.

NOTE: Compressor may be inclined to any angle between 90 degrees and 0 degrees but only toward the side for which it was designed (right or left).

---

*   The following text and diagrams, in part, are reprinted with permission from the York Corporation.

252

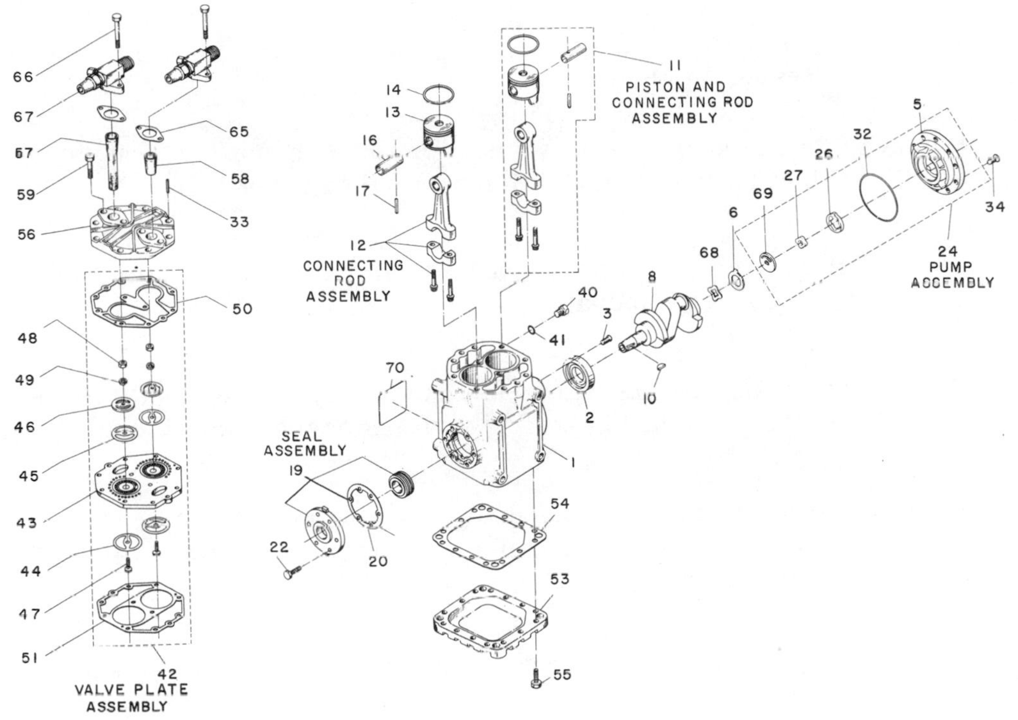

Key No.	Description	Key No.	Description
1	Crankcase Body	43	Valve Plate, Bare
2	Bearing, Ball	44	Valve, Suction
3	Screw	45	Valve, Discharge
4	Housing Assembly (Rear Bearing)	46	Retainer, Discharge Valve
6	Washer, Thrust	47	Stud, Valve Plate
8	Crankshaft	48	Nut, Stud
10	Key, Woodruff	49	Washer, Stud
11	Piston and Connecting Rod Assembly	50	Gasket, Plate to Head
12	Connecting Rod Assembly	51	Gasket, Plate to Body
13	Piston	53	Plate, Base
14	Ring, Piston	54	Gasket, Base Plate
16	Wrist Pin	55	Cap Screw
17	Retainer, Wrist Pin	56	Head, Cylinder
19	Seal Assembly	57	Tube, Suction, With Screen
20	Gasket, Seal Retainer Plate	58	Tube, Suction or Discharge
22	Screw, Cap	59	Screw, Cap, Head to Body
24	Oil Pump Assembly	60	Gasket Kit, Not Shown
26	Gear, Outer, Oil Pump	65	Gasket, Service Stop Valve
27	Gear, Inner, Oil Pump	66	Screw, Cap
32	"O" Ring, Pump Cover	67	Valve, Service Stop
34	Screw	68	Washer, Wave
40	Plug, Oil Filler	69	Washer, Oil Pump
41	"O" Ring, Oil Filler Plug	70	Name Plate
42	Valve Plate Assembly, Complete		

FIG. 39-1   EXPLODED VIEW   TYPICAL YORK COMPRESSORS, MODELS A206, A209, AND A210

PROCEDURE

SHAFT SEAL ASSEMBLY SERVICING

Parts required: Seal assembly kit

This kit includes the front seal plate, seal nose, spring assembly, and gasket O-ring set for front seal plate.

1. Remove the clutch and Woodruff key from the compressor crankshaft. Use a 5/8″ NC bolt to remove the clutch to avoid damage.

2. Remove the clutch coil if seal mounted. If boss mounted, the seal may be serviced without its removal.

3. Remove the seal plate capscrews and gently pry the seal plate loose, being careful not to scratch the flat sealing surfaces or the polished shaft surfaces.

4. Remove the shaft seal from the shaft by prying behind the drive ring which is that portion of the seal assembly farthest back on the shaft. Take care not to scratch the crankshaft.

5. Clean all parts and surfaces of all foreign material and gasket or O-ring material.

6. Place new seal assembly and gaskets in clean refrigeration oil.

7. Inspect all mounting surfaces for nicks and burrs. Coat all surfaces with clean refrigeration oil.

8. Place the seal plate gasket(s) or O-ring in position on the seal housing face (it will be necessary to insert the O-ring into the compressor crankcase).

9. Push the seal assembly, less the carbon ring if it is free, over the end of the crankshaft with the carbon ring retainer facing out. Now place the carbon ring into the seal assembly with the polished surface facing outward. The indentations in the outside edge of the carbon ring must engage the tangs in the retainer. Install seal plate.

10. Insert the capscrews fingertight. Make sure that there is equal clearance between the crankshaft and seal plate.

11. Tighten all capscrews in a sequence so that capscrews diagonally opposite each other are evenly drawn to a torque of 13-17 foot-pounds.

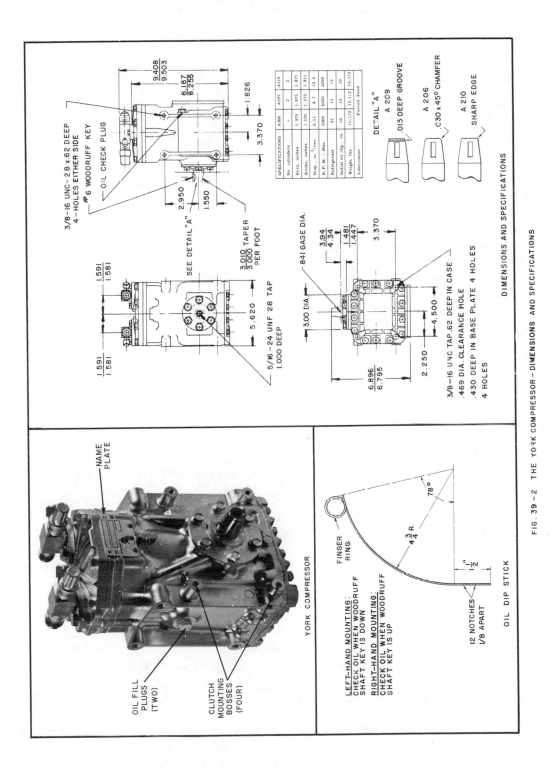

FIG. 39 - 2   THE YORK COMPRESSOR — DIMENSIONS AND SPECIFICATIONS

HEAD AND VALVE PLATE SERVICING

Parts required: Valve plate kit

This kit includes the valve plate, discharge valves, suction valves, valve retainer parts, valve plate and cylinder head gasket, and service valve gaskets.

1. Remove the capscrews from the flanged-type service valves. Note that these four capscrews are longer than the remaining head capscrews. If the valves are of the Rotolock type, remove by loosening the hex nuts which are a part of the Rotolock valve assembly.

2. Remove the remaining capscrews and washers in the head and remove the valve plate and head from the cylinder by prying or tapping under the ears which extend from the valve plate. The head is made of aluminum. Take care not to damage it.

3. Remove all foreign material and gaskets from the head and compressor crankcase. Take care not to mar or scratch any mating surfaces.

4. Do not disassemble valves. Reed valves and valve plate come as an assembly and are not serviced separately.

5. Apply a thin coat of refrigeration oil on all gaskets and surfaces.

6. Place a valve plate gasket over the compressor crankcase so the dowel pins go through the dowel pin holes in the gasket.

7. Place the valve plate assembly in position over the gasket and make sure that the discharge valves face up to avoid piston damage (the smaller of the two reeds is the discharge valve). Position over the dowel pins.

8. Place the head gasket over the valve plate so that the dowel pins pass through the holes provided in the gasket.

9. Place the head on the cylinder head gasket so the dowel pins line up with the holes in the head.

10. Insert all capscrews through head, valve plate, and gaskets. Tighten finger-tight.

11. Insert discharge tube and suction screen through the head and push into place.

12. Lay service valve gaskets into place and install service valves on the proper side. Insert capscrews holding service valves in place and tighten fingertight.

13. Tighten the head and service valve capscrews to a torque of 14-18 ft.-lbs.

14. Tighten inside service valve capscrews first, then outside service valve capscrews. Then tighten the remaining head capscrews in a sequence so that capscrews diagonally opposite each other are evenly drawn to the above specified torque. Retorque after two hours.

PISTONS AND CONNECTING RODS

Parts required: Piston and connecting rod assembly, gasket kit and oil charge. Piston and connecting rod assembly includes the rod, cap, screws, piston, piston rings, piston pins and pin retainers

1. Remove head and valve plate assembly (procedure on page 236, steps 1 and 2).

2. Drain oil and remove baseplate.

3. Remove damaged piston assembly by removing capscrews holding rod cap in place.

4. If the connecting rod(s) are to be reused, before removing the connecting rod bolts, match and mark the rod, cap and crankshaft throw to insure proper reinstallation.

5. Clean all gasket and foreign material from the crankcase, baseplate, valve plate and head.

6. Insert the new piston(s) assembly through the top of the compressor.

   NOTE: The wrist pin roll pin must be positioned toward the center of the compressor. If positioned toward the outside, the roll pin may make contact with the crankshaft when the piston is at the bottom of its stroke.

7. Install the connecting rod caps. Install the connecting rod cap bolts and torque to 90-100 in.-lbs.

8. Replace the bottom plate and gasket. Replace the capscrews fingertight, then tighten in a sequence so that capscrews diagonally opposite each other are evenly drawn to a torque of 11-14 ft.-lbs.

9. Replace the valve plate and head assembly. Follow procedure as outlined in Head and Valve Plate Servicing, steps 5 through 14.

10. Replace oil as necessary to bring it to the proper level.

CRANKSHAFT AND MAIN BEARINGS

Parts required: Crankshaft and/or main bearing or rear bearing as required, gasket kit and oil charge, seal assembly kit

The rear main bearing is a bronze-sleeve bearing with a steel outer shell which is a press fit in the bearing cavity in the rear bearing cover plate. The rear bearing is replaced only with the cover plate as an assembly.

The seal end main bearing is a ball-type bearing which is mounted in the bearing recess machined in the inside wall of the crankcase. The bearing is a shrink fit, being inserted in the recess after the crankcase is oven-heated to 150-300°F.

The inner race of the bearing is a press fit on the crankshaft.

When replacing the crankshaft, the seal end main bearing should also be replaced since the existing bearing may be damaged in dismantling.

1. Remove crankcase base and drain oil.

2. Mark the rod caps, rods, and crankshaft throw to insure proper reinstallation. Remove the rod caps.

3. Remove the compressor shaft seal and the rear bearing housing.

4. Remove the head and valve plate assembly. Remove the piston and rod assemblies.

5. Wash in a clean solvent to remove all foreign matter from the crankcase. Blow dry.

6. Oven-heat the crankshaft-crankcase assembly to 300°F. Heat the complete assembly. Localized heating may crack the assembly.

7. At 300°F., the crankshaft and ball bearing assembly can be removed from the crankcase with little applied pressure.

8. If the crankshaft is to be reused, remove the bearing.

9. Press new bearing on crankshaft by exerting pressure on inner race only.

10. Oven-heat the crankcase to 300°F. Slide crankshaft and bearing assembly into place. Using the opening in the bottom of the crankcase as a point of entry, place the bearing in the recess. If necessary, apply force to the outer race to be sure that it is seated in the bottom of the recess.

NOTE: On one side of the bearing, faces of the inner and outer races are flush. On the other side, the face of the inner race is set in since the races are not of the same width. Refer to the sketch for the proper positioning in the crankcase. Allow the crankcase to cool, and insert crankshaft through the rear bearing cover plate opening and guide the flywheel end through the inner race of the ball bearing.

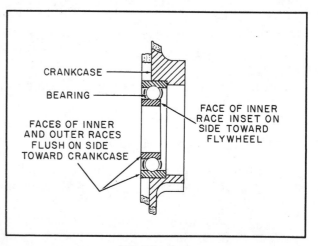

FIG. 39-3

11. Position the crankcase in such a manner that it is completely supported on the inner race of the bearing. Then press the shaft into place until the cheek of the shaft contacts the inner bearing race.

12. Replace the rear bearing O-ring and assembly. Torque to **7-10 ft.-lbs.**

13. Replace pistons in proper position, as removed, and replace rod caps. Torque to **90-100 in.-lbs.**

14. Replace seal, baseplate, valve plate, and head assembly as outlined previously.

OIL PUMP ASSEMBLY

Parts required: Oil pump assembly

This assembly includes housing, gears, spacers, washers, and O-ring.

1. Place the compressor so that it is resting on the baseplate and the front of the crankshaft. Place the wave washer in the crankshaft cavity, then place the thrust washer on top of the wave washer; the tang of the thrust washer must be in the drive slot of the crankshaft.

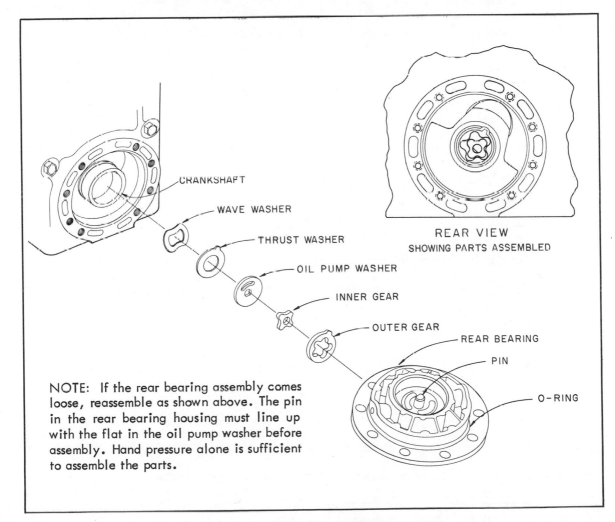

REAR VIEW
SHOWING PARTS ASSEMBLED

NOTE: If the rear bearing assembly comes loose, reassemble as shown above. The pin in the rear bearing housing must line up with the flat in the oil pump washer before assembly. Hand pressure alone is sufficient to assemble the parts.

FIG 39-4 OIL PUMP ASSEMBLY

2. Place the oil pump washer into the cavity with the kidney-shaped slot toward the top head of the compressor and the half circle slot off center toward the left side.

3. Place the outer gear into the cavity with the tang on this gear in the drive slot of the crankshaft. Next, place the inner gear within the outer gear in a position where the hole through the gear is in alignment with the half circle of the oil pump washer.

4. Insert the rear bearing housing with the pin in the housing lined up with the hole in the inner gear.

5. With the bearing housing partially entered, rotate it slightly right and left until you feel the parts slide into position.

6. Now insert completely the rear bearing housing and rotate slowly to the proper position. Be careful not to damage the O-ring.

7. Insert screws and tighten to 7-10 ft.-lbs.

REVIEW QUESTIONS

1. How is the rear bearing replaced? _____

_____

2. How do you remove the shrink fit front bearing from the crankcase?

_____

_____

3. Name five parts of the oil pump.

    a. _____   d. _____

    b. _____   e. _____

    c. _____

4. What parts must be removed in order to replace a piston assembly?

_____

_____

_____

5. What parts is it necessary to remove to replace the oil pump?

_____

_____

SERVICE PROCEDURE 40

To Rebuild the Tecumseh Compressor, Models HA-850 and HA-1000 *

The following procedure may be followed when it is necessary to tear down a Tecumseh compressor for overhaul. This procedure will be given in eight steps, as follows:

1. Valve Plate Replacement
2. Seal Assembly Replacement
3. Rear Bearing Installation
4. Front Bearing Installation
5. Crankshaft Installation
6. Connecting Rod Installation
7. Piston Assembly Installation
8. Oil Pump Installation

TOOLS

Set of 1/4" drive sockets to 9/16", hard rubber hammer, small screwdriver, needle nose pliers, snap ring pliers, single edge razor blades, piston ring compressor, torque wrench, Allen wrench set

MATERIAL

Ample supply of refrigeration oil, gasket set, seal set, and any other part that may be found defective

PROCEDURE

VALVE PLATE REPLACEMENT PROCEDURE

Parts required: Valve plate kit

This kit includes the valve plate, discharge valves, suction valves, valve retainer parts, valve plate gasket, cylinder head gasket and suction screen.

1. Isolate compressor from system.

2. Remove all bolts from cylinder head.

3. Remove valve plate and cylinder head assembly from crankcase by tapping sidewise against valve plate edge. Do not hit or tap against cylinder head or crankcase body for damage will result to those parts.

4. Remove valve plate from cylinder head by holding cylinder head and tapping sidewise against valve plate.

5. Remove all particles of gasket, dirt, and foreign material from surface of cylinder head and cylinder face being careful not to scratch or nick mating surfaces.

---

* Text and diagrams used with the permission of Tecumseh Products Company.

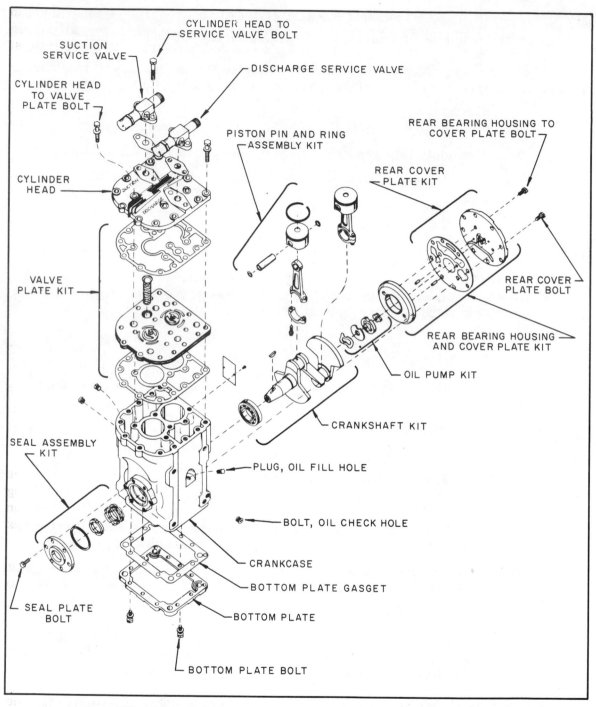

FIG. 40-1   EXPLODED VIEW OF TECUMSEH COMPRESSOR

6. Insert all mounting bolts, except for service valves, through cylinder head.
    Dip new cylinder head gasket into clean refrigeration oil and properly locate
    over mounting bolts. Properly locate new valve plate assembly over mount-
    ing bolts. Dip valve plate gasket into clean refrigeration oil and properly lo-
    cate it over mounting bolts

7. Immediately after dipping the gaskets and assembling the plate as noted in step 6, properly locate the assembly on the cylinder face and tighten down the bolts in sequence as shown below to a specified torque of **15-19 ft.-lbs.** Retorque after a minimum of two hours.

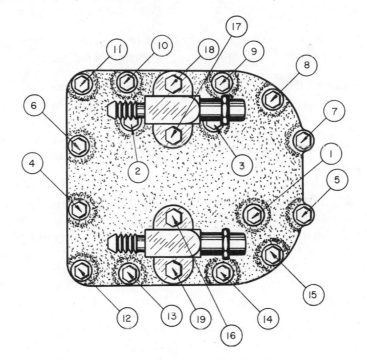

FIG. 40-2   TIGHTENING SEQUENCE OF HEAD BOLTS

8. Insert bolts through mounting holes of service valves. Dip new service valve gaskets in refrigeration oil and immediately insert valve mounting bolts through them and properly locate valves on cylinder head. Tighten bolts in sequence shown and torque to a specified **15-19 ft.-lbs.** for hex head bolts and **10-12 ft.-lbs.** for **12-point** and Allen head bolts.

9. After a period of two hours from the time of assembly of the valve plate and service valves, retorque the bolts of these parts in sequence shown to the limits as specified.

SEAL ASSEMBLY REPLACEMENT PROCEDURE

Parts required: Seal assembly kit

This assembly includes front seal plate, seal nose and spring assembly, and the O-ring for front seal plate.

1. Isolate compressor from system.

2. Wash and clean seal plate and adjoining surfaces of dirt and foreign matter.

3. Remove seal plate nose assembly by removing the six bolts in the plate and gently pry plate loose being careful not to scratch crankcase mating surfaces.

4. Remove carbon nose and spring assembly from shaft by prying behind the drive ring which is that portion of the seal assembly farthest back on the shaft. When prying the seal assembly from the shaft, do not scratch crankshaft. If rubber seal around shaft does not come out with carbon nose and spring assembly, remove it with long nose pliers on edge of grommet.

5. Remove all gasket material, dirt and foreign matter from crankcase mating surfaces, exposed crankshaft and adjacent surfaces.

6. Remove new shaft seal washer from bellows seal assembly. Coat the exposed surface of crankshaft with clean refrigeration oil. Dip new bellows seal assembly and shaft seal washer in clean refrigeration oil. Place bellows seal assembly over shaft with end for holding shaft seal washer going on last. By hand, push bellows seal assembly onto the crankshaft to a position beyond taper of shaft.

7. Assemble shaft seal washer in bellows seal assembly, checking to see that bellows seal assembly and shaft are free from dirt and foreign material. Assemble seal washer so that raised rim is away from bellows seal assembly and that the notches in washer line up with the nibs in bellows seal assembly. Cover exposed surface of shaft seal washer with clean refrigeration oil.

8. Insert new O-ring in crankcase mating surface for seal plate.

9. Place new front seal plate over shaft. Properly line up mounting holes. With hands on each side of front seal plate, push up against crankcase. Insert the six capscrews and screw in evenly. Tighten capscrews in circular sequence to **9-12 ft.-lbs.**

REAR BEARING INSTALLATION

Parts required: Rear bearing housing and cover plate kit, oil charge and gasket kit

1. Isolate compressor and remove from system.

2. Place compressor in upside-down position. Remove all dirt, grease, oil and foreign matter from bottom plate, rear cover plate and surface next to these plates.

3. Remove the bottom baseplate by removing the twelve bolts in the base and gently tapping side of base. When removing the bolts, observe type of bolts removed from various locations for it is necessary that they be reassembled in the same manner. Take care not to scratch, mar, or nick the mating surfaces.

4. Remove rear bearing cover plate and bearing assembly by removing all capscrews in plate and inserting edge of thin screwdriver between plate and compressor crankcase. Remove the plate by prying up evenly on all edges. When removing screws, observe type and location of each for it is necessary that they be replaced in the same location.

5. Remove any gasket material from bottom baseplate, crankcase, bottom surface and crankcase mating surface to rear seal plate, being careful not to scratch surfaces.

6. Flush out inner exposed parts of compressor with solvent. Drain thoroughly.

7. Soak new cover plate gasket in clean refrigeration oil from one to two hours. Position oil-soaked gasket over dowel pins in new cover plate, being careful to insure that all holes line up properly. Insert the 1/4" diameter by 3/8" long capscrew through the cover plate to housing and tighten fingertight.

8. Check to see that oil pump parts (spring, washer and rotor) are properly located in crankshaft end.

9. Properly locate rear bearing housing and cover plate assembly over crankshaft, being sure oil pump shaft is inserted in oil pump rotor and all mounting holes line up.

10. Insert the eight capscrews in rear cover plate using new copper washers over screws in holes which are not blind. Tighten all screws in cover plate in sequence shown to 12-14 ft.-lbs., except for the two center bolts which should be 10-12 ft.-lbs.

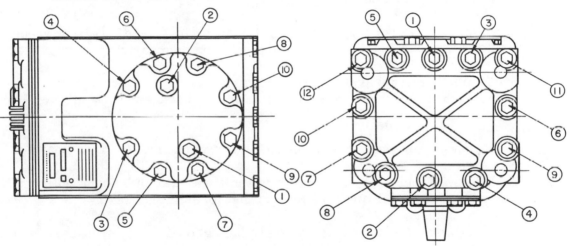

FIG. 40-3   REAR AND BASE TIGHTENING SEQUENCE

11. Soak new bottom plate gasket in clean refrigeration oil for one to two hours.

12. Properly locate and place bottom baseplate on bottom plate gasket.

13. Insert the twelve 1/4" × 11/16" bolts with washers in bottom baseplate mounting holes. Use three new copper washers on bolts adjacent to rear bearing when using kit K669-1, and use one copper washer on bolt in center adjacent to rear bearing when using kit K669-2 or K669-3. Use steel washers on all other hex-head base mounting bolts. Tighten in sequence shown to 12-14 ft.-lbs. on all hex-head bolts, and 9-11 ft.-lbs. on all button-head bolts. Retorque after two hours.

14. With the compressor in the upright position, remove one of the oil fill plugs and charge with the quality and quantity of oil as specified on **page 250**.

FRONT BEARING INSTALLATION

Parts required: Front bearing number 26546, rear cover plate, seal kit, gasket kit and oil charge as specified

1. Follow Seal Assembly Replacement Procedure, steps 1 through 5.

2. Follow Rear Bearing Installation Procedure, steps 2 through 6, and Valve Plate Replacement Procedure, steps 2 through 5.

3. Remove the two caps from the connecting rods by removing the four screws that hold them. Identify the removed caps so that they will be reassembled to the same rod and in the same position as removed. A dot is cast on one side of each rod and cap for easy identification and correct mating of the parts. The parts should be assembled so that the dots are on the same side.

4. With connecting rod caps removed, push connecting rod, piston pin, and ring assembly up and out of the crankcase.

5. Remove front bearing retainer setscrew by inserting setscrew wrench for 6-32 screw in 1/4" untapped hole in base on side adjacent to front bearing.

6. Supporting crankshaft rear bearing end, gently tap front bearing end of crankshaft toward compressor until front bearing has moved out of crankcase housing.

7. Remove crankshaft from crankcase through opening for rear bearing.

8. Remove front bearing from crankshaft with aid of bearing puller. Clean crankshaft of all oil, grease, dirt and foreign material.

9. Install new front bearing by first placing bearing in crankcase with end nearest retainer groove in outer race going in first. Supporting front end of crankcase against a flat, smooth surface, press bearing into crankcase. Press perpendicular to crankshaft centerline and against outer race of bearing. Position bearing against crankcase shoulder.

10. Insert crankshaft into front bearing as assembled into crankshaft.

11. Remove dowel pins from rear bearing housing and place over rear crankshaft journal with side of bearing plate having holes for dowel pins next to crankshaft counterweight. Using rear bearing housing as a guide for centrally lining up crankshaft, press crankshaft into front bearing by pressing on rear end of crankcase with inner race supported until bearing inner race seats against shoulder of housing.

12. Insert retainer setscrews for securing front bearing removed under step 5 and hand-tighten with a setscrew wrench.

13. Install connecting rod, piston and ring assembly per Connecting Rod Installation Procedure, step 8 and steps 12 through 18.

14. Remove rear bearing housing used for aligning crankshaft and follow Rear Bearing Installation Procedure, steps 7 through 14.

15. Install new seal assembly per Seal Assembly Replacement Procedure, steps 5 through 9.

CRANKSHAFT INSTALLATION

Parts required: Crankshaft kit, rear cover plate kit, gasket kit and seal kit

1. Use same procedure as Front Bearing Installation, except step 9.

2. Use new front bearing and crankshaft included in kits.

CONNECTING ROD INSTALLATION

Parts required: Connecting rod and cap assembly, gasket kit and oil charge

1. Follow Rear Bearing Installation Procedure, steps 1 through 4.

2. Remove the connecting rod cap from the connecting rod by removing the two screws holding it.

3. Position compressor on crankcase base after first draining the oil from the compressor.

4. Follow Valve Replacement Procedure, steps 2 through 5.

5. Remove piston, pin, ring and connecting rod assembly from crankcase by pressing them out through the top of the crankcase assembly.

6. Remove one snap ring retaining piston pin from side of piston.

7. With a slight press, push piston pin out so as to clear one side of the piston and connecting rod bearing and remove connecting rod.

8. Clean piston of all foreign matter.

9. Remove new connecting rod cap from rod assembly. Insure that their proper position in relation to each other is maintained as described under step 3 of Front Bearing Installation Procedure.

10. Properly locate new connecting rod in piston and push piston pin in until it rests against installed snap ring.

11. Reinstall snap ring removed in step 6.

12. Insert piston and connecting rod assembly, less rod caps, into cylinder bores positioned so that connecting rod bearings line up with crankshaft journals.

13. With the aid of a piston ring compressor, collapse ring against piston and complete entrance of piston and rod assembly into cylinder bore.

14. Dip new valve plate gasket into refrigeration oil and properly locate it on top of the compressor crankcase.

15. Locate cylinder head and valve plate assembly on crankcase.

16. Insert head valve plate bolts and tighten as outlined in step 7 of Valve Plate Replacement Procedure.

17. Turn compressor over, resting on cylinder head. .

18. Position connecting rod bearings around crankshaft journals and properly locate connecting rod caps over journals, being sure that the parts are mated properly. Insert screws and torque to 9-11 ft.-lbs.

19. Rotate crankshaft several times to insure that connecting rod does not bind.

20. Assemble bottom plate as outlined in Rear Bearing Installation Procedure, steps 11 through 14.

PISTON ASSEMBLY INSTALLATION

Parts required: Piston, pin, and ring assembly kit, gasket kit, and oil charge

1. Use Connecting Rod Installation Procedure, steps 1 through 7.

2. When removing connecting rod caps, be sure to maintain their proper relationship to each other as they are to be reused.

3. Clean connecting rod and caps of all foreign matter.

4. Select correct piston, pin, and ring assembly. The assembly for a standard HA-850 is identified by the number 20520 cast on the inner top surface of the piston; for a model HA-1000, the number will be 20521. The .020 oversize can be identified by the above noted figures cast on the piston's inner surface, plus the figure .020 stamped on the piston top.

5. Locate connecting rod in new piston assembly and push piston pin in against installed snap ring.

6. Follow Connecting Rod Installation Procedure, steps 11 through 18.

7. Assemble bottom plate as outlined in Rear Bearing Installation Procedure, steps 11 through 14.

OIL PUMP INSTALLATION

Parts required: Oil pump kit as specified

For compressors with bills of material 99110, 99111, 99112 and 99113

1. To change the oil pump on compressors of these bills of material will require changing and installing a new crankshaft. A new crankshaft is included in the oil pump kit specified for compressors under these bills of material. Follow procedure for Crankshaft Installation when changing the oil pump in these compressors.

For compressors with bills of material number 99114 and higher, use the following procedure for changing oil pump.

1. Follow procedure in Rear Bearing Installation Procedure, steps 1 and 4.

2. Remove used oil pump parts from end of crankshaft.

3. Dip the new oil pump parts in refrigeration oil and place them in the end of the crankshaft in the order noted:
   a. Wave washer
   b. Flat washer, polished side out
   c. Outer rotor
   d. Inner rotor

4. Follow steps 8, 9 and 10 in Rear Bearing Installation Procedure.

REVIEW QUESTIONS

1. What component part must be removed to replace the valve plate assembly?

2. Name the parts of the seal assembly.

3. What should the torque of the seal plate be?

4. The compressor should be retorqued after _____ hour(s).

SERVICE PROCEDURE 41

To Rebuild the Tecumseh Compressor, Models HG-500, HG-850 and HG-1000 *

The following procedure should be followed when it is necessary to tear down a Tecumseh compressor for overhaul. This procedure will be given in seven steps as follows:

1. Valve Plate Replacement
2. Seal Assembly Replacement
3. Rear Bearing Installation
4. Front Bearing Installation
5. Crankshaft Installation
6. Connecting Rod Installation
7. Piston Assembly Installation

This compressor, unlike the HA-850 and HA-1000 which are made of cast aluminum, is made of cast iron with aluminum connecting rods and pistons. Main bearings are ball type. Lubrication by differential pressure eliminates the need for an oil pump.

The HG series compressors have superseded the HA-850 and HA-1000 compressors. Complete interchangeability is assured by the manufacturer; crankshaft tapers and mounting dimensions are the same.

TOOLS

Set of 1/4" drive sockets to 9/16", hard rubber hammer, small screwdrivers, needle nose pliers, snap ring pliers, single edge razor blades, piston ring compressor, Allen wrench set, torque wrench

MATERIAL

Ample supply of clean refrigeration oil, gasket set, seal assembly, and other parts that may be found defective

OIL CHARGE

Compressor Position	Oil Height Hg.	Remarks
Vertical	1 5/16"	Factory charge of 11 fluid oz.
Horizontal	1 9/16"	Factory charge of 11 fluid oz.
Vertical	7/8"	Minimum recommended height *
Vertical	1 1/16"	Maximum recommended height *
Horizontal	7/8"	Minimum recommended height *
Horizontal	1 1/8"	Maximum recommended height *

* After connection to system and run

---

* Text and diagram reprinted with the permission of Tecumseh Products Company.

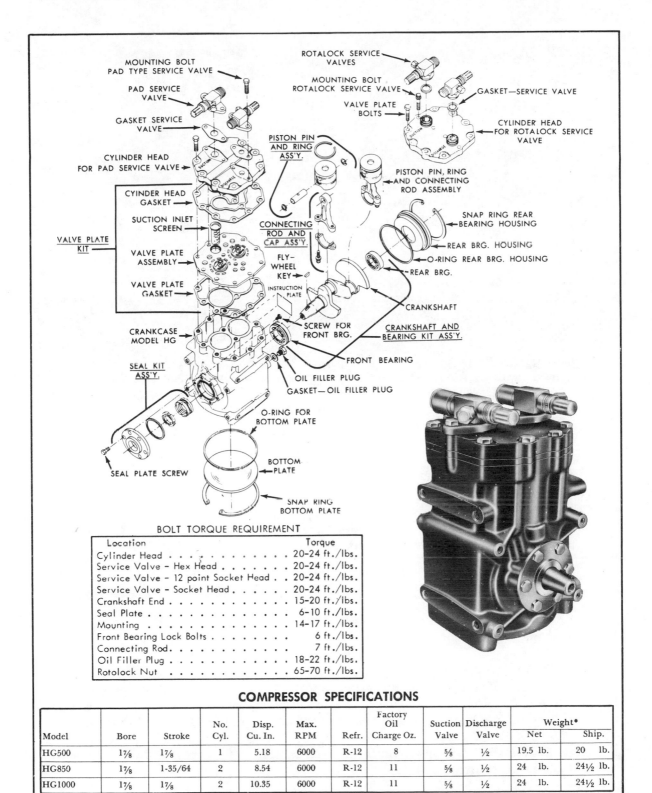

BOLT TORQUE REQUIREMENT

Location	Torque
Cylinder Head	20-24 ft./lbs.
Service Valve – Hex Head	20-24 ft./lbs.
Service Valve – 12 point Socket Head . .	20-24 ft./lbs.
Service Valve – Socket Head	20-24 ft./lbs.
Crankshaft End	15-20 ft./lbs.
Seal Plate	6-10 ft./lbs.
Mounting	14-17 ft./lbs.
Front Bearing Lock Bolts	6 ft./lbs.
Connecting Rod	7 ft./lbs.
Oil Filler Plug	18-22 ft./lbs.
Rotolock Nut	65-70 ft./lbs.

COMPRESSOR SPECIFICATIONS

Model	Bore	Stroke	No. Cyl.	Disp. Cu. In.	Max. RPM	Refr.	Factory Oil Charge Oz.	Suction Valve	Discharge Valve	Weight* Net	Weight* Ship.
HG500	1⅞	1⅞	1	5.18	6000	R-12	8	⅝	½	19.5 lb.	20 lb.
HG850	1⅞	1-35/64	2	8.54	6000	R-12	11	⅝	½	24 lb.	24½ lb.
HG1000	1⅞	1⅞	2	10.35	6000	R-12	11	⅝	½	24 lb.	24½ lb.

*oil and valves

FIG. 50-1 EXPLODED VIEW AND PARTS ASSEMBLY KIT
MODELS HG500, HG850 & HG1000 AUTOMOTIVE COMPRESSORS

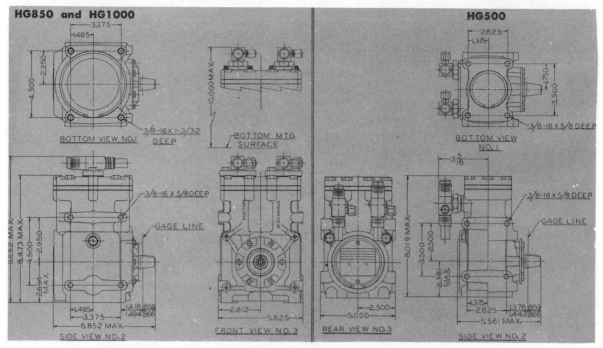

FIG. 41-2 COMPARISON OF COMPRESSORS. NOTE THE LOCATION OF THE SERVICE
VALVES ON THE HG-500 COMPRESSOR.

PROCEDURE

VALVE PLATE REPLACEMENT PROCEDURE

Parts required: Valve plate kit

This kit includes the valve plate, discharge valves, suction valves, valve retainer parts, valve plate and cylinder head gaskets.

1. Follow steps 1 through 5 in Valve Plate Replacement Procedure, Models HA-850 and HA-1000, Service Procedure 40, page 261.

2. Take the new valve plate gasket and, keeping it dry, place it over the crank-case cylinder face.

3. Place the new valve plate assembly over the valve plate gasket so that the letter "S" stamped on the valve plate is visible and on the same side as the word "Suction" on the front of the crankcase. Place so that its mounting holes are properly in line with those of the valve plate gasket and cylinder face.

4. Insure that the suction inlet screen is clean and insert it into the counter-bore of the valve plate.

5. Keep the new cylinder head gasket dry and locate it over the valve plate so that the largest opening (circle) is over top of the screen and the other circu-lar holes line up with the holes in the valve plate.

6. Locate the cylinder head over the head gasket so that the side of the head with the word "Suction" is on the same side as the word "Suction" on the front of the crankcase.

7. Insert eight or twelve (as applicable) bolts through the cylinder head and valve plates. Tighten fingertight, then torque in a sequence so that bolts diagonally opposite each other are evenly drawn to torque limits. Torque to 20-24 ft.-lbs.

8. Mount service valves:

   a. Rotalock type. Connect service valves to correct ports and tighten to a torque of 65-70 ft.-lbs. Use new gaskets.

   b. Pad base type. Take a new service valve gasket and insert valve mounting bolts through it. Properly locate valve over correct service valve ports. Tighten bolts to a torque of 20-24 ft.-lbs.

9. After a period of about two hours from time of assembly, retorque cylinder head and pad-type service valves.

SEAL ASSEMBLY REPLACEMENT PROCEDURE

Parts required: Seal assembly kit. This kit includes the front seal plate, seal nose, spring assembly, and O-ring for front seal plate.

1. Follow complete procedure outlined in Seal Assembly Replacement Procedure, Tecumseh HA-850 and HA-1000 compressors.

REAR BEARING INSTALLATION

Parts required: Rear bearing, gasket kit, and oil charge as specified

1. Isolate compressor and remove from the system.

2. Remove all dirt and foreign matter from rear and base cover plates and adjoining surfaces.

3. Remove oil filler plug and drain crankcase of oil.

4. With appropriate snap ring pliers, remove the snap ring which secures the rear bearing housing in position. Remove the end plate.

5. Remove rear O-ring and discard.

6. Remove the rear bearing by using two offset screwdrivers with their ends inserted diametrically apart under the inner edge of the bearing outer race and prying out evenly on both sides.

7. Remove baseplate by turning compressor upside-down and, using appropriate snap ring pliers, remove the snap ring holding the bottom cover in place. Remove cover next.

8. Remove and discard O-ring.

9. Clean all exposed parts and surfaces with solvent. Drain and blow out.

10. Support compressor on drive end of shaft and place the new bearing over the end of the crankshaft. Press until its inner race rests against the shaft shoulder. PRESS ON THE INNER RACE OF THE BEARING ONLY.

11. Insert new O-ring into counterbored hole for rear bearing cover plate. Be sure it is seated at the bottom of the bore and against its sides.

12. With the rear bearing housing properly aligned and positioned on top of the bearing, press the bearing housing into the compressor crankcase counterbore until it is inserted to full depth. Insert the snap ring.

13. Insert new O-ring into the crankcase base groove. Position baseplate, with bracket on the outside, into the base counterbore. Insert the snap ring. With the aid of a hammer or press, tap or press on the base allowing the snap ring to enter the crankcase groove.

14. With the compressor again in the upright position, charge with the proper amount of oil, 11 ounces, or until the level is 1 5/16″ on a dipstick with the compressor in a vertical position.

FRONT BEARING INSTALLATION

Parts required: Front bearing, seal kit, gasket kit, and oil charge, as required

1. Follow Seal Assembly Procedure, Tecumseh HA-850 and HA-1000 compressors, steps 1 through 5.

2. Follow Rear Bearing Installation Procedure to remove rear bearing plate and baseplate cover.

3. Remove cylinder head and valve plate assembly by following procedure outlined in Valve Plate Replacement Procedure, Models HA-850 and HA-1000, steps 2 through 5.

4. Identify rod caps and rods to insure that they will be reassembled in the same position. Remove the two rod caps by removing the four screws holding them.

5. Push connecting rod-piston assemblies out of the crankcase.

6. Support the crankcase from the rear and gently tap the front of the crankshaft with a rubber or fiber mallet until it has moved out of the front bearing.

7. Remove crankshaft and rear bearing from compressor.

8. From the rear of the compressor, remove the two bolts that hold the front bearing in place. Remove front bearing by placing a wood or metal rod against the front end of the bearing inner race and gently tapping the rod.

9. Clean all parts with solvent; let drain and blow out.

10. Install new front bearing into crankcase by entering bearing, properly aligned, into the counterbore and pressing or gently tapping outer race to full depth of bore.

11. Install the two bolts holding the bearing into place. Torque to 6 ft.-lbs.

12. Insert the crankshaft into the front bearing assembly. Properly align crankshaft and press or gently tap on rear end of crankshaft until it has moved into full length of the bearing journal and bottomed on it.

13. Install connecting rod, piston and ring assembly as outlined in Connecting Rod Assembly, Tecumseh Models HA-850 and HA-1000, steps 12, 13, 18, and 19.

14. Install rear bearing, bearing housing and cover plate as outlined in Rear Bearing Installation, steps 11 and 12.

15. Install new seal assembly as outlined in Seal Assembly Replacement, Tecumseh HA-850 and HA-1000, steps 5 through 9.

16. Install baseplate by inserting the new O-ring into the counterbore. Position baseplate, with bracket to the outside, and press into counterbore. Insert snap ring.

CRANKSHAFT INSTALLATION

Parts required: Crankshaft kit, gasket kit and seal kit

1. Follow Front Bearing Installation Procedure, steps 1 through 7.

2. Install new rear bearing on new crankshaft by pressing or tapping on inner race of bearing.

3. Follow Front Bearing Installation Procedure, steps 12 through 16.

CONNECTING ROD INSTALLATION

Parts required: Connecting rod and cap assembly, gasket kit and oil charge

1. Isolate compressor from system.

2. Remove all dirt and foreign material from the compressor, particularly from around the base and head areas.

3. Remove the baseplate by turning the compressor upside-down and, using appropriate snap ring pliers, remove the snap ring holding the bottom cover in place. Remove cover.

4. Drain oil from compressor. Discard. Flush exposed parts with solvent. Drain and blow off.

5. Identify the rod caps and rods to insure their proper replacement. Remove the two rod caps by removing the four screws holding them. If one rod only is to be replaced, remove only that rod cap.

6. Remove the valve plate and head. Follow procedure as outlined in Valve Plate Replacement Procedure, Tecumseh HA-850 and HA-1000, steps 2 through 5.

7. Remove piston and connecting rod assembly by pressing them out through the top of the crankcase.

8. Using snap ring pliers, remove the piston pin snap ring.

9. Push the piston pin out so as to clear one side of the piston and connecting rod bearing. Remove connecting rod.

10. Clean all foreign material from parts to be reused.

11. Remove cap from new connecting rod assembly to be installed. Insure identification of original position so that it will be installed properly.

12. Locate new connecting rods in the pistons and push the piston pin in until it rests against the installed snap ring.

13. Reinstall snap ring into piston.

14. Follow procedure as outlined in Connecting Rod Installation, Tecumseh Compressors, Models HA-850 and HA-1000, steps 12, 13, 18, and 19.

15. Insert the new O-ring into the crankcase base groove. Position baseplate with bracket to the outside into the groove. Insert the snap ring. Tap or press on the base, allowing the snap ring to enter the crankcase groove.

16. Replace the valve plate and head assembly by following procedure outlined in Valve Plate Replacement Procedure, steps 2 through 9.

PISTON ASSEMBLY INSTALLATION

Parts required: Piston, pin and ring assembly kit, gasket kit and oil charge

1. Use Connecting Rod Installation Procedure, steps 1 through 11.

2. Select correct piston, pin and ring assembly. A .020″ oversize can be identified by a figure 2 stamped on the piston top.

3. Follow Connecting Rod Installation Procedure, steps 12 through 16.

REVIEW QUESTIONS

1. List three physical differences between the HG and HA series Tecumseh compressors. _____

_____

2. What is the normal factory charge of oil? _____

3. What are two types of service valves used on the Tecumseh compressor ?

   a. _____ b. _____

4. What parts are included in the valve plate kit? _____

_____

_____

5. What torque should the valve plate and head be? _____

SERVICE PROCEDURE 42

To Rebuild the Chrysler Air-Temp V-2 Compressor *

The following procedure may be followed when it is necessary to rebuild the Chrysler Air-Temp compressor. Specifications of this compressor are: 9.45 cubic inches displacement with a bore of 2 5/16″ and a stroke of 1 1/8″. The "V" type compressor uses reed-type valves located in each head. This two-cylinder compressor has an oil charge of eleven ounces.

TOOLS

Hand wrenches, EPR valve wrench, internal and external snap ring pliers, quarter-inch drive set to 9/16″, Allen wrench set, razor blades, rubber hammer, screwdrivers, pilot studs, arbor press, torque wrenches and ring compressor (Special tools obtained from the Kelsey-Hayes Company, Detroit, Michigan.)

MATERIAL

Refrigeration oil, compressor shaft seal kit, gasket kit and other parts that may be found to be defective

PROCEDURE

COMPRESSOR PREPARED FOR SERVICE

1. All operations will be performed with the compressor removed from the car. Carry out necessary isolation or purging procedures as outlined in this book.

2. Remove compressor from car.

3. Remove 5/16″ bolt from crankshaft located at the center of the clutch hub.

4. Using a 5/8″ NF (or NC) bolt, remove the clutch rotor.

5. If stationary field, remove the field. If rotating field, remove the brush set.

6. Clean external surfaces of the compressor to prevent contamination by foreign particles.

7. Remove oil plug and drain oil from compressor into a graduate. Make a note of the amount of oil removed, then discard the oil. New oil will be used to recharge the compressor.

---

* Text and diagrams are, in part, by courtesy of the Chrysler Motor Corporation.

COMPRESSOR DISASSEMBLY PROCEDURES

A. Cylinder Head and Valve Plate Assembly

1. Remove the seven cylinder head bolts from each head. If the head and valve plate assembly does not separate easily from the crankcase, tap with a rubber hammer. DO NOT use a screwdriver to pry them apart as scoring of the mating surfaces may result.

2. Remove all gasket material from mating surfaces and check for scratches and burrs. Light scratches may be removed with a crocus cloth.

3. Make no attempt to disassemble reed valves from valve plate. Inspect reed valves for bent or broken reeds. Replace complete assembly if necessary. CAUTION: Do not touch or pry the reed valves.

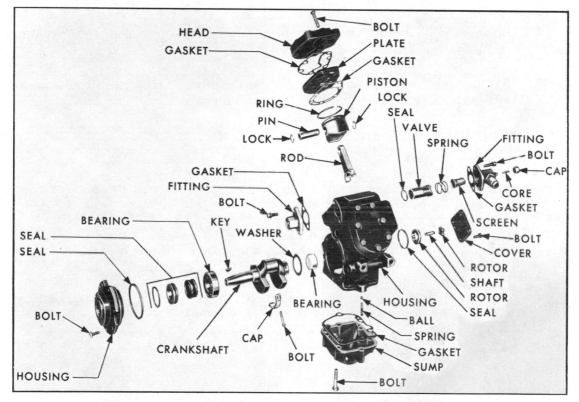

FIG. 42-1 EXPLODED VIEW OF THE V-2 COMPRESSOR

B. Piston and Connecting Rods

1. Remove the six bolts holding the sump onto the compressor crankcase.

2. Remove the sump. Do not pry. Tap with a rubber hammer if necessary. Be careful not to damage the oil pressure spring (note location in the exploded view).

279

3. Remove the oil pressure spring and rubber ball from the crankcase.

4. Clean the sump cover and compressor crankcase mating surfaces of all gasket material.

5. Note the position of the rod caps and remove the four bolts holding the two caps onto the connecting rods.

6. Remove the rod caps. Remove the piston and rod assemblies from the cylinders.

7. Replace caps on the rods in their correct position.

8. Inspect rods and caps for scoring. If worn or damaged, replace as an assembly.

9. Inspect the pistons for damage. Replace damaged or broken rings.

10. Inspect cylinder walls for damage. Slight scuffing or scratches may be removed with a crocus cloth.

11. After conditioning the cylinder bores, clean the surfaces of the block with mineral spirits and coat with clean refrigeration oil.

C. Crankshaft Bearing Housing and Shaft Oil Seal

1. Remove the six bolts from the crankshaft bearing housing.

2. Remove the bearing housing from the crankcase by using two screwdrivers inserted in the slots provided.

3. Remove the O-ring seal from the bearing housing. Remove the stationary seal and O-ring from inside the housing. Discard these parts.

4. Remove the shaft seal from the crankshaft using a screwdriver if necessary. Take care not to scratch the crankshaft. Small scratches and burrs may be removed from the crankshaft with a crocus cloth.

FIG. 42-2. CRANKCASE BEARING HOUSING
REMOVAL

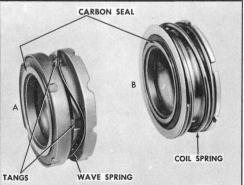
FIG. 42-3 (A) CARTRIDGE-TYPE SEAL
(B) UNITIZED-TYPE SEAL

D. Crankshaft and Ball Bearing

1. Remove the crankshaft and thrust washer from the crankcase. Make sure that the pistons and rods are completely removed.

2. The bearing may be removed from the crankshaft by using a small arbor press. If bearing is not to be replaced, do not remove it from the crankshaft.

3. Note the oil pump shaft. If it remains in the crankshaft, remove it to insure that it will not get lost.

E. The Oil Pump

1. Remove the oil pump cover plate and seal by removing the four bolts holding the plate in position.

2. Discard the seal.

3. Remove the internal and external rotor. Note relation of installation to insure their proper replacement.

4. If the oil pump shaft did not come out with the crankshaft, remove it at this time to insure that it will not be lost.

INSPECTION

NOTE: Reinspect all parts. Any parts found to be damaged beyond repair should be replaced.

1. Inspect all parts for excessive wear.

2. Inspect all parts for cracks and breaks.

3. Inspect all parts for scoring, burrs, or scratches. Small scratches should be removed with crocus cloth. If scratch cannot be removed, part must be replaced.

4. The valve plates and heads, and the sump cover, must not be bent or warped.

5. Replace all damaged parts.

COMPRESSOR REASSEMBLY PROCEDURES

A. Parts Prepared for Reassembly

1. Clean and inspect all parts. Replace defective parts.

2. Submerse new seal kit in clean refrigeration oil.

3. Submerse gasket kit in clean refrigeration oil.

4. Coat all surfaces with a light coat of clean refrigeration oil.

B. Install Crankshaft and Bearing

1. Using a small arbor press, slide the bearing onto the crankshaft. Apply pressure to the inner race of the bearing only.

2. Install a thrust washer at the rear of the crankshaft.

3. Install crankshaft into rear bushing, through front opening.

C. Install Shaft Seal and Bearing Housing

1. Place bearing housing O-ring into groove provided. Install stationary seal and O-ring into the housing. Take care not to damage the seal surface.

2. Slide the shaft seal onto the crankshaft. Hold seal firmly on the outside edges. DO NOT TOUCH THE FACE OF THE CARBON SEAL.

3. Install the bearing housing, making sure it is in proper alignment with screw holes in the crankcase.

4. The seal assembly may be damaged if bearing housing is rotated after the housing seal contacts the carbon seal.

5. Replace the six bolts. Tighten in diagonal sequence to torque of 10-13 ft.-lbs.

FIG. 42-4 SLIDING THE SHAFT SEAL INTO POSITION

D. Replace the Oil Pump

1. Install the oil pump drive shaft through the rear housing and into the crankshaft. The drive shaft may have to be rotated to engage into the crankshaft properly.

2. Install the internal and external rotors.

3. Install the O-ring into the groove provided. Install oil pump cover plate.

4. Replace four bolts holding cover plate into position. Torque to 10-13 ft.-lbs.

E. Replace Piston and Connecting Rods

1. Remove the rod caps and install pistons into the bores. If original rods are used, install them in the same position as removed.

2. Using a ring compressor to prevent damage, slip the pistons into their bores.

3. Replace rod caps. Torque to 52-56 in.-lbs.

4. Rotate crankshaft and check for binding.

5. Check crankshaft axial movement.

FIG. 42-5 CHECKING THE CRANKSHAFT AXIAL MOVEMENT

F. Replace the Cylinder Head and Valve Plate Assembly

1. Install pilot studs into compressor crankcase.

2. Position valve plate gasket over studs.

3. Position reed valve and valve plate assembly over studs.

4. Position head gasket over studs.

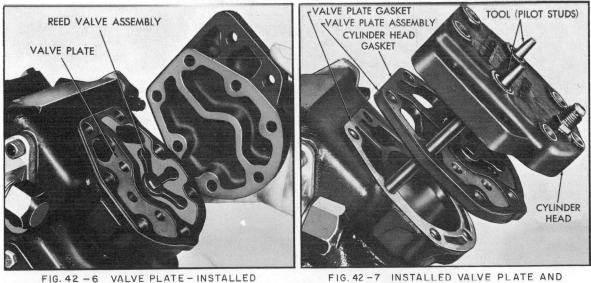

FIG. 42-6 VALVE PLATE - INSTALLED POSITION

FIG. 42-7 INSTALLED VALVE PLATE AND CYLINDER HEAD

5. Position head over studs.

6. Install five bolts and tighten fingertight.

7. Remove the two studs.

8. Install the other two bolts and tighten fingertight.

9. Repeat with the other head.

10. Tighten each bolt alternately and evenly to 23-27 ft.-lbs. torque.

11. Retorque after about two hours.

G. Install the Sump Cover

1. Turn the compressor up-side-down.

2. Drop the rubber ball into hole drilled into crankcase. Place spring on top of ball.

3. Insert pilot studs into two of the crankcase holes.

4. Position the sump gasket over the studs.

5. Position sump cover over the studs.

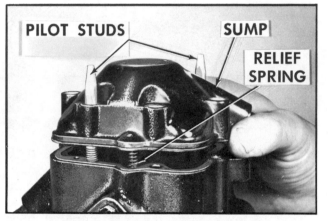

FIG. 42 – 8   INSTALLING THE SUMP

6. Install four bolts into the sump cover and tighten fingertight.

7. Remove the pilot studs and install the other two bolts fingertight.

8. Alternately tighten sump bolts to a torque of 15-19 ft.-lbs.

CHARGE WITH OIL

NOTE: Recharge with the proper amount of oil.

1. Remove oil plug.

2. If compressor is going back into service on the vehicle it was removed from, reinstall same amount of oil as removed.

3. If compressor is intended for service compressor (going into stock), install eleven ounces of oil.

4. Use only approved refrigerant oil.

TORQUE REFERENCE

	Foot-Pounds	Inch-Pounds
Compressor Bearing Housing Bolt	10-13	
Compressor to Bracket Bolt	50	
Compressor Connecting Rod Screw		52-56
Compressor Cylinder Head Cover Bolt	23-27	
Compressor Cylinder Head Cover (nameplate bolt)	20-24	
Compressor Discharge Adapter Bolt	14-18	
Compressor to Engine Bolt	30	
Compressor Oil Pump Cover Bolt	10-13	
Compressor Oil Sump	15-19	
Compressor to Strut Bolt	30	
Compressor Suction Adapter Bolt	10-14	
Magnetic Clutch to Compressor Bolt	20	

REVIEW QUESTIONS

1. When removing the sump, what parts should be looked for? _____

   _____

2. Where is the EPR valve located? _____

   _____

3. Name two types of shaft seal.

   a. _____ b. _____

4. Why is it important not to touch the carbon face of the seal? _____

   _____

   _____

5. What is the charge of oil recommended if the compressor is going into stock?

   _____

SERVICE PROCEDURE 43
To Rebuild the General Motors' 6-Cylinder Compressor *

Rebuilding the General Motors' 6-cylinder compressor is considered to be a major service operation. The compressor must be removed from the car and placed on a clean workbench, preferably one that has been covered with a clean piece of white paper.

Orderliness and cleanliness cannot be overstressed when working on the internal assembly of the compressor.

An adequate service parts stock must be maintained in order to service the six-cylinder compressor. Some of the more important parts to stock are as follows:

1. Piston drive balls
2. Shoe discs, ten sizes
3. Thrust races, fourteen sizes
4. Pistons
5. Piston rings
6. Main shaft bearings
7. Thrust bearings
8. Compressor shaft drive shaft assembly
9. Suction reed valves
10. Discharge reed valves
11. Gasket set
12. Seal Kit
13. Retainer rings, all sizes
14. Service discharge crossover tube
15. Pulley bearings
16. Oil pump drive and driven gears
17. Oil inlet tube

The following procedures are based on the use of the proper service tools and on the condition that an adequate stock of service parts is at hand.

Special service tools, as required to service the six-cylinder compressor, are available from the Draft Tool Co., or Kent Moore Tool Co., or through your air conditioning supply house. The following list of tools may be a guide; however, it may be found that some tools are not desired or will be unnecessary for your type of operation while others will be needed. The following list includes all tools suggested by the equipment manufacturers as being essential for proper compressor service.

TOOLS

Nonmagnetic feeler gage, snap ring pliers, compressor holding fixture, compressing fixture, pulley puller, clutch hub holding tool, 9/16″ thin wall socket with handle, hub and drive plate remover, hub and drive plate installer, pulley bearing remover, pulley bearing installer, internal assembly support block, oil pickup tube remover, needle bearing installer, suction crossover seal installer, pressure test connector, parts tray, O-ring installer, hand wrenches, screwdrivers, micrometer, dial indicator, spring tension scale and feeler gage stock

----

* Some of the illustrations and charts are by permission of Cadillac Motor Car Division and Oldsmobile Division of General Motors Corporation, as well as other divisions.

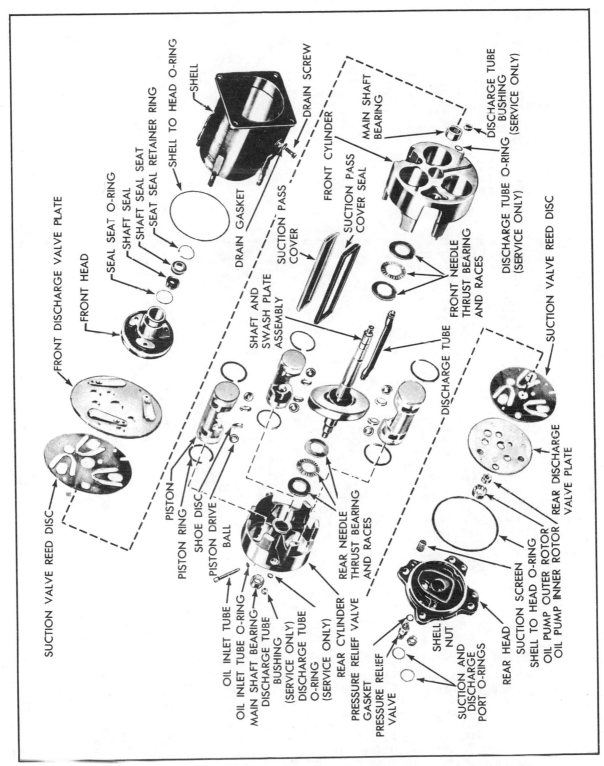

FIG. 43 - 1

MATERIAL

Gasket set and seal kit, clean refrigeration oil and any other parts as may be required

PROCEDURE

HUB AND DRIVE PLATE REMOVAL

1. Mount compressor in a holding fixture and secure the fixture in a vise.

2. Using a drive plate holding tool and a 9/16″ thin wall socket, remove the lock-nut from the shaft.

3. Remove hub and drive plate with hub and drive plate remover.

4. Use snap ring pliers to remove the retainer ring and hub spacer.

FIG. 43-2   REMOVING HUB AND DRIVE PLATE ASSEMBLY

FIG. 43-3   REMOVING PULLEY RETAINING RING

PULLEY AND BEARING ASSEMBLY REMOVAL

1. Using snap ring pliers, remove the pulley and bearing snap ring (retainer).

2. Place a puller pilot over crankshaft. Using a pulley puller, remove the pulley.

    NOTE: Be sure the pilot is in place. Never place puller against crankshaft. Damage to the internal assembly will be the result.

FIG. 43-4   REMOVING PULLEY

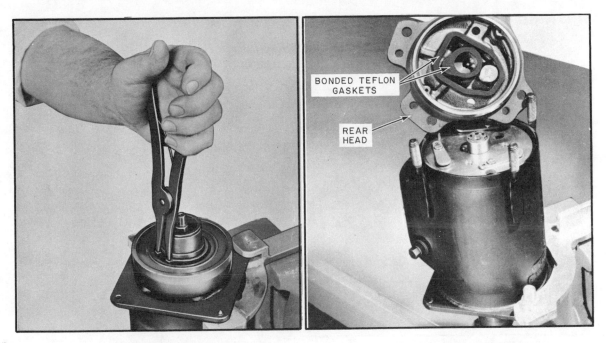

FIG. 43 – 5 REMOVING COIL HOUSING   FIG. 43 – 6 REAR HEAD REMOVAL
              RETAINER RING

3. If the bearing is to be replaced, use a sharp instrument, such as a small screwdriver, and remove the wire retaining ring.

4. From the rear of the pulley, press or drive bearing out.

COIL HOUSING ASSEMBLY

1. Scribe the location of the coil housing to the compressor body. This operation will insure that the reassembly will result in proper electrical location.

2. Using snap ring pliers, remove the coil housing retainer ring.

3. Remove the coil housing assembly.

REMOVE SHAFT SEAL ASSEMBLY

1. Using snap ring pliers, remove the snap ring retainer.

2. Using the shaft seal seat remover, remove the shaft seal seat.

3. Remove the shaft seal, using the shaft seal remover.

4. Remove the shaft seal seat O-ring. This may be done by hooking it with the oil pickup tube remover. Take care not to scratch the inner bore of the assembly when removing the O-ring.

REAR HEAD, OIL PUMP AND VALVE PLATE REMOVAL

1. Remove the oil sump plug. Remove the compressor from the holding fixture and drain the oil into a graduated container.

2. Note the quantity of oil removed, and discard the oil.

3. Return compressor to holding fixture, rear head up.

4. Remove the four nuts from the shell studs.

5. Remove the rear head. Take care not to scratch or nick the Teflon surface.

6. Remove the oil pump drive and driven gears. Keep the gears matched to insure proper reassembly.

7. Remove the rear head-to-shell O-ring and discard.

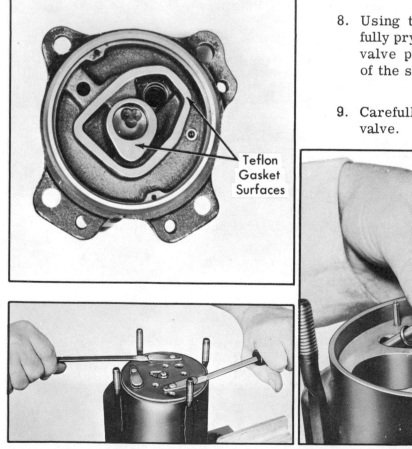

Teflon Gasket Surfaces

8. Using two screwdrivers, carefully pry up on the rear discharge valve plate assembly. Lift out of the shell.

9. Carefully lift off the suction reed valve.

FIG. 43-7 REMOVING REAR DISCHARGE VALVE PLATE

FIG. 43-8 REMOVING OIL INLET TUBE AND O-RING

REMOVE INTERNAL MECHANISM FROM SHELL

1. Remove the oil inlet tube and O-ring with an oil inlet tube remover.

    NOTE: This operation must be carried out before proceeding to the next step. Failure to do so may result in compressor shell damage as well as ruining the oil inlet tube.

2. Carefully remove the compressor assembly from the holding fixture and lay it on its side

3. DO NOT ATTEMPT TO REMOVE THE INTERNAL ASSEMBLY WITHOUT REMOVING THE FRONT HEAD. SERIOUS DAMAGE TO THE TEFLON SURFACES CAN RESULT.

FIG.43 – 9 REMOVE INTERNAL ASSEMBLY, HELD ON SUPPORT BLOCK, COMPLETE WITH FRONT HEAD

4. Gently tap the head casting with a soft hammer to slide internal assembly and head out of the shell.

5. Place internal assembly and front head on the support block.

6. Carefully remove the front head. Use extreme caution not to damage the Teflon-coated surface of the front head.

7. Remove discharge valve plate and suction valve plate from internal assembly.

8. Remove and discard the front O-ring gasket.

DIAGNOSIS

1. Replace six-cylinder internal assembly if indicated, or rebuild internal assembly as outlined in Service Procedure 44.

2. Examine front and rear discharge valve plates for broken or damaged valves.

3. Examine front and rear suction valve plates for damaged or broken valves.

4. Examine Teflon surfaces on front and rear heads. If either surface is damaged by nicks or scratches, the head must be replaced.

5. Examine the suction screen in the rear head. If contaminated or damaged, clean or replace.

6. Examine oil pump gears; if either shows signs of damage or wear, replace both gears.

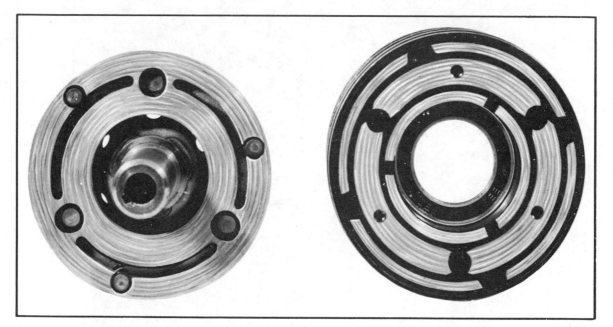

DRIVEN PLATE   DRIVE PLATE

FIG. 43 – 10   SCORING OF DRIVE AND DRIVEN PLATES IS NORMAL.
DO NOT REPLACE FOR THIS CONDITION.

7. Inspect the seal and seal seat for gouges or serrations of any kind. If damage is noted, replace complete seal assembly.

8. Check coil for loose connectors or cracked insulation. Amperage should not be more than 3.2 amps. at 12 volts at room temperature.

9. Check the appearance of the pulley and bearing assembly. If the frictional surface of the pulley shows signs of warpage due to excessive heat, the pulley should be replaced.

10. If the pulley bearing shows signs of excessive noise or looseness, it must be replaced.

11. Inspect the hub and drive plate. If the frictional surface shows signs of warpage due to excessive heat, replace it.

REASSEMBLE COMPRESSOR

1. Replace all defective parts.

2. Secure a new gasket kit from stock.

3. Secure a new seal kit from stock if indicated.

4. Reverse procedures outlined and reassemble the compressor.

REPLACE INTERNAL MECHANISM

1. Place internal mechanism, oil pump end down, into the support block.

2. Place suction valve plate into place over the dowel pins.

3. Place discharge valve into place over the dowel pins.

4. Carefully place the front head in place over the dowel pins. TAKE CARE NOT TO DAMAGE THE TEFLON SURFACES.

5. Place front O-ring into position. This O-ring is located between the head and the discharge valve plate.

6. Locate oil pickup tube hole with center of shell and slide shell over internal assembly.

7. Gently tap into place. Take care not to pinch or distort the O-ring.

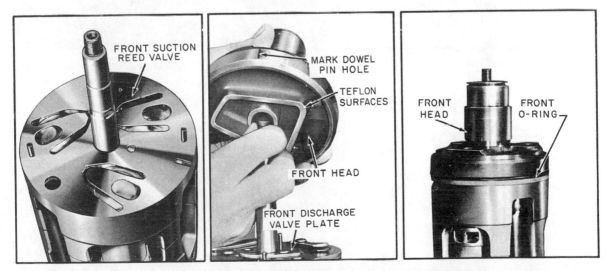

FIG. 43 -11   INSTALLING FRONT REED VALVE, HEAD AND O-RING.

INSTALL PICKUP TUBE, REAR VALVE PLATES AND OIL PUMP

1. Holding the internal mechanism securely in the shell, invert and place, service valve side up, in the holding fixture.

2. Making sure the internal mechanism is in proper position, drop the oil pickup tube into place. If equipped with an O-ring, make sure it is in place.

3. Hold suction valve plate in proper location and drop into place.

4. Locate discharge valve plate and put into place.

5. Install oil pump gears.

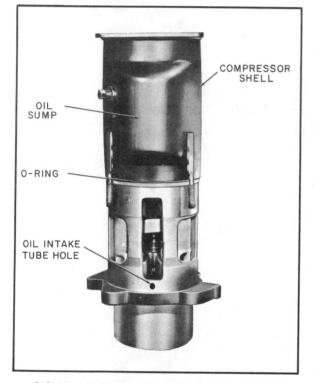

FIG.43-12 REPLACING SHELL OVER INTERNAL ASSEMBLY

FIG.43-13 INSTALLING OIL INTAKE (PICK-UP) TUBE

FIG.43-14 INSTALLING REAR HEAD

INSTALL REAR HEAD AND TORQUE

1. Position the rear head casting to align with the dowel pins.

2. Note what position the outer oil pump gear will have to be in to insure that damage does not occur to the Teflon surface of the rear head.

3. Position oil pump and slide rear head into place.

4. Install nuts and torque to 19-23 ft.-lbs.

REPLACE SEAL

1. Using an O-ring installer, install new seal seat O-ring.

2. Using a shaft seal installer, install the shaft seal. Turn it clockwise until it is felt to slide into the proper position.

3. Twist the installing tool counterclockwise and remove the tool.

4. Using the seal seat remover, install the seal seat. The remover is used to insure that the seal seat is not installed backward.

5. Replace the snap ring.

6. The system can now be leak tested.

LEAK TEST COMPRESSOR

1. With the test fitting in place, connect the manifold gage hoses to the test ports.

2. Tap a can of refrigerant and purge lines of air.

3. Open high- and low-side manifold hand valves to allow refrigerant pressure to enter the compressor.

4. With a leak detector, check both ends of the compressor shell and shaft seal for an indication of refrigerant leakage.

5. If a leak is detected at the shaft seal area, rotate the crankshaft a few turns to seat the seal.

6. Recheck if leak reoccurs; replace the seal.

7. If either internal O-ring leaks, the assembly must be disassembled to correct.

8. If no leaks are found, continue with the next procedure.

REPLACE COIL HOUSING

1. Note original position of the coil housing by the scribe marks.

2. Slip the coil housing into place.

3. Replace snap ring.

REPLACE PULLEY AND BEARING ASSEMBLY

1. Press new bearing into pulley and replace wire retaining ring.

2. Using the proper tool, press or drive the pulley and bearing assembly onto the compressor neck.

3. Install retainer ring.

FIG. 43—15   INSTALLING PULLEY AND DRIVE
PLATE BEARING

FIG. 43—16   INSTALLING PULLEY AND DRIVE
PLATE ON COMPRESSOR

REPLACE HUB AND DRIVE PLATE

1. Position key in keyway. Allow about 3/16″ of the key to stick out of keyway.

2. Align the keyway in hub and drive plate with the key and slide into position. Take care not to force the drive key into the shaft seal.

3. Using a hub and drive plate installer, press this part onto the crankshaft. There should be about .030″ clearance between the drive plate and rotor.

4. Replace spacer and clutch hub retainer ring.

5. Replace the shaft nut.

CHECK FOR FREE OPERATION

1. Turn the clutch hub by hand and feel for drag or binding.

2. Spin the pulley. It should turn freely.

RETURN COMPRESSOR TO SERVICE

1. Return compressor to stock or service.

2. Refill with 525 viscosity refrigeration oil, the same quantity as removed.

3. Add one ounce of oil if drier is replaced.

REVIEW QUESTIONS

1. What is considered to be an important factor, aside from having the proper tools, in rebuilding the compressor? _____

2. If scoring is indicated when removing the hub and drive plate, should these parts be replaced? _____

3. What precaution should be observed when removing the rear head?

_____

4. What precaution should be observed before removing the internal assembly?

_____

_____

5. Why must the front head assembly be removed with the internal assembly?

_____

_____

_____

6. If the internal assembly is damaged to the point that repair is not practical, what may be done? _____

7. When ready to install the internal assembly into the shell, where must the oil pickup hole be? _____

8. Care must be taken when installing the rear head to avoid damaging the Teflon surface gasket on the _____

9. Torque the rear nuts to _____ ft.-lbs.

10. What is the clearance between the drive plate and rotor? _____

SERVICE PROCEDURE 44

To Rebuild Internal Assembly, General Motors' 6-Cylinder Compressor

The following unit deals with the disassembly, testing and reassembly procedures on the General Motors' six-cylinder internal compressor assembly. It is a continuation of Service Procedure 43. Refer to Procedure 43 for opening comments, service tools required, material required, and acknowledgments.

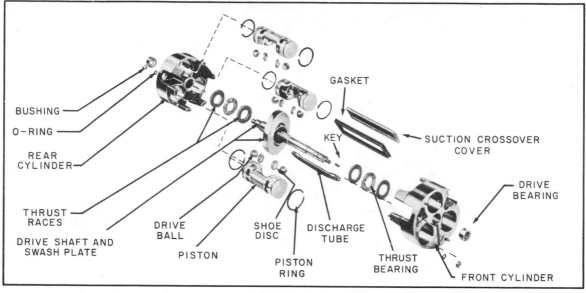

FIG. 44 —1

If the mechanism has sustained major damage, due possibly to loss of refrigerant and oil, it may be necessary to replace it with a complete service internal assembly rather than to replace individual parts. If further disassembly is considered worthwhile, proceed as follows.

PROCEDURE

SEPARATE CYLINDER HALVES

1. To insure replacement in their original position, mark pistons and cylinder bores. DO NOT MARK OR PUNCH MARK A MACHINED SURFACE.

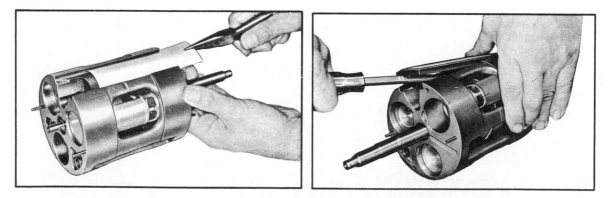

FIG. 44 - 2 REMOVING SUCTION CROSSOVER COVER

2. Remove suction crossover cover.

3. Using the discharge remover tool, drive the discharge tube out of the cylinder by driving it toward the rear of the assembly.

4. Position wobble plate so that the low part is under the crossover tube toward the rear of cylinder assembly.

5. Drive the cylinder halves apart and free from the dowel pins and discharge crossover. Use a fiber or wooden block and a hammer in this operation. Do not hit the internal assembly with a steel hammer, Figure 44-3.

6. Carefully remove the rear half of the cylinder from the pistons and set the front cylinder half, with internal parts, into the holding fixture.

7. Push up on the shaft and, one at a time, remove pistons with balls and shoes.

8. Remove rings, balls and shoes from the pistons. Note the notch at one end of the piston identifying the front end of the piston, Figure 44-5.

9. Place pistons, rings and balls into their proper positions in the parts tray. Figure 44-6.

10. Lay aside the ball shoes.

11. Remove the rear combination of thrust washers and bearing and place them in their proper positions in the parts tray.

12. Remove the shaft and wobble plate from the front cylinder half.

13. Remove the front combination of thrust washers and bearing from the front cylinder half and place them in their proper positions in the parts tray.

14. If it has been determined that the front and/or rear main bearing is to be replaced, use the main bearing tool and drive them from the cylinder halves. If they are not to be replaced, do not remove them.

INSPECTION AND DIAGNOSIS

1. Keeping them in proper position to insure that they will be reassembled as they were originally, examine the front and rear thrust washers and bearings. If any or all show signs of wear or damage, discard all of them. Otherwise return them to the parts tray.

2. If thrust washers and bearings are to be replaced, return to parts tray two new thrust bearings and four new ZERO thrust races.

3. Examine rings. Replace in the parts tray any that were damaged or broken.

4. Examine all balls. It any are damaged, replace them in the parts tray.

5. Examine all pistons for chips or cracks. Examine the ball sockets for damage. Replace those found to be damaged in the parts tray.

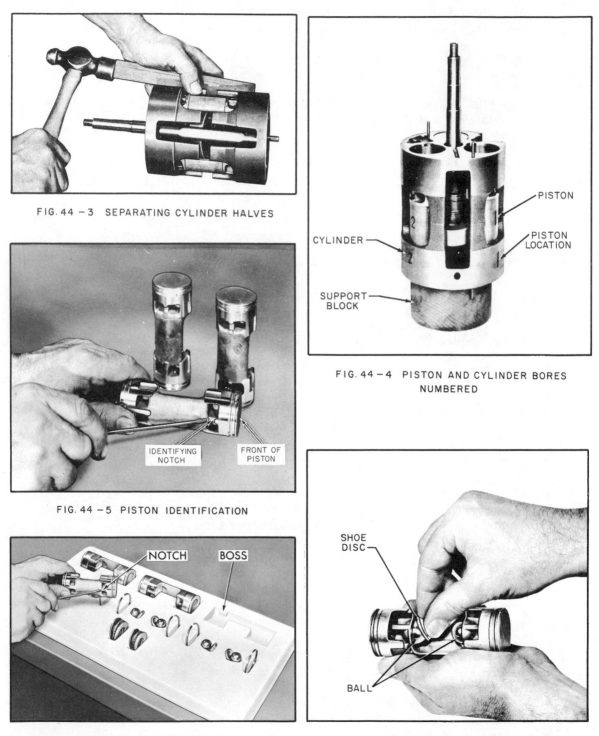

FIG. 44 – 3   SEPARATING CYLINDER HALVES

FIG. 44 – 5   PISTON IDENTIFICATION

IDENTIFYING NOTCH

FRONT OF PISTON

FIG. 44 – 4   PISTON AND CYLINDER BORES NUMBERED

PISTON

PISTON LOCATION

CYLINDER

SUPPORT BLOCK

FIG. 44 – 6   PARTS TRAY

NOTCH   BOSS

FIG. 44 – 7   ZERO SHOE AND BALL AT FRONT OF PISTON

SHOE DISC

BALL

6. Place in the tray, with the front piston ball, a zero ball shoe with each. If zero ball shoes are not used, select ball shoes of .017. Method of obtaining correct ball shoes will be covered at the end of this unit.

7. Examine shaft and wobble plate. If either shows signs of damage, it must be replaced as an assembly.

8. Examine both cylinder halves. Note that these halves are identified with a number stamped into the casting. This insures perfect mating and alignment. If either half is damaged, both must be replaced.

9. Wash all parts in a good cleaner, such as clean mineral spirits, and blow dry.

PREPARATION FOR GAGING

1. Place front half of compression fixture in holding fixture.

2. Place front head in fixture. Note that the front head is the one that is not drilled for the oil pickup tube.

3. Secure, from the parts tray, the front thrust washers and bearing and put in place on the front cylinder half.

4. Slide the long end of the shaft through the washers, bearing and front cylinder half.

5. Place the rear thrust washers and bearing into place at the rear of the shaft.

6. Do not install piston rings for gaging operation.

7. Place a ball and a ZERO ball shoe into the front part of the piston.
NOTE: ZERO ball shoes are usually .017" and may be secured by measuring the thickness of shoes removed from compressors. Procedure for gaging ball shoes is covered under Service Procedure 37.

8. Into the rear of the piston, place a ball only. Clean lubricant will aid in holding the balls in their sockets.

9. Slide this assembly onto the wobble plate and slip the front of the piston into the cylinder bore.
NOTE: The front of the piston is identified with a notch.

10. Repeat this operation, steps 7, 8 and 9, with the other two pistons.

11. Affix the four compression fixture vertical bolts and tighten them.

12. Align the rear cylinder half with the dowel pins and slide it into place.

13. Install the rear half of the compression fixture. Install the nuts and tighten to 19-23 ft.-lbs. torque.

GAGING PROCEDURES

NOTE: All gaging procedures are carried out using feeler gages that are un-damaged, and using a spring or dial scale of known calibration. Coat the feeler gages with clean refrigeration oil to insure smooth operation.

1. Start with the number one piston. Use a feeler gage inserted between the ball and wobble plate that will require between four and eight ounces of pull to remove. If less than four ounces are required, increase the thickness of the stock. If more than eight ounces are required, use a thinner stock.

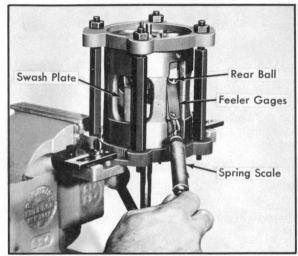

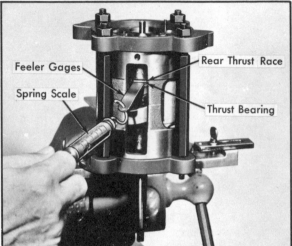

FIG. 44-8 CHECKING CLEARANCE BETWEEN REAR BALL AND WOBBLE PLATE

FIG. 44-9 CHECKING CLEARANCE BETWEEN REAR THRUST BEARING AND OUTER THRUST RACE

SHOE CHART

SERVICE *PART NUMBER	IDENTIFICATION NO. STAMPED ON SHOE
6557000	0
6556180	18
6556190	19
6556200	20
6556210	21

* The last three digits indicate identification number on shoes.

THRUST BEARING RACE CHART

Service *Part Number	Thickness Dimension	Identification No. Stamped on Race
6556000	.0920	0
6556060	.0970	6
6556070	.0980	7
6556080	.0990	8
6556090	.1000	9
6556100	.1010	10
6556110	.1020	11
6556120	.1030	12

* The last three digits indicate identification number on race.

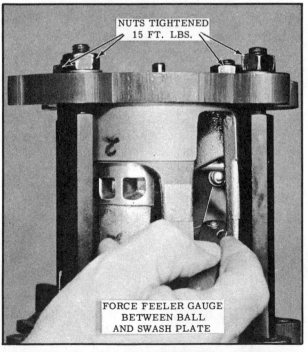

FIG. 44-10 CHECKING DRIVE BALL-TO-SWASH PLATE CLEARANCE

2. Make a note of the thickness of the stock required to cause a pull of four to eight ounces.

3. Rotate the shaft **120** degrees and recheck number one cylinder. Make a note of the thickness of the stock required to cause a pull of four to eight ounces in this position to remove the stock.

4. Rotate the shaft another **120** degrees and repeat the procedure. Make a note of the stock thickness.

5. Repeat procedure steps 1, 2, 3 and 4 with pistons two and three.

6. If new thrust bearings and races are used, proceed with step 7; if old bearings and races are used, proceed with step 8.

7. Use a feeler gage between the thrust bearing and the upper rear thrust race of a thickness to cause four to eight ounces pull on the scale. Make a note of the thickness of the gage.

8. Insure that all pistons are gaged and identified.

DISMANTLE ASSEMBLY

1. Remove the nuts and rear ring from the compression fitting.

2. Remove the internal assembly and lay it flat on the bench.

3. Carefully drive the cylinder halves apart, using a fiber or wooden block and a hammer.

4. Place front cylinder half with internal parts into the holding fixture.

5. Carefully remove the pistons and place them together with the balls and ball shoes into their proper positions in the parts tray.

6. It is not necessary to remove the thrust races or bearings.

7. If original thrust races and bearings are used, disregard the following step. If new ZERO races are used, remove the rear ZERO race and select a race corresponding with the feeler gage reading. (If feeler gage was .0095", use a thrust race stamped 9 1/2; if gage was .011", use a race stamped 11.) Substitute this race for the ZERO race removed.

8. Into the parts tray, place a rear ball shoe to correspond with the lesser of the three readings obtained when checking between ball and plate.

    EXAMPLE: If readings on piston one were .019", .0195" and .019", use a shoe reading 19; if readings were .022, .021 and .022, use a shoe reading 21.

9. Assemble rings onto the pistons. The scraper groove is assembled toward the center of the piston.

10. Insure that all parts are clean and free of all foreign matter and in their proper positions in the parts tray.

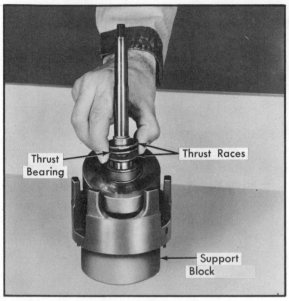

FIG. 44-11 FRONT THRUST RACES AND BEARING

ASSEMBLE INTERNAL ASSEMBLY

1. Rotate the wobble plate so the high point is above number one cylinder bore.

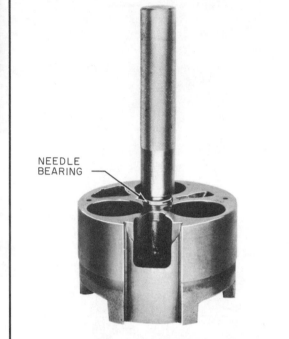

FIG. 44-12 INSTALLING DRIVE SHAFT BEARING

2. Place a ball in each end of the piston. Place the ZERO ball shoe at the front end of the piston and a selected ball shoe at the rear end of the piston. NOTE: Balls and shoes can be held in place by using a thin coat of clean petroleum jelly.

3. Locate ball shoes onto the wobble plate. Carefully compress the front ring and enter the piston into the front cylinder half.

4. Repeat steps 1, 2 and 3 with pistons two and three.

5. Enter the discharge crossover tube into the front cylinder half. Be sure that the flattened portion of this tube faces the inside of the compressor to allow for wobble plate clearance.

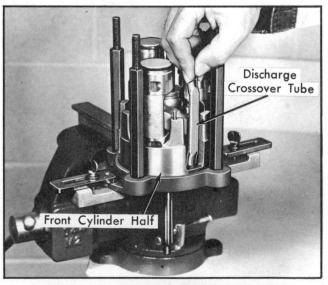

FIG. 44-13 INSTALLING SERVICE DISCHARGE CROSSOVER TUBE

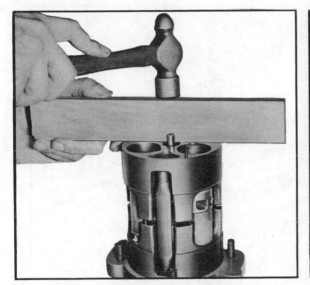

FIG. 44-14 ASSEMBLING CYLINDER HALVES

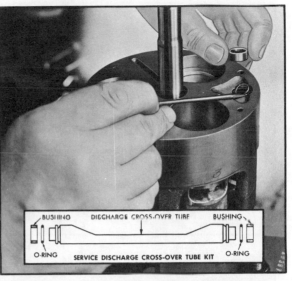

FIG. 44-15 INSTALLING SERVICE DISCHARGE
CROSSOVER PARTS

6. Carefully place the rear cylinder half in position and insert the pistons into the bores one by one, compressing the rings on each to permit its entrance.

7. When all parts are in proper alignment, tap with a wooden block and hammer to seat the rear cylinder half over the dowel pins. If necessary, clamp assembly in the compression fixture to completely draw the halves together.

8. Install the rear portion of the compression fixture and tighten the nuts to 19-23 ft.-lbs. torque.

9. Generously lubricate the internal mechanism.

10. Check for free operation. If any binding or tight spots are felt, they must be corrected.

11. Remove internal assembly from the compression fixture and lay it on a flat surface.

12. Install suction crossover cover. If cover is equipped with a gasket, use a piece of flat spring steel (.015″ to .020″) as a shoehorn to press the gasket in place. This "shoehorn" is a part of the regular compressor tool assortment.

INSTALL INTERNAL ASSEMBLY

1. Internal assembly is now ready for reinstallation into the compressor shell.

2. Follow procedure as outlined in Service Procedure 43.

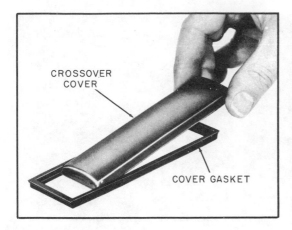

CROSSOVER COVER

COVER GASKET

FIG. 44-17 INTERNAL MECHANISM

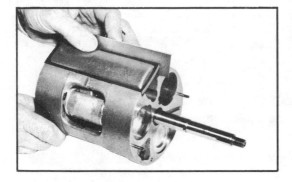

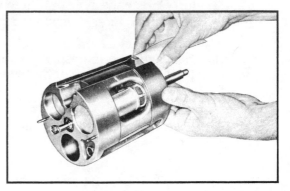

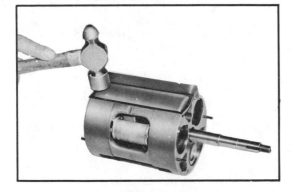

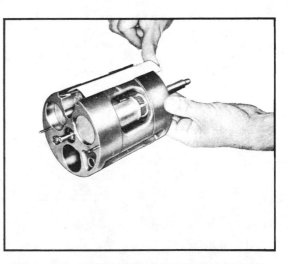

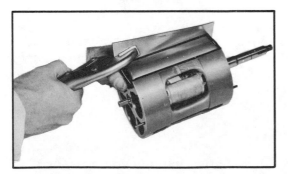

FIG. 44-16 INSTALLING SUCTION CROSSOVER
AND GASKET ASSEMBLY

FIG. 44-18 INSTALLING SUCTION CROSSOVER
COVER

REVIEW QUESTIONS

1. What instrument is used to separate cylinder halves? _____

2. What is the thickness of a ZERO ball shoe? _____

3. Toward which end of the compressor does the notch in the piston rest?

   _____

4. Which way does the scraper of the ring point? _____

5. When gaging for ball shoes, a pull of less than four ounces indicates a _____ shim may be tried.

6. If, when gaging, a shim of .018 allows a pull of six ounces to remove it on all three checks, which ball shoe would be used? _____

7. Why are the rings removed for gaging operations? _____

   _____

8. Are shaft bearings replaced as a matter of practice? _____

9. What is the purpose of the discharge crossover tube? _____

   _____

10. Do all suction crossover covers have a gasket? _____

SERVICE PROCEDURE 45
To Perform Functional Test — Automatic Temperature Control
(General Motors' Electro-Pneumatic System)

The following procedure is typical, and may be followed for holding the functional test on the electro-pneumatic automatic temperature control systems used by General Motors. Manufacturer's wiring and/or vacuum diagrams should be consulted to determine color coding if different from that given in Figure 45-1. This diagram applies only to this service procedure.

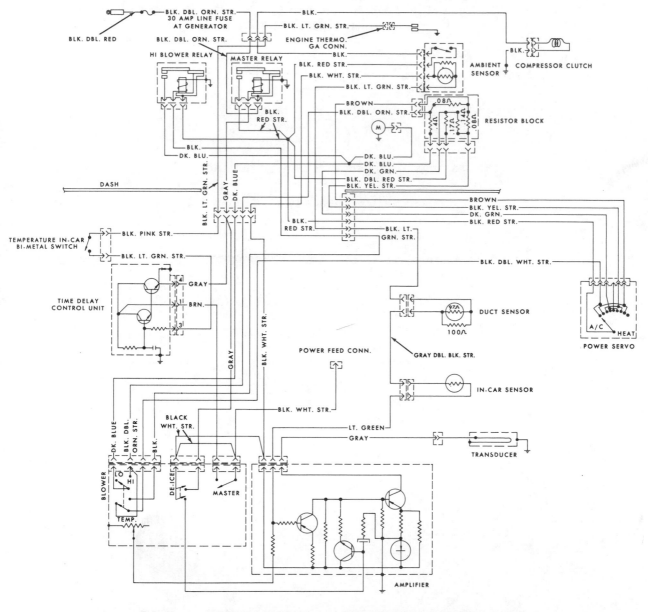

FIG. 45 - 1   CIRCUIT DIAGRAM — AUTOMATIC TEMPERATURE CONTROL
(TYPICAL GENERAL MOTORS)

Before holding this test, place an auxiliary fan in front of the automobile, directing air across the condenser. Place the automatic transmission in PARK (manual transmission in neutral) with the emergency brake set. Study Figure 45-2 carefully to learn how the various parts of the test relate to each other. To hold this test, proceed according to instructions given in charts A through K, pages 310 through 314.

TOOLS   MATERIAL

Voltmeter, ammeter, test light, jumper lead   As may be required

Air Conditioning Automatic Temperature Control Functional Test

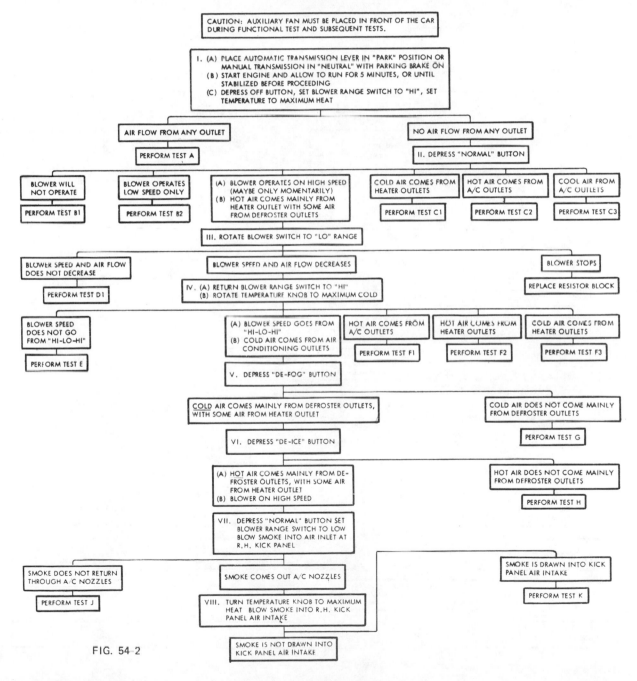

FIG. 54-2

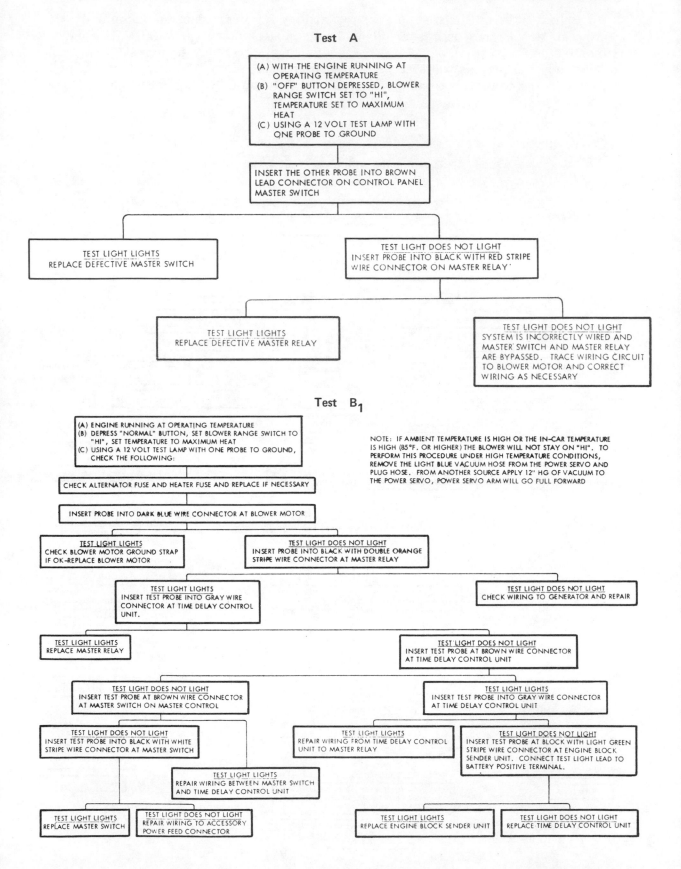

Test A

(A) WITH THE ENGINE RUNNING AT OPERATING TEMPERATURE
(B) "OFF" BUTTON DEPRESSED, BLOWER RANGE SWITCH SET TO "HI", TEMPERATURE SET TO MAXIMUM HEAT
(C) USING A 12 VOLT TEST LAMP WITH ONE PROBE TO GROUND

INSERT THE OTHER PROBE INTO BROWN LEAD CONNECTOR ON CONTROL PANEL MASTER SWITCH

TEST LIGHT LIGHTS
REPLACE DEFECTIVE MASTER SWITCH

TEST LIGHT DOES NOT LIGHT
INSERT PROBE INTO BLACK WITH RED STRIPE WIRE CONNECTOR ON MASTER RELAY

TEST LIGHT LIGHTS
REPLACE DEFECTIVE MASTER RELAY

TEST LIGHT DOES NOT LIGHT
SYSTEM IS INCORRECTLY WIRED AND MASTER SWITCH AND MASTER RELAY ARE BYPASSED. TRACE WIRING CIRCUIT TO BLOWER MOTOR AND CORRECT WIRING AS NECESSARY

Test B₁

(A) ENGINE RUNNING AT OPERATING TEMPERATURE
(B) DEPRESS "NORMAL" BUTTON, SET BLOWER RANGE SWITCH TO "HI", SET TEMPERATURE TO MAXIMUM HEAT
(C) USING A 12 VOLT TEST LAMP WITH ONE PROBE TO GROUND, CHECK THE FOLLOWING:

NOTE: IF AMBIENT TEMPERATURE IS HIGH OR THE IN-CAR TEMPERATURE IS HIGH (85°F. OR HIGHER) THE BLOWER WILL NOT STAY ON "HI". TO PERFORM THIS PROCEDURE UNDER HIGH TEMPERATURE CONDITIONS, REMOVE THE LIGHT BLUE VACUUM HOSE FROM THE POWER SERVO AND PLUG HOSE. FROM ANOTHER SOURCE APPLY 12" HG OF VACUUM TO THE POWER SERVO, POWER SERVO ARM WILL GO FULL FORWARD

CHECK ALTERNATOR FUSE AND HEATER FUSE AND REPLACE IF NECESSARY

INSERT PROBE INTO DARK BLUE WIRE CONNECTOR AT BLOWER MOTOR

TEST LIGHT LIGHTS
CHECK BLOWER MOTOR GROUND STRAP IF OK-REPLACE BLOWER MOTOR

TEST LIGHT DOES NOT LIGHT
INSERT PROBE INTO BLACK WITH DOUBLE ORANGE STRIPE WIRE CONNECTOR AT MASTER RELAY

TEST LIGHT LIGHTS
INSERT TEST PROBE INTO GRAY WIRE CONNECTOR AT TIME DELAY CONTROL UNIT.

TEST LIGHT DOES NOT LIGHT
CHECK WIRING TO GENERATOR AND REPAIR

TEST LIGHT LIGHTS
REPLACE MASTER RELAY

TEST LIGHT DOES NOT LIGHT
INSERT TEST PROBE AT BROWN WIRE CONNECTOR AT TIME DELAY CONTROL UNIT

TEST LIGHT DOES NOT LIGHT
INSERT TEST PROBE AT BROWN WIRE CONNECTOR AT MASTER SWITCH ON MASTER CONTROL

TEST LIGHT LIGHTS
INSERT TEST PROBE INTO GRAY WIRE CONNECTOR AT TIME DELAY CONTROL UNIT

TEST LIGHT DOES NOT LIGHT
INSERT TEST PROBE INTO BLACK WITH WHITE STRIPE WIRE CONNECTOR AT MASTER SWITCH

TEST LIGHT LIGHTS
REPAIR WIRING FROM TIME DELAY CONTROL UNIT TO MASTER RELAY

TEST LIGHT DOES NOT LIGHT
INSERT TEST PROBE AT BLOCK WITH LIGHT GREEN STRIPE WIRE CONNECTOR AT ENGINE BLOCK SENDER UNIT. CONNECT TEST LIGHT LEAD TO BATTERY POSITIVE TERMINAL.

TEST LIGHT LIGHTS
REPAIR WIRING BETWEEN MASTER SWITCH AND TIME DELAY CONTROL UNIT

TEST LIGHT LIGHTS
REPLACE MASTER SWITCH

TEST LIGHT DOES NOT LIGHT
REPAIR WIRING TO ACCESSORY POWER FEED CONNECTOR

TEST LIGHT LIGHTS
REPLACE ENGINE BLOCK SENDER UNIT

TEST LIGHT DOES NOT LIGHT
REPLACE TIME DELAY CONTROL UNIT

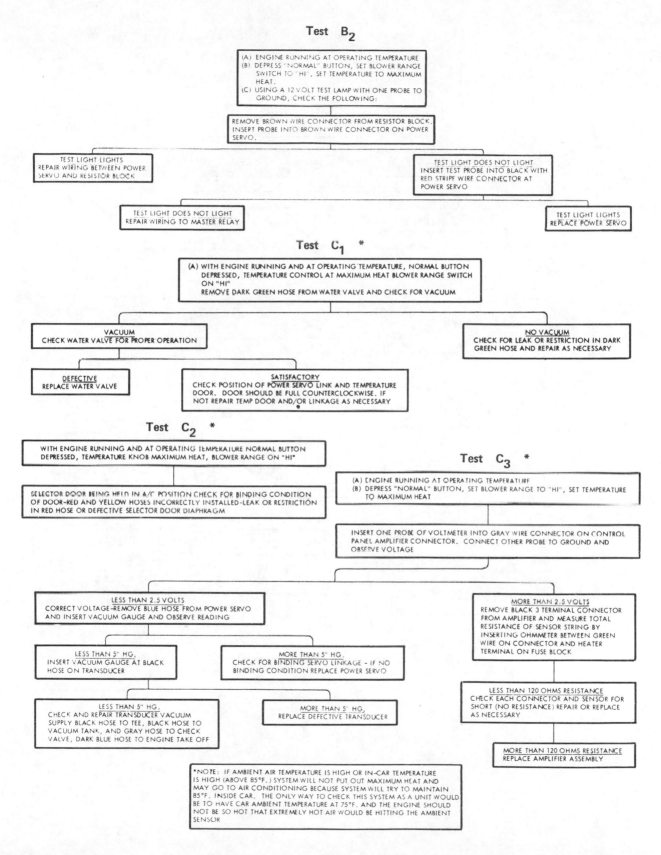

Test B₂

(A) ENGINE RUNNING AT OPERATING TEMPERATURE
(B) DEPRESS "NORMAL" BUTTON, SET BLOWER RANGE SWITCH TO "HI", SET TEMPERATURE TO MAXIMUM HEAT.
(C) USING A 12 VOLT TEST LAMP WITH ONE PROBE TO GROUND, CHECK THE FOLLOWING:

REMOVE BROWN WIRE CONNECTOR FROM RESISTOR BLOCK. INSERT PROBE INTO BROWN WIRE CONNECTOR ON POWER SERVO.

TEST LIGHT LIGHTS
REPAIR WIRING BETWEEN POWER SERVO AND RESISTOR BLOCK

TEST LIGHT DOES NOT LIGHT
INSERT TEST PROBE INTO BLACK WITH RED STRIPE WIRE CONNECTOR AT POWER SERVO

TEST LIGHT DOES NOT LIGHT
REPAIR WIRING TO MASTER RELAY

TEST LIGHT LIGHTS
REPLACE POWER SERVO

Test C₁ *

(A) WITH ENGINE RUNNING AND AT OPERATING TEMPERATURE, NORMAL BUTTON DEPRESSED, TEMPERATURE CONTROL AT MAXIMUM HEAT BLOWER RANGE SWITCH ON "HI"
REMOVE DARK GREEN HOSE FROM WATER VALVE AND CHECK FOR VACUUM

VACUUM
CHECK WATER VALVE FOR PROPER OPERATION

NO VACUUM
CHECK FOR LEAK OR RESTRICTION IN DARK GREEN HOSE AND REPAIR AS NECESSARY

DEFECTIVE
REPLACE WATER VALVE

SATISFACTORY
CHECK POSITION OF POWER SERVO LINK AND TEMPERATURE DOOR. DOOR SHOULD BE FULL COUNTERCLOCKWISE. IF NOT REPAIR TEMP DOOR AND/OR LINKAGE AS NECESSARY

Test C₂ *

WITH ENGINE RUNNING AND AT OPERATING TEMPERATURE NORMAL BUTTON DEPRESSED, TEMPERATURE KNOB MAXIMUM HEAT, BLOWER RANGE ON "HI"

SELECTOR DOOR BEING HELD IN A/C POSITION CHECK FOR BINDING CONDITION OF DOOR-RED AND YELLOW HOSES INCORRECTLY INSTALLED-LEAK OR RESTRICTION IN RED HOSE OR DEFECTIVE SELECTOR DOOR DIAPHRAGM

Test C₃ *

(A) ENGINE RUNNING AT OPERATING TEMPERATURE
(B) DEPRESS "NORMAL" BUTTON, SET BLOWER RANGE TO "HI", SET TEMPERATURE TO MAXIMUM HEAT

INSERT ONE PROBE OF VOLTMETER INTO GRAY WIRE CONNECTOR ON CONTROL PANEL AMPLIFIER CONNECTOR. CONNECT OTHER PROBE TO GROUND AND OBSERVE VOLTAGE

LESS THAN 2.5 VOLTS
CORRECT VOLTAGE-REMOVE BLUE HOSE FROM POWER SERVO AND INSERT VACUUM GAUGE AND OBSERVE READING

MORE THAN 2.5 VOLTS
REMOVE BLACK 3 TERMINAL CONNECTOR FROM AMPLIFIER AND MEASURE TOTAL RESISTANCE OF SENSOR STRING BY INSERTING OHMMETER BETWEEN GREEN WIRE ON CONNECTOR AND HEATER TERMINAL ON FUSE BLOCK

LESS THAN 5" HG.
INSERT VACUUM GAUGE AT BLACK HOSE ON TRANSDUCER

MORE THAN 5" HG.
CHECK FOR BINDING SERVO LINKAGE - IF NO BINDING CONDITION REPLACE POWER SERVO

LESS THAN 120 OHMS RESISTANCE
CHECK EACH CONNECTOR AND SENSOR FOR SHORT (NO RESISTANCE) REPAIR OR REPLACE AS NECESSARY

LESS THAN 5" HG.
CHECK AND REPAIR TRANSDUCER VACUUM SUPPLY BLACK HOSE TO TEE, BLACK HOSE TO VACUUM TANK, AND GRAY HOSE TO CHECK VALVE, DARK BLUE HOSE TO ENGINE TAKE OFF

MORE THAN 5' HG.
REPLACE DEFECTIVE TRANSDUCER

MORE THAN 120 OHMS RESISTANCE
REPLACE AMPLIFIER ASSEMBLY

*NOTE: IF AMBIENT AIR TEMPERATURE IS HIGH OR IN-CAR TEMPERATURE IS HIGH (ABOVE 85°F.) SYSTEM WILL NOT PUT OUT MAXIMUM HEAT AND MAY GO TO AIR CONDITIONING BECAUSE SYSTEM WILL TRY TO MAINTAIN 85°F. INSIDE CAR. THE ONLY WAY TO CHECK THIS SYSTEM AS A UNIT WOULD BE TO HAVE CAR AMBIENT TEMPERATURE AT 75°F. AND THE ENGINE SHOULD NOT BE SO HOT THAT EXTREMELY HOT AIR WOULD BE HITTING THE AMBIENT SENSOR

Test D

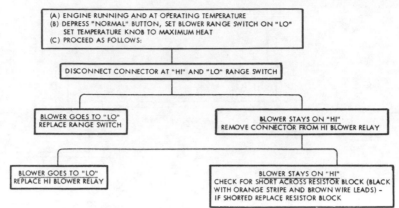

(A) ENGINE RUNNING AND AT OPERATING TEMPERATURE
(B) DEPRESS "NORMAL" BUTTON, SET BLOWER RANGE SWITCH ON "LO"
    SET TEMPERATURE KNOB TO MAXIMUM HEAT
(C) PROCEED AS FOLLOWS:

DISCONNECT CONNECTOR AT "HI" AND "LO" RANGE SWITCH

BLOWER GOES TO "LO"
REPLACE RANGE SWITCH

BLOWER STAYS ON "HI"
REMOVE CONNECTOR FROM HI BLOWER RELAY

BLOWER GOES TO "LO"
REPLACE HI BLOWER RELAY

BLOWER STAYS ON "HI"
CHECK FOR SHORT ACROSS RESISTOR BLOCK (BLACK
WITH ORANGE STRIPE AND BROWN WIRE LEADS) -
IF SHORTED REPLACE RESISTOR BLOCK

Test E

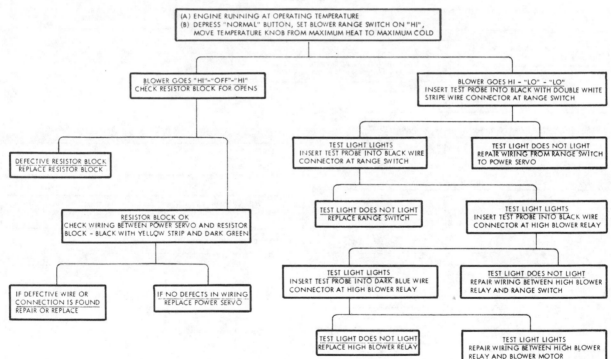

(A) ENGINE RUNNING AT OPERATING TEMPERATURE
(B) DEPRESS "NORMAL" BUTTON, SET BLOWER RANGE SWITCH ON "HI",
    MOVE TEMPERATURE KNOB FROM MAXIMUM HEAT TO MAXIMUM COLD

BLOWER GOES "HI"-"OFF"-"HI"
CHECK RESISTOR BLOCK FOR OPENS

BLOWER GOES HI - "LO" - "LO"
INSERT TEST PROBE INTO BLACK WITH DOUBLE WHITE
STRIPE WIRE CONNECTOR AT RANGE SWITCH

DEFECTIVE RESISTOR BLOCK
REPLACE RESISTOR BLOCK

RESISTOR BLOCK OK
CHECK WIRING BETWEEN POWER SERVO AND RESISTOR
BLOCK - BLACK WITH YELLOW STRIP AND DARK GREEN

IF DEFECTIVE WIRE OR
CONNECTION IS FOUND
REPAIR OR REPLACE

IF NO DEFECTS IN WIRING
REPLACE POWER SERVO

TEST LIGHT LIGHTS
INSERT TEST PROBE INTO BLACK WIRE
CONNECTOR AT RANGE SWITCH

TEST LIGHT DOES NOT LIGHT
REPAIR WIRING FROM RANGE SWITCH
TO POWER SERVO

TEST LIGHT DOES NOT LIGHT
REPLACE RANGE SWITCH

TEST LIGHT LIGHTS
INSERT TEST PROBE INTO BLACK WIRE
CONNECTOR AT HIGH BLOWER RELAY

TEST LIGHT LIGHTS
INSERT TEST PROBE INTO DARK BLUE WIRE
CONNECTOR AT HIGH BLOWER RELAY

TEST LIGHT DOES NOT LIGHT
REPAIR WIRING BETWEEN HIGH BLOWER
RELAY AND RANGE SWITCH

TEST LIGHT DOES NOT LIGHT
REPLACE HIGH BLOWER RELAY

TEST LIGHT LIGHTS
REPAIR WIRING BETWEEN HIGH BLOWER
RELAY AND BLOWER MOTOR

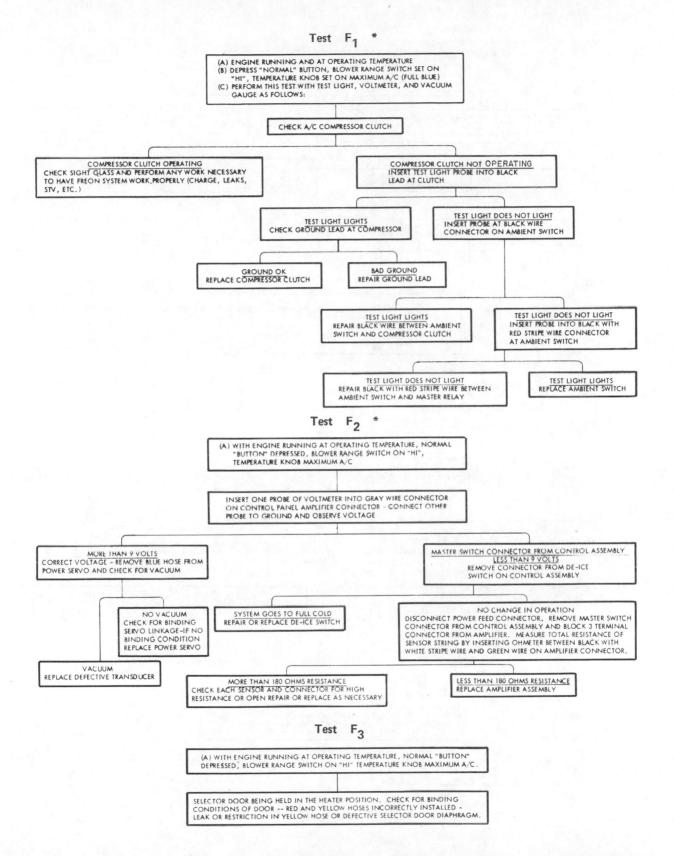

Test F$_1$ *

(A) ENGINE RUNNING AND AT OPERATING TEMPERATURE
(B) DEPRESS "NORMAL" BUTTON, BLOWER RANGE SWITCH SET ON "HI", TEMPERATURE KNOB SET ON MAXIMUM A/C (FULL BLUE)
(C) PERFORM THIS TEST WITH TEST LIGHT, VOLTMETER, AND VACUUM GAUGE AS FOLLOWS:

CHECK A/C COMPRESSOR CLUTCH

COMPRESSOR CLUTCH OPERATING
CHECK SIGHT GLASS AND PERFORM ANY WORK NECESSARY TO HAVE FREON SYSTEM WORK PROPERLY (CHARGE, LEAKS, STV, ETC.)

COMPRESSOR CLUTCH NOT OPERATING
INSERT TEST LIGHT PROBE INTO BLACK LEAD AT CLUTCH

TEST LIGHT LIGHTS
CHECK GROUND LEAD AT COMPRESSOR

TEST LIGHT DOES NOT LIGHT
INSERT PROBE AT BLACK WIRE CONNECTOR ON AMBIENT SWITCH

GROUND OK
REPLACE COMPRESSOR CLUTCH

BAD GROUND
REPAIR GROUND LEAD

TEST LIGHT LIGHTS
REPAIR BLACK WIRE BETWEEN AMBIENT SWITCH AND COMPRESSOR CLUTCH

TEST LIGHT DOES NOT LIGHT
INSERT PROBE INTO BLACK WITH RED STRIPE WIRE CONNECTOR AT AMBIENT SWITCH

TEST LIGHT DOES NOT LIGHT
REPAIR BLACK WITH RED STRIPE WIRE BETWEEN AMBIENT SWITCH AND MASTER RELAY

TEST LIGHT LIGHTS
REPLACE AMBIENT SWITCH

Test F$_2$ *

(A) WITH ENGINE RUNNING AT OPERATING TEMPERATURE, NORMAL "BUTTON" DEPRESSED, BLOWER RANGE SWITCH ON "HI", TEMPERATURE KNOB MAXIMUM A/C

INSERT ONE PROBE OF VOLTMETER INTO GRAY WIRE CONNECTOR ON CONTROL PANEL AMPLIFIER CONNECTOR - CONNECT OTHER PROBE TO GROUND AND OBSERVE VOLTAGE

MORE THAN 9 VOLTS
CORRECT VOLTAGE - REMOVE BLUE HOSE FROM POWER SERVO AND CHECK FOR VACUUM

MASTER SWITCH CONNECTOR FROM CONTROL ASSEMBLY LESS THAN 9 VOLTS
REMOVE CONNECTOR FROM DE-ICE SWITCH ON CONTROL ASSEMBLY

NO VACUUM
CHECK FOR BINDING SERVO LINKAGE-IF NO BINDING CONDITION REPLACE POWER SERVO

SYSTEM GOES TO FULL COLD
REPAIR OR REPLACE DE-ICE SWITCH

NO CHANGE IN OPERATION
DISCONNECT POWER FEED CONNECTOR, REMOVE MASTER SWITCH CONNECTOR FROM CONTROL ASSEMBLY AND BLOCK 3 TERMINAL CONNECTOR FROM AMPLIFIER. MEASURE TOTAL RESISTANCE OF SENSOR STRING BY INSERTING OHMETER BETWEEN BLACK WITH WHITE STRIPE WIRE AND GREEN WIRE ON AMPLIFIER CONNECTOR.

VACUUM
REPLACE DEFECTIVE TRANSDUCER

MORE THAN 180 OHMS RESISTANCE
CHECK EACH SENSOR AND CONNECTOR FOR HIGH RESISTANCE OR OPEN REPAIR OR REPLACE AS NECESSARY

LESS THAN 180 OHMS RESISTANCE
REPLACE AMPLIFIER ASSEMBLY

Test F$_3$

(A) WITH ENGINE RUNNING AT OPERATING TEMPERATURE, NORMAL "BUTTON" DEPRESSED, BLOWER RANGE SWITCH ON "HI" TEMPERATURE KNOB MAXIMUM A/C.

SELECTOR DOOR BEING HELD IN THE HEATER POSITION. CHECK FOR BINDING CONDITIONS OF DOOR -- RED AND YELLOW HOSES INCORRECTLY INSTALLED - LEAK OR RESTRICTION IN YELLOW HOSE OR DEFECTIVE SELECTOR DOOR DIAPHRAGM.

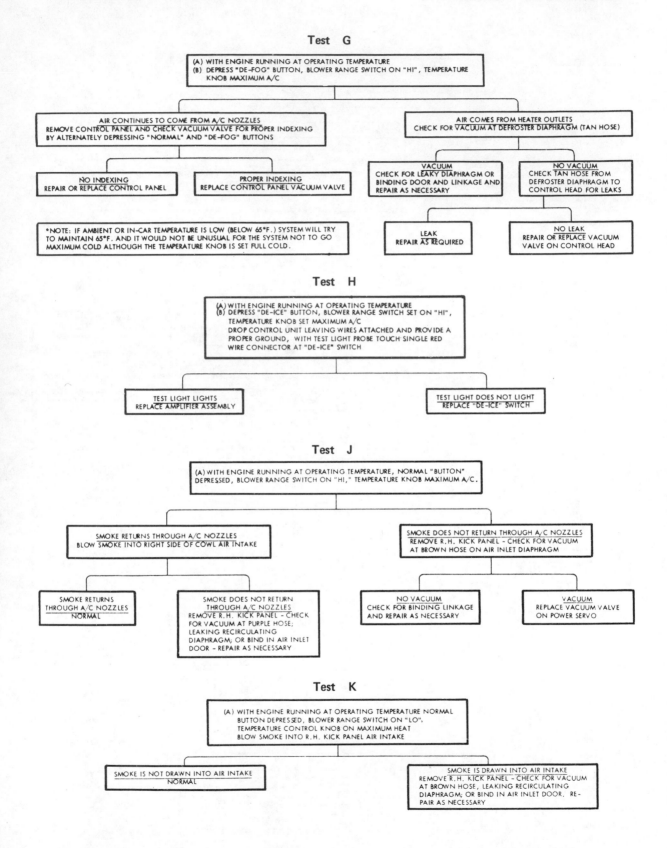

Test G

(A) WITH ENGINE RUNNING AT OPERATING TEMPERATURE
(B) DEPRESS "DE-FOG" BUTTON, BLOWER RANGE SWITCH ON "HI", TEMPERATURE KNOB MAXIMUM A/C

AIR CONTINUES TO COME FROM A/C NOZZLES
REMOVE CONTROL PANEL AND CHECK VACUUM VALVE FOR PROPER INDEXING BY ALTERNATELY DEPRESSING "NORMAL" AND "DE-FOG" BUTTONS

AIR COMES FROM HEATER OUTLETS
CHECK FOR VACUUM AT DEFROSTER DIAPHRAGM (TAN HOSE)

NO INDEXING
REPAIR OR REPLACE CONTROL PANEL

PROPER INDEXING
REPLACE CONTROL PANEL VACUUM VALVE

VACUUM
CHECK FOR LEAKY DIAPHRAGM OR BINDING DOOR AND LINKAGE AND REPAIR AS NECESSARY

NO VACUUM
CHECK TAN HOSE FROM DEFROSTER DIAPHRAGM TO CONTROL HEAD FOR LEAKS

*NOTE: IF AMBIENT OR IN-CAR TEMPERATURE IS LOW (BELOW 65°F.) SYSTEM WILL TRY TO MAINTAIN 65°F. AND IT WOULD NOT BE UNUSUAL FOR THE SYSTEM NOT TO GO MAXIMUM COLD ALTHOUGH THE TEMPERATURE KNOB IS SET FULL COLD.

LEAK
REPAIR AS REQUIRED

NO LEAK
REPAIR OR REPLACE VACUUM VALVE ON CONTROL HEAD

Test H

(A) WITH ENGINE RUNNING AT OPERATING TEMPERATURE
(B) DEPRESS "DE-ICE" BUTTON, BLOWER RANGE SWITCH SET ON "HI", TEMPERATURE KNOB SET MAXIMUM A/C
DROP CONTROL UNIT LEAVING WIRES ATTACHED AND PROVIDE A PROPER GROUND, WITH TEST LIGHT PROBE TOUCH SINGLE RED WIRE CONNECTOR AT "DE-ICE" SWITCH

TEST LIGHT LIGHTS
REPLACE AMPLIFIER ASSEMBLY

TEST LIGHT DOES NOT LIGHT
REPLACE "DE-ICE" SWITCH

Test J

(A) WITH ENGINE RUNNING AT OPERATING TEMPERATURE, NORMAL "BUTTON" DEPRESSED, BLOWER RANGE SWITCH ON "HI," TEMPERATURE KNOB MAXIMUM A/C.

SMOKE RETURNS THROUGH A/C NOZZLES
BLOW SMOKE INTO RIGHT SIDE OF COWL AIR INTAKE

SMOKE DOES NOT RETURN THROUGH A/C NOZZLES
REMOVE R.H. KICK PANEL - CHECK FOR VACUUM AT BROWN HOSE ON AIR INLET DIAPHRAGM

SMOKE RETURNS THROUGH A/C NOZZLES
NORMAL

SMOKE DOES NOT RETURN THROUGH A/C NOZZLES
REMOVE R.H. KICK PANEL - CHECK FOR VACUUM AT PURPLE HOSE; LEAKING RECIRCULATING DIAPHRAGM; OR BIND IN AIR INLET DOOR - REPAIR AS NECESSARY

NO VACUUM
CHECK FOR BINDING LINKAGE AND REPAIR AS NECESSARY

VACUUM
REPLACE VACUUM VALVE ON POWER SERVO

Test K

(A) WITH ENGINE RUNNING AT OPERATING TEMPERATURE NORMAL BUTTON DEPRESSED, BLOWER RANGE SWITCH ON "LO", TEMPERATURE CONTROL KNOB ON MAXIMUM HEAT BLOW SMOKE INTO R.H. KICK PANEL AIR INTAKE

SMOKE IS NOT DRAWN INTO AIR INTAKE
NORMAL

SMOKE IS DRAWN INTO AIR INTAKE
REMOVE R.H. KICK PANEL - CHECK FOR VACUUM AT BROWN HOSE, LEAKING RECIRCULATING DIAPHRAGM; OR BIND IN AIR INLET DOOR. REPAIR AS NECESSARY

REVIEW QUESTIONS

1. What does the term electro-pneumatic mean? _____

   _____

2. What tools are required to hold tests? _____

   _____

3. What are the precautions to take before holding this test? _____

   _____

4. Why do you think such precautions are necessary? _____

   _____

   _____

SERVICE PROCEDURE 46

To Perform Functional Test — Automatic Temperature Control
(Chrysler Motors' Electro-Pneumatic System)

The following procedure is typical and may be followed for holding the functional test on the Chrysler automatic temperature control system. Manufacturer's wiring and/or vacuum diagrams should be consulted to determine color coding or arrangement if different from those given in Figures 46-1 and 46-2. These two diagrams apply only to Service Procedure 46. Before holding this test, place an auxiliary fan in front of the automobile, directing air across the condenser. Place the automatic transmission in PARK (manual transmission in neutral) with the emergency brake set.

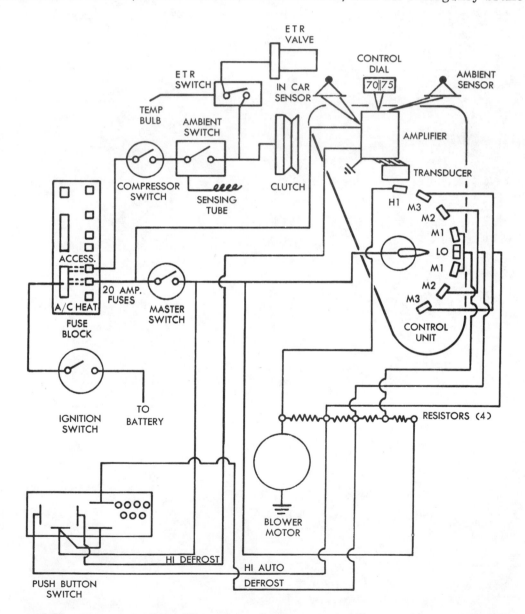

FIG. 46-1 TYPICAL CHRYSLER AUTOMATIC TEMPERATURE CONTROL WIRING DIAGRAM

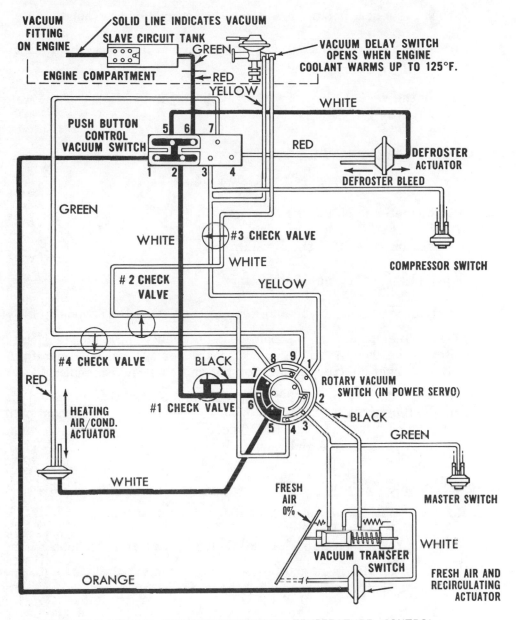

FIG. 46-2 TYPICAL CHRYSLER AUTOMATIC TEMPERATURE CONTROL
VACUUM SYSTEM — SYSTEM "OFF"

TOOLS

Kelsey-Hayes tester (Chrysler #C-4064)

MATERIAL

As may be required

PROCEDURE

TO CONNECT THE TESTER

1. Insert the tester connectors in series with the system harness and control
   unit harness.

2. Attach the tester ground lead (white) to a good body ground.

3. Attach the tester hot lead (black) to tan wire at the three-terminal connector on the blower motor resistor block.

4. Tee-in the vacuum line of tester at the right-hand port of the water valve thermostat.

TO CALIBRATE THE TESTER

1. Start engine and set speed to 1000 r.p.m.

2. Set voltmeter knob to OFF position.

3. Set vacuum control knob to minimum.

4. Depress the AUTO pushbutton.

5. Slowly rotate tester vacuum knob to the CALIBRATE position.

   NOTE: The vacuum gage should read between 4 and 6 inches. This reading indicates whether the amplifier and transducer are reducing manifold vacuum to the correct control vacuum for a given electrical signal.

   If the correct reading is not received, make sure that manifold vacuum is being delivered to the control unit assembly. (Check for kinked or damaged vacuum hoses.) If full manifold vacuum is being received, the control unit assembly is defective and should be replaced.

TO TEST AMBIENT SENSOR

1. Move voltmeter knob to the ambient sensor position.

2. Note position of voltmeter needle. It should be in the center green area.

   NOTE: If needle is in red to the right of center, the sensor is open; if to the left of center, the sensor is shorted.

   CAUTION: Do not allow voltmeter knob to remain in any of the sensor positions more than 30 seconds. If so, sensors could be damaged.

TO TEST TEMPERATURE CONTROL DIAL

1. Set instrument panel dial at 75° F.

2. Set tester voltmeter knob to TEMP. CONTROL position.

3. Note position of voltmeter needle. It should be in the green area.

   NOTE: If needle is in either red area, the temperature control is "open" or "shorted" or, in some cases, out of calibration.

AUTO TEMP. SEQUENCE CHART

Pushbutton Position	Control Vacuum	Fresh Air Door Position	AC/Heat Door Position	Defrost Door Position	Blower Motor Speed
OFF	Below 8 inches Hg.	0% F/A	A/C (open)	Closed	Off
	Above 8 inches Hg.	0% F/A	Heater (closed)	Bleed	Off
AUTO	MINIMUM (0)	20%	A/C	CLOSED	HI
SLOWLY ROTATE		20%	A/C	CLOSED	HI to M3
VACUUM CONTROL	3.5	100%	A/C	CLOSED	M3
KNOB FROM		100%	A/C	CLOSED	M3 to M2
MINIMUM TO					
MAXIMUM		100%	A/C	CLOSED	M2 to M1
		100%	A/C	CLOSED	M1 to LO
	8.0	100%	HEAT	BLEED	LO
		100%	HEAT	BLEED	LO to M1
		100%	HEAT	BLEED	M1 to M2
	12.0	100%	HEAT	BLEED	M2 to M3
		100%	HEAT	BLEED	M3
		100%	HEAT	BLEED	M3
SLOWLY ROTATE	12.0	100%	HEAT	BLEED	M3
VACUUM CONTROL					
KNOB FROM	7.0	100%	A/C	CLOSED	LO
MAXIMUM TO	2.5	20%	A/C	CLOSED	M3
MINIMUM	0	20%	A/C	CLOSED	HI
HI-AUTO	MINIMUM (0 HG.)	20%	A/C	CLOSED	HI
SLOWLY ROTATE		20%	A/C	CLOSED	HI to M3
VACUUM CONTROL		100%	A/C	CLOSED	M3
KNOB FROM	3.5				
MINIMUM TO		100%	A/C	CLOSED	M3
MAXIMUM					
	0.0	100%	HEAT	BLEED	M3
		100%	HEAT	BLEED	M3
	12.0	100%	HEAT	BLEED	M3
		100%	HEAT	BLEED	M3
		100%	HEAT	BLEED	M3
SLOWLY ROTATE	12.0	100%	HEAT	BLEED	M3
VACUUM CONTROL	7.0	100%	A/C	CLOSED	M3
KNOB FROM					
MAXIMUM TO	2.5	20%	A/C	CLOSED	M3
MINIMUM	0	20%	A/C	CLOSED	HI
DEFROST	MINIMUM (0" HG.)	20%	HEAT BLEED	OPEN	HI
SLOWLY ROTATE		20%	HEAT BLEED	OPEN	HI to M3
VACUUM CONTROL	3.5	100%	HEAT BLEED	OPEN	M3
KNOB FROM		100%	HEAT BLEED	OPEN	M3 to M2
MINIMUM TO					
MAXIMUM		100%	HEAT BLEED	OPEN	M2
		100%	HEAT BLEED	OPEN	M2
SLOWLY ROTATE	8.0	100%	HEAT BLEED	OPEN	M2
VACUUM CONTROL		100%	HEAT BLEED	OPEN	M2
KNOB FROM MAXIMUM		100%	HEAT BLEED	OPEN	M2
TO MINIMUM					
	12.0	100%	HEAT BLEED	OPEN	M2 to M3
		100%	HEAT BLEED	OPEN	M3
HI-DEFROST	12.0" OR	100%	HEAT BLEED	OPEN	M3
(TEMP. CONTROL	ABOVE				
DIAL HAS NO EFFECT)					

FIG. 46-3 AUTO-TEMP SEQUENCE CHART

4. An ohmmeter may be used to check calibration of the temperature control dial. The meter should read 300 ohms with the dial set at 75.

TO TEST IN-CAR SENSOR

1. Set voltmeter knob to the IN-CAR position.

2. Note position of voltmeter needle. It should be in the green area.

   NOTE: If needle is in red, the sensor is either "open" or "shorted." Do not allow voltmeter knob to remain in this position for more than 30 seconds to avoid damage to the sensor.

SEQUENCE TEST

   NOTE: This test puts the system through all of its paces from air conditioning with high blower to heating with high blower.

1. Set voltmeter knob to voltage position.

2. Set vacuum knob to minimum position.

3. Refer to Figure 46-3, Auto Temp Sequence Chart, to determine the position of doors and changes in blower speed as the vacuum control knob is rotated.

REVIEW QUESTIONS

1. What is the precaution taken when holding the sensors tests? _____

   _____

2. Briefly, how is the calibration of the temperature control dial checked?

   _____

3. What would prevent a vacuum "signal" from reaching the control unit?

   _____

4. What tool(s) are used to hold this test? _____

   _____

5. What is the purpose of the "Auto Temp Sequence" test? _____

   _____

   _____

SERVICE PROCEDURE 47
To Perform Functional Test — Automatic Temperature Control
(Ford Motors' Automatic Climate Control System)

The following procedure is typical and may be used for holding the functional test on Ford automatic climate control systems. This procedure gives the testing sequence for performing seven tests on system components. Figures 47-1 and 47-2 give vacuum and electrical diagrams for this system; however, the manufacturer's service manuals should be consulted to determine color coding and arrangement if different from those given.

Before holding either test, determine that there are no vacuum or wiring problems outside of the units being tested. Place an auxiliary fan in front of the condenser. Place the transmission in PARK (manual transmission in neutral) with the emergency brake set.

Tools and material required are outlined in each test procedure. The tests are:

- A. Instrument Panel ACC Functional Control Switch test
- B. Automatic Climate Control Box Test
- C. High-Range Relay Test
- D. Power-Servo Assembly Test
- E. Temperature Sensors and Control Rheostat Test
- F. Heater Water Control Valve Test
- G. Water Valve Solenoid Test

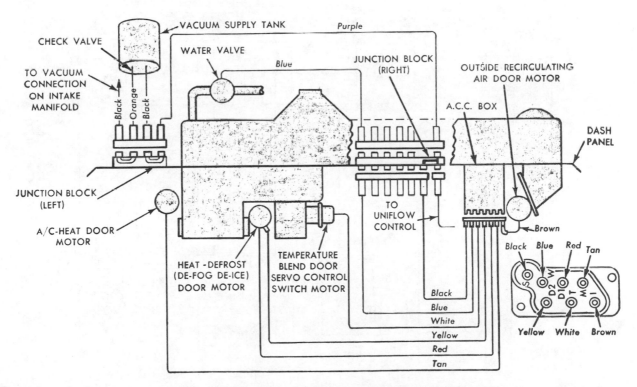

FIG. 47-1 AUTOMATIC CLIMATE CONTROL VACUUM SYSTEM

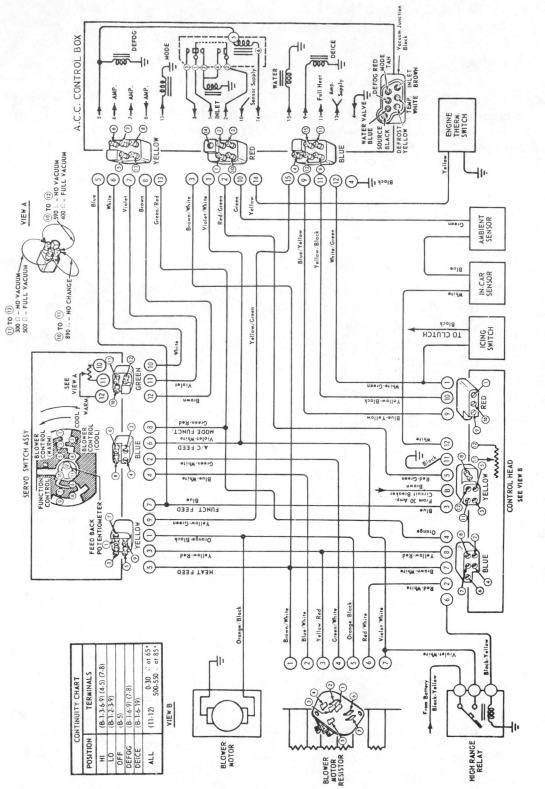

FIG. 47-2 AUTOMATIC CLIMATE CONTROL ELECTRICAL SYSTEM SCHEMATIC

TEST A — INSTRUMENT PANEL ACC FUNCTIONAL CONTROL SWITCH TEST

To test the switch and connecting wiring for continuity and proper resistance, it is necessary to remove the control assembly from the instrument panel. Refer to the wiring diagram for location of test points given in this procedure.

NOTE: When testing for continuity, there should be continuity only between those points given. If procedure indicates there should be continuity between terminals 4 and 5, there should not be continuity between, say, B and 5.

TOOL   MATERIAL

    Ohmmeter   As may be required

PROCEDURE

TO TEST "HIGH" POSITION

1. Check for continuity between terminals B, 1, 3, 6, and 9.

2. Check for continuity between terminals 4 and 5.

3. Check for continuity between terminals 7 and 8.

4. If there is no continuity in any of the three steps above, repair or replace switch. If OK, proceed with next test.

TO TEST "LOW" POSITION

1. Check for continuity between terminals B, 1, 2, 3, and 9.

2. If there is no continuity in any of these terminals, repair or replace switch. If OK, proceed with the next test.

TO TEST "OFF" POSITION

1. Check for continuity between terminals B and 5.

2. If OK, proceed with next step. If not, repair or replace as necessary.

TO TEST "DE-FOG" POSITION

1. Check for continuity between terminals B, 1, 6, and 9.

2. Check for continuity between terminals 7 and 8.

3. If OK, proceed with next test. If not, repair or replace as necessary.

TO TEST "DE-ICE" POSITION

1. Check for continuity between terminals B, 1, 6, and 10.

2. If OK, proceed with next test. If not, repair or replace as necessary.

TEST ALL POSITIONS FOR —

1. Continuity between terminals 11 and 12 of 0-30 ohms with temperature control set at 65° F.

2. Continuity between terminals 11 and 12 of 500-550 ohms with temperature control set at 85° F.

3. If not as specified, repair or replace as necessary.

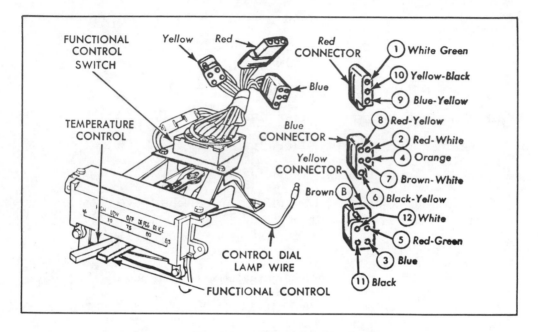

FIG. 47-3   FUNCTIONAL CONTROL SWITCH

TEST B — AUTOMATIC CLIMATE CONTROL (ACC) BOX TEST

The ACC box can be quickly checked for malfunction. If the ACC box fails to pass any one of the tests, it must be replaced as a unit. If the ACC box passes all of the tests, there is trouble elsewhere in the system.

TOOLS

One 6″ jumper wire with an alligator clip on one end and a double female connector on the other, one 3′ jumper wire with an alligator clip on each end, one 12″ jumper wire with a female connector on one end and an alligator clip on the other, two 1/8″ × 2′ vacuum hoses, one 1/8″ × 3″ vacuum hose, four vacuum connectors, one vacuum gage.

MATERIAL

ACC box, if required

PROCEDURE

PREPARE SYSTEM FOR TEST

1. Remove glove box for easy access to ACC box.

2. Ground the ACC box.

3. Disconnect the three multiple electrical connectors from the ACC box.

4. Disconnect the vacuum harness from the ACC box.

5. Connect the 1/8″ × 3″ jumper hose between the harness and the ACC box (S black).

6. Start engine and operate at 1500 r.p.m.

INLET DOOR SOLENOID TEST

1. Apply 12 volts to terminal 2 of the red connector.

2. Connect a vacuum gage to vacuum port I on the ACC box.

3. A solenoid "click" should be heard in the ACC box and a vacuum should be indicated on the gage.

4. If no click is heard, the ACC box is defective and should be replaced. If click is heard, proceed with the next test.

DE-FOG SOLENOID TEST

1. Apply 12 volts to terminal 5 of the yellow connector.

2. Connect a vacuum gage to port D1 of the ACC box connector.

3. A solenoid click should be heard in the ACC box and a vacuum should be indicated on the gage.

4. If no click is heard, the ACC box is defective and should be replaced. If a click is heard, proceed with the next test.

DE-ICE SOLENOID TEST

1. Apply 12 volts to terminal 9 of the blue connector.

2. Connect a vacuum gage to port D2.

3. A solenoid click should be heard in the ACC box and a vacuum should be indicated on the gage.

4. If no click is heard, the ACC box is defective and must be replaced. If a click is heard, proceed with the next test.

MODE SOLENOID TEST

1. Apply 12 volts to terminal 13 of the yellow connector.

2. Connect the vacuum gage to port M of the ACC box.

3. A solenoid click should be heard and a vacuum should be indicated on the gage.

4. If no click is heard, the unit is defective and should be replaced. If a click is heard, proceed with the next test.

WATER VALVE SOLENOID TEST (Units built after 2/19/68)

1. Apply 12 volts to terminal 15 of the blue connector.

2. Connect a vacuum gage to port W.

3. A solenoid click should be heard and a vacuum should be indicated on the gage.

4. If no click is heard, the unit is defective and must be replaced. If a click is heard, proceed with the next test.

COLD WATER BLOWER CUTOFF RELAY TEST

1. Apply 12 volts to terminal 5 of the yellow connector.

2. Ground terminal 14 of the red connector.

3. A relay click should be heard in the ACC box when grounding the wire.

4. If no click is heard, the unit is defective. If a click is heard, proceed with the next test.

TRANSDUCER TEST

1. Connect the power servo yellow connector to the ACC box yellow connector.

2. Connect the vacuum gage to port T of the ACC box connector.

3. Apply 12 volts to terminal 12 of the blue connector.
NOTE: There should be no vacuum reading on the gage at this point.

4. Ground terminal 10 of the red connector.
NOTE: There should now be full vacuum on the gage at this point.

CONCLUSION

   1. If everything checks out properly, reassemble unit as follows:

      a. Connect red and blue multiple connectors of the wiring harness to the red and blue connectors of the ACC box.

      b. Remove ground jumper lead.

      c. Remove vacuum gage.

      d. Reconnect vacuum harness.

      e. Replace glove box.

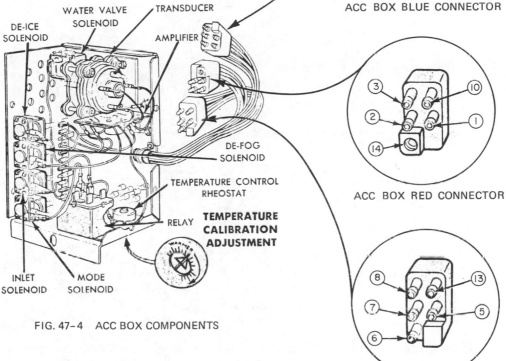

FIG. 47-4   ACC BOX COMPONENTS

TEST C — HIGH-RANGE RELAY TEST

    The high-range relay test is best accomplished by substitution. If the relay is not functioning properly, it should be replaced.

TOOLS

    None

MATERIAL

    High-range relay

PROCEDURE

REPLACE HIGH-RANGE RELAY

1. Disconnect relay harness.

2. Connect new relay into harness.

3. Ground new relay and check for proper operation.

4. If OK, discard old relay and install new relay.

   NOTE: If new relay does not work, check for wiring problems and correct as necessary.

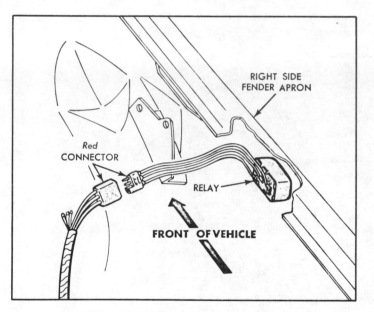

FIG. 47-5   HIGH-RANGE RELAY INSTALLATION

TEST D — POWER-SERVO ASSEMBLY TESTS

The following procedure may be used to test the power-servo assembly for proper operation.

TOOLS

Vacuum gage, ohmmeter

MATERIAL

As may be required

PROCEDURE

PREPARE SYSTEM FOR TEST

1. Disconnect the three multiple connectors from the power-servo connectors.

2. Connect a vacuum gage to an outside vacuum source and the power-servo vacuum actuator.

3. Place transmission in PARK.

4. Start engine and operate at idle speed.

SERVO SWITCH POTENTIOMETER OPEN OR SHORT TEST

1. With an ohmmeter, check the resistance:

   a. From 10 to 11
   b. From 11 to 12
   c. From 10 to 12

2. Resistance should be as follows:

   a. From 10 to 11 — 890 ohms, plus/minus 10%
   b. From 11 to 12 — 300 ohms with no vacuum and 500 ohms with full vacuum, plus/minus 60 ohms
   c. From 10 to 12 — 590 ohms with no vacuum and 400 ohms with full vacuum, plus/minus 60 ohms

SERVO SWITCH POTENTIOMETER WEAR TEST

1. Check resistance from terminals 12 to 10, slowly increasing vacuum from zero to maximum.

   NOTE: Resistance readings should be smooth and continuous.

2. Check resistance from terminals 12 to 11 slowly increasing vacuum from zero to maximum.

   NOTE: Resistance readings should be smooth and continuous.

3. If not as specified, potentiometer must be replaced.

SERVO SWITCH OPEN OR SHORT TEST

1. Check resistance of the following terminals to ground — 1 through 12.

   NOTE: All readings should be open (one megohm or higher).

SERVO SWITCH WARM OPERATION WITH NO VACUUM TESTS

1. Check the continuity from terminal 5 to terminals 1, 2, 3, 4, and 6.

2. Terminals 1 through 4 should show continuity.

3. Terminal 6 should read open.

SERVO SWITCH WARM OPERATION WITH INCREASE/DECREASE VACUUM TEST

1. Check the continuity from terminal 5 to terminals 1 through 4, while vacuum is slowly increased.

2. Circuits 5-1, 5-2, 5-3, and 5-4 should each open in sequence.

NOTE: Circuit 5-4 should open before the crank reaches midway position.

SERVO SWITCH COOL OPERATION WITH NO VACUUM TEST

1. Check continuity from terminal 6 to terminals 1 through 5.

2. All five circuit checks should show open.

SERVO SWITCH COOL OPERATION WITH INCREASE/DECREASE VACUUM TESTS

1. Check continuity from terminal 6 to terminals 1 through 4 in sequence while vacuum is slowly increased.

2. Circuits 6-4, 6-3, 6-2, and 6-1 should close in sequence.

3. Circuit 6-4 should close just after the crank arm reaches mid-position.

SERVO SWITCH FUNCTIONAL OPERATION AT HIGH VACUUM TESTS

1. Check continuity between terminals 7 to 8, 7 to 9, and 8 to 9.

2. Continuity should exist between these terminals.

3. No continuity should exist between these three terminals and any other terminal.

SERVO SWITCH HIGH VACUUM TO ZERO VACUUM OPERATIONAL TEST

NOTE: This test is given in two parts. Part 1 covers the ACC box with a water control valve solenoid and Part 2 covers the ACC box without a water solenoid.

PART 1

1. Check the continuity from terminals 7 to 8, 7 to 9, and 8 to 9 in sequence as vacuum is slowly decreased to zero.

2. Continuity between 8 and 9 should be unbroken.

3. Continuity between 7 and 8 should open at about the midway position of crank arm movement.

4. Continuity between 7 and 9 should open at about the midway position of crank arm movement.

PART 2

1. Check the continuity, as outlined in Part 1, step 1.

2. Continuity between 7 and 9 should open soon after crank arm starts to move.

3. Continuity between 7 and 8 should open at about the midway position of the crank arm.

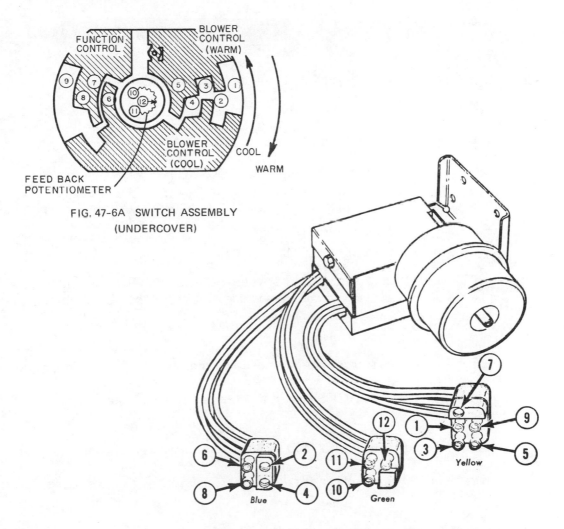

FIG. 47-6A SWITCH ASSEMBLY
(UNDERCOVER)

FIG. 47-6B POWER SERVO

TEST E — TEMPERATURE SENSORS AND CONTROL RHEOSTAT TESTS

The resistance of the two sensors should be tested together with the control assembly rheostat to determine if they are operating properly.

Use the following procedure to determine if the sensors and rheostat are operating properly. The automobile and sensors should be at a temperature of 70° to 80° for accurate test results.

TOOL

Ohmmeter

MATERIAL

As may be required

PROCEDURE

TO TEST SENSORS AND RHEOSTAT

1. Disconnect battery ground cable.

2. Set temperature control dial to 75° F.

3. Disconnect red wiring connector from the ACC box.

4. Connect an ohmmeter between the green wire of the electrical harness and ground.

5. Observe the resistance.

   NOTE: Resistance should be between 1200 and 1300 ohms. If somewhat higher or lower, individual sensors and rheostat resistance should be checked.

TO TEST THE RHEOSTAT

1. Measure total resistance with temperature dial set at 85° F. Note reading.

2. Measure the total resistance with the temperature dial set at 65° F. Note the reading.

3. A resistance differential of 400 to 500 ohms indicates rheostat is good.

4. If less than 400 ohms, check for loose shaft set screw. If it is loose, tighten and recheck.

5. If screw is tight and resistance is less than 400 ohms or more than 500 ohms, the rheostat is defective and must be replaced.

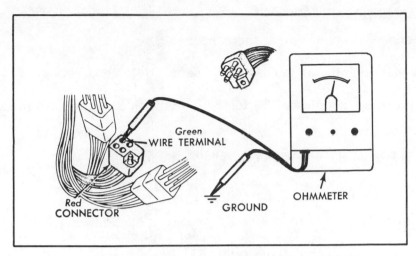

FIG. 47-7A   TEMPERATURE SENSORS AND CONTROL
RHEOSTAT RESISTANCE TEST

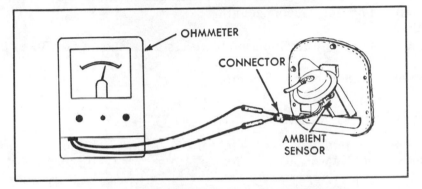

FIG. 47-7B   AMBIENT SENSOR RESISTANCE TEST

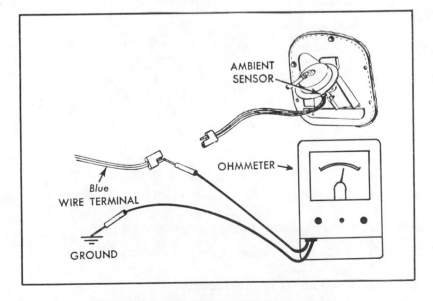

FIG. 47-7C   IN-CAR SENSOR RESISTANCE TEST

TO TEST AMBIENT SENSOR

1. Disconnect connector at the sensor.

2. Connect ohmmeter across the sensor. Note reading.

3. Resistance should be 165 to 185 ohms with an ambient temperature of 70° to 80° F.

4. If not as specified, replace sensor.

TO TEST IN-CAR SENSOR

1. Test the rheostat to insure its proper operation.

2. Set temperature control dial at 65° F.

3. Connect ohmmeter between ground and the blue wire at the ambient sensor (ambient sensor disconnected).

4. Note reading on the ohmmeter. Resistance should be 750 to 900 ohms.

5. If not as specified, replace sensor.

TEST F — HEATER WATER CONTROL VALVE TEST

Before holding this test, always test the water valve solenoid for proper operation. Refer to Test G, "Water Valve Solenoid Test" for the proper procedure.

TOOL

Vacuum gage

MATERIAL

As may be required

PROCEDURE

PREPARE FOR TEST

1. Start engine. Set temperature control to 85° F.

2. Set functional lever to LOW. Allow engine to run until water is warm.

3. Check blend door vacuum motor position.
   NOTE: It should be between mid- and full-vacuum position.

4. Check discharge air from heater ducts.
   NOTE: It should be warm. If not, check water control valve.

TO TEST WATER CONTROL VALVE

1. Remove 1/8″ vacuum line from valve.

2. Install a vacuum gage between the line and water control valve. Note reading on the vacuum gage.

3. If no vacuum and no heat is noted, the water control valve is defective, or the heater core is restricted.

4. Replace control valve or clean heater core as necessary.

TEST G — WATER VALVE SOLENOID TEST

This tests the ability of the solenoid to operate the heater water control valve.

TOOL	MATERIAL
Vacuum gage	As may be required

PROCEDURE

1. Apply 12 volts to terminal 15.

2. Connect vacuum gage to port "W."

3. Listen for "click" and note the vacuum reading on the gage.

4. If no "click" is heard and/or there is no vacuum reading on the gage, the ACC box is defective.

REVIEW QUESTIONS

1. What name does Ford give the automatic temperature control system?

   _____

2. If the inlet door solenoid proves to be defective when holding the ACC box test, how is it repaired? _____

   _____

3. Briefly, how is the high-range relay test made? _____

   _____

4. In the servo switch potentiometer test, resistance from 10 to 11 should be 890 ohms, plus/minus 10%. This means the resistance should be from

   _____ ohms to _____ ohms.

5. Does one megohm reading on an ohmmeter indicate an open or short circuit?

   _____

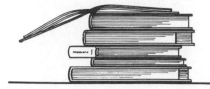

HOSES, LINES AND FITTINGS

This section will deal with the various types of hoses, hose fittings, metal tubing and tube ends as used in automotive air conditioning. Various sizes and types of hose, line and hose fittings are identified. Proper assembly and flare procedures are covered in the Service Procedures, Section III.

REFRIGERANT HOSE

Refrigerant hose is one of the most difficult to formulate. The best assurance you can have against refrigerant loss due to leaking hoses is to insist on refrigeration hose that has been thoroughly tested and engineered for this use.

Some hydraulic hoses are being offered as refrigerant hoses; however, they only meet the requirements prescribed for refrigerant pressure. This type of hose should not be used on automotive air conditioning applications, particularly with insert fittings.

Refrigerant hose, offered by the Murray Corporation, approved for automotive air conditioning work is shown here. This hose is available in both single- and double-braid construction.

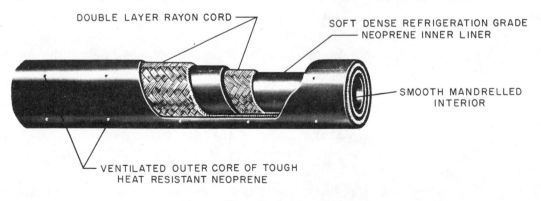

DOUBLE LAYER RAYON CORD

SOFT DENSE REFRIGERATION GRADE NEOPRENE INNER LINER

SMOOTH MANDRELLED INTERIOR

VENTILATED OUTER CORE OF TOUGH HEAT RESISTANT NEOPRENE

DOUBLE — BRAIDED REFRIGERANT HOSE

The R. H. Series double-braid hose is the better of the two hoses offered. It is washed, dried and both ends are sealed to aid in avoiding entrance of dirt or moisture. This hose may be used on all General Motors' units, as well as on most Ford and Chrysler products.

It is available in the following sizes, which should fit any requirement for automotive air conditioning replacement hose.

R. H. Series	Inside Diameter	Outside Diameter
Double Braid	5/16″ 13/32″ 1/2″ 5/8″	3/4″ 15/16″ 1 1/16″ 1 3/16″

The 99 series, or single-braid hose, is not as rigid as the R.H. series. This hose, while it meets the general requirements of refrigeration hose, is not recommended for all automotive applications.

It is available in the following sizes, and is recommended for limited application only.

R. H. Series	Inside Diameter	Outside Diameter
Single Braid	5/16″ 13/32″ 1/2″ 5/8″	3/4″ 29/32″ 1″ 1 3/16″

INSERT FITTINGS

Insert fittings are made of aluminum alloy specially designed to simplify hose assembly and replacement or repair. The fitting selected should have a rating of refrigerant loss of one pound every forty years.

Insert fittings are available in male and female flare as well as male and female O-ring applications. The illustrations on page 338 demonstrate the various types of insert fittings available. Correct cutting and assembly procedures are covered in the Service Procedures, Section III.

TUBING

An aluminum tube is specially processed for refrigeration work and is available at most refrigeration supply houses, though most servicemen prefer soft-drawn copper tube.

In either case, tubing should only be used in automotive applications where vibration will be kept to a minimum, such as the liquid line. Tubing can never be used as any line running to the compressor because of the engine vibration. Tubing can, however, be run to a point just before the compressor and a piece of rubber hose added to take up the shock of the engine.

Copper tube is available in several sizes, many that are not standard in the automobile air conditioner. Those sizes that are standard are: 1/4″, 3/8″, 1/2″ and 5/8″. These are outside diameters as this is the method used in identification.

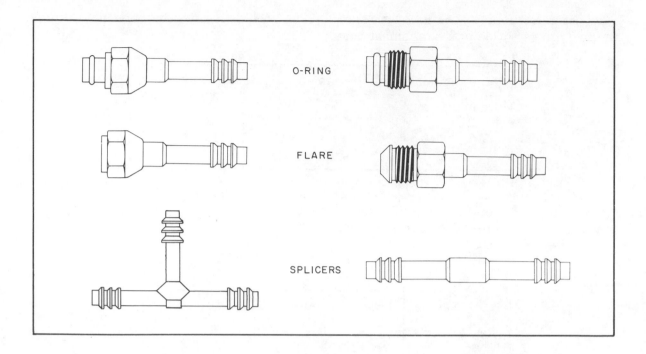

TUBE NUTS AND FITTINGS

Tube nuts, reducers, fittings, sweat and compression fittings, as well as flare, male and female, are available in all sizes to meet every requirement of the air conditioning mechanic. These fittings and adapters are too numerous to list here. Your refrigeration supply house should be contacted for their catalog of fittings for your requirement.

PURPOSE AND METHODS OF FLARING

Leak-proof flares are important to the efficient operation of any refrigeration system. Flares, which fit against machined surfaces are prepared by one of two common methods: They are either formed by a spinning action or punched and blocked. While there are many manufacturers of flaring tools, only one type is illustrated as being typical of the construction and operation of each.

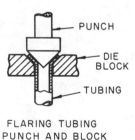

FLARING TUBING
PUNCH AND BLOCK

SINGLE THICKNESS FLARES

Flaring tools contain a series of blocks, usually ranging from 3/16″ to 5/8″, to accommodate tubing of these sizes. The tubing is inserted in the proper block and projects above the face of the block to whatever distance is recommended by the manufacturer. The better tools eliminate guesswork in positioning the tubing. Means are provided in positioning the tubing formed with top of die blocks for accurate flare diameters. The flare is formed as the cone is advanced into the tubing, forcing the tubing against the die block opening. A drop of lubricating oil should be placed between the cone and the tubing.

Precision flaring tools are also available for flaring tubing above the die blocks. This method maintains the original tubing wall thickness at the base of the flare, eliminating flare failures at this point. These tools are usually designed with a faceted flaring cone that tends to smooth out any surface imperfections on the flare seat by a burnishing action.

The term "single thickness flare" means that the part of the tubing that forms a flare is the thickness of the tubing. A "double thickness flare" indicates that the flare thickness is made up of two thicknesses of tubing.

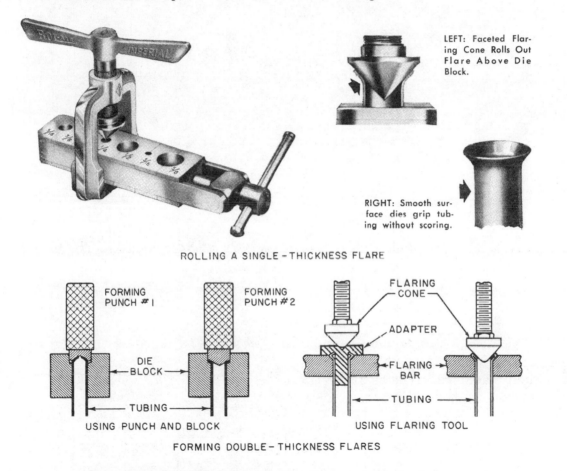

LEFT: Faceted Flaring Cone Rolls Out Flare Above Die Block.

RIGHT: Smooth surface dies grip tubing without scoring.

ROLLING A SINGLE-THICKNESS FLARE

FORMING PUNCH #1

FORMING PUNCH #2

DIE BLOCK

TUBING

USING PUNCH AND BLOCK

FLARING CONE

ADAPTER

FLARING BAR

TUBING

USING FLARING TOOL

FORMING DOUBLE-THICKNESS FLARES

DOUBLE THICKNESS FLARES

The double thickness flare is used on larger sizes of tubing and, especially, where an extra strong joint is required to withstand vibration. The double thickness flare may be made by the punch and block method or by using a double flaring tool. The point of the flaring cone is brought down against an adapter which forces the tubing to become bell-shaped. The cone is backed off, the adapter is removed, and the flaring cone is rotated against the top edge of the tube until it forms the double shoulder flare.

WIRING DIAGRAMS

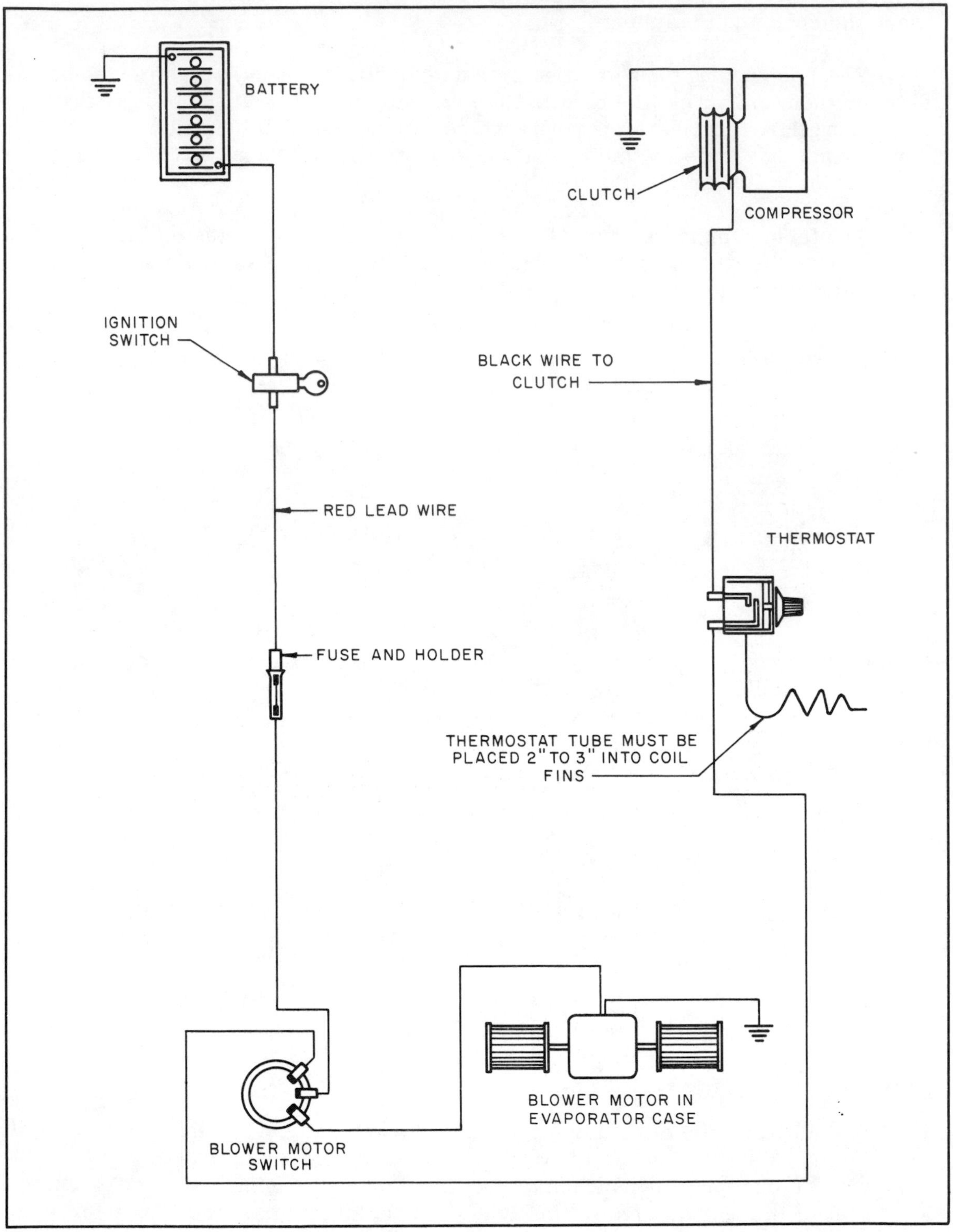

BATTERY

CLUTCH

COMPRESSOR

IGNITION
SWITCH

BLACK WIRE TO
CLUTCH

RED LEAD WIRE

THERMOSTAT

FUSE AND HOLDER

THERMOSTAT TUBE MUST BE
PLACED 2" TO 3" INTO COIL
FINS

BLOWER MOTOR IN
EVAPORATOR CASE

BLOWER MOTOR
SWITCH

Basic Wiring Diagram

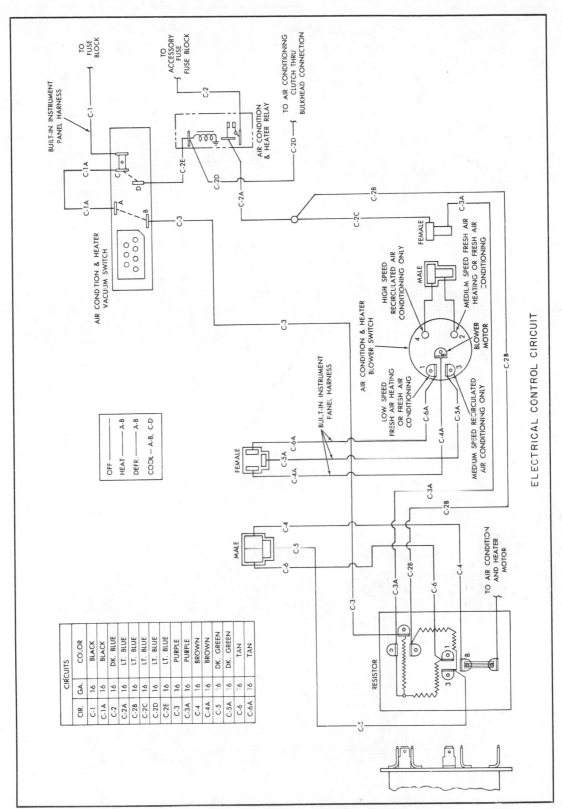

Typical Chrysler Wiring Diagram

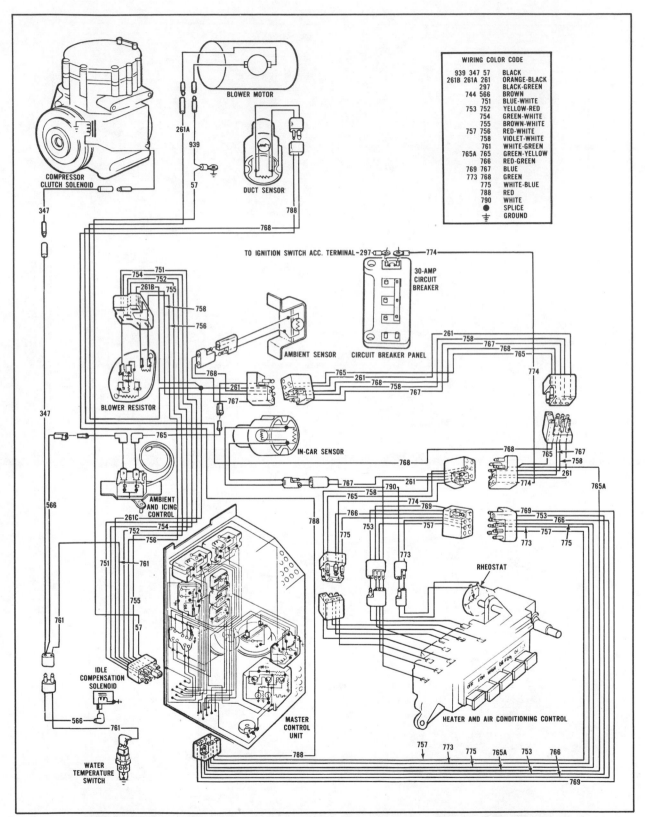

Ford Motor Company's Automatic Temperature Control Diagram

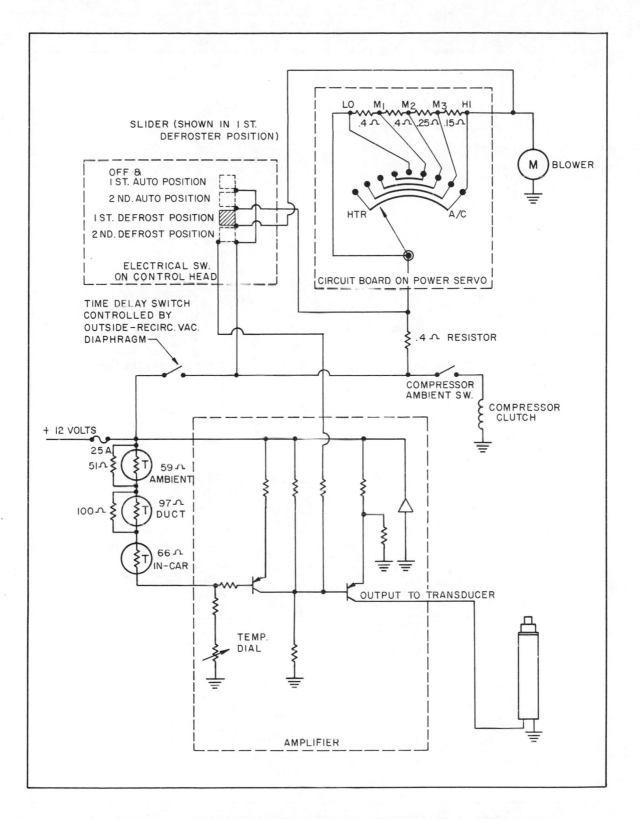

General Motors' Automatic Temperature Control Wiring Diagram

VACUUM DIAGRAMS

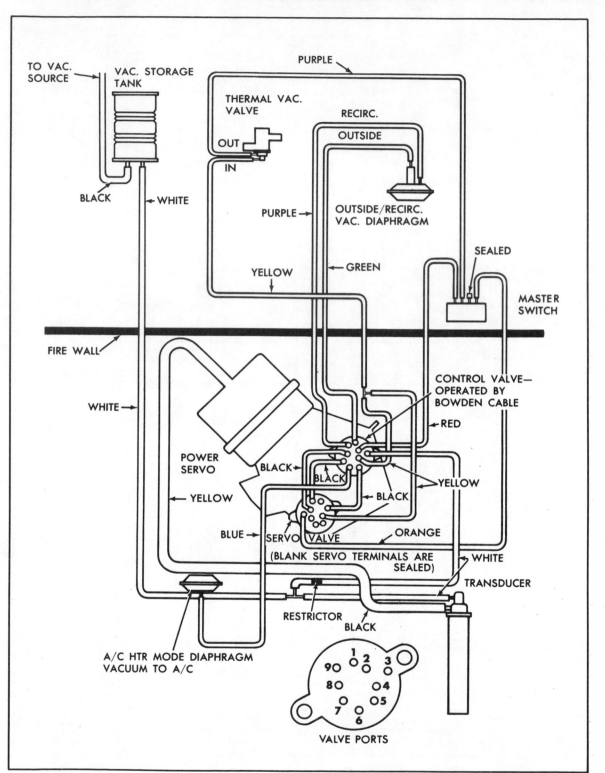

General Motors' Automatic Temperature Control Vacuum Diagram

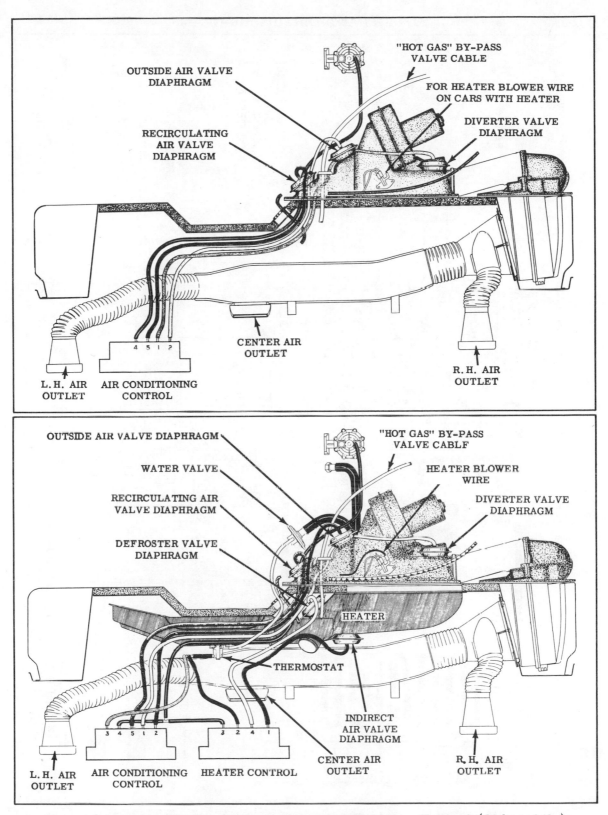

General Motors' Air Conditioning Vacuum Diagram - Typical (Oldsmobile)

REFRIGERANT CIRCUIT DIAGRAMS

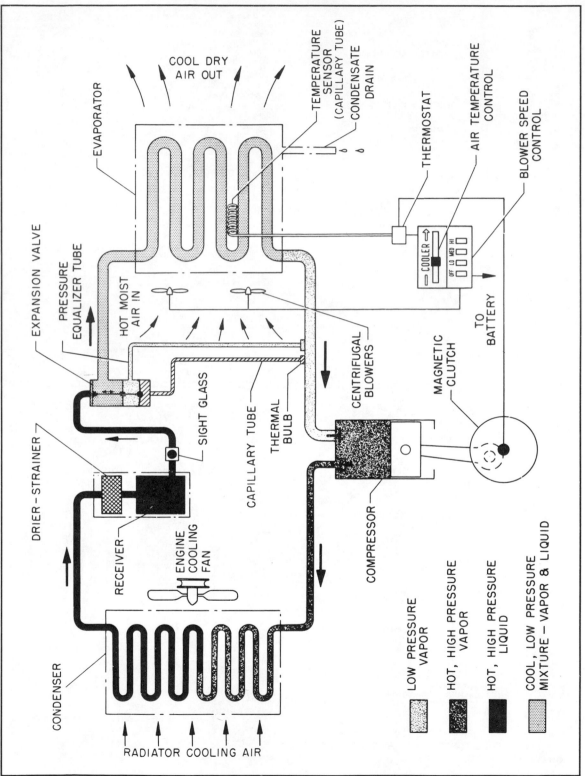

Chrysler MoPar Air Conditioning Circuit

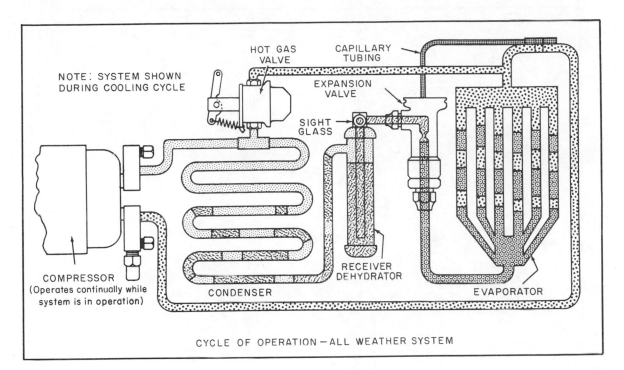

NOTE: SYSTEM SHOWN
DURING COOLING CYCLE

HOT GAS
VALVE

CAPILLARY
TUBING

EXPANSION
VALVE

SIGHT
GLASS

COMPRESSOR
(Operates continually while
system is in operation)

CONDENSER

RECEIVER
DEHYDRATOR

EVAPORATOR

CYCLE OF OPERATION — ALL WEATHER SYSTEM

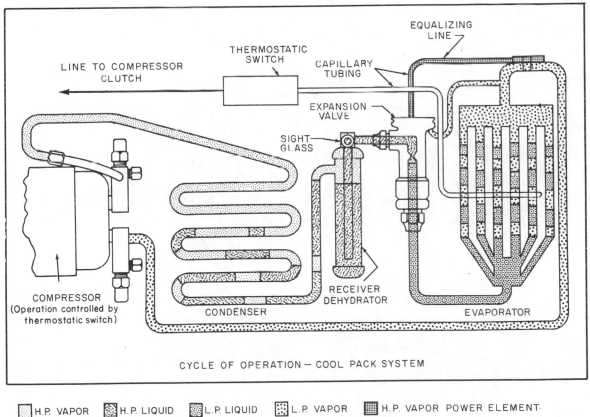

LINE TO COMPRESSOR
CLUTCH

THERMOSTATIC
SWITCH

EQUALIZING
LINE

CAPILLARY
TUBING

EXPANSION
VALVE

SIGHT
GLASS

COMPRESSOR
(Operation controlled by
thermostatic switch)

CONDENSER

RECEIVER
DEHYDRATOR

EVAPORATOR

CYCLE OF OPERATION — COOL PACK SYSTEM

H.P. VAPOR   H.P. LIQUID   L.P. LIQUID   L.P. VAPOR   H.P. VAPOR POWER ELEMENT

General Motors' Air Conditioning Circuit

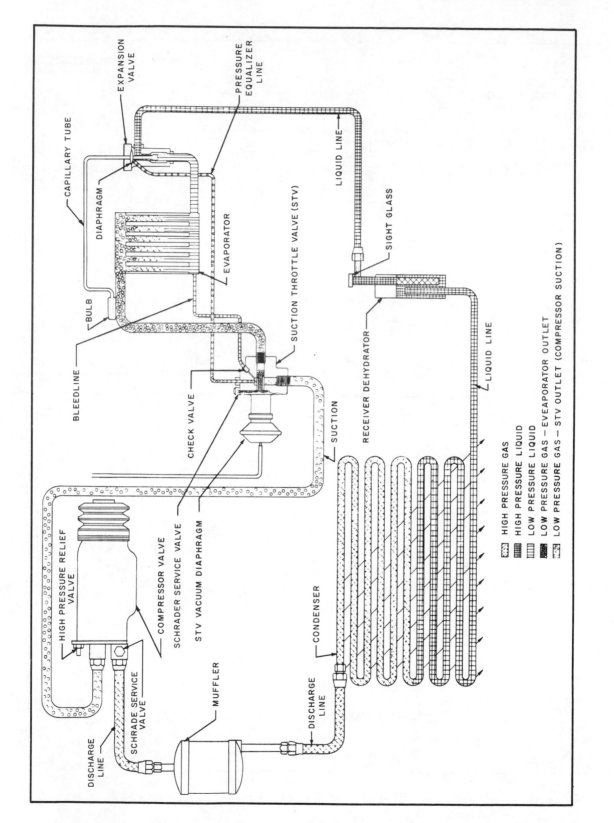

General Motors' Air Conditioning Circuit with Suction Throttling Valve

YORK COMPRESSOR IDENTIFICATION

Compressor identification is important to insure that when mounted in the car, proper operation of the oil pump is possible.

Compressor models can be identified by their color. Six cubic inch York compressors are blue. Nine and ten cubic inch compressors are grey, or black; nine cubic inch compressors have a groove around the crankshaft end; ten cubic inch compressors do not have a groove.

Left-hand mounted compressors have four mounting holes drilled on your left-hand side as you look at the rear of the cover plate. Conversely, right-hand mounted compressors have four holes drilled on the right. Universal mount compressors have drilled and tapped mounting bosses on both sides of the crankcase.

The year of manufacture and reverse rotation compressors may be identified from the nameplate as follows:

1958 Black on Silver

1959 Red on Silver

1960 Dark Blue on Silver - standard

1960 Yellow on Silver - reverse

1961 Green on Silver - Universal mount also has Red on Silver

1962 Green on Silver - Universal mount also has Red on Silver, and a "C" suffix in serial number

1963 Light Blue on Silver - at rear of compressor; also will have a "D" suffix in serial number

1964 and later - Metal plate mounted on top front surface with date of manufacture stamped on it

MOUNTING DESIGNATIONS

L	Left-hand mount compressor
R	Right-hand mount compressor
UL	Universal mount. Factory shipped for left-hand mount
UR	Universal mount. Factory shipped for right-hand mount
LR	Left-hand mount. Reverse rotation compressor
RR	Right-hand mount. Reverse rotation compressor
U	Universal mounting. Beginning with 1963 model, compressors have no mounting designations as they can be mounted universally and run in either direction, clockwise or counterclockwise.

SERVICE VALVES

Service valves may be standard hand shutoff valves or Schrader-type service valves. While the hand shutoff valve and Schrader-type valve are interchangeable, distinction must be made between the type of mounting desired; swivel pad or swivel Rotalock.

TO CHANGE MOUNTING POSITIONS

Universal left and Universal right compressors may be changed for opposite mounting by changing the rear oil pump plate, or with the series 1962 compressor, changing the oil passage screws at the rear of the compressor.

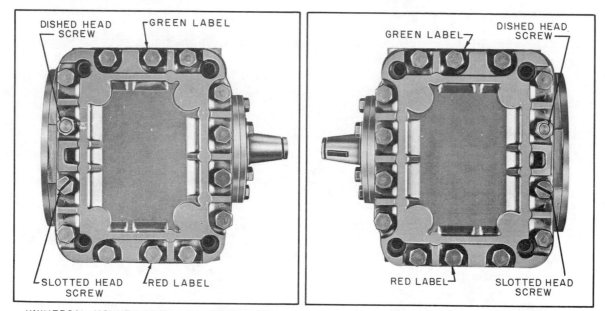

UNIVERSAL MOUNT — SERIES 62 BASEPLATE
VIEW, UNIVERSAL LEFT

UNIVERSAL MOUNT — SERIES 62 BASEPLATE
VIEW, UNIVERSAL RIGHT

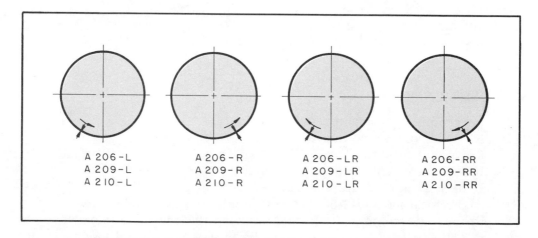

COMPRESSOR ROTATION WHEN FACING REAR OF COMPRESSOR
(END OPPOSITE FLYWHEEL).

COMPRESSOR DISPLACEMENT IDENTIFICATION

The compressor may be identified by the crankshaft and cubic inch displacement determined even if all other identification is removed. The six cubic inch compressor will have a .030 × 45° chamfer at the end of the crankshaft; the nine cubic inch compressor will have a .015 groove cut into the end; the ten cubic inch compressor will have sharp corners at the end of the crankshaft.

NOMENCLATURE

The following designation is given to York compressors by the manufacturer.

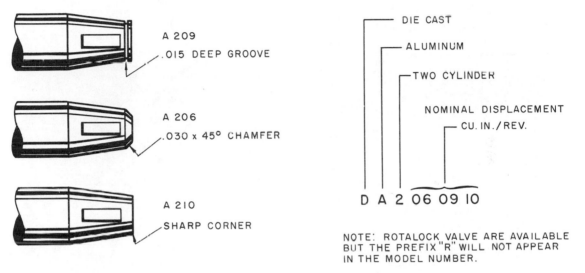

A 209
.015 DEEP GROOVE

A 206
.030 x 45° CHAMFER

A 210
SHARP CORNER

DISPLACEMENT IDENTIFICATION

DIE CAST
ALUMINUM
TWO CYLINDER
NOMINAL DISPLACEMENT
CU. IN./REV.

D A 2 06 09 10

NOTE: ROTALOCK VALVE ARE AVAILABLE BUT THE PREFIX "R" WILL NOT APPEAR IN THE MODEL NUMBER.

NOMENCLATURE

MODEL A-209

Car Speed, MPH	Idle	10	20	30	40	50	60	70
Compressor Speed, RPM	350	456	1090	1640	2185	2740	3280	3820
BTU/HR	2600	3800	8500	13500	17500	21250	22600	25000
HP Required by Compressor	.4	.70	1.3	2.2	2.85	3.8	4.6	5.1

MODEL A-206

Car Speed, MPH	Idle	10	20	30	40	50	60	70
Compressor Speed, RPM	350	456	1090	1640	2185	2740	3280	3820
BTU/HR	1100	1800	5000	8200	11000	13800	15200	16200
HP Required by Compressor	.25	.43	.79	1.33	1.72	2.30	2.8	3.1

MODEL A-210

Car Speed, MPH	Idle	10	20	30	40	50	60	70
Compressor Speed, RPM	350	456	1090	1640	2185	2740	3280	3820
BTU/HR	3100	5000	11500	15800	19500	23500	25000	27000
HP Required by Compressor	.6	.75	1.5	2.5	3.0	3.9	4.75	5.2

HEAVY-DUTY FANS

Because of the added heat load placed on a car with an air conditioner, it is, in some cases, necessary to add a heavy-duty fan to increase air flow across the radiator and air conditioning condenser. Manufacturers' recommendations should be followed as to the type and size of the fan to use.

The following chart, typical specifications, is of a 25° pitch, six-blade thinline fan, manufactured by the Fort Worth Pressed Steel Corporation. It is easy to see the increase in air flow from this chart.

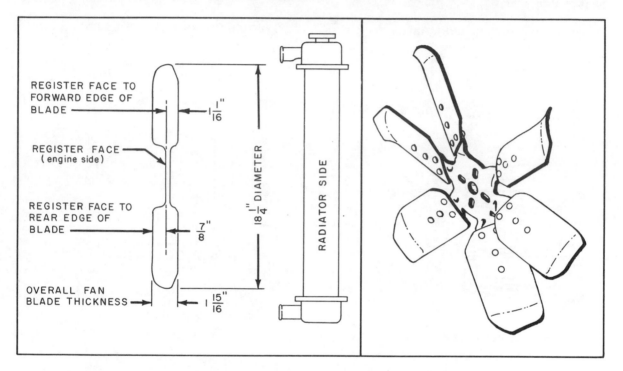

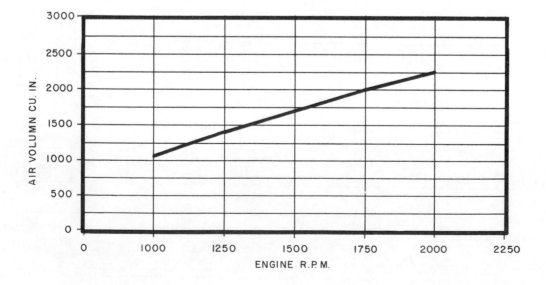

REFERENCE BOOKS

Harrison Automotive Air Conditioning Training Manual by Harrison
    Radiator Division, General Motors Corp., Lockport, New York

Modern Refrigeration and Air Conditioning by A. D. Althouse and C. H.
    Turnquist, Goodheart-Willcox Co., Chicago, Illinois.

Principles of Air Conditioning by V. Paul Lang, Delmar Publishers,
    Albany, New York.

Principles of Refrigeration by R. Warren Marsh and C. Thomas Olivo,
    Delmar Publishers, Albany, New York.

Refrigeration Servicing by Paul F. Goliber, Delmar Publishers, Albany,
    New York.

Direct Current Fundamentals by Orla E. Loper, Delmar Publishers,
    Albany, New York.

Manufacturers' shop manuals published by all automobile manufacturers.

GLOSSARY

A

Absolute Pressure – Pressure measured from absolute zero instead of normal atmospheric pressure.

Absolute Temperature – Temperature measured on the Rankine thermometer calibrated from absolute zero. The freezing point of water on the Rankine Scale is 492° R.

Absolute Zero – The complete absence of heat, believed to be -459.67° F. This is shown as 0° on the Rankine and Kelvin Scales.

Accumulator – A tank located in the tail pipe to receive the refrigerant that leaves the evaporator. This device is so constructed as to insure that no liquid refrigerant will enter the compressor.

Air Conditioner – A device used in the control of temperature, humidity, cleanness, and movement of air.

Air Conditioning – The control of the temperature, humidity, cleanness, and movement of air.

Air Inlet Valve – A movable door in the plenum blower assembly that permits the selection of outside air or inside air for both heating and cooling systems.

Air Outlet Valve – A movable door in the plenum blower assembly that directs air flow into the heater core or into duct work that leads to the evaporator.

Ambient Air – Air surrounding an object.

Ambient Air Temperature – See "Ambient Temperature."

Ambient Temperature – Temperature of surrounding air. In air conditioning work it refers to outside air temperature.

Ambient Sensor – A thermistor used in automatic temperature control units for sensing ambient temperature. Also see "Thermistor."

Ambient Switch – A switch used to control compressor operation, turning it on or off, regulated by ambient temperature.

Amplifer – A device used in automatic temperature control units providing an output voltage which is in proportion to its input voltage from the sensors.

Annealed Copper – Copper used in refrigeration systems that has been heat treated to render it workable.

Atmospheric Pressure – Air pressure at a given altitude. At sea level, atmospheric pressure is 14.696 p.s.i.

Atom – The smallest possible particle of matter.

Auxiliary Seal – Used on General Motors compressors through 1960, this seal mounted outside the seal housing, prevents refrigeration oil from entering the clutch assembly.

B

Back Idler – A pulley to tighten the drive belt that rides on the back or flat side of the belt.

Back Seat – (Service Valve) Turning the valve stem to the left all the way backseats the valve. The valve outlet to the system is open and the service port is closed.

Bellows – An accordian-type chamber which will expand or contract with temperature changes creating a mechanical controlling action such as in a thermostatic expansion valve.

Bi-metal – Two dissimilar metals fused together which expand (or contract) at different temperatures causing a bending effect. Used in temperature sensing controls.

Bi-metal Thermostat – A thermostat using bi-metal strips instead of a bellows for making or breaking contact points.

Bleeding – Slowly releasing pressure in the air conditioning system by drawing off some liquid or gas.

Blower – See "Squirrel Cage Blower."

Blower Fan – See "Squirrel Cage Blower" or "fan."

Boiling Point – The temperature at which a liquid changes to a vapor.

Bowden Cable – A wire cable inside a metal or rubber housing used to regulate a valve or control from a remote place.

Brazing – A high-temperature metal joining process satisfactory for units with relatively high internal pressures.

British Thermal Unit (B.T.U.) – The amount of heat necessary to raise one pound of water one degree Fahrenheit.

B.T.U. – See "British Thermal Unit."

C

Calorie – The smallest measure of heat energy. One calorie is the amount of heat energy required to raise one gram of water one degree Centigrade.

Can Tap – A device used to pierce, dispense, and seal small cans of refrigerant.

Can Valve – See "Can Trap."

C

Capillary – A small tube with calibrated length and inside diameter used as a metering device.

Capillary Attraction – The power possessed by tubular bodies of drawing up a fluid.

Capillary Tube – A tube with calibrated inside diameter and length used to control the flow of refrigerant. In automotive air conditioning the tube connecting the remote bulb to the expansion valve or to the thermostat is called the capillary tube.

Capacity – Refrigeration produced, measured in tons or B.T.U.s per hour.

Centigrade – A thermometer scale using the freezing point of water as zero. The boiling point of water is 100° C.

Change of State – Rearrangement of the molecular structure of matter as it changes between any two of the three physical states; solid, liquid, or gas.

Charge – A specific amount of refrigerant or oil by volume or weight.

Charging – The act of placing a charge of refrigerant or oil into the air conditioning system.

Charging Cylinder – A container with a visual indicator for use where a critical, or exact, amount of refrigerant must be measured.

Charging Hose – A small diameter hose constructed to withstand high pressures between the unit and manifold set.

Charging Station – A unit containing a manifold gage set, charging cylinder, vacuum pump, and leak detector, for servicing air conditioners.

Check Valve – A device located in the liquid line or inlet to the drier to prevent liquid refrigerant from flowing the opposite way when the unit is shut off.

Chemical Instability – An undesirable condition caused by the presence of contaminants in the refrigeration system.

Circuit Breaker – A bi-metallic device used instead of a fuse to protect a circuit.

Clutch – A coupling device which transfers torque from a driving to a driven number when desired.

Clutch Armature – That part of the clutch that is pulled in when engaged.

Clutch Coil – See "Clutch Field."

Clutch Field – Consists of many windings of wire and is found fastened to the front of the compressor. Current applied sets up a magnetic field that pulls the armature in to engage the clutch.

Clutch Plate – Found in General Motors' clutches prior to 1961 and is referred to as "Ball-and-Ramp" clutch.

Clutch Rotor – That portion of the clutch that the belt rides in and is freewheeling until engaged. On some clutches the field is found in the rotor, the electrical connection being made by the use of brushes.

Cold – The absence of heat.

Compound Gage – A gage that will register both pressure and vacuum, used on the low side of the systems.

Compressor – A component of the refrigeration system that pumps refrigerant and increases the pressure of refrigerant vapor.

Compressor Displacement – A figure obtained by multiplying displacement of compressor cylinder or cylinders by a given RPM, usually average engine speed of 30 MPH, or 1750 RPM.

Compressor Shaft Seal – An assembly consisting of springs, snap rings, O-rings, shaft seal, seal sets, and gaskets, mounted on the compressor crankshaft permitting the shaft to be turned without loss of refrigerant or oil.

Condensate – Water taken from the air which forms on the exterior surface of the evaporator.

Condensation – The act of changing a vapor to a liquid.

Condenser – The component of a refrigeration system in which refrigerant vapor is changed to a liquid by the removal of heat.

Condenser Comb – A comb-like device used to straighten fins on the evaporator or condenser.

Condenser Temperature – The Temperature at which compressed gas in the condenser changes from a gas to a liquid.

Condensing Pressure – Head pressure as read from the gage at the high-side service valve; pressure from the discharge side of the compressor into the condenser.

Conduction – Transmission of heat through a solid.

Conduction of Heat – The ability of a substance to conduct heat.

Contaminants – Anything other than refrigerant and refrigeration oil in the system.

GLOSSARY

C

Convection – The transfer of heat by the circulation of a vapor or liquid.

Custom System – A delux automotive air conditioning system that uses both inside and outside air.

Cycling Clutch System – Referring to a system which uses a clutch, thermostatically controlled, as a means of temperature control.

Cylinder – A circular drum used to store refrigerant.

D

Declutching Fan – An engine cooling fan mounted on the water pump with a temperature sensitive device to govern or limit terminal speed.

De-Ice Switch – A switch used to control compressor operation to prevent evaporator freezup.

Density – Weight or mass of a gas, liquid, or solid.

Desiccant – A drying agent used in refrigeration systems to remove excess moisture.

Design Working Pressure – The maximum allowable working pressure for which a specific system component is designed to work safely.

Deoxidized – Referring to a tubing or metal surface that is free of oxide formations, which may have been caused by action of air or other chemicals.

Diagnosis – The procedure followed to locate the cause of a malfunction.

Diaphragm – A rubber-like piston or bellows assembly dividing the inner and outer chambers of back pressure-regulated air conditioning control devices.

Dichlorodifluoromethane – See "Refrigerant - 12."

Discharge – To bleed some or all of the refrigerant from a system by opening a valve or connection and permitting the refrigerant to escape slowly.

Discharge Air – Conditioned air as it passes through the outlets and enters the passenger compartment.

Discharge Line – Connects the compressor outlet to the condenser inlet.

Discharge Pressure – Pressure of the refrigerant being discharged from the compressor. High-side pressure.

Discharge Side – That portion of the refrigeration system under high pressure, extending from the compressor outlet to the thermostatic expansion valve inlet.

Discharge Valve – See "High-Side Service Valve."

Displacement – In automotive air conditioning referring to the compressor stroke X-bore.

Distributor – A device used to divide the flow of liquid refrigerant between parallel paths in an evaporator.

Double Flare – A flare on the end of a piece of copper tubing or other soft metal that has been folded over to form a double face.

Drier – A device containing desiccant placed in the liquid line to absorb moisture in the system.

Drive Pulley – A vee pulley attached to the crankshaft of an automobile used to drive the compressor clutch pulley by use of a belt.

Drip Pan – A shallow pan located uner the evaporator core used to catch condensation. A drain hose is fastened to the drip pan and extended to the outside to carry off the condensate.

Drying Agent – See "Desiccant."

E

E.P.R. – See "Evaporator Pressure Regulator."

Equalizer Line – A line or connection used specifically for obtaining required operation from certain control valves. Very little, if any, refrigerant flows through this line.

E.T.R. – See "Evaporator Temperature Regulator."

Evacuate – To create a vacuum within a system to remove all trace of air and moisture.

Evaporation – Changing from a liquid to a vapor.

E

Evaporator – The component of an air conditioning system that conditons the air.

Evaporator Pressure Regulator – A back pressure regulated temperature control device used by Chrysler products.

Evaporator Temperature Regulator – A temperature regulated device used by Chrysler Air-temp to control evaporator pressure.

Expansion Valve – "Thermostatic Expansion Valve."

External Equalizer – See "Equalizer Line."

F

Fahrenheit – A thermometer scale using 32° as the freezing point of water.

Fan – A device having two or more blades attached to the shaft of a motor, mounted in the evaporator, to cause air to pass over the evaporator. A device having four or more blades, mounted on the water pump, to cause air to pass through the radiator and condenser.

Field – A coil with many turns of wire located behind the clutch rotor. Current passing through this coil sets up a magnetic field and causes the clutch to engage.

Filter – A device used with the drier or as a separate unit to remove foreign material from the refrigerant.

Fitz-All – A can tap designed to be used on screw top and flat top refrigerant cans.

Flare – A flange or cone-shaped end applied to a piece of tubing to provide a means of fastening to a fitting.

Flash Gas – Gas resulting from the instantaneous evaporation of refrigerant in a pressure-reducing device such as an expansion valve.

Flooding – A condition caused by too much liquid refrigerant being metered into the evaporator.

Fluid – A liquid, gas, or vapor.

Flush – To remove solid particles such as metal flakes or dirt. Refrigerant passages are purged with refrigerant.

Flux – A substance used in the joining of metals when heat is used to promote fusion of metals.

Foaming – The formation of a froth of oil and refrigerant due to rapid boiling out of the refrigerant dissolved in the oil when the pressure is suddenly reduced.

Foot-Pound – A unit of energy required to raise one pound one foot.

Freeze Protection – Controlling evaporator temperature so moisture on its surface will not freeze and block the air flow.

Freezeup – Failure of a unit to operate properly due to the formation of ice at the expansion valve.

Freezing Point – The temperature at which a given liquid will solidify. Water will freeze at 32° F.; this is its freezing point.

Freon Refrigerant – Registered trademark of E. I. Dupont.

Freon 12 – See "Refrigerant 12."

Front Idler – A vee groove pulley used in automotive air conditioning as a means of tightening the drive belt. The belt rides in the vee groove pulley.

Front Seat – Closing of the compressor service valves by turning them all the way in, clockwise.

Front Seating – Closing off the line leaving the compressor open to the service port fitting. This allows service to the compressor without purging the entire system. Never operate the system with the valves front seated.

Frosting Back – The appearance of frost on the tail pipe and suction line extending back as far as the compressor.

Fuse – An electrical device used to protect a circuit against accidental overload or unit malfunction.

Fusion – The act of melting.

G

Gas – A vapor having no particles or droplets of liquid.

Gage Manifold – See "Manifold."

Gage Set – Two or more instruments attached to a manifold and used for measuring or testing pressure.

Genetron 12 – Refrigerant 12 by ALLIED Chemicals Company. A registered trademark.

H

Halide Leak Detector — A device consisting of a tank of acetylene gas, a stove, chimney, and search hose used to detect leaks by visual means.

Headliner — That part of the automobile interior overhead or covering the roof inside. Some early air conditioners had duct work in the headliner.

Head Pressure — Pressure of the refrigerant from the discharge reed valve through lines and condenser to the expansion valve orifice.

Heat — **Energy.** Any temperature above absolute zero.

Heat Exchanger — An apparatus in which heat is transferred from one fluid to another, on the principle that heat will move to an object with less heat.

Heat Intensity — The measurement of heat concentration with a thermometer.

Heat Quantity — Amount of heat as measured on a thermometer. See "British Thermal Unit."

Heat Radiation — The transmission of heat from one substance to another while passing through, but not heating, intervening substances.

Heat of Respiration — The heat given off by ripening vegetables or fruits in the conversion of starches and sugars.

Heat Transmission — Any flow of heat.

Heliarc — The act of joining two pieces of aluminum or stainless steel using a high-frequency electric weld and an inert gas, such as helium. This weld is made electrically while the inert gas is fed around the weld. This gas prevents oxidation by keeping the surrounding air away.

Hg. — Chemical symbol for Mercury.

High Head — A term used when the head, or high side, pressures of the system is excessive.

High Load Condition — Refers to times when the air conditioner must operate continuously at maximum capacity to provide the cool air required.

High-Pressure Lines — The lines from the compressor outlet to the expansion valve inlet that carry high-pressure liquid and gas.

High Side — See "Discharge Side."

High-Side Service Valve — A device located on the discharge side of the compressor to allow the serviceman to check high-side pressures and perform other necessary operation.

High Suction — Low-side pressure higher than normal due to a malfunction of the system.

High Vacuum — A vacuum below 500 microns or 1/2 mm. Hg.

High-Vacuum Pump — A two-stage vacuum pump that has the capability of pulling below 500 microns. Many vacuum pumps will pull to 25 microns, or 29.999 of mercury.

Hot Gas — The condition of the refrigerant as it leaves the compressor until it gives up its heat and condenses.

Hot Gas Bypass Line — The line that connects the hot gas bypass valve outlet to the evaporator outlet. Metered hot gas flows through this line.

Hot Gas Bypass Valve — A device used to meter hot gas back to the evaporator through the bypass line to prevent condensate from freezing on the core.

Hot Gas Defrosting — The use of high-pressure gas in the evaporator to effect the removal of frost.

Humidity — See "Moisture."

Hydrolizing Action — The corrosive action within the air conditioning system induced by a weak solution of hydrochloric acid formed by excessive moisture reacting with the refrigerant chemically.

I

Ice Melting Capacity — Refrigerant equal to the latent heat of fusion of a stated weight of ice at 144 B.T.U. per pound.

Ideal Humidity — A relative humidity of 50%.

Ideal Temperature — Temperature from $68°$ to $72°$.

Idler — A pulley device to keep belt whip out of the drive belt of an automotive air conditioner. Also used as a means of tightening the belt.

Idler Eccentric — A device used with idler pulley as a means of tightening the belt.

I

In-Car Sensor – A thermistor used in automatic temperature control units for sensing in-car temperature. Also, see "Thermistor."

Inches of Mercury – A unit of measure when referring to a vacuum.

Inch Pound – Unit of energy required to raise one pound one inch.

In-Duct Sensor – A thermistor used in automatic temperature control units for sensing in-duct return air temperature. Also, see "Thermistor."

Insulate – To isolate or seal off with a nonconductor.

Insulation Tape – Tape, rubber or cork, used to wrap refrigeration hoses and lines to prevent condensate drip.

Isotron 12 – Refrigerant 12 by Penn Salt Company. A trademark.

K

Kinetic – Pertaining to motion.

Kelvin – A thermometer scale using 273° K as the freezing point of water. Absolute zero on this thermometer is the start; 459.67° F. or 0° K.

L

Latent Heat – The amount of heat required to cause a change of state of a substance without changing its temperature.

Latent Heat of Condensation – The quantity of heat given off while changing a substance from vapor to a liquid.

Latent Heat of Evaporation – The quantity of heat required to change a liquid into a vapor without raising the temperature of the vapor above that of the original liquid.

Latent Heat of Fusion – The amount of heat that must be removed from a liquid to cause it to change to a solid without causing a change of temperature.

Latent Heat of Vaporization – See "Latent Heat of Evaporation."

Leak Detector – See "Halide Leak Detector."

Liquid – A column of fluid without gas pockets or solids.

Liquid Line – Line connecting the drier outlet with the expansion valve inlet. The line from the condenser outlet to the drier inlet is sometimes referred to as a liquid line also.

Load – The required rate of heat removal in a given time.

Low-Head Pressure – High-side pressure lower than normal due to a malfunction of the system.

Low Side – See "Suction Side."

Low-Side Service Valve – A device located on the suction side of the compressor to allow the serviceman to check low-side pressures or perform other necessary service operations.

Low-Suction Pressure – Pressure lower than normal in the suction side of the system due to a malfunction of the unit.

Lubricant – See "Refrigeration Oil."

M

Magnetic Clutch – A coupling device used to turn compressor on and off electrically.

Manifold – A device equipped with a hand shutoff valve that gages may be connected to for use in system testing and servicing.

Manifold Gage – A calibrated instrument used for measuring pressures of the system.

Manifold Gage Set – A manifold complete with gages and charging hoses.

Mean Altitude – 900 feet is used as the mean, or average, altitude by engineers.

Melting Point – The temperature above which a solid cannot exist at a given pressure.

GLOSSARY

M

Mercury – See "hg."

Micron – A unit of measure .1,000 microns equal 1 millimeter, or .03937 inches.

Millimeter – A unit of measure .1 millimeter is 1/1000 of a meter.

Mobil Sorbead – A desiccant used in General Motor's driers.

Molecular Sieve – A drying agent. See "Desiccant."

Monochlorodifluoromethane – See "Refrigerant 22."

Mount and Drive – Pulleys, mounting plates, belts, and fittings necessary to mount a compressor and clutch assembly onto an engine.

Muffler – A hollow tubular device used in the discharge line of some air conditioners to minimize compressor thumping sounds transmitted to the inside of the car. Some use a muffler on the low side as well.

O

Oil Bleed Line – An external line usually bypassing an expansion valve, evaporator pressure regulator, or bypass valve to insure positive oil return to the compressor at high compressor speeds and under a low charge or clogged system condition.

Oil Bleed Passage – Internal orifice bypassing an expansion valve, evaporator pressure regulator, or bypass valve to insure positive oil return to the compressor.

Operational Test – See "Performance Test."

Overcharge – Indicating too much refrigerant or refrigeration oil in the system.

Oxidize – The formation of crust on certain metals due to the action of heat and oxygen.

P

Package Tray – Shelf behind the rear seat in a sedan. Trunk units have ducts through the package tray for intake and outlets from the unit.

Performance Test – The taking of temperature and pressure readings under controlled conditions to determine if an air conditioning system is operating at full efficiency.

Plenum Blower Assembly – Located on the engine side of the fire wall, it contains air ducts, air valves, and a blower that permits selection of air from the outside or inside of the car and directs it to the evaporator or to the heater core if desired.

P.O.A.S.T.V. – See "Positive Absolute Suction Throttling Valve."

P.O.A. Valve – See "Positive Absolute Suction Throttling Valve."

Positive Absolute Suction Throttling Valve – A suction throttling valve used by Frigidaire having a bronze bellows under a near-perfect vacuum which is not affected by atmospheric pressure.

Power Servo – A servo unit used in automatic temperature control operation by a vacuum or an electrical signal.

Pressure – Force per unit of area. The pressure of refrigerant is measured in pounds per square inch.

Pressure Drop – The difference in pressure between any two points that may be caused by a restriction or friction.

Pressure Sensing Line – See "Remote Bulb."

Prestone 12 – Refrigerant 12 by Union Carbon and Carbide Chemical Company. A trademark.

Primary Seal – A seal between the compressor shaft seal and shaft to prevent refrigerant and oil from escaping.

Propane – A flammable gas used in the Halide Leak Detector.

P. s. i. – Abbreviation for pounds per square inch.

P.s. i. g. – Abbreviation for pounds per square inch gage.

Psychrometer – See "Sling Psychrometer."

Pulley – A flat wheel with a vee groove machined around its outer edge, attached to the drive and driven number, provides a means of driving the compressor.

Pump – The compressor. Also refers to the vacuum pump.

Pumpdown – See " Evacuate."

Purge – To remove moisture and air from a system or a component by flushings with a dry gas refrigerant.

R

Radiation – The transition of heat without heating the medium through which it is transmitted.

Ranco Control – A tradename used when referring to a thermostat. See "Thermostat."

Rankine – A thermometer using a scale for the freezing point of water as 492° R. Absolute zero is the start of this thermometer.

Ram Air – Air that is forced through the condenser coils by the movement of the vehicle or action of the fan.

Receiver – A container for the storage of liquid refrigerant.

Receiver-Dehydrator – A combination container for the storage of liquid refrigerant and a desiccant.

Receiver-Drier – See "Receiver-Dehydrator."

Reciprocating Compressor. – A positive displacement compressor with pistons that travel back and forth in a cylinder.

Reed Valves – Thin leaves of screen located in the valve plate of automotive compressors to act as suction and discharge valves. The suction valve is located on the bottom of the valve plate and the discharge on top.

Refrigerant. – The chemical compound used in a refrigeration system to produce the desired cooling.

Refrigerant 12 – The refrigerant used in automotive air conditioners. Proper name; Dichlorodifluoromethane. Chemical symbol; $C Cl_2 F_2$.

Refrigerant 22 – A refrigerant used in some early automotive applications. Not used today because of high pressures. Proper name; Monochlorodifluoromethane. Chemical symbol; $C H Cl F_2$.

Refrigeration Cycle – The complete cycle of the refrigerant back to the starting point, evidenced by temperature and pressure changes.

Refrigeration Oil – Highly refined oil free from all contaminants, such as sulfur, moisture, and tars.

Relative Humidity – The actual moisture content of the air in relation to the total moisture that the air can hold at a given temperature.

Remote Bulb – A sensing device connected to the expansion valve by a capillary tube to sense tail pipe temperature and transmit pressure to the expansion valve for its proper operation.

Resistor – A voltage-dropping device, usually wire wound, to provide a means of controlling fan speeds.

Rheostat – A wire-wound variable resistor used in the control of blower motor speeds.

Rotor – The rotating or freewheeling portion of a clutch on which the belt rides.

S

Saddlebag – Air chambers or openings in the left and right front corners of the car body between the kickpads and the exterior of the car. The General Motors' evaporator is usually located in the right saddlebag.

Saturated Vapor – Saturation indicates that the space holds just as much vapor as it possibly can. No further vaporization is possible at this particular temperature.

Saturated Temperature – The boiling point of a refrigerant at a particular pressure.

Schrader Valve – A spring-loaded valve similar to a tire valve located inside the service valve fitting and used on some control devices to hold refrigerant in the system. Special adapters must be used with the gage hose to allow access to the system.

Screen – A metal mesh located in the receiver, expansion valve and compressor inlet to prevent particles of dirt from being circulated through the system.

Sensible Heat – Heat that causes change in temperature of a substance but not a change of state.

Sensor – A temperature-sensitive unit such as a remote bulb or thermistor. See "Remote Bulb" and "Thermistor."

Service Port – A quarter-inch fitting on the service valves and some control devices to allow manifold set charging hoses to be connected.

Service Valve – See "High-Side (Low-Side) Service Valve."

Shaft Seal – See "Compressor Shaft Seal."

Short Cycling – May be caused by poor air circulation of a thermostat out of adjustment and cause the unit to run for very short periods.

Sight Glass – A window in the liquid line or in top of the drier used to observe the liquid refrigerant flow.

GLOSSARY

S

Silica Gel — A drying agent found in many automotive air conditioners because of its great ability to absorb large quantities of water.

Silver Solder — An alloy of silver containing from 35% to 45% silver. Silver solder melts at 1120° F and flows at 1145°F.

Sling Psychrometer — A device using mercury-filled thermometers to obtain the relative humidity reading.

Slugging — The return of liquid refrigerant or oil to the compressor.

Soft Solder 50/50 — A metallic alloy 50% tin and 50% lead used to repair or join refrigeration parts for temperatures up to 250° F.

Soft Solder 95/05 — A metallic alloy 95% tin and 5% antimony used to repair or join refrigeration parts for temperatures below 30° F.

Solder — A metallic alloy for uniting metals.

Solenoid Valve — An electromagnetic valve controlled remotely by energizing and de-energizing a coil.

Solid — A state of matter, not liquid, not gas or vapor.

Sorbead — A "desiccant."

Specifications — Information provided by the manufacturer that describes an air conditioning system function.

Specific Heat — The quantity of heat required to change one pound of a substance one degree Fahrenheit.

Squirrel Cage — A blower case designed for use with the Squirrel Cage Blower.

Squirrel Cage Blower — A blower wheel designed for providing a large volume of air with a minimum of noise. The blower is more compact than the fan and air may be directed more efficiently.

Standard Ton — See "Ton."

Strainer — See "Screen."

S.T.V. — See "Suction Throttling Valve."

Subcooler — A section of liquid line used to insure all liquid refrigerant to the expansion valve. This line may be a part of the condenser or lay in the drip pan of the evaporator.

Substance — Any form of matter.

Suction Line — The line connecting the evaporator outlet to the compressor inlet.

Suction line Regulator — See "Suction Throttle Valve" or "Evaporator Pressure Regulator."

Suction Service Valve — See "Low-Side Service Valve."

Suction Side — That portion of the refrigeration system under low pressure extending from the expansion valve to the compressor inlet.

Suction Throttling Valve — A back pressure-regulated device that prevents evaporator core freezing up, used by General Motors.

Suction Pressure — Compressor inlet pressure. Reflects the pressure of the system on the low side.

Super Heat — Adding heat intensity to a gas after complete evaporation of a liquid.

Superheated Vapor — Vapor at a temperature higher than its boiling point for a given pressure.

Swaging — A means of shaping soft tubing so that two pieces of the same size can be joined without the use of a fitting. The inside diameter of one tube is increased to accept the outside diameter of the other.

Sweat — The use of a soft solder to join two pieces of tubing or fittings by the use of heat.

Sweat Fitting — A fitting designed to be used in sweating.

Sweeping — See "Purge."

System — All the components and lines together make up an air conditioning system.

T

Tail Pipe — The outlet pipe from evaporator to compressor. See "Suction Line."

Taps All Valve — See "Fits All Valve."

Temperature — Heat intensity measured on a thermometer.

Temperature Regulated Valve — See "Hot Gas Bypass Valve."

T

Thermistor — A temperature-sensing resistor having the ability of changing valves with changing temperature.

Thermostat — A device used to cycle the clutch to control the rate of refrigerant flow as a means of temperature control. The driver has control over temperature desired.

Thermostatic Expansion Valve — A component of a refrigeration system that regulates the rate of flow of refrigerant into the evaporator as governed by action of the remote bulb-sensing tail pipe temperatures.

Thermostatic Switch — See "Thermostat."

Throttling Valve — See "Suction Throttling Valve" and "Evaporator Pressure Regulator."

Tinning — Coating two surfaces to be joined with solder.

Ton of Refrigeration — The effect of melting one ton of ice in 24 hours. One ton equals cooling at 12,000 B.T.U. per hour.

Total Heat Load — The human heat load, plus heat entering through the floor, glass, roof and sides.

Torque — A turning force such as that required to seal a connection measured in foot-pounds or inch-pounds.

Trace — A colored dye suitable for use in a refrigeration system for the detection of leaks.

Transducer — A vacuum valve used to transfer the electrical signal from the amplifier into a vacuum signal. This vacuum signal regulates the power servo unit in automatic temperature control units.

Trunk Unit — An automotive air conditioning evaporator that mounts in the trunk compartment and inducted through the package tray.

U

Ucon — Refrigerant 12. A trademark.

Undercharge — A system short of refrigerant which will result in proper cooling.

Unloading Solenoid — An electrically-controlled valve for operating the throttling valve or bypass valve in some applications.

V

Vacuum — Referring to less than atmospheric pressure, expressed in inches of mercury.

Vacuum Power Unit — A device for operating doors and valves of air conditioner using vacuum as a source of power.

Vacuum Pump — A mechanical device used to evacuate the refrigeration system to rid it of excess moisture and air.

Vapor — See "Gas."

Vapor Lines — Lines that are used to carry refrigerant gas or vapor.

Vee Pulley — Used in automotive applications for the driving of the accessories; water pump, generator, alternator, power steering, etc.

Viscosity — The thickness of a liquid or its resistance to flow.

Volatile Liquid — One that evaporates readily to become a vapor.

W

Water Valve — A shutoff valve, mechanically or vacuum operated, for stopping the flow of hot water to the heater.

Woodruff Key — An index key used to prevent a pulley from turning on a shaft.

INDEX

INDEX

ACKNOWLEDGMENTS

Publications Director
Alan N. Knofla

Editor-in-Chief
Marjorie A. Bruce

Sponsoring Editor
Marjorie A. Bruce

Revision
Boyce Dwiggins

Production Director
Frederick Sharer

Production Specialist
Lee St.Onge

Illustrations
Anthony Canabush
Michael Kokernak

The following companies and organizations, listed in alphabetical order, contributed generously in supplying illustrations and technical data for this book.

American Standard, Controls Division, Detroit, Michigan

Cadillac Motor Car Division, General Motors Corporation, Detroit, Michigan

Chrysler Motors Corporation, Detroit, Michigan

Controls Company of America, Heating and Air Conditioning Division, Milwaukee, Wisconsin

Delco-Remy, Division of General Motors, Anderson, Indiana

E.I. duPont de Nemours and Company, Freon Products Division, Wilmington, Delaware

Fort Worth Pressed Steel Corporation, Fort Worth, Texas

Harrison Radiator Division, General Motors Corporation, Lockport, New York

General Electric Company, Lynn, Massachusetts

John E. Mitchell Company, Inc., Dallas, Texas

Murray Corporation, Towson, Maryland

Oldsmobile, Division of General Motors Corporation, Lansing, Michigan

Tecumseh Products Company, Tecumseh, Michigan

Warner Electric Brake and Clutch Company, Beloit, Wisconsin

York Corporation, Subsidiary of Borg-Warner Corporation, York, Pennsylvania

---

The author and editorial staff at Delmar Publishers are interested in continually improving the quality of this instructional material. The reader is invited to submit constructive criticism and questions. Responses will be reviewed jointly by the author and source editor. Send comments to:

Editor-in-Chief
Box 5087
Albany, New York 12205